STUDIES ON ETHNIC GROUPS IN CHINA

Stevan Harrell, Editor

A LANDSCAPE OF TRAVEL

The Work of Tourism in Rural Ethnic China

JENNY CHIO

UNIVERSITY *of* WASHINGTON PRESS | SEATTLE *&* LONDON

Publication of this book was supported by a generous grant from the
Association for Asian Studies First Book Subvention Program.

© 2014 by the University of Washington Press
Printed and bound in the United States of America
Composed in Minion Pro, typeface designed by Robert Slimbach
17 16 15 14   5 4 3 2 1

University of Washington Press
PO Box 50096, Seattle, WA 98145, USA
www.washington.edu/uwpress

Library of Congress Cataloging-in-Publication Data
Chio, Jenny.
A landscape of travel : the work of tourism
in rural ethnic China / Jenny Chio.
p.   cm.
(Studies on ethnic groups in China)
Includes bibliographical references and index.
ISBN 978-0-295-99365-2 (cloth : alk. paper);
ISBN 978-0-295-99366-9 (pbk. : alk. paper)
1. Rural tourism—China.   2. Ethnicity—China.   3. China—Ethnic
relations.   4. China—Rural conditions.   I. Title.
G155.C55C4828   2014
338.4'79151—dc23
2013046931

To Teacher Pan, C. Q., W. Q.,

and their families in Upper Jidao

and

the families of Yulong, Yueliang Wan,

and Hong Lajiao guesthouses in Ping'an.

Thank you.

CONTENTS

FOREWORD

STEVAN HARRELL

Jenny Chio's *A Landscape of Travel* is about China becoming a nation that travels. Its rural workers by the hundreds of millions travel yearly to the cities to make clothes, to build skyscrapers, to serve diners, and to clean hotel rooms. Its consumers bought almost seventeen million cars in 2012, causing both monumental traffic jams and perhaps the world's worst urban air pollution. Its premier high-speed train now takes travelers from Beijing to Guangzhou in eight hours, while its freeways are engineering marvels, allowing travelers to glide through, rather than over or around, formidable mountain ranges.

One way of traveling is to be a tourist, and China is also becoming a nation that tours. In 2010 Chinese tourists took an estimated 2.1 billion domestic tourist trips. They go to big cities to see historical and nationalist sites; they go to national parks and nature reserves to see scenery and to escape the city; they even go to the countryside to experience nostalgically that rough rural life that their grandparents and today's migrant workers have fought so hard to escape. And increasingly, they go to China's ethnic minority towns and villages to experience difference: the difference between their fast-paced, urban life and the bucolic rhythms of a longed-for simpler time; the difference between their cosmopolitan world, which can be a little gray, and the local world replete with colorful songs, dances, and clothing; the difference between their own affluence, with its noise and pollution, and what they imagine to be the minority people's "backwardness" with clean water, clear air, and expansive views.

Tourists do not, of course, go to ethnic minority regions to experience the poverty, the underdevelopment, the drug addiction, or the longing to leave that plague much of rural China these days. They go rather to experience a benign and colorful difference—a difference that local people must continuously shape and reshape to keep attracting the tourists. *A Landscape of Travel* tells the story of two communities occupied in creating and maintaining this gentle and alluring difference. Ping'an, a Zhuang village in Guangxi, and Upper Jidao, a Miao village in Guizhou, are two villages that are constantly remaking themselves to realize the tourist ideal of difference, so that they can eliminate the undesirable differences of wealth, education, and access to the rest of the world.

To meet their own goals, the villagers of Ping'an and Upper Jidao must "do tourism" (*gao lüyou*), as they themselves put it; they must maintain their landscapes to look attractively bucolic for photographers, regulate their architecture to look quaint and local, dress themselves to look exotic and ethnic, and perform songs and dances that people will want to listen to and watch. They must also provide clean, attractive rooms with indoor plumbing and comfortable beds; serve meals that have a hint of the exotic but still meet the particular tastes of the urban tourists; build roads and parking lots where tour buses and private cars can reach the villages without too much pothole-bumping or uphill hiking; and adjust their own schedules to make sure to be there, looking good, when the tourists arrive.

In other words, ethnic and scenic tourism in Southwest China is about maintaining difference while making it accessible, about how people do the work of tourism in order to allow tourists to bridge the geographic, economic, and ethnic differences between tourist and villager without eliminating that difference. It is about how to be modern, to participate actively in the modern economy of mobility while portraying themselves as un-modern, un-urban, and un-Han enough to stay interesting to the tourists. *A Landscape of Travel* is both a story and a portrait of this process of calibrating difference. Chio tells the story in a combination of vivid vignettes and fluent analysis, and displays the portrait in a series of stunning photographs, every one of which flashes both the irony of calibrating difference and the fun of tourism that is shared by the tourists, the villagers, and us the readers.

A Landscape of Travel also reminds us how much ethnicity in China has changed since the first volume in the series Studies on Ethnic Groups in China, published in 1995: *Cultural Encounters on China's Ethnic Frontiers.* That book also contained both stories and portraits of difference, but the stories were about the encounter between state and local community, and the portraits were of differences that had been created by the long history of ecological adaptation and the shorter history of state projects of nation-building. How different the differences are now in the 2010s, as affluent urbanites and increasingly cosmopolitan villagers dance both the circle-dances that still symbolize minorities and the dance of difference that keeps them attracting and visiting each other. Certainly tourism is only one mode through which China's mobility expresses itself, and we must remember that most villages have no tourists at all. But if we want to understand why tourists see and experience what they do on many of those two billion tourist trips, and how this reflects China as a nation that travels, Chio's *A Landscape of Travel* is both delightful and essential.

PREFACE

On a bright summer afternoon in 2007, a group of Chinese travel-media photographers, editors, and publishers gathered in a Beijing bookstore for a casual brainstorming session. Their task at hand was to discuss the creation of a Chinese-language guidebook to China for the domestic tourism market, but under the imprint of an iconic Western travel guide brand, which I'll call "Travelprints."[1] I was invited along by a magazine photographer, a friend of a friend, who knew that I had been living in two rural ethnic tourism villages in Southwest China and that I wanted to know more about the Chinese travel industry. In the villages, I learned just how vital good publicity is in creating and maintaining the success of a tourism destination. Village residents in each place loved to recall stories about the photographers, writers, and television crews (domestic and foreign) who had visited and who inevitably had become enamored with the warm hospitality of the local community as well as the beauty of the surrounding landscape. These villagers were proud of being seen by the media and by people across the country and the world. Now in Beijing, I wanted to listen in on how Chinese travel-media producers talked about their work, which in large part was promoting and selling the experience of tourism to potential travelers.

The discussion focused on how to create a Chinese-language edition of an internationally established travel guide brand for domestic tourism in

China. This inverted the common association of the brand with "off the beaten track" travel in exotic, far-flung destinations for budget-conscious, presumably "Western" tourists (*xifang*, i.e., from North America, Western Europe, Australia, and New Zealand). The publishers wanted to see if they could take the Travelprints brand and localize it just enough to appeal to the exploding market for in-country tourism without losing the cachet of its perceived distinction as a Western, and therefore more cosmopolitan, perspective on travel. Up to this point, they had already published a number of Chinese-language Travelprints guidebooks to destinations outside of China. In large part, this was achieved by translating the English editions into Chinese and editing out certain parts that might be irrelevant for a Chinese audience (or potentially sensitive to Chinese censors) but leaving the bulk of the content intact. But in the case of a China guidebook for in-country tourism, the lead publisher explained that they could not simply translate the existing English-language Travelprints guidebook into Chinese and sell it in the Chinese market. How could they "domesticate" an international travel guide to China? Was there something different about Chinese domestic tourism?

Travelprints—indeed anyone interested in profiting from the domestic Chinese tourism market—faced a number of contradictory conditions. By the mid-2000s the staggering growth and market potential of domestic tourism in China could not be ignored. In 2006 the China National Tourism Administration (CNTA) reported that there were nearly 1.4 billion domestic tourist trips taken, or approximately 1.06 trips taken per person (CNTA 2007).[2] In 2010 the National Bureau of Statistics (NBS) reported 2.1 billion domestic tourism trips taken, which, given China's official population of 1.34 billion, translated to about 1.6 trips per person (NBS 2011). Chinese were traveling domestically in enough numbers to more than justify, and indeed to demand, a China guide from Travelprints. But such a guide had to offer its potential consumers something different, something distinctive, which in this case would be a certain status based off its brand. While the English-language Travelprints guidebook to China was associated with budget-minded, foreign "backpackers," the travel-media publishers pointed out that the Chinese-language Travelprints guidebooks were generally purchased by a more well-to-do segment of the Chinese population: those who could afford to travel internationally and who wanted to do so in a more independent, *worldly* manner. After all, the Chinese-language Travelprints guidebooks were some of the most expensive on the market—typically twice the price of other guides.

The problem with selling travel and tourism was its relationship to the actual content. For example, the point was raised that many Chinese tourists prefer to travel in groups with tour guides arranged through travel agencies, and as a result, these tourists often don't bother with guidebooks. Of course, organized groups of tourists are not the target audience for Travelprints; the publisher acknowledged that this guide, even more than others, would ultimately be about branding. The Travelprints guide to domestic travel in China would need to emphasize its desirability as an international brand by appealing to the Chinese tourist who wanted to travel around China in a "Travelprints" kind of way. What might this kind of Chinese tourists want? Travelprints needed to figure out how to offer something just different enough from the current guidebook marketplace, but how were travel-media producers and others involved in the tourism industries, tasked with providing (or describing) the travel experience, supposed to give the tourist what they thought he or she wanted?

A suggestion was made that perhaps they could start by translating into Chinese the English-language Travelprints guidebook to Southwest China, because this region was already popular with both domestic and international tourists looking for a culturally exotic experience in some of China's ethnic minority areas. But to the notion of simply duplicating the existing Travelprints guide written by non-Chinese authors, one travel magazine editor exclaimed: "Why would I want to hear what a foreigner has to say about Guizhou [one of the provinces covered in the English-language guide to Southwest China]?" This editor's outburst revealed a deeper problem: how were they to provide interesting, different information about China to a domestic audience who already had a strong sense of what to expect and what they wanted to experience? In the marketplace for travel guides, the best-selling domestic guidebook at the time was a series called China Independent Travel (Zhongguo Zizhu You). Inexpensive and mostly full of practical details on distances, travel times, and hotels, these guides offered very little background information on destinations. However, the publisher scorned, without a history and culture section in a guidebook, tourism was just "getting out of the bus to take a picture, getting on the bus to take a nap" (*xiache paizhao, shangche shuijiao*). Relatively speaking, the existing Chinese-language Travelprints guidebooks to other countries and world regions contained quite a lot of background information; this was part of their perceived distinctiveness and would need to be written anew for a domestic audience.

When I interviewed the Travelprints publisher a few days after this brainstorming session, he said that although they still had no concrete plans, the ideas had been helpful. He mentioned that a Chinese-language Travelprints guidebook to China might include "foreign voices" to provide new perspectives and to promote "different types of discoveries" (*bu yiyang de faxian*) for Chinese tourists while maintaining the brand's international flair. This was one of the first attempts by an international travel guide brand, he said, to "go native" in the Chinese travel guidebook market. After listening to the publisher's musings on what his books might offer a domestic tourist that would be "different," I was struck by the similarities between his concerns and those expressed to me by the residents of Ping'an and Upper Jidao villages, where I had been conducting fieldwork on tourism, development, and rural social change for the previous year and a half.

While the travel-media producers in Beijing strove to find the most appealing and distinctive means of describing the tourism experience in order to sell more guidebooks, villagers in Ping'an and Upper Jidao voiced uncertainties over how to "do tourism" (*gao lüyou*), or more precisely, how to do the work of tourism successfully. For village residents this entailed, in part, being different enough from other nearby tourism destinations to attract tourists, but it also meant calculating whether or not they could earn more money working as a migrant outside the village. For both villagers and guidebook publishers, the work of tourism was to make travel desirable as a consumable experience for tourists and therefore profitable for themselves. Whether in a rural ethnic tourism village or in a publisher's office in Beijing, the issues raised at the Travelprints meeting highlight the contested meanings of tourism and the difficulty of making sense of the experience of travel. From these perspectives tourism was no longer an activity engaged in by *tourists* but rather something enacted and made possible by those who have to do the work of tourism.

This book explores the myriad ways in which rural ethnic minority village residents are doing tourism in China today, in response to and entrenched in the country's dramatic socioeconomic transformations, programs for rural development and modernization, and global concerns for cultural heritage preservation. Like the travel-media producers I met in Beijing in 2007, the people who reside in tourism villages such as Ping'an and Upper Jidao confronted similar questions about how to create, construct, and provide tourism experiences for tourists; they debated and occasionally doubted the possible benefits of doing tourism for themselves, their families, and their communities. Tourism is never just leisure or economics but rather a matter of perspective, representation, and imagination. Guidebook publishers in Beijing, guesthouse owners in Ping'an, and members of the Upper Jidao Tourism Association were all engrossed in the common project of teasing out the constituent parts of tourism as they envisioned their opportunities and ambitions within this moment in contemporary China. As they imagined what tourists might want, they engaged in acts of imagining what tourism and travel meant to themselves, as individuals, framed by their own experiences and desires. As tourism was produced and problematized by village residents, travel itself became meaningful in revealing ways. By paying close attention to the concerns and aspirations expressed by Ping'an and Upper Jidao residents as they lived in, through, and with tourism, this book presents these circumstances as a landscape of travel—a landscape in which the act and the imagination of travel become key nodes through which tourists, migrants, ethnic minorities, mainstream majorities, rural villagers, and urban dwellers negotiate and make sense of current social, economic, and political conditions.

This book aims to build an anthropological understanding of the contemporary regimes of labor and leisure in China today by approaching tourism as one part, and at present one very integral part, of life in rural ethnic China. In tourism, after all, one person's leisure is another person's labor. At stake is our knowledge of the work and debates involved in making tourism possible and how these intersect with, or interrupt, the ongoing formation of rural, ethnic subjectivities and livelihoods in China today. The focus is the *doing* of tourism—in other words, the work that is conducted and debated by village residents as they pursue their own life goals and aspirations within the growing tourism economy. The analytical and practical significance of not privileging the *tourist* in tourism studies is emphasized throughout this book; meaning-making in tourism is not the exclusive purview of those who travel from destination to destination, from site to sight. Rather, as my ethnography shows, the people and communities who do the work of tourism are just as, if not more, invested in making tourism meaningful. The "front stage" of tourism (MacCannell 1999 [1976], building on Goffman 1990 [1959])—or what is seen by a tourist—cannot be interpreted without due diligence to the "backstage," or what creates the conditions of possibility for tourism. What happens in the backstage occurs in relation to a host of other imperatives, claims, and desires. These backstage conditions determine how tourism can, should, and will be *done* in rural ethnic villages like Ping'an and Upper Jidao.

FIELDWORK, METHODOLOGY, AND THE VILLAGES

It shouldn't surprise me how much things have changed each time I return to Ping'an and Upper Jidao, and yet every trip leaves me somewhat astonished. In 2012, the number of multistory, concrete hotels in Ping'an (an ethnic Zhuang village in Guangxi) had doubled while the number of village residents who ran family guesthouses appeared to have decreased. Many villagers had found new opportunities in the tourism backstage— for example, by buying produce and meat from regional markets and reselling them at a markup in the village to restaurants and hotels, which were increasingly run by outside entrepreneurs. From the looks of it, business was still very good in Ping'an; tourists streamed up and down the mountainside in regular waves, and the entire Guilin Longji Terraced Fields Scenic Area (Guilin Longji Titian Jingqu), of which Ping'an is a part, was expanding its tourism offerings and sights.[3] Clearly, villagers were invested, both emotionally and financially, in the ongoing success of tourism in Ping'an, but at the same time the village elementary school had closed due to low enrollment. Families with school-aged children were moving to the nearby township and county towns, in Heping and Longsheng, and subleasing their businesses to relatives or other contractors.

In Upper Jidao (an ethnic Miao village in Guizhou), construction plans for a new parking lot, granaries, and the village sewage system were under way, funded in large part by a World Bank project loan to the provincial government.[4] A much anticipated village hotel had not been completed because of mismanaged funds; instead, six furnished guestrooms and an indoor shower and toilet had been built on the third floor of a village house, paid for by a philanthropist from Hong Kong who had connections with provincial tourism officials. Some tourists still came to Upper Jidao, but the general opinion throughout the village was that tourism numbers had fallen since 2008, when the nearby Xijiang Thousand Households Miao Village (Xijiang Qianhu Miaozhai) had been redeveloped and reopened as the region's premier Miao ethnic tourism destination. The World Bank project promised a number of much needed and desired infrastructure improvements to Upper Jidao, but residents expressed doubts about the future benefits of tourism on their everyday lives and livelihoods.

This book represents an effort at making sense of the transformations in the lives and expectations of residents in these two rural ethnic minority villages in the early years of the new millennium. When I began fieldwork in Ping'an and Upper Jidao in 2006, the Chinese government had just released its 11th Five Year Plan, in which they foregrounded rural development as a key national policy, dubbed Build a New Socialist Countryside (*jianshe shehui zhuyi xin nongcun*). The development of rural tourism was widely promoted as a significant means of achieving the stated goals of improving rural-urban relations and rural living conditions. But what did the building of a New Socialist Countryside and this attention to rural life mean for the residents of Ping'an and Upper Jidao villages? Were village residents satisfied with the ideas and suggestions put forward in government policy? What else did they want from tourism? Has tourism, which was so hotly promoted in 2006 as an integral part of the strategy for developing rural China, ultimately made a difference to them?

Instead of locating the tourist at the center, as the active subject who "does tourism," my analysis takes the "hosts" as the primary actors who do tourism. It is the host communities, in conjunction with and in response to diverse local, regional, and state imperatives, who create the conditions of possibility for tourism. This was reflected in the way village residents talked about tourism; in China, rural tourism is often referred to as *nong jia le*, which I loosely translate as "peasant family happiness" for reasons outlined in chapter 2. This is a name and category used generally to describe tourism businesses that involve family-run rural guesthouses, rural-themed restaurants, and the experience of relaxation and leisure in a rural, homey environment. Village residents frequently use the phrase *nong jia le* as an activity; for example, when talking about how they might further develop tourism, they would sometimes say "we could do *nong jia le*" (*women keyi gao nong jia le*).

To examine tourism from the perspectives of village residents and not tourists, I situate the transformative experience of tourism *as* development within what I call a landscape of travel. The notion of a landscape—criss-crossed by travel routes for tourists and migrants as well as all of the hopes, dreams, desires, and disappointments associated with these types of mobility—provides a framework for understanding how tourism is designed to and indeed does become a part of everyday experiences in places like Ping'an and Upper Jidao. Moreover, as I elaborate in the introduction, by bringing together the concept of landscape with the idea of travel, my analysis integrates two fundamental characteristics of tourism itself: sightseeing (visuality) and human movement (mobility). Much of the literature in tourism studies demonstrates how visuality and mobility are important for *tourists*, but my purpose is to understand how visuality and mobility are equally, if not more, significant and transformational for destination communities.

By "visuality," I am referring to the "social fact of vision" (Foster 1988; Mitchell 2005; and Mirzoeff 2011), which is exemplified in the frequent arguments over the outward appearance of a village (*waimao*) or how terraced fields should be maintained in order to reproduce well in photographs. By "mobility," I am considering multiple forms of, and diverse reasons for, travel, including tourism and migration. Thus the landscape of travel I map is an ethnographic project in taking seriously how travel influences individual understandings of opportunity and identity; how rural ethnic villagers acquire the skills and knowledge to renovate their homes to better suit tourism and achieve modern living conditions; and how village residents learn to be touristic to successfully adapt their tourism industries to attract potential visitors.

My fieldwork took place primarily in Ping'an, in the Guangxi Zhuang Autonomous Region, and Upper Jidao, in Guizhou (see map). Both Guangxi and Guizhou are equivalent as provincial-level administrative units in China. Guangxi and Guizhou share a border, and regular public bus services connect towns throughout the region. The villages were chosen for their current participation in tourism industries and tourism-based development programs, their popularity (as evidenced in provincial, national, and international media coverage, in guidebooks, and in numbers of incoming tourists), and their promoted status as rural ethnic tourism destinations. Ping'an (population approximately 850) is a single surname village, Liao, and residents who trace their lineages to families within the village are all ethnically Zhuang; it is located an hour and a half north of Guilin, a well-known city of cultural, historical, and touristic significance in China. Ping'an is administratively part of Guilin, a prefecture-level city. In Upper Jidao (population approximately 400), local village families are ethnically Miao and the village is comprised of two lineages, surnamed Pan and Huang. Upper Jidao is located in the Qiandongnan Miao and Dong Autonomous Prefecture, whose administrative capital is Kaili, a county-level city about forty minutes by bus from Upper Jidao. Kaili is three hours by bus from Guiyang, the provincial capital of Guizhou.

Fieldwork in Ping'an and Upper Jidao was initially conducted over twenty-three months between 2006 and 2007, when I lived with a local family in each village for an extended period. Between 2007 and 2012, I visited the villages on average once a year, staying anywhere from three days to three weeks. I have also spent time outside of Ping'an and Upper Jidao with village residents, as they themselves traveled for work and sometimes leisure to regional towns near their home villages and to factories in Guangdong. I met, interviewed, and discussed tourism, rural development, media representations, and ethnic identity in China with university professors, government officials (including tourism bureau officials), tour guides, journalists, and graduate students in cities across the country, including Beijing, Chengdu, Guangzhou, Guilin, Guiyang, Kunming, and Xiamen. These conversations, across the spaces of village and urban China, helped me to comprehend the broader intersections of domestic tourism, rural development, and discourses of ethnicity in China today. Ultimately, however, it was my long-term ethnographic fieldwork in the villages—including participant observation, a household survey, and semistructured interviews—that illuminated the simple fact that what these villagers are participating in is best understood as a process of learning how to be ethnic and rural in particular ways that have emerged in tension and in tandem with larger national policies for development and modernization. Doing tourism is therefore a deeply significant means through which village residents are making sense of their place and role in these broader transformations.

My initial encounter with rural ethnic tourism in China occurred in 2002, when I visited Ping'an for the first time. The day I went to see the terraced fields was cold and foggy, and although I hadn't planned well enough in advance to stay overnight, the place stuck out in my mind not only because the terraced fields were truly breathtaking but because of the ticket offices. The idea of charging entry to a "real" village both baffled and fascinated me. It was enough to prompt me to revisit the village in the summer of 2004, when I stayed for a few nights at a local family's guesthouse, chosen simply because the mother of the household was the brashest, most insistent, and most unrelenting woman who immediately approached me as I stepped off the public bus at the village parking lot. Since then, I have almost always stayed with her family whenever I visit Ping'an. In 2008, her family began building a large, concrete hotel just steps away from their older wooden home, and in the summer of 2012, I was honored to be their first overnight guest in one of the new rooms.

Over the past decade, I have followed the ways in which Ping'an has attempted, perhaps unintentionally, to transform itself from a destination for landscape photography based on sight-seeing into a more ethnic tourism scenic area. This is in large part a response to the changing discourses of tourism, rural development, and ethnicity in China. The history of tourism in Ping'an is grounded in a particular way of looking at the terraced fields that surround the village, and these fields remain the village's most highly valued asset. They are now highly contested, however, because they are the least capable aspect of tourism in the village for generating income for residents, as discussed in chapter 1. Discord characterizes the political and economic relationships between the village of Ping'an, the tourism management company in charge of the Longji Scenic Area of which Ping'an is a part, and the local county government.

My first visit to Upper Jidao was in March 2006, at the suggestion of Zhang Xiaosong of Guizhou Normal University and the Guizhou Tourism Bureau. By then, Upper Jidao had already been marked as a site for tourism development. Under the guise of a World Bank project loan application and a program implemented in the early 2000s by the World Tourism Organization (UNWTO), which is part of the United Nations, Upper Jidao was selected by a team of consultants and government officials to be a part of a "demonstration project" (UNWTO 2006, 41–44). The plan for Upper Jidao was consciously constructed in light of experiences from other tourism villages, including Ping'an; in fact, in 2004, organizers of this rural tourism development program in Guizhou arranged for a group of villagers, including two men from Upper Jidao, to visit Ping'an as part of a study tour. In many ways, Upper Jidao is a relative newcomer to the rural village-as-ethnic tourism destination trend in China. However, it is located within a few kilometers of the most well-known and long-standing ethnic Miao tourism villages in southeastern Guizhou: Upper Langde and Xijiang (on the former, see Donaldson 2007 and 2011 as well as Oakes 1998 and 2011; on the latter, see Schein 2000).

With the involvement of regional, provincial, national, and international organizations and agencies, the pace and impact of tourism-related changes in this corner of Guizhou have been large scale. The bigger idea is to turn the entire prefecture, Qiandongnan, into an ethnic tourism "heartland," while raising the standard of living in both Kaili and the surrounding rural countryside. A wider, straighter highway has shortened travel times between Kaili and Upper Jidao from an hour to about forty minutes. The construction of this highway was timed with the 2008 Beijing Olympics; village residents in Upper Jidao recall with pride the Olympic torch procession that passed by the village. The difficulty for villagers has been in negotiating their newcomer status within the already existing ethnic tourism market in southeastern Guizhou, while grappling with the continued daily concerns that face households who still rely on subsistence farming and migrant remittances. Since 2010, whenever I visit, I find myself spending more and more time in Kaili with friends from Upper Jidao who have since moved to the city. Their travels back and forth between Upper Jidao and Kaili are reshaping the fabric of everyday life in the village. The new, improved roads certainly do facilitate more continuous movement between the city and the village for both tourists and village residents, thus demonstrating the continued complexity of understanding mobility as a social process.

In many respects, the individuals from Upper Jidao who choose to migrate are no different than other migrant laborers across China; they leave often with the intent to return and return often with a desire to leave again. What made Upper Jidao and Ping'an so fascinating, however, was the layering of mobilities in each place, the interwoven trajectories of tourists and migrants cross-cutting everyday village livelihoods. Migrants from Upper Jidao and Ping'an were returning home to find their homes transformed into tourist destinations for urbanites from some of the places they had themselves worked and lived in. As I lived in each village community, I found myself drawn to the stories of travel told by returned migrants; their narratives of where they had been and what they had seen across China highlighted, and indeed asserted, their subjectivities and their village socialities in rural ethnic tourism—a perspective I explore in chapter 3. Like research conducted by Tamara Jacka (2006) with migrant women in Beijing and by Rachel Murphy (2002) among returnees in rural Jiangxi, I became interested in the individual stories of travel and how, from these narratives, potential, current, and former migrants were giving form to and making sense of contemporary social and economic opportunities. In Upper Jidao and Ping'an, these opportunities are in tourism, which operates in ways particular to the contemporary regimes of labor and leisure in China. Thus mobility is doubly revealing as an analytical perspective on both individual, subjective experiences of encountering the world beyond one's home and as a shared, community chance for an active, productive role in national modernization agendas.

Whether discussing migration or tourism, one conceptual figure around which many of the village residents shaped their stories of travel was that of home. The element of "home" is often invoked in popular forms of homestays and family-run guesthouses (Yu Wang 2007) and frequently plays a central role in the marketing of rural tourism. The push to develop village hotels and guesthouses in Ping'an and Upper Jidao was representative of this trend, encompassed in the promotion of rural tourism as *nong jia le*, or peasant family happiness, where the middle character *jia* stands for both family and home. For returned migrants, however, the concept of "home" was complicated by their own travels and by their perspectives on leaving home and then returning to create and sell their "home" to tourists. For these people there was one personal, remembered understanding of home from not-being-at-home and then another layer of collective nostalgia added upon return when their homes were changing to meet tourist demands for the fulfillment of urban nostalgic longings. Participating in rural, ethnic tourism was inevitably entrenched in a need to reconfigure local ideas and ideals about what kinds of home were desired, by whom, and to fulfill what needs.

As an ethnographer trained in visual anthropology, I entered my field research sites with the clear intention of recording footage that would eventually be edited into an ethnographic film (Chio dir. 2013). Throughout my fieldwork I shared clips and sequences from my footage with village residents; these collective viewings of video recordings made in each village provided a deeper sense of how tourism was cultivating a particular "way of seeing" in the communities. Using visual media in this way allowed me to explore not only how people in Ping'an and Upper Jidao responded to my own visual representations of their communities but also to discover their expectations of what tourism, and rural villages-as-ethnic tourism destinations, should look like. Collaborative visual research was a multivalent learning process for me as an anthropologist and for residents in both Ping'an and Upper Jidao as stakeholders in China's rural, ethnic tourism industry.[5] Much of my thinking on and analysis of visuality in the context of tourism has been deeply shaped by the comments, reactions, and questions of the villagers who watched my footage and, in 2010 and 2012 as the film took shape, reviewed rough and final cuts of the film itself.

Over the course of my research, I integrated video production into the ethnographic flesh of my project by using digital video's portability and its visibility as a means of creating data about living in, through, and beyond tourism in China. I also realized that by sharing footage of one village with residents of the other, I made my project more transparent to the villagers and myself. They could see where I was when I wasn't in their village and get a sense of what I was doing. We talked about how to produce images and what images are good for. Not only did this model the tourism "sight-seeing" experience but it became a part of how we all were learning about what tourism entailed. Discussions with village residents in Ping'an and Upper Jidao about the visual representation of rural Chinese villages revealed the lasting importance of knowing how to be seen in tourism. This in turn focused my data collection and analysis on the moments and sites at which this visual knowledge emerged during encounters with tourists or when this knowledge was invoked for the purposes of understanding where tourism was headed. My analysis thus benefited immensely from using video as a research method and later through the process of editing the film itself.

It was apparent that local village perspectives on tourism and travel were greatly influenced and shaped by mass media representations (beyond my own footage). This is what prompted me to spend time with travel-media producers in Beijing after completing many months of ethnographic fieldwork in the villages. So many of the conversations I had and opinions that had been expressed in Ping'an and Upper Jidao dovetailed with larger, media-based narratives of travel, and indeed residents were always quick to engage with any and all media personnel who showed up in the villages. Television programs beamed in idealized images of urban living, while tourism travel shows demonstrated to the villagers just what tourists want to see and do when in a rural village. As Arjun Appadurai (1996, 53–54) has noted, "more persons throughout the world see their lives through the prisms of the possible lives offered by mass media in all their forms."

Pushing this notion further, Tim Oakes and Louisa Schein (2006, 22) have pointed out that "messages about other places are being transmitted through all these media at a remarkable pace and density. And desires to tour or live in these places seem to have burgeoned concomitantly."[6] Notions of place and home are increasingly complicated by the transmission of images and stories of "other" places through media representations. Coupled with the occasional researcher or development consultant who showed up unannounced and usually asked too many questions, villagers were learning from a plethora of sources just what constituted contemporary tourism practices and discourses. I came to understand the value village residents placed on learning about tourism through a variety of means—from direct interaction with tourists to training sessions funded by international donors to media portrayals of their villages, their ethnic group, and rural tourism activities. The residents of Ping'an and Upper Jidao depended on "being seen" for their local tourism industries to be profitable. For the tourists who visited these places, seeing ethnic, rural livelihoods in all of their olfactory, tactile realities was a part of the anticipated and desired experience. Learning how to be seen was therefore integral to the future success of tourism in these villages.

SCOPE OF THE BOOK

Drawing on critical approaches in tourism studies as well as anthropological perspectives on contemporary Chinese culture and society, this book investigates the spheres of power, modernization, and nation-building latent in tourism with the goal of understanding how rural ethnic Chinese village residents make sense of their livelihoods and formulate new aspirations. I situate my analysis at the nexus of mobility and visuality precisely because these are the two social processes I found to be most influential and dominant in shaping resident opinions on how best to do tourism in Ping'an and Upper Jidao. The introduction lays out the conceptual framework of this book, focusing on how an anthropological approach to landscape expands the critical study of tourism for understanding both the physical practices and material spaces through which travel is imagined and realized. I delve more deeply into notions of mobility and visuality to account for, and to account with, the multiple social actors in tourism as a transformative social phenomenon for destination communities, in contrast to many earlier works in tourism studies that have tended to emphasize the *tourist* experience of tourism.

Chapter 1 situates these villages within the contexts of ethnic identity and visual representations of ethnicity in China since 1949, drawing attention to how the knowledge and discourses produced in the Ethnic Classification project (*minzu shibie*) influenced the later development and promotion of domestic tourism—in particular, tourism about the nation's official ethnic minorities—since "reform and opening" (*gaige kaifang*) in the late 1970s. I describe the history of tourism and current conditions in the two villages, Ping'an and Upper Jidao. Chapter 2 discusses how tourism has fit into recent national policies and goals for rural development, in part by drawing on earlier, dominant discourses of rural livelihoods in China, to justify tourism *as* development and to produce a desirable, consumable rural ethnic tourism commodity for the contemporary market. I focus on the national campaign to build a New Socialist Countryside incorporated into the 11th Five Year Plan from 2006 to 2010 and the popular tourism trend dubbed *nong jia le*—the catchy gloss used to describe rural household-based tourism enterprises.

One of the major domestic issues that both the New Socialist Countryside policy and the national-level support for *nong jia le* tourism were intended to address was rural-to-urban internal migration and the attendant social consequences of "the largest voluntary migration in the history of the world" for both rural and urban China (Wasserstrom 2010, 122).[7] The goal in the mid-2000s was to create enough opportunities in the countryside to convince able-bodied rural residents to stay, or to return, home. In chapter 3, I explore the perspectives of some returned rural migrants in Ping'an and Upper Jidao on tourism and development in their home villages. It is crucial to recognize and take seriously the multiple, overlapping mobilities that Ping'an and Upper Jidao residents must account for on an everyday basis in order to acknowledge that tourism development itself holds very powerful, if frequently unarticulated, assumptions about who should and who should not travel.

Chapter 4 considers the *visual* work undertaken in each village as a part of doing tourism—from architectural renovations as homes are transformed into guesthouses and hotels to the migrants who come to Ping'an to find employment as ethnic minority models. Not everything is as it looks on the surface of a tourism village, and this chapter details how village residents conceive of and make sense of what I call "the politics of appearance" in ethnic tourism. This is a politics that ultimately determines who and what looks appropriately ethnic and rural enough for tourism and tourists, and village residents by necessity have had to learn how to work within these changing expectations. Chapter 5 examines the internal politics of tourism on relationships within each village and between nearby villages (some of which may or may not also be doing tourism). The importance of being able to present oneself as just different enough from neighboring villages becomes a key factor in achieving success and profits in the competitive tourism marketplace.

Finally, I conclude by considering how doing tourism for Ping'an and Upper Jidao residents is a process of learning how to be ethnic and rural, and this learning process is very much entrenched in their identities as modern, rural, and ethnic minority Chinese citizens. The conclusion centers on a short study tour I organized for a group of residents from Upper Jidao to visit Ping'an in 2007. I close by thinking through some of the more recent changes that have occurred in each village as a result of shifting local and national politics as well as individual aspirations and ambitions. Tourism is as much about the physical process of movement as it is about the imagination of meaningful experiences to be lived—and for the people I have met and befriended in Ping'an and Upper Jidao, their labors at providing a memorable leisure experience for tourists demand both respect and further attention to the complex and often contradictory factors involved in the work of tourism.

ACKNOWLEDGMENTS

This project has taken me from the United States to China to Australia and back, and the book would never have emerged without the endless stream of encouragement from family, friends, and colleagues near and far. First and foremost, I am deeply inspired by and indebted to Nelson H. H. Graburn, who taught me that a little bit of enthusiasm goes a very long way. He has never let me forget that tourism matters. William Schaefer offered his time and suggestions on everything from writing to how to take pictures more seriously. Liu Xin challenged me to think critically about the fundamental assumptions of my research, and Chris Berry generously provided resources, contacts, and guidance. Wanning Sun mentored my research as it expanded in new directions. My writing has benefited in countless ways from Stevan Harrell's input, and his work on ethnicity and rural life in China shaped my own thinking from early on. The encouragement I received from colleagues, students, and the anthropology office staff at Emory University helped bring this book to completion.

In China, I thank Yang Hui at Yunnan University, who first supported my project and whose unflagging energy and dedication to promoting anthropology in China continues to inspire. Peng Zhaorong provided me with countless introductions in the field, and Xu Ganli was a constant source of ideas in Guilin. Zhang Xiaosong facilitated many important contacts throughout Guizhou. In Guiyang, Guilin, Kaili, Kunming, and

Beijing, I depended upon many old and new friends for places to sleep, rides, meals, and conversation. I most regret that I am not able to share this book or my film with Yang Kun, who taught me so much about the city of Kunming and the art of filmmaking. I am truly lucky to have been his friend. Finally, I am forever thankful for the friendship of the residents of Ping'an and Upper Jidao villages. They have accepted my presence and my questions as just another part of life's unpredictable changes, and for that I am utterly grateful. This book is dedicated to the individuals and families who welcomed me into their homes and lives.

Over the years my thinking has benefited enormously from the perceptive comments and questions of audiences at the Australian National University, Chinese University of Hong Kong, Duke University, Emory University, Haverford College, the 2013 Irmgard Coninx Foundation Berlin Roundtable on Transnationality, Kanazawa University, Macquarie University, National University of Singapore, University of California–Berkeley Tourism Studies Working Group, University of Pennsylvania, University of Sydney, University of Victoria, and the University of Western Sydney. Portions of this work were presented as early drafts at the Society for Visual Anthropology's 2008 Visual Research Conference and at annual meetings of the American Anthropological Association and the Association for Asian Studies.

More specifically, I am thankful for the insights, advice, generosity, and inspiration from Mayling Birney, Ben Blanchard, Tami Blumenfield, Alexis Bunten, Carlo Caduff, Charles Carroll, Cindy Chang, Susette Cooke, Jennifer Deger, Devleena Ghosh, Maris Gillette, Samantha Goodner, Guo Jing, Yingjie Guo, Zeynep Gürsel, Joyce Hammond, Jonathan Hassid, He Xiaoxun, He Yuan, Christina Ho, Stephanie Malia Hom, Li Xin, Jen Lin-Liu, Peter Little, Ling Liu, Lü Bin, Luo Yifang, Dean MacCannell, Yasmine Musharbash, Pál Nyíri, Tim Oakes, Goldie Osuri, Ou Chou Chou, Michael Peletz, Luke Robinson, Noel Salazar, Erynn Sarno, Louisa Schein, Graeme Smith, Julie Starr, Rachel Stern, Liv Stutz, Margaret Swain, Jessica Anderson Turner, Chris Vasantkumar, Eileen Walsh, Leslie Wang, Wang Xiaomei, Wang Yu, Monique Wollan, Xu Wenkun, Yi Sicheng, Zeng Han, Li Zhang, and Zhong Jian.

Earlier versions of parts of this book have appeared previously in "The Internal Expansion of China: Tourism and the Production of Distance," in *Asia on Tour: Exploring the Rise of Asian Tourism*, edited by Tim Winter, Peggy Teo, and T. C. Chang (New York: Routledge, 2009), 207–20; "China's

Campaign for Civilized Tourism: What to Do When Tourists Behave Badly," *Anthropology News* (November 2010), 41 (8): 14–15; "Know Yourself: Making the Visual Work in Tourism Research," in *Fieldwork in Tourism: Methods, Issues, and Reflections*, edited by C. Michael Hall (New York: Routledge, 2011), 209–19; and "The Appearance of the Rural in China's Tourism," *Provincial China* (2011) 3 (1): 60–79. A shorter version of chapter 3 was published as "Leave the Fields without Leaving the Countryside: Modernity and Mobility in Rural, Ethnic China," *Identities: Global Studies in Culture and Power* (2011), 18 (6): 551–75. Figure 1.5 appeared in "2008 AAA Photo Contest Winners and Finalists," *Anthropology News* (March 2009), 50 (3): 23. I would like to acknowledge the publishers for permission to use these materials.

My analysis of Chinese historical ethnographic films in chapter 1 first began as a coauthored paper, written with John Alexander, whose critical insights on documentary and ethnicity have been greatly influential on my own thinking. At the University of Washington Press, I thank Lorri Hagman for her encouragement and support for this book, as well as Jacqueline Volin and Tim Zimmermann for their assistance with publication details both large and small. Ellen Walker created the map, and Amy Smith Bell provided meticulous copyediting. I am also grateful for the extensive comments and critiques on the manuscript provided by Stevan Harrell and one anonymous reviewer. Of course, all mistakes and omissions are my own.

Financial support for research and writing came from the University of California–Berkeley, and in particular the Department of Anthropology, the Graduate Division, the Institute for East Asian Studies, and the Center for Chinese Studies; a Fulbright-Hays research award; the Wenner-Gren Foundation for Anthropological Research; and the University of Technology, Sydney. I also acknowledge generous additional support from Emory College of Arts and Sciences and the Laney Graduate School in the form of a faculty subvention, and a grant from the Association for Asian Studies First Book Subvention program.

My family has visited me in every place I have ever lived, and I am certain that my interest in travel stems from them. Heartfelt thanks go to my parents, Amy and Shiu-Shin, as well as to Sandy and Steve, for always coming to visit no matter how long the flight or how short the trip.

And for everything, I thank John, my partner in life, love, and travel. With him, these years have been the best kind of journey imaginable, and I am so glad that we are in it together.

A LANDSCAPE OF TRAVEL

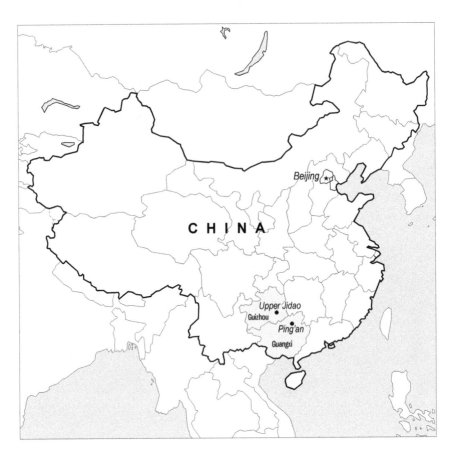

China, showing Guizhou and Guangxi (shaded) and the locations of Ping'an and Upper Jidao.

INTRODUCTION

Landscape, Mobility, Visuality

From 2006 to 2007, a billboard declaring, "Develop Rural Tourism, Build a New Socialist Countryside" (*Fazhan xiangcun lüyou, jianshe shehui zhuyi xin nongcun*), stood on the side of the Gui Xin highway—a smooth, recently constructed four-lane highway linking Guiyang, the capital of Guizhou, to cities in the southeastern prefectures and beyond (figure I.1). The slogans would have been familiar to anyone following the news in China: the placement of this particular billboard was clearly timed with the new state policies for rural development announced in early 2006. The Chinese government had revealed plans to build a New Socialist Countryside as a part of the 11th Five Year Plan (2006–2010), with a renewed emphasis on policies that would help rural people and communities to take part in, and benefit from, China's rapid modernization.[1] At the same time, 2006 was deemed the year of "China Rural Tourism" (*Zhongguo xiangcun you*) by the China National Tourism Administration (CNTA), thus firmly situating tourism within new national priorities (Xinhua 2005).

Such slogans promoting rural development and national progress are common across China, whether plastered on signs in characters large enough to read from passing vehicles or painted on the sides of buildings, houses, or schools. As a literal extension of the rural landscape, a billboard like this was a visible, material sign of the times. In the southeastern corner of Guizhou, where this particular billboard stood, the ambition was

FIGURE I.1. A billboard in Guizhou promotes rural tourism development and building the New Socialist Countryside (2006). Photo by the author.

to integrate the region's participation in the New Socialist Countryside policies with the development of rural tourism. Attracting tourists to the area was not a new idea.[2] Billboards lining highways and roads in rural Guizhou before 2006 also advertised particular regions, with the dual goal of attracting both tourists and investors (figure I.2). Therefore, while the promotion of rural tourism development in 2006 was not entirely new to the area, the deliberate, heavily publicized incorporation of tourism into larger programs for building a New Socialist Countryside gave rural tourism an even brighter patina of doing something not only for the rural communities involved but also for the nation as a whole.

In reality, the national designation of 2006 as the year of China Rural Tourism was a way for policy to "catch up" with tourism trends in China. At stake in bringing rural tourism together with rural development was both the relative success or failure of a New Socialist Countryside as well as an affirmation of the state's expectations for what rural China could contribute to the modernizing nation. The campaign to build a New Socialist Countryside together with the China Rural Tourism year suggested a concerted effort to reconceptualize the relationship between rural and urban

FIGURE I.2. A billboard in Huangping, Guizhou, beckons both tourists and investors (2004). Photo by the author.

regions in China. Rural tourism was lauded by the CNTA as an ideally balanced socioeconomic formula that could increase rural incomes while simultaneously boosting urban leisure. It would help establish the role of tourism in building a New Socialist Countryside, and it would provide new destinations for domestic tourism for urban residents who needed relief from the stresses of modern city living (CNTA 2007, 93). But what were the assumptions and expectations suggested in this straightforward association between rural tourism and rural development? What would it mean to develop rural tourism *and* build a New Socialist Countryside? Who were these billboards really addressing, and more important, who was supposed to actually *do* these things?

DOING TOURISM: REGIMES OF LABOR AND LEISURE

The photographs of the billboards in figures I.1 and I.2 were taken near Upper Jidao, an ethnic Miao village in southeastern Guizhou, where provincial government officials, including the tourism bureau, have promoted tourism development as a means of alleviating rural poverty since the early 2000s. These plans were developed with the knowledge of how tourism in other ethnic minority regions of China, including the ethnic Zhuang village of Ping'an in neighboring Guangxi, which had started its own tourism industry more than a decade earlier, had benefited local economies and communities by providing opportunities for rural ethnic minority households to earn cash incomes closer to home. The corollary that such development could promote local and national awareness about ethnic minority cultural traditions while also stimulating a desire to preserve and protect ethnic heritage was touted as a significant reason for promoting tourism *as* development in such areas. The question of *how* to do all of these things remained unanswered, however. For villagers in Upper Jidao and Ping'an, the two communities studied in this book, tourism development has been experienced and understood by village residents as "doing tourism" (*gao lüyou*), which involves an ever growing number of expectations, ambitions, and logistics.

Village residents talked about tourism as an active experience, as a process in which they clearly saw themselves playing a part (no matter how big or small). Their reflections on doing tourism should be understood as a critical means of asserting their own agency in the building and maintenance of their villages as desirable, consumable tourism destinations. Understanding how tourism is "done" in rural ethnic minority villages like Upper Jidao and Ping'an exposes the odd configuration of labor and leisure that creates and sustains tourism in China. To succeed, village residents have to comprehend not only what constitutes leisure for the relatively new and rapidly expanding domestic tourism market, but they also need to create ways to translate this concept of leisure into profitable and desirable forms of labor for themselves. For those individuals and communities who continue to be directly affected by tourism and rural development programs, the policies and politics of rural tourism reach deeply into notions of belonging and community, values and understandings of rural and urban as categories of place and subjectivity, the social impact of mobility in postreform China, and, of special importance in Ping'an and Upper Jidao, the consequences of being seen as rural ethnic minorities in contemporary Chinese society.

The experience of tourism for village residents extends beyond short-lived, momentary encounters with tourists to encompass learning how to be distinctly modern as rural and ethnic Chinese subjects. Tourism as a practice allows the ethnic minority residents to claim belonging in processes of national modernization, while reconfiguring the contemporary value of ethnic distinctiveness. The commodification and mediatization of ethnic and rural identities reveals a politics of appearance at work in this complex of labor and leisure, a politics in which an overriding concern with looking good encompasses the range of complicated and often contradictory developmental impulses in China's domestic modernization policies. Under these conditions, identity becomes increasingly contingent upon processes of visuality, involving not only how people and places are seen by others but also how people prepare themselves (and their home villages) to be seen. Residents of Ping'an and Upper Jidao are very concerned with finding the appropriate and most desirable ways to present themselves and their village environments (including architecture and the surrounding landscape) to tourists. Indeed, visuality is especially significant and consequential in tourism, and the work of "looking good" doubles onto individual senses of self, subjectivity, and shared cultural characteristics. Furthermore, the role of rural ethnic minority villagers in national programs for development through tourism is conditioned by shared understandings of why tourism is desirable, who should be a tourist, and who should be the "toured."

Rural tourism development, as the CNTA and other government bodies readily explain, could help to reverse the recent trend of rural-to-urban migration. But tourism travel illuminates another side of the myriad forces propelling internal migration in China. Tourism provides an analytical counterpoint for understanding rural-to-urban migration; it encapsulates a context in which to examine how mobility itself can be rendered both socially meaningful and politically suspect. In a country that has aimed to control the movement of its population through the household registration system (*hukou*; see Chan and Zhang 1999; F. Wang 2005), tourism travel within China has been nonetheless underexplored in terms of its discursive effects on the social significance of mobility domestically and among the overseas Chinese diaspora.[3] Statistics on internal migration and domestic tourism attest to the sheer enormity of how mobility in China has become part and parcel of everyday life. In 2003, the number of people not registered in their place of residence in China was 140 million, and 114 million individuals "participated in internal migration" (Huang and Zhan 2005, 2). Comparatively, in 2004, there were 1.1 billion domestic tourist trips taken in China, totaling 84.8 percent of the population (CNTA 2007) and increasing to more than 1.4 billion tourist trips taken in 2006 (CNTA 2008a).[4] By 2010, the official population of China was 1.34 billion. The number of internal migrants, or rural workers (*nongmin gong*), in China that year was 252 million, and the number of domestic tourism trips taken in the country reached 2.1 billion.[5]

Residents of rural ethnic minority villages like Ping'an and Upper Jidao have come to negotiate with tourism and migration as elements of their livelihoods and life experiences; in their everyday musings on what tourists might want to buy or where they themselves might like to visit, mobility is part of their participation in contemporary Chinese society. In such touristed places, being mobile and being seen are integral to local senses of belonging and opportunity; mobility and visuality, as social processes, deeply shape the contested meanings of travel for those whose lives and livelihoods are most at stake in the tourism industries and for whom migration away from the village remains a very real, very imaginable, alternative for achieving some economic stability. By interrogating the social and political arenas in which rural tourism has been promoted, the unacknowledged frictions embedded in the relationship between mobility and modernity are rendered more apparent. Ultimately, tourism has been made meaningful by village residents as a chance to transform their homes into better places to visit and ideally into better places to live.

This book is a portrait of the relationships between tourism, politics, and representation in an era when the freedom of movement has been declared a universal human right by the United Nations (Article 13).[6] In Ping'an and Upper Jidao, being seen and being mobile are deeply intertwined with how individuals perceive their life chances, but any opportunities that emerge remain in tension with national narratives of progress and development. Doing tourism has become a way for these communities and individuals to make sense of their contemporary contexts and to imagine future prospects. By examining, ethnographically, the regimes of labor and leisure in these two rural ethnic minority villages, it is thus possible to recognize the risks and opportunities emerging as China grapples with its rapid transformations and seemingly untold potential. I call this context a landscape of travel.

UNDERSTANDING A LANDSCAPE OF TRAVEL

To fully comprehend the extent of what doing tourism entails as well as to acknowledge that tourism is much more than building roads, serving meals, and greeting tourists, there is a need to understand how all of these activities take place under particular material and imagined circumstances. The transformations occurring in rural ethnic China are embedded in a landscape of travel, where mobility and visuality as social processes have come to frame the opportunities, possibilities, and meanings of tourism for village residents. It is within this landscape where tourists and village residents meet, where one person's leisure becomes another person's labor, and where imaginations and desires materialize as very real experiences. After all, for residents of Ping'an and Upper Jidao, mobility and visuality are daily tasks to be reckoned with; they constitute such mundane activities as sweeping village paths or making sure to be at the parking lot in time to meet the first tour bus of the day. Although the physical landscape around a village is largely experienced visually by tourists, this is a deeply and often troublesome *physical* matter for village residents who are expected to perform the labor necessary to maintain an appropriately rustic, rural appearance to their villages and fields and to imagine (and try to visualize) what *else* might appeal to potential tourists.

However, a landscape of travel is more than just the effects of tourism on the land and its people; this conceptual framework casts a wider gaze onto the multiple forms of and reasons for travel in China. Tourism is not just leisure, and travel should be engaged with as discourse, as constituent of subject formation, and as life opportunity. For village residents, tourism was merely one of many forms of mobility, and by extension possibilities, with which they lived. Thus a landscape of travel is not entirely the same as what has been called tourism landscapes by Claudio Minca and Tim Oakes (2006) or touristed landscapes by Carolyn Cartier and Alan A. Lew (2005). Tourism landscapes, following Minca and Oakes, are conceptualized with a greater emphasis on the subjectivity of the tourist; the concept of touristed landscapes, as described by Cartier (2005, 3), "concerns the possibilities of landscapes as toured and lived, places visited by their own residents, the dialectic of moving in and out of 'being a tourist.'" The latter concept extends landscape to include not only tourists but also all others present at the site of tourism, but I seek here to draw attention to how multiple forms of mobility overlap with one another, beyond the limits of a touristed place. More important, by not focusing on the mobility of tourists, this serves as a reminder that the agency and subjectivities of those who live in touristed places may not necessarily have much to do with the idea of "being a tourist" but they do figure prominently into what tourism means.

A landscape of travel is an ethnographic effort to take seriously how travel influences individual understandings of opportunity and identity; how rural ethnic villages undergo material, structural alterations to better suit tourism and achieve ideal modern, sanitized living conditions; and how village residents learn to be touristic in order to successfully build their village-based tourism industries to attract potential visitors. The seductiveness of rural ethnic villages in China is rooted in the circuits of a (trans)national nostalgia for a landscape that appears to embody, nourish, and sustain a more fundamental relationship between nature and human society. This desire for a particular form of romantic rurality drives political and social calls for international rural development, economic rationalizations of global and domestic tourism, and cultural celebrations of "national" ethnic diversity and the subsequent mainstreaming of minority identities. The resulting landscape is constructed to be generic enough *and* specific enough to satisfy the foreign tourist's desires for the exotic, the national urban dwellers' longing for a "simpler life," the regional daytripper's need for a brief escape, and even the village residents' aspirations for a place in modern China.

As a framework for conceptualizing the everyday experience of tourism, a landscape of travel therefore encompasses the physical and material transformations brought about by tourism development in villages and also the social changes and cultural politics of leisure, labor, and identity in China today. In employing landscape as an analytical device, landscape should be understood as both a literal component of the tourism experience (in terms of tourists coming to a village to look at the rural landscape) and a means for understanding the terrain of experiences, including migration, embedded in this ethnographic moment of tourism growth in China's ethnic minority villages.[7] At the heart of landscape's complexity is the tension between landscape as a material form and landscape as a process. This illuminates precisely how and why landscapes can become so contested; landscapes are shaped and made meaningful through human intervention, whether directly through agriculture or symbolically through stories and interpretation, and yet landscapes are most frequently approached and apprehended as static sights (perhaps best exemplified by the popularity of "landscape photography"). But the apparent stability of a landscape is deceptive, and, as Denis Cosgrove (2006, 56–57) has argued, "it is thus a simple and predictable step from promoting the pictorial or scenic qualities of specific regions as embodying essential qualities of a nation's territory and people, to seeking to fix their origins and preserve and protect them from change."

The relationship between land and human is equally obscured and revealed in a landscape; landscape is both a "field" of social action and agency (following Bourdieu 1977) and an already existing plane of possibilities and relationships embodied in the copresence of people and the land. Therefore, a primary goal in utilizing landscape as a framework for understanding travel is to develop a more comprehensive perspective on the complex, intersecting, and overlapping dynamics of tourism. Landscapes are a symbolic and physical manifestation of the perceived relationships between actuality (lived experiences) and potentiality (expected, or imagined, possibilities; Hirsch 1995, 5). To negotiate between actuality and potentiality thus places emphasis on analyzing landscape as "a means of conceptual ordering that stresses relations . . . acting so as to encompass rather than exclude" (Tilley 1994, 34) and makes it possible to recognize the structural forces at work in a phenomenon such as tourism and the spaces for agency and subject formation within these conditions.

There are multiple forces embedded in any sociopolitical context; Arjun Appadurai's oft-cited model of "scapes" that shape global cultural flows has been influential in highlighting the disjunctures of modern life.[8] He contends that "these [scapes] are not objectively given relations that look the same from every angle of vision but, rather, that they are deeply perspectival constructs, inflected by the historical, linguistic, and political situatedness of different sorts of actors" (Appadurai 1996, 33). Amid these disjunctures, however, mobility is one underlying constant in this formulation, as Louisa Schein has argued. She writes: "[Appadurai's] emphasis is on the mobility—of persons and of signs—effected through these contemporary modes and hence on the varied interconnections between peoples and spaces rather than their homogenous unities. His key point is not that people live increasingly similar lives under modernity but, rather, that they can imagine—and sometimes actualize—more and more different lives through the potentials of media consumption and geographic mobility" (Schein 1999, 362–63). Schein offers an important reminder that despite all of the apparent connections made possible in modernity, the consequences may be increased differences and scatter.

For those involved in village-based tourism development—from tourists to tour guides, government officials, consultants, and village residents—tourism and landscapes indeed look different from various perspectives. For example, in analyzing landscapes as an intersection of social relations in Norway, "rural tourism can be seen as an arena where landscape views and perceptions are negotiated between farmers and tourists" (Daugstad 2008, 404). Farmers, in Karoline Daugstad's study, viewed the landscape in terms of economic restructuring; tourists saw the landscape in terms of a romantic, nostalgic external view based on visual qualities as seen from a distance. In tourism development in northern Thailand, the "landscaping" of the rural becomes a cultural process of constructing a desirable, attractive, and pleasurable "Other": "Under the influence of an idyllic, traditionalist and nostalgic vision of the countryside, rural spaces [in Thailand] have been reinvented and transformed into appealing visual and conceptual archetypes which sustain discourses on national identity and history. Such 'landscaping' processes are qualitatively different from those which occurred at the end of the nineteenth century: while cultural difference was at that time encountered, it is now sought after; while it was equated with backwardness and danger, it is now considered as something picturesque and pleasurable" (Evrard and Leepreecha 2009, 245). Landscape in this sense suggests an ongoing process of control and mastery of rural areas and the people who live there, for the sake of the landscaper's or the tourist's (visual) pleasure and enjoyment.[9] The construction of a landscape is grounded in the matrix of social expectations it contains and the processes by which these ideas are rendered as socially acceptable ideas and dominant discourses. This approach to landscape tacks back and forth between the general and the particular, the imagined and the real, the similar and the different.

Moreover, through its very materiality, landscape is inextricably tied to images and representations of the land and human experiences of it. Given that the English word "landscape" was first introduced by painters in the late sixteenth century, "what came to be seen as landscape was recognized as such because it reminded the viewer of a painted landscape" (Hirsch 1995, 2). The idea of landscape shifts between the representational ideal of the painted landscape and the reality of the lived experience, thus allowing for the simultaneous consideration of social relations and mobility (Appadurai 1996 and Ingold 1993) and of imagery and visuality (Cosgrove 1984 and Mitchell 2002).[10] The power of landscape, as a representational form, demands attention to particular ways of seeing and how the act of seeing engages with and engenders structures of power. W.J.T Mitchell (2005, 337) glosses visuality as "practices of seeing the world and especially of seeing other people." The distinctions between vision and visuality are important in establishing a fundamental understanding of how the processes of seeing affect what is seen.

Examining vision as a social process allows for exploring how certain visions become more socially and politically significant than others. In other words, "the difference between the terms [vision and visuality] signals a difference within the visual—between the mechanism of sight and its historical techniques, between the datum of vision and its discursive determinations—a difference, many differences, among how we see, how we are able, allowed, or made to see, and how we see this seeing or the unseen therein" (Foster 1988, ix). The significance of understanding vision and visuality in modernity, which is "resolutely ocularcentric," as the art historian Martin Jay (1988, 3) has argued, cannot be overlooked.[11] After all, if the term "landscape" stems from pictorial practices of representation— namely, landscape paintings—then landscapes are by definition subjectively experienced through techniques of observation (following Crary 1990). In this way, landscapes are created and made meaningful through visual practices and processes of seeing and, in the case of tourism villages, of literally creating the proper, desired countryside and inhabitants *to be seen.*

Images of landscapes straddle the real and virtual; they gain efficacy and discursive power by virtue of their connection to "real" spaces, which then are perceived as natural and given. The supposed naturalness of landscape imagery effectively masks the inequalities, imbalances, and tensions existent in the very relationships engendered by the process of visual representation. As W.J.T. Mitchell (2002, 1–2) reminds us, it is important not to underestimate how landscape "is an instrument of cultural power, perhaps even an agent of power that is (or frequently represents itself as) independent of human intentions. Landscape as a cultural medium thus has a double role with respect to something like ideology: it naturalizes a cultural and social construction, representing an artificial world as if it were simply given and inevitable. . . . Thus, landscape always greets us as space, as environment, as that within which 'we' find—or lose—ourselves."[12] The politics of appearance are encapsulated in landscapes and imagery, and the often virulent debates over who could, or should, control the literal *look* of a tourism village—whether it should be government officials, the village residents themselves, or the media—reveal deeper issues at stake in terms of political power, social relations, and perceived economic opportunities.

By taking into consideration how landscape offers a conceptual framework for tracing social relations, a landscape of travel illuminates the complex networks of ambitions, expectations, and opportunities that are shaping transformations in toured places like Ping'an and Upper Jidao. This approach extends the idea of tourism as the "sacred journey" (Graburn 1989 [1977]). Drawing on Emile Durkheim (1912) and Edmund Leach (1961), Nelson Graburn (1989 [1977], 24–25) has argued that for tourists, touristic experiences take place within a structural formation of tourism and work that is constituted by opposing ends of the sacred (tourism, the nonordinary experience) and the profane (work, or the ordinary everyday). People move through phases of the sacred (tourism) and the profane (work) throughout their lifetimes, sometimes being tourists and sometimes not. As a result, Graburn has asserted, tourism should be understood as an integral part of life experience rather than as an anomaly.[13]

Pushing these ideas beyond tourists to the people who are the toured, the residents of destinations, it is crucial to recognize that tourism has not been an "added-value" project onto a presumably stable "everyday" village life. Destination communities should not be analyzed in simplistic binary terms of "before" or "after" tourism because neither the communities nor the tourism experiences in these communities are static. Rather, tourism is incorporated into narratives of past experiences, current livelihoods, and future aspirations for village residents, just as tourism is made meaningful for tourists over the course of a lifetime. There is one major difference, however; for the residents of tourist villages, experiencing tourism at home (as the toured, or as hosts) comprises the profane, the mundane everyday experience of work. The sacred, or nonordinary experience, for these village residents is actually the imagination and fulfillment of a "life worth living" (a key function of tourism in Graburn's formula (1989 [1977], 26) through the symbolic, social, economic, and political shifts brought about by being a tourism destination—which sometimes also included the possibility of imagining *being* a tourist (Harrison 2003) rather than *doing* tourism, once enough money was earned.

MOBILITY AND VISUALITY IN PING'AN AND UPPER JIDAO

In many ways, mobility and visuality are as deeply implicated in the experience of tourism for the residents of tourism villages as they are for the tourist.[14] For residents of rural tourism villages in China, tourism and migration have become ways of envisioning and mediating current circumstances. Concurrent surges in domestic urban-to-rural tourism and in internal rural-to-urban migration since the early 1990s attest to the point that mobility is constitutive of rural social lives rather than a "disruption" to an otherwise stable, static condition (Greenblatt et al. 2009). Tourism and migration are integrated into personal expectations and ambitions for rural tourism village residents and raise new questions about the sociopolitical force of imagining being able to travel. But in many rural tourism development programs, the unspoken expectation is that village residents will stop being mobile in order to participate in local tourism industries. Indeed, the entire purpose of rural tourism development often seems centered on stopping, or slowing, the "flow" of rural-to-urban laborers and migrants. Thus mobility becomes a socially ordered concept of opportunity for the villagers who are valued by the nation-state and by domestic and international tourists for their potential immobility. This discursive value of mobility hints at much larger issues of the sociopolitical differences between and attributes of being rural or being urban, being culturally mainstream or ethnically a minority, and being rich or being poor.

Visuality is likewise as significant as mobility in the lives and livelihoods of tourism village residents. While practices of seeing are deeply rooted in tourism and the commonplace activity of sightseeing (Adler 1989 and Urry 2002b [1990]) reflects "modern ocularcentrism" (Jay 1988) precisely because of the value placed on "seeing it for yourself," the labor involved in creating a sight to be seen often goes unnoticed. The close-knit relationship between visual experiences, everyday life, and dominant ideologies is embedded in what I call the politics of appearance; one means of understanding this has been to focus on the visual economy of touristic images and representations.[15] However, an even more significant aspect of the politics of appearance in tourism development is the work, discursive and material, involved in creating representative landscapes, experiences, and appearances *for* tourism. These are the images and surfaces created specifically for visual consumption by tourists and, in an era of ever increasing media outlets and forms, they play a critical role in how places are made suitable for development into tourist attractions. Such features promise to communicate knowledge and meaning *visually*, and to that end, tourism village residents (among others) debate and work to create and maintain an appropriate appearance.

This approach to understanding the impact and efficacy of visual images, following Deborah Poole (1997, 7), "stress[es] simultaneously the material and social nature of both vision and representation," where "relationships of referral and exchange among images themselves, and the social and discursive relations connecting image-makers and consumers" come together to be understood as an "image world." Examining the image world of Ping'an and Upper Jidao thus includes consideration of a range of materialities and technologies—from photographs to architecture to clothing—in order to demonstrate how the visual economy of tourism moves not only among potential tourists but also among those who work in tourism. Through the labor and imagination of tourism workers, the visual environments and experiences of tourism are produced. But whereas visual economy, in Poole's usage, depends in large part upon the existence of material images that physically move in circulation, the visuality of tourism includes the opinions and decisions involved in putting together a view, a scene, or a landscape that has the potential to exude a meaningful representativeness when made into a material image, such as a souvenir print or photograph. For those doing tourism, their attention remains focused on how to look good for tourists, an act that reveals complex processes of exchange, relations, and consumption embedded within the production of these good-looking villages.[16]

Proposed programs for rural tourism development in Ping'an and Upper Jidao almost always begin with and include a significant amount of work directed at improving the "look" of the villages, referencing the visual features that can be immediately seen from the roadside or parking lot, with the primary goal of looking good as a tourism destination. This bias toward visual experience in tourism—especially in these places that promote sightseeing and ethnic culture as their main tourist attractions—has led to a heightened attention to the construction and maintenance of photographic opportunities and visually recognizable differences. Certain visual motifs and practices are considered expedient to the success of a village; these visual expediencies draw on a complex of expectations, beliefs, and representational strategies that are visually rendered in tourism development and that, as a result, shape understandings of place and identity. The visual expediencies of tourism in rural ethnic villages include such elements as local styles of architecture, ethnic dress, agricultural features like terraced fields, natural décor, as well as general cleanliness and tidiness in public spaces. All of these things have to look good, not only outwardly for national or regional media such as television programs, magazines, and travel guides, but also to express the appropriate notions of "home" and hospitality. The idea of "looking good" has extended inwardly into notions of individual character, civilized (*wenming*) behavior, and modern attitudes. Indeed, village residents are exhorted to "look good," not just for the sake of tourists but for their own futures as well.

The question of the "look" of a tourism village is also where a number of conflicts have risen in relation to the effects of development, progress, and growth that might damage the "visual impact" of a destination. "Looking good" is crucial to tourism planning, and there is no shortage of information and approaches from the field of landscape architecture on how to create the greatest visual impact.[17] According to the Landscape Institute, a U.K.–based professional organization for landscape architects, the visual impact of a landscape is the product of its visual effect and visual amenity; the assessment of visual impact is frequently a core feature of development programs and policies.[18] In the *Strategic Environmental Assessment Study* on tourism development in Guizhou published as part of a World Bank project for the province, landscape and visual impact in rural tourism villages are directly addressed in terms of potential positive and negative effects on the tourist experience (World Bank 2007, 47–48). The architectural styles of homes, restaurants, and shops in tourism villages are considered for their compatibility with ideal forms of heritage tourism, and highways and road construction or upgrades are specifically cited as potentially "detract[ing] from the visual amenity of tourist sites" (ibid., 47). The implicit suggestion is that tourism destinations are not meant to reveal their fundamental dependence, or reliance, on transport and mobility. Roads might suggest that not only can tourists travel into these otherwise "traditional" destinations, but the residents of these destinations might actually be able to travel out of these places as well.[19] However contradictory, it is perhaps unsurprising that in the discourse of heritage preservation, the removal or avoidance of the trappings of mobility is considered desirable and preferable in the ideal visuality of rural tourism.

By approaching visuality as a social process, it becomes apparent that being seen is not merely a passive, inherently given condition of tourism. Rather, when considering the consequences of tourism on village architecture, vernacular rural landscapes, and the bodies of the village residents themselves, being seen is an active, productive process that makes identity meaningful in certain ways and communicates these notions through visual means. Identity becomes tied up in the dual nature of tourism as an act of movement and an act of seeing, where travel and image intersect in the formation of socially recognizable subjectivities. In Ping'an and Upper Jidao, one's cultural and social identities are molded by existing discourses and new, local ways of imagining being ethnic and being rural. Current practices and recent histories of image-making, media production, and tourist photography of ethnic minorities continue to inform and contribute to the construction of meaningful identities for these communities. The close study of the relationship between visual images and tourism in China thus sheds new light on how categories such as "ethnic minority" and "rural" have been woven into the fabric of the contemporary Chinese nation through tourism for the purposes of socioeconomic development. John L. Comaroff and Jean Comaroff (2009, 38; italics in original) have dubbed this process as "Ethnicity, Inc.," where in their formula "ethnicity" is taken as "the equation *ethnicity = culture + identity*," which "interpolates itself into the domain of capital, thus constituting the *Inc.*" Tourism is just one way in which ethnicity, or as they put it, "identity-as-difference," comes to accrue base material value toward the accumulation of wealth and prestige.

Because appearances are posited as central to tourism success, the onus of visual representation falls upon village residents to look, and to appear, ethnic and rural. In these instances, being seen is politically and materially important. As the Chinese national government attempts to stem rural-to-urban migration by promoting urban to rural tourism, it is becoming increasingly possible to literally see how the rural has been reconceived, represented, and reimaged as a desirable place for urbanites to visit and for rural villagers to stay. In this landscape of travel, the visual sensuousness of landscape and the mobile sensibility of travel are intertwined with village transformations and individual aspirations. Changes to the look of a particular landscape suggest major changes occurring at larger national levels (Lewis 1979, 21), and an ethnographic approach to this landscape allows for the exploration of the wholeness of a phenomenon (such as national programs for tourism development) and of particular issues of relatedness occurring within that contextual whole (such as intravillage conflicts and contests over the consequences of tourism growth).

By participating in a mainstream activity such as tourism, rural ethnic minority villagers have been learning to imagine and to place themselves in the whole of China—economically, socially, and politically. At the same time, however, they need to find ways of promoting their villages' own distinctiveness within the national tourism market, and the histories of tourism development shed light on how these villages have come to their specific forms as rural ethnic tourism destinations. For village residents, successfully doing tourism in Ping'an and Upper Jidao means referencing shared national ideas of what it means to be a rural ethnic minority in contemporary China and finding ways to represent and to sell these qualities to incoming tourists.

大同小异

CHAPTER 1

SIMILAR, WITH MINOR DIFFERENCES

A Tale of Two Villages

"Doing tourism" in Ping'an and Upper Jidao entails pragmatic and discursive understandings of both being an ethnic minority and being rural in China today.[1] After all, the potential success of tourism in these communities rests upon their ability to turn a profit from the tourist's experience of encountering ethnic difference in a visually and physically distinctive rural landscape. While similarities between many ethnic tourism destinations around the world speak to the standardizing effects of tourism as a commercial enterprise, studies of ethnic tourism often emphasize the role of national government policies and programs that direct and regulate ethnic encounters. This regulatory feature of ethnic tourism points to contestations over the governance of ethnic identity in contemporary nation-states, including China. For village residents who must do tourism, their identities as ethnic and rural are more than performative roles to be enacted in the presence of tourists; these subjectivities provide a moral understanding of the changes and conflicts experienced in each community over the past decades of socioeconomic transformation.

HAVE YOU LOST YOUR ETHNIC IDENTITY?

It took me a few months in Ping'an to work up the nerve to approach Lao, one of the elder leaders of the village, for an interview. Everyone said I needed to speak with him to get the whole story on how tourism started in the village. I was worried about not being taken seriously by someone so well respected within the village, even though I knew his family fairly well. Trained as a doctor, Lao was a Party cadre and had been privy to the first discussions on tourism in Ping'an in the late 1970s. He opened the village's second guesthouse, named Li Qing after his two daughters, in the early 1990s. By the mid-2000s, Li Qing was a veritable brand-name enterprise by Ping'an standards, with three guesthouses and a steady stream of foreign and domestic customers.

The first time I asked Lao if he was willing to be interviewed, he said yes but he was busy that day; he suggested that I find him another time. Meanwhile, without my prompting, he wrote out the history of the village's tourism development for me, and when I returned to interview him, he read the document aloud and I asked questions to clarify certain points.[2] When he reached the end, I asked what he thought about the future of tourism in the village. Lao pointed out four problems that needed to be addressed: more equitable monetary compensation for villagers who worked on maintaining the terraced fields; more public infrastructure, such as village paths and toilets for tourists; better management of water resources; and treating tourists with greater respect. On this last point, Lao said that the Zhuang used to be known for their hospitality, generosity, and cleanliness, but over time, as a result of tourism, these "special characteristics" (tese) of the Zhuang were fading fast. This prompted me to ask, as I had started to do jokingly with some of my friends in the village, if Lao thought that the villagers had stopped "being Zhuang" as a result of tourism in Ping'an. Many scholars, journalists, and tourists write about this idea, I added—namely, that tourism is causing people to lose their ethnic identity. Did he agree? Without a moment's pause, Lao responded, "No."

He elaborated on his point a few days later, when I went back to his house to pick up a copy of his history of tourism development in Ping'an. He was at home with his wife and one of his grandsons. (During the week, Lao's wife and grandson lived in the county seat, Longsheng, so that the grandchildren could attend primary school in town. They were back in Ping'an for a weekend visit.) Lao handed me a carefully rewritten copy of his account, and I looked through it. Then, Lao suddenly added that he had thought of something that had really changed in village life and affected their "folk customs" (*minsu*) since tourism had begun twenty-five years ago: the environment and sanitation in the village were much, much worse now than before, he declared.

Before a lot of tourism, Lao continued, the surroundings and the water in the village were "very lovely, very nice," but with "development, and doing tourism, the garbage hasn't been taken care of—the water in the ravines, streams . . . now you don't even dare to wash your hands or feet [in that water]; the environment is really bad." This was a matter of custom, he added, because the environment's decline directly affected the life and the look of the village. "The original atmosphere, the original appearance [*yuanfeng yuanmao*] of the village has changed," and he put part of the blame for this squarely on the villagers themselves. "The people's habits are bad—human waste, sewage, animal waste, everything is dumped in the ravine" to flow down the mountainside to the river below. I suggested that perhaps it was the numbers of tourists who were contributing to the environmental problems, but Lao disagreed. To him, the problems of sanitation and the decline of the environment in Ping'an were the problems of the people who lived in Ping'an. The inference was clear: for the Zhuang, his community, to neglect the environment was a crisis rooted in the core of their consciousness as a people. To be Zhuang, Lao implied, was to take pride in the environment and thus to maintain its cleanliness; the degradation of the latter, therefore, was an indication of the decline of Zhuang identity itself. This was a comment not only on individual behavior and bad decisions; this was a matter of their collective, shared identity as a part of the Zhuang ethnic group.

My initial surprise at the apparent disconnect between the changes Lao associated with ethnic identity in the village and what I assumed to be "ethnic" reveals both the wide applicability of the term "ethnic" to describe myriad human behaviors and attributes and the specificity and the seriousness of these claims. When I joked about "losing your ethnic identity" with others in Ping'an, the only concrete aspect of Zhuang life that we usually agreed was being "lost" was knowledge of the Zhuang language among younger generations. The children now spoke standard Chinese (Mandarin, *putonghua*) in school and in their interactions with tourists; some children even preferred to use standard Chinese instead of the local, regional dialect (called Guilinhua, named after the near-est major city).[3] Historically, language provided a recognized "boundary" (following Barth 1969) between the ethnic identities of the tourists (who generally were not Zhuang or did not know the northern dialect of Zhuang spoken in Ping'an) and the village residents.[4] How was sanitation and the treatment of wastewater somehow also an ethnic characteristic, or at least tied to local senses of collective community and belonging, as Lao seemed to suggest?

Ethnic tourism has been defined as a type of tourism "marketed to the public in terms of the 'quaint' customs of indigenous and often exotic peoples . . . [including] visits to native homes and villages, observation of dances and ceremonies, and shopping for primitive wares and curios" (Smith 1989 [1977], 4). "As long as the flow of visitors is sporadic and small," Valene Smith (ibid., 4) has written, "host-guest impact is minimal." However, Ping'an received more than two hundred thousand visitors in 2006, and by resident reports the numbers have continued to increase since; for a village of approximately 850 regular residents, the impact of this many tourists can hardly be minimal. Lao's concern over the environment in Ping'an tied his worries about the effects of environmental degradation to the material, cultural lives of village residents and to the ways in which the Zhuang would be perceived by national and international visitors. In his assessment, the problems boiled down to ethnicity. He was proud of being Zhuang but disappointed in the community's behavior that reflected poorly on their collective identity. After all, Ping'an was a Zhuang village—it said so in all of the tourism brochures and on a sign at the entrance to the village. Beyond the importance of maintaining pride in one's own community, even more pressing at the time was the fact that in response to greater market competition from other tourism villages in the region, Ping'an residents themselves were actively trying to make the place more "ethnic" for tourists.

Lao's perspective on Zhuang ethnicity revealed both a local understanding of ethnic identity that diverged from dominant national discourses of ethnic minorities (*shaoshu minzu*) and a cautious eye to the demands and requirements of the current politics of tourism and development. "Sanitation" and "cleanliness" are keywords of rural tourism and rural development more generally, and by linking Zhuang identity to the imperative to be clean, Lao in turn reaffirmed the significance of Zhuang ethnicity to both a personal, subjective sense of self and belonging to this place and to the broader imperatives of the national tourism marketplace. The codification of ethnicity in contemporary postreform China, particularly in cultural productions and place-based naming strategies, has marked the ethnic as a particular type of commodified characteristic within the greater national narrative of China's development since the establishment of the People's Republic in 1949.[5] These techniques and stereotypes are fully exploited in tourism today.

MAKING *SHAOSHU MINZU*

While studies of tourism often emphasize the appeal of the ethnic "Other" as a factor in tourist motivations, the institutional state history of ethnic classification and minority identity in China requires a closer examination of the relationships between ethnicity and national modernization policies (Sautman 1999), how the state has constructed ethnic difference, and how these relate to the ways ethnicity is used in Chinese tourism. Two interlocking aspects of ethnic identity construction and representation frame the circumstances now faced by rural ethnic tourism villages. First, early discourses of non-Chinese populations within the Chinese imperial imagination informed modern nationalist sentiments in China, most notably during the establishment of the Republican government in the early twentieth century. Second, the Ethnic Classification project (*minzu shibie*) of the 1950s and 1960s began the process of formally determining the number, boundaries, and characteristics of the ethnic minority groups recognized by the Chinese Communist state.[6] The inherent difficulty of such a project, and the complexities involved in determining a finite number of ethnicities, are visually illustrated in documentary and feature films of the 1950s and 1960s that depict ethnic minorities. In these films, ethnicity was made visually knowable and recognizable, as the country's forward-looking development was rendered into visual narrative form. This emphasis on the visible evidence of ethnicity and modernization has left lingering traces on how tourism development in rural ethnic minority regions is expected to unfold and ultimately succeed.

Concern over, or at least an expressed interest in, the non-Chinese populations at the borders of the Chinese empire has been recorded since as early as the first century BCE, in the *Records of the Historian,* by Sima Qian (Harrell 2001, 36). The mythology of barbarian tribes occupying the empire's edges and borderlands was also a feature of a Confucian worldview (Dikötter 1992, 2–7). Notions of classification and identification already existed in imperial records, and embedded in these writings were politically driven ideas of barbarian populations as capable of being "transformed" or becoming "Chinese" (*hanhua*) (Dikötter 1992 and Leibold 2007).[7] Visual representations were significant as a tool for classifying and knowing difference. Ethnological reporting in the Ming and Qing dynasties generally appeared in one of two genre forms: gazetteer accounts or pictorial descriptions, such as the "Miao Albums."[8]

During the late Qing dynasty, the growing presence and activities of Western missionaries in China also contributed to conceptualizations of race, drawn from Western theories of racial types.[9] In southwestern China especially, Western missionaries working in Guizhou and Yunnan recorded their own tribal classifications of the local populations (see Clarke 1911) while adding to local understandings of group identity during this tumultuous period of imperial decline and revolution (Cheung 1995 and Swain 1995). The effects of these discursive changes were extensive and deep. By the late nineteenth century, challenges to the Qing empire increasingly began to be formulated in racialized terms.[10] The term *minzu* first appeared in China around 1895, as a Chinese pronunciation of the Japanese *minzoku*. *Minzu* was first used to refer to the majority Han people, as opposed all other minority groups, and later, by extension, to the notion of a Han nation-state in the Republican era (Y. Zhang 1997, 76), glossed by Sun Yat-sen's principle of nationalism (*minzu zhuyi*).[11]

Minzu zhuyi was an inclusive discourse of racial amalgamation, small in scale yet large in scope, in which, according to Sun Yat-sen, the new Chinese Republic would unite the Han, Manchu, Mongol, Hui, and Tibetan territories, subsequently uniting these five races into a single people (Leibold 2007, 38). Not surprisingly, these five races were associated with the territorial boundaries of the new Chinese Republic. As a result, discourses of *minzu* shifted from relating to notions of the nation-state, in the political sense of autonomous rule and governance, to concepts of ethnicity and identity, rooted in shared social traits and histories (Y. Zhang 1997, 76). These pre-Communist strategies of knowing and classifying ethnic difference in the modern Chinese nation-state deeply informed the policies of the early Chinese Communist government (Harrell 2001, 37; and Mullaney 2004a and 2011).

The Chinese Communist Party was concerned with ensuring the unity of the nation while representing the new nation-state as one founded on the will of people. The granting of autonomy to regions inhabited by ethnic minorities—a decision included in Communist policies before the People's Republic of China was formally established in October 1949—meant only that "in regions where one ethnic group exercised autonomy, a member of that group should head the [local] government" (Mackerras 2004, 304–5; see also Heberer 1989). By 1953, the plan to develop People's Congresses at national, provincial, county, and local levels with one representative from each minority group in the National People's Congress meant that a limited number of minority groups was needed to construct the congress. However, censuses taken between 1953 and 1954 under an original policy that allowed groups to self-identity and self-name produced more than four hundred different ethnic group names nationwide (Fei 1981, 64; and Schein 2000, 81).[12]

To determine a more manageable number, at least in terms of the composition of the National People's Congress, linguists and social science researchers were commissioned to identify and classify the various ethnic minority groups within China's political borders in the campaign known as the Ethnic Classification project. The 1956 text of the drafted policy on national minorities and the "national question" (Moseley 1966) revealed the careful and deliberate movements of the young Chinese Communist Party government toward shifting the significance of *minzu* from nationality, and its possible corollary of nationhood for minority groups within China, toward the classification of these groups as "minority nationalities," or ethnic minorities. The 1950s Ethnic Classification project therefore had the effect of relegating *minzu* to the status of ethnic minorities in order to assert the political legitimacy of the new government over minority populations (Tapp 2012). It also sparked ongoing debates over the definition of the term "nationality" with regard to the unity of the Chinese state, which was perceived as a national body (Cai 1987 and Wang Lei 1983).

Although this project was new in the sense that it was justified and undertaken as a part of the Communist government's effort to establish its organizing structures and governing principles, these classifications were conceptually linked to earlier ideas of sociocultural difference and imaginations of the new sociopolitical order.[13] The Zhuang ethnic group provides a particularly illuminating example of ethnic classification as ethnic *creation* (Kaup 2000). Despite relatively low numbers of people declaring themselves to be Zhuang in the first census of 1953, the number of individuals identifying as Zhuang steadily increased over the ensuing decades at a rate of about 1.5 percent annually (ibid., 91). This change was in large part spurred by the political establishment of the Guangxi Zhuang Autonomous Region in 1958, the country's first autonomous region, and the attendant perceived benefits of this political identity, particularly in contrast to the neighboring provinces of Guizhou and Yunnan.

Researchers working in the Ethnic Classification project drew upon Stalin's 1913 four "common criteria" for the identification of nations—namely, a common language, a common territory, a common mode of economic production, and a common culture or psychological makeup (Gladney 1996, 66–67; Mullaney 2004b, 200; and Schein 2000, 83)—in order to identify groups and assign each group to a notched rank on a scale of human social development. This scale was based on a schema of the evolution of human history and social progress developed by Lewis Henry Morgan (1963 [1877]).[14] The entrenchment of these ideas of social evolution and economic production in the pursuit of socialism resulted in ethnic groups being assigned to one of five economic production types—primitive, slave, feudal, capitalist, and socialist—with the assumption that the Han ethnic majority was in a state of late feudalism (Schein 2000, 83). Thus the Ethnic Classification project was not only intended to reduce the four hundred self-identified ethnic groups into a more manageable number by emphasizing similarities but also to position the officially recognized groups along a unidirectional scale of social progress and development, under the guidance of the Chinese Communist Party.

VISUALIZING ETHNICITY

The codification of ethnic difference in China was the result of careful action and policy; studies of these newly classified groups were published as government reports, scholarly studies, and documentary films. The films were intended to form a comprehensive visual record of all official ethnic minority groups, and they reveal much about the intersection of politics, science, and art at the time (Krüger 2003).[15] These films created and shaped the visually recognizable ethnic characteristics that still dominate media representations today. Production began in 1957, when film crews operating under the orders of the central government and with support from provincial nationalities institutes traveled to ethnic minority areas. The project was terminated at the onset of the Cultural Revolution in 1966, although a few films were later completed and released in 1976.[16]

These films not only contributed to the classification of ethnic groups in China, but they also contributed to the classification of knowledge about ethnicity. The production of the films brought into question fundamental concerns over science, authenticity, aesthetics, politics, and what constitutes "documentary" (Alexander 2005). In 1961, in the middle of the film production period, a series of evaluation forums took place during which the relevant teams and scholars involved with the films debated the distinctions between "general documentary films," "popular science films," and "scientific documentary films." During this same period, fictional, narrative "minority films" (*shaoshu minzu dianying*) were also made by central film agencies, thus necessitating that the films of the Ethnic Classification project be distinguished as scientific documents lest they be confused with their fictional counterparts. The classification project films were ultimately categorized as "scientific documentary films" and were intended to be understood as depictions of the social and cultural lives of ethnic minority groups in their "original" state before liberation by the Communist Party. While representing the livelihoods, religious beliefs, and social structures of specific ethnic groups, voice-over narratives in the films were highly critical of these practices and typically concluded with statements about the bright futures awaiting these ethnic groups as a result of Communist liberation. According to an official abstract issued by the present-day Institute for Nationality Studies, these films were explicitly not to address post-1949 conditions. The statement declared: "It should be confirmed that scientific documentaries are to record the social aspects before Liberation. . . . To reflect the new social aspects after Liberation is a task of documentary films and feature films and other kinds of films, and not of scientific documentaries" (Krüger 2003, Appendix 1, 44).

According to Karsten Krüger (ibid., Appendix), who has assembled a range of interviews with some of the filmmakers involved in the production of these scientific documentaries, reports, and transcribed discussions about the films, reenactments were used in the films to represent life conditions before 1949, but any possible contradictions between the use of reenacted scenes and the production of these scientific films as authentic documents were cast aside because ethnographers and researchers were involved in the actual production process, bestowing scientific validity to the films' content. Scripts were written and approved by the ethnographers and film studios before any shooting took place. Teams of cameramen and sound recorders worked with ethnographers, and every film project was subjected to extensive external editing and review from the beginning to the end.

After 1961, directors had to come up with a shooting outline, essentially a visualization of the entire film, before any actual filming could occur. Most productions were proofed twice, once as a rough edit and once again after the final cut. Changes could be asked for during either of these phases. Those doing the proofing were experts, scientists and other high-level leaders at the studios and institutes. These classification films were envisioned only for scholarly audiences; they were distributed to universities, institutes, and museums in the areas where the films had been produced and kept centrally at the Institute for Nationality Studies in Beijing. Universities and research groups with scientific and educational purposes could borrow the films (for example, for classes on Marxism-Leninism and ethnology, and courses on attaining a socialist society). Ostensibly the scholarly audiences for which the films were intended would be able to "see past" the reenacted scenes and therefore be capable of accepting and analyzing the films as wholly authentic representations of ethnic minority livelihoods before 1949. The films were not shown publicly to a general audience, and until 1988 they were not screened outside of China.[17]

The limited distribution of the Ethnic Classification films belies the broader context of film production in the early decades of the Chinese Communist government. At this time, as today, film studios were extremely active due to a belief in the potential of film to serve national purposes. Although a majority of the films produced during the early Communist period dealt with such common socialist themes as the proletariat struggle against oppressive bourgeoisie, land reform, and military might, by 1955 there was also a noticeable number of "minority films" featuring ethnic minority themes and actors (see Li Zhuangming 1997). The coincidence of the ethnographic film project and of the "minority film" genre of feature films should not be overlooked. Approximately twenty minority films were made in the 1950s, and another twenty in the first half of the 1960s (Y. Zhang 1997, 79–81). For example, *Five Golden Flowers*

(*Wuduo Jinhua,* directed by Wang Jiayi)—a film about socialist modernization, agricultural collectivization, and women's liberation among the Bai of Yunnan—was released in 1959 (Notar 2006, 47).[18]

Another popular film from this era is *Third Sister Liu* (*Liu San Jie,* directed by Su Li, released in 1960), which is about a Zhuang woman who seeks liberation from oppressive landlords. Despite the relatively small percentage of actual ethnic minority peoples in China, their role in Chinese cinema was important for the national agenda; minority feature films "purported to show the way of life of these minority peoples, and their enthusiasm for socialism, [and] contributed to the policy of national integration" (Clark 1987, 19). Paradoxically, these minority films were often celebrated for their commitment to promoting a distinct Chinese "national style" (*minzu fengge*), where "the outcome of locating 'national style' in ethnic cultural practices was never a restoration of 'minority' cultures to 'majority' status, but always a legitimation of minority peoples as part of the 'solidarity' of the Chinese nation" (Y. Zhang 1997, 79–80; see also Gladney 1994).[19]

The production of scientific documentary and minority feature films in the early years of Communist China has had a noticeable impact on contemporary constructions of ethnic minority identity and continues to legitimate Han cultural and political hegemony. Thus, when considered alongside the minority films genre, the authenticity of the scientific documentaries of the Ethnic Classification Project, which used reenactments to visualize ethnicity and render ethnic difference knowable, is located precisely in the fact that ethnography at this time was in the service of the Communist Party—the films are quite reasonably authentic Communist ethnographies.[20] The visual images and socialist narratives of ethnic minority groups presented in scientific films were produced and circulated alongside a broader trend in "images of minorities" that "melded surface features of minority customs with various socialist agendas" (Schein 2000, 87), such as pictorial illustrations of ethnic peoples engaged in political or militaristic activities or, as in feature films like *Five Golden Flowers,* Bai ethnics celebrating their socialist liberation.[21]

ETHNIC BORDERS AND BOUNDARIES

Although the Ethnic Classification project formally began in the 1950s, the work of classifying China's ethnic groups did not conclude until the early 1980s, when fifty-six ethnicities were officially recognized (including fifty-five ethnic minorities and the majority Han ethnic group). The project spanned a number of decades and discursive modes depending on the political exigencies of each era, which Louisa Schein (2000, 80–99) has defined as the years 1949–57 (the original census and classifications), 1958–76, and the 1980s–90s. Ethnic distinctiveness was "leveled" during the Cultural Revolution (1967–76) in favor of socialist unity, Schein (ibid., 86) argues, a move that began to redraw the borders and boundaries of what constituted acceptable and unacceptable differences. In the postreform years, the ways in which ethnicity and ethnic identities are understood and experienced have continued to shift according to current social and political conditions.

A collective effect of the Ethnic Classification project was to define the boundaries and borders of ethnic identity (see Barth 1969). Some groups were distinguished from each other and assigned different names to concretize differences, while some self-identified groups were brought together on the basis on apparent linguistic or shared social similarities (though, as the Zhuang exemplify, this was politically motivated from above and below). The classification of ethnic groups relegated each group's socioeconomic conditions to a place along a continuum of development, based on Marxist-Leninist formulations of class and labor, thus linking all ethnic groups into a singular historical narrative of socialist progress. This classification was intended to assist in the direct intervention by government policies for the purposes of socioeconomic reform. For many ethnic groups, the classifications were quite new; the Miao, in particular, are noted as an example of a single-name group comprising communities who speak mutually unintelligible languages and are spread over enormous distances, from Hunan to Guizhou to Yunnan and even across the border to Laos and Thailand.[22] What bound together various individuals within a defined ethnic minority group was a more abstract and broader notion of culture and ethnicity that could extend across huge swaths of physical land and geography. This formulation of ethnicity did not need to reflect actual lived networks of exchange and social interaction, but it did provide a useful category for political organization and structures by the central Chinese state, as well as new areas of study for contemporary scholars both in China and abroad.[23]

Of course, it was not only the minority groups who were affected by ethnic classification. Certain preferential policies directed at ethnic minorities boosted the number of self-identified Zhuang in the early years of the Communist regime, while in more recent cases some Han have shown a preference toward marrying Hui Muslims to access rights and privileges for themselves and their families, despite ongoing public criticisms of the perceived government favoritism shown toward minorities (Gladney 1996, xv–xvi). How ethnicity is deployed as a category potentially affects all social and political relations; indeed, being ethnic as a "way of being" (Harrell 2001) illuminates the integral role of and interrelations between the Chinese state, its official history, and concepts of ethnicity. For instance, Susan Blum's work (2001) has recontextualized ethnicity in China by taking into account majority views of various minority groups. Examining the language used by the Han to speak about ethnic minorities, Blum (ibid., 13) invokes the idea of "portraits" to emphasize the selectivity of representations of difference.[24] She presents four "prototypes" of otherness at work in Yunnan: the fetishized ethnic other (represented by the Dai), the resistant, disliked ethnic other (represented by the Wa, Zang/Tibetan, and Hui), the colorful, harmless ethnic other (the Naxi and the Yi), and the "almost-us" (meaning almost Han: the Bai). Such typologies often reveal more about those in charge of creating the prototypes than those included within them, of course; "the minority nationalities help the Han to see themselves" (ibid., 176). However, although "minority nationalities in general are often lumped together, in distinction to the Han . . . it is clear upon inquiry that some are more distinct than others" (ibid.).

It is neither sufficient to simply accept the boundaries of difference as posited by dominant perspectives, nor to refuse entirely the structures that guide and inform ethnic identity constructions in China today. The changes and attributes ascribed onto ethnic identity in China are reflective of mainstream Chinese social imaginaries, and they in turn hold meaning for the communities involved. These latter significances may be contested or made complicated by local contexts, as suggested earlier in this chapter in Lao's story on cleanliness and Zhuang identity. In another example, "the Miao . . . have embraced some of these [external] definitions in a dialogic accommodation with the modes by which they were typified," and therefore "the defining of the Miao is not reducible to a form of knowledge/power in which external agents script and draw the boundaries of Miao identity for them" (Schein 2000, 62). A number of characteristics attributed to Miao culture and customs are often raised by Miao themselves, including the *lusheng* (a bamboo reed instrument), drinking, song, attire, and conventions of sociality (including "highly codified norms of reciprocity, offering food with bare hands and drink with two hands, improvised singing back and forth between host and guest, and copious amounts of drinking" [ibid., 63]).[25]

These internal typologies of Miao identity work alongside external definitions, sometimes coinciding and sometimes not. The tension between the multiple possible meanings of "being Miao" render the group name, Miao, a "composite sign" (Rack 2005, 62–65), where the ethnic way of being Miao can simultaneously operate as a referent both to the nation (and national unity) and to local distinctiveness. In Mary Rack's research, she found that a regional university in western Hunan highlighted images of the Miao in its official publicity campaigns, as the university was located in the capital city of West Hunan Miao and Tujia Autonomous Prefecture. These "images of the Miao were both an attraction in themselves and an indication of the role of the university in the development of the region" (ibid., 63–64) and, by extension, the role of the university in acting in conjunction with national agendas and imperatives. That said, Rack (ibid., 66) adds, it is important to recognize and acknowledge that such representations and references to ethnic identity can be just as frequently ignored instead of interpreted. The effectiveness of ethnic identity as a composite sign is reflected in how ethnic difference becomes identified as a resource for tourism development, as both a marker of what is to be valued in a tourism destination and of associated conditions and differences that the central state is poised to address through development. This occurs in a manner not dissimilar to the scientific films of the Ethnic Classification period that represented ethnic difference within a narrative of progress under the leadership of the government. The key objective is to restrict ethnic identity into a series of bounded, limited features ("special characteristics") that can either be transformed, if needed, or celebrated—or both.

The boundaries and borders of what could or would be acceptable as ethnic are mutually maintained, internally and externally, as a process of negotiation between national, mainstream, local, and individual imaginations and aspirations. When being ethnic becomes a part of doing tourism, how this is actually achieved refers back to and relies upon existing forms and categories of ethnic identity. In Ping'an and Upper Jidao, the need to be distinctive and to adhere to certain expected characteristics of ethnic difference is deeply internalized into local perspectives on doing tourism. Tourism, development, and ethnicity are thus wound up in overlapping relations of understanding how identities are forged and what opportunities are imaginable in China today.

THE ETHNIC IN TOURISM

If ethnic identity is seen as the result of negotiations over the perceived limits and boundaries of sociocultural difference, then the process of creating meaningful ethnic experiences for tourists always runs up against the possibility of disappointment. Jing Li has recounted a case of ethnic tourism blues: a young, male, non-Dai tourist returned to a Dai ethnic tourism village in Xishuangbanna, Yunnan, in search of the local "Dai bride" he had met previously. To his dismay, he learned that the "bride" was doubly false—she was not in fact Dai, and she was not actually going to marry him. This story became a joke among the local women who run tourism businesses. Li concludes by suggesting that "the distance between regret and laughter [in this anecdote] reveals processes of fantasizing the Other by consumers and the simultaneous deconstruction of these fantasies by hosts" (Jing Li 2003, 52). Indeed, it is precisely this "distance between regret and laughter" that characterizes ethnic tourism encounters, which rely upon inherent discrepancies, deceptions (playful or serious), and deliberate attempts to mold the interaction for the mutual satisfaction of all parties involved.[26]

Authenticity in tourism is paradoxical, and this paradox is experienced in senses of disappointment (Oakes 2006a). In ethnic tourism, the notion of encountering an authentic, exotic ethnic is impossible; the "Heisenberg effect is inevitable. The search for the exotic is self-defeating because of the overwhelming influence of the observer on the observed" (van den Berghe and Keyes 1984, 345–46). Nevertheless, as suggested earlier among some Miao who adopted with pride certain features of dominant, mainstream characterizations of Miao ethnicity, the ethnic other in tourism often must self-consciously construct and maintain an ethnic boundary so as to sustain tourism activities, often in conjunction with a middleman travel guide (ibid., 347).[27]

Ethnic tourism has always been involved in and dependent upon strategies of representation; it is "the marketing of tourist attractions based on an indigenous population's way of life" (Swain 1989 [1977], 85). What drives ethnic tourism are the connections between fantasy and reality enacted between village residents and tourists at the borders or "contact zones" (Clifford 1997 and Pratt 2008 [1992]) of tourism destinations, which are made visible and tangible in the village through material means. The exotic ethnic other becomes a carrying vessel for the resolution of these tensions in a popular, positive format that celebrates difference as a form of entertainment and enlightenment. As Li Yang and Geoffrey Wall (2009, 560) have argued: "With the broad integration of ethnicity into tourism worldwide, the representation, consumption, and experience of ethnicity have become fashionable. 'Ethnic' has become a popular tourist icon, consumed and produced locally and afar, from ethnic restaurants, neighborhoods, and markets to ethnic museums, theme parks, and tourist villages." As an icon of otherness, the ethnic in tourism straddles discursive conceptualizations of nature and culture (Cohen 2001), past and present, but ethnic boundaries require constant negotiation and production, however, by both the tourist and the toured. For example, in Indigenous performances on Wala Island, Vanuatu, "a good performance of the show is not simply to please tourists, and for them to evaluate. It is a dialogic encounter which is as much about self-worth and self-evaluation" for the local performers as well (Tilley 1997, 84). The dynamics of tourism encounters thus produce "touristic culture," in which the multiplicity of meanings made possible by ethnic boundary maintenance allows for identity to become newly significant in varied ways.[28]

Ethnic tourism is often folded into more encompassing narratives of heritage, nationhood, and belonging, and both heritage and ethnic tourism tend to be located in rural peripheries that are perceived as far away (in time and space) from the modern urban center.[29] Indeed, the gulf between the past and the present prompts tourists to seek authentic experiences in other places, through other people.[30] Thus the rural, the ethnic, and notions of heritage draw upon familiar modernist binaries of traditional/modern, authentic/fake, real/copy in tourist experiences shaped by nostalgia and longing. Nostalgia marks the regret of the forlorn groom in Xishuangbanna, and it is nostalgia, of a different order, that links the environmental problems of Ping'an with Zhuang ethnic identity for a village elder like Lao. Nostalgia provides a meaningful connection between the search for authenticity, the marketing of ethnic otherness as an enjoyable experience, and the rural as past and urban as future.[31] And while different types of nostalgia can be defined in relation to varied perspectives on tourism, nostalgic longings are central to the pursuit of authentic experiences in modernity (Graburn 1995, 167)—an authenticity that is displaced both physically (onto an "Other," whose culture and society are not like that of the modern person) and temporally (onto a pastoral past of "simpler" times) by the modern subject.[32]

Nostalgia is not merely a passive sort of longing but an active engagement with the world.[33] It is inherently social, and shared, which makes nostalgia all the more ripe for exploitation in the marketing of ethnic tourism; it is the result of a collective recognition of a temporal "break" between present and past conditions. This type of memory of the past is a memory "transformed by its passage through history" (Nora 1989, 13) and a form of remembering that moves history, and habitus, into the realm of heritage (Kirshenblatt-Gimblett 2006). In ethnic tourism, those who do the work of tourism bear the burden of producing consumable signs of ethnic difference that can then be experienced as nostalgic by tourists, exemplified in "traditional" performances, "local" handicrafts (Graburn, ed. 1976), or even a rural landscape. The souvenir, in particular, can be read instantly as a tangible, visible, present thing that is a trace of what is recognizably (and regrettably) no longer present, just as photography and photographs have also been understood.[34]

Nostalgia can also exacerbate social tensions when it takes the form of a national heritage that is celebrated in and through the representation of ethnic minorities who may become "fixed" in a timeless, unchanging state as the object of nostalgic longings.[35] As a technology of cultural representation, ethnic tourism relies upon these yearnings of nostalgia that become mediated through icons of the ethnic. But the form and content of an ethnic icon are never completely open for interpretation. The specific "ethnic options" available in tourism illuminate the often contentious relationships between tourism, ethnicity, and the state.[36] Ethnic options are "manifestations of ethnicity that arise from a complex process of symbolic construction" involving multiple social actors, from local communities and tourism industries to the government representatives (Wood 1997, 19). It is possible that new ethnic options may emerge from the confrontation of competing discourses and agendas (Cohen 2001, 42), but the structures of power that determine and enable a particular bounded set of options, of ways of being appropriately different, are rarely challenged. In this way, ethnic tourism is often promoted in multiethnic states precisely for the purposes of fostering social cohesion and national unity through the guise of celebrating a common national heritage, at a super-structural level above and beyond the recognition of difference. The ethnic theme park, in particular, offers an ideal controlled space for the construction of appropriate national narratives of diversity and unity and the consumption of this knowledge in an entertaining environment.[37]

The theme park model for ethnic tourism was adopted in China in the late 1980s and early 1990s, and some of the country's more well-known ethnic theme parks include the China Folk Cultures Village (FCV) in Shenzhen, the Ethnic Culture Village in Beijing, the Yunnan Folk Culture Village in Kunming, and the Xishuangbanna National Minority Park in Jinghong.[38] Each park is spatially organized by ethnic group; in each, a number of the fifty-six officially recognized ethnic groups in China are presented through life-sized model village displays, usually centered around a typical village house that tourists can enter and walk through, and each village contains a space for scheduled performances.[39] The villages in the parks are staffed by young men and women, often recruited from corresponding ethnic minority communities across the country, and in many parks, native architects were hired to design and build the villages. To further emphasize the authenticity of the theme park village structures, some houses include photographs taken by researchers from central institutes and universities who have visited the regions.[40]

In these parks, the ethnic options available are exactly, and only, those made possible in official government classifications. But, as Tim Oakes (2006b, 181, following Hitchcock, Stanley, and Chung 1997) has written about the FCV in Shenzhen, "there is much more to FCV than this display of official nationality ideology. FCV offers a display of a more timeless and authentic multinationalism in which replication of specific styles and forms becomes an important principle in and of itself." The timelessness of the ethnic options in the Chinese parks reinforces both national ideologies of the linear progression of sociocultural groups toward an ideal socialist end, but also the authority and unquestionable unity of the Chinese nation-state with all of its diverse constituent parts. The styles and visible forms of ethnic identity in the parks reduces the "ethnic options" of identity in China to precisely those on display, codifying not only the names of these groups but also the characteristics associated with each ethnic identity.

In addition to providing a visual reflection of Chinese domestic politics and an idealized nationalism, the technologies of display at work in the ethnic theme park exemplify what has been called "Chinese Style Tourism"—a particular mode of experiencing tourism that weaves together landscape, architecture, and performance (Stanley 1998, 65). The intended effect of "Chinese Style Tourism" is a "form of ethnographic realism: the visitor is invited not only to inspect but to enter the theatrical sense of the occasion" (ibid., 65). In turn, it is unsurprising that already existing ethnic villages throughout China have adopted a "Chinese Style Tourism" ethnic theme park model in their own local efforts. "The village as theme park" (Oakes 2006b) model potently and poignantly integrates landscape, architecture, and performance into the three-dimensionality of everyday life itself. Places such as the Manchunman Dai village in Xishuangbanna, Yunnan, and Huashishao, Guizhou, in fact have deliberately modeled their own village tourism industries after the FCV (ibid., 167).[41] The notion of the village-as-ethnic tourism destination is both holistic, in that this model attempts to frame and include everything about village life as worthwhile for the tourism experience, and selective, by determining which features of the village should be highlighted.

The ways of doing tourism in Ping'an and Upper Jidao villages fall in line with this general formula of "village as theme park" through landscape, architecture, and performance, although the emphasis differs in each place. As relatively self-contained spaces, these two villages are advertised as places to see, experience, and enjoy an ethnic encounter through a variety of activities, such as watching a song-and-dance performance, gazing at the landscape, eating a meal cooked by a local resident, staying overnight in a local family's home, or, better yet, all of the above. For tourists, everything about the experience of being in one of these villages is coated with the veneer of "being ethnic" simply by virtue of being *there* in the village. Advertised names of the villages contain an ethnic moniker, such as "Jidao Miao Village" and "Ping'an Zhuang Minority Terraced Fields Scenic Area," to further emphasize the "ethnic-ness" of these places.

The categorization of tourism as ethnic, heritage, cultural, rural, or otherwise is, on the one hand, merely an academic convenience. Ping'an, for instance, has been variously analyzed as an ethnic tourism destination (Luo 2006a, 34) and an "agro-tourism" site (Gao, Huang, and Huang 2009, 6).[42] Although the exact differences between ethnic tourism and agro-tourism might be inconsequential for most tourists, they matter quite a lot in the livelihoods of those involved in maintaining, and seeking benefit from, the tourism industries. Advertising ethnic tourism to a village places the onus of representation and display on the people themselves, whereas "agro-tourism" shifts the focus of attention onto the land and landscape maintenance. However, as Lao's comment at the outset of this chapter about being Zhuang in Ping'an suggested, to him, both the land and the people were implicated in their community's identity and tourism prospects. The "ethnic" in tourism is therefore as singular as the person or object on display and as all-encompassing as the entire village scene and surroundings.

But the fundamental motivations for doing tourism in Ping'an and Upper Jidao have less to do with ethnicity and more to do with economics; tourism development in these villages has been intended to alleviate poverty, which is often associated with being both rural and an ethnic minority.[43] The discursive links between the ethnic, the rural, and the poor continue to frame and structure the tourism efforts in each place. Ping'an village began its engagement with tourists and tourism as early as the late 1970s, starting with local involvement and investments by village leaders such as Lao who largely viewed the developments as a means of earning some income to supplement agricultural and other labor. Upper Jidao, conversely, was brought into provincial-level plans for tourism development in the early 2000s, under the dual goals of poverty alleviation and heritage preservation. The persistence of dominant discourses of ethnic minority difference and rural underdevelopment, however, continue to underscore and, to a large extent, define how village residents have been doing tourism in postreform China.[44]

A TALE OF TWO VILLAGES
Ping'an, Guangxi Zhuang Autonomous Region

Ping'an village is located in the northern part of Guangxi, in the Longsheng Multiethnic Autonomous County, and is administratively located within the prefectural level city of Guilin. Although the Zhuang are the numerically largest recognized ethnic minority group in China with a total population of about sixteen million concentrated in Guangxi and neighboring Yunnan, Longsheng is a multiethnic autonomous county with communities of Zhuang, Yao, Miao, Dong, and Han. Major industries in Longsheng are talc, timber, and tourism; tourism destinations in the county include the national "AAAA" rated Guilin Longji Terraced Fields Scenic Area (shortened here to Longji Scenic Area), where Ping'an is located, a hot springs resort and vacation village, and Silver Water Dong minority village (Yinshui Dongzhai).[45]

The Longji Scenic Area is comprised of a number of villages, four of which are the most frequently advertised and visited: Ping'an Zhuang Terraced Fields Scenic Spot (Ping'an Zhuangzu Titian Guanjingqu), Jinkeng Red Yao Terraced Fields Scenic Spot (Jinkeng Hong Yao Titian Guanjingqu), Longji Old Zhuang Village Cultural Terraced Fields Scenic Spot (Longji Gu Zhuang Titian Wenhua Guanjingqu), and Huanglo Yao Village (Huangluo Yao Zhai).[46] The Longji Scenic Area is about ninety kilometers from Guilin and frequent bus connections link Guilin and Longsheng. According to local tour guides in Ping'an, the village population is around 850, divided into 180 households.[47] In addition to the resident population, there were an estimated 50 to 100 nonlocal full-time residents in the village, including restaurant owners, hotel managers, and other employees hired from outside regions who were living and working in Ping'an.

This account of tourism development in Ping'an is drawn from a variety of sources, including Lao's written history (completed in May 2007); scholarly studies conducted by Chinese scholars on Ping'an; pamphlets, brochures, and the website from the management company for the Longji Scenic Area (figures 1.1 and 1.2); websites from area tour agencies; interviews with the scenic area company managers; and conversations with village residents.[48] Because of its long engagement with tourism, Ping'an is frequently studied by Chinese academics, although the village has received significantly less attention from foreign scholars (with the notable exception of Turner 2010).

Tourism to Ping'an and to the Longji Scenic Area as a whole is largely based on sightseeing and photographing the terraced fields that have been constructed out of the mountainsides around the villages in the region. The construction of the terraced fields surrounding Ping'an began during the Yuan dynasty (1271–1368) and was completed during the Qing dynasty

FIGURE 1.1. A brochure for the Longji Scenic Area created by the tourism management company (2007).

(1644–1911). During the first two decades of Communist rule post-1949, the village was divided into eight subunits (based on preexisting kin groups), and land was collectivized. Some village residents recalled trying to achieve two rice harvests annually during the Cultural Revolution, a project that failed.[49] According to Lao, the first visitor to come to Ping'an and grasp at the potential for tourism to the village was a government official from the Longsheng county propaganda department who took photographs of the terraced fields and the village in the spring of 1976. Three of these photographs were published in the *Guangxi Daily*, and the same official returned later that year with more government representatives from the municipality. Three articles about Ping'an and more photographs were subsequently published in the same newspaper, and Lao regarded these visitors as the first three tourists in Ping'an. By the spring of 1977, more people came to photograph the terraced fields, and the first three foreign tourists arrived in 1978.[50] A popular phrase used nowadays to describe the terraces—"Longji terraces are unique under the heavens"

FIGURE 1.2. Images of the terraced fields around Ping'an, ethnic Yao performers in Huangluo, and village scenes are featured on a brochure (top) and entry ticket (bottom) for the Longji Scenic Area (2007).

(*Longji titian tianxia yi jue*)—was coined by one of the foreign visitors, Lao said.

He had been privy to these early visits because of his status in the village as a doctor and as a Party cadre. Occupying a higher-status position within local political spheres, the village cadres in Ping'an were "tipped off" to tourism plans by the government early on. According to Wen Tong (2002, 27), as representatives of the Party and the government, village cadres were also personally more open to new ideas and regularly attended local government meetings at the county and township levels, where they learned about the importance of tourism and the county government's burgeoning priorities in building tourism industries.[51] The village secretary built the first guesthouse in the early 1980s offering twelve beds—when there were more tourists, Lao said, they would simply sleep in local homes. At the time, there were no roads into the village, so travel to Ping'an from Longsheng involved a bus ride to Huangluo and then a hike up into the mountains; staying overnight was necessary. In 1983, an official from the Longsheng propaganda department published an article in the *Guangxi Daily* titled "Mountain People Also Use Foreign Money," marveling over how Ping'an had become a desirable destination for foreign tourists and how quickly village residents had picked up on the economic benefits of tourism.[52]

In the early years, photography was the primary tourist activity in the village. Most of the tourists came to photograph the fields in the height of the spring and early summer, when the terraces are flooded with water prior to transplanting rice seedlings. Many of these tourist-photographers sent copies of their pictures back to families in the village, and nowadays these images (or copies of the originals) are often displayed inside guesthouses and homes. The aesthetic potential of the terraces for photography continues to drive tourism in Ping'an today. Village residents say that many visitors are drawn to Ping'an by the photographs they have seen elsewhere, desiring to re-create the photographic experience through their tourism encounter, and fulfilling what John Urry (2002b [1990], 140) has called the "hermeneutic circle" of tourism, photography, and "the tourist gaze."[53] From the perspective of residents, photography brought tourism to Ping'an by motivating photographers to visit the village repeatedly to achieve that perfect picture. Villagers, even nowadays, will offer to take tourists to the place where "that picture was made," referencing existing postcards or other widely circulated images of the terraces.[54] According to Xu Ganli (2005, 197) and corroborated in my own conversations with residents, the terraced fields were never explicitly valued by the villagers for their aesthetic appeal; indeed, villagers said that they did not "see" the beauty in the terraces until they saw the photographs taken by tourists. Only after photography and tourism was the value of the *terraces as images* introduced into the consciousness of village residents. In discussions with villagers about the beauty of the terraces, people agreed that the terraces were often considered undesirable because for farmers, terraced fields are much difficult and tiring to work. Accessing some fields frequently involves a long uphill hike, and many fields are too narrow for oxen to plow.

Through the 1980s and early 1990s, the economic impact of tourism was relatively minimal but not unnoticed—in this period, many villagers worked manual labor or other jobs elsewhere, but with increased remittances, households gradually had more money to invest in remodeling their homes into hotels (Wen 2002, 27). Lao built his Li Qing guesthouse, the second family-run guesthouse in the village, in the early 1990s. In 1994, the Longsheng government held a regional conference about tourism development. This meeting coincided with the first wave of national attention to tourism's potential contribution to local economies and poverty alleviation in rural areas (see chapter 2). Yet in 1994, there was still no road to Ping'an. As tourist arrivals steadily increased, the county began discussing plans to build a road directly to the base of Ping'an in the fall of 1995; around the same time, villagers in Ping'an began organizing the sale of entry tickets, charging domestic Chinese tourists ¥3 and foreign tourists ¥5. Construction on the road to Ping'an began in the fall of 1997; the county government provided funds to build the first 3 kilometers, and the villagers contributed labor to complete the final stretch of about 1.5 kilometers. In 1998, as the road was finished, the county government restructured its tourism enterprises, creating the Longsheng Tourism Development Company as a separate business enterprise from the Longsheng Tourism Bureau, which remained a branch of the county government. The newly formed company took over the day-to-day management of and ticket sales to Ping'an. According to Wen (2002, 27), between 1997 and 1998, three more family-run guesthouses opened in Ping'an.

The year 2001 was a watershed for Ping'an: the Longsheng Tourism Bureau created the Longji Terraced Fields Scenic Area, which encompassed Ping'an and other villages in the area, and sold a 60 percent majority share of the Longsheng Tourism Development Company to the privately run Guilin Tourism Company Ltd. This Guilin-based investment company in turn established the Guilin Longsheng Hot Springs Tourism Company Ltd., which at the time managed both the Longji Scenic Area and the nearby hot springs resort. Ticket sales were now handled by the Guilin Tourism Company, whose branch office in charge of the Longji Scenic Area is referred to as the Guilin Longji Tourism Company Ltd. The daily operations of the previous Longsheng Tourism Development Company were devolved into a local management office for the newly created scenic area, which was tasked with overseeing relations between the management company and villages, as well as working with the government tour-

TABLE 1.1. Visitor numbers to the Longji Scenic Area, 1997–2006

	1997	1998	1999	2000	2001
Visitor numbers[a]	3,900	4,100	14,100	25,000	47,300
Percent increase	5.4	5.1	243.9	77.3	89.2
	2002	2003[b]	2004	2005	2006
Visitor numbers	84,700	92,000	143,000	183,000	237,000
Percent increase	79.1	8.6	55.4	28.7	28.8

Source: Guilin Shi Qikexing Lüyou Guihua Zixun Youxian Gongsi 2008.
[a] Approximately 65 percent of all visitors to the scenic area go to Ping'an.
[b] The outbreak of SARS in early 2003 closed tourism to the region for some months.

ism bureau on such logistical issues as public transport, toilets, and other facilities in each village scenic spot. A large fire broke out in one section of the village in 2001, damaging nearly twenty houses beyond repair and spurring many village residents to rebuild their homes as guesthouses in light of an anticipated rapid growth in tourism. Also in 2001, the Longji Scenic Area was deemed one of Guangxi's twenty "Grade A" tourism sites.

The approach to tourism development and management in Ping'an from the 1990s on reflects a persistent belief that the primary attraction for tourists would be the terraced fields, and all maps, brochures, and other promotional materials featured the terraces prominently. But charging an entry fee to a tourism scenic area named for the terraced fields implied that the price paid was for the privilege of seeing the terraces and reinforced the centrality of the fields, rather than the village, to tourism. This approach has had serious ramifications for Ping'an. Individual entry tickets to the Longji Scenic Area cost ¥20–30 in the early 2000s, ¥50 in the mid-2000s, and ¥80 in 2012.[55] Visitor numbers to Ping'an skyrocketed with the completion of the road in 1998 and the investment of the Guilin Tourism Company, whose connections with the larger tourism market in Guilin allowed for increased promotion of the region more widely (table 1.1). When the local Longsheng government company took over tickets sales in 1998, a set amount from the annual profits was allotted for distribution to village residents (table 1.2).[56] This amount increased with the entry of the Guilin-based investors, but nonetheless conflicts over the amount received by the village from the ticket sales hampered relations between the company, the county government, and the village. Individual village

TABLE 1.2. Amounts received by
Ping'an from ticket sales, 1998–2004

Year	Amount Received by Ping'an (in RMB)
1998	15,000
1999	25,000
2000	30,000
2001	150,000
2002	150,000
2003	150,000
2004	350,000

Source: Data compiled from my interview with
Lao and figures stated in Huang H. 2006.

residents who had contributed either labor or land to help build the road
to Ping'an in 1997 were allotted a certain number of workpoints, which
were then calculated into individual shares of the profits from ticket sales.
Nevertheless, most villagers still consider their cut to be an unequal,
unfair share of the total profits from tickets.

The distribution of profits from ticket sales has been an ongoing source
of tension between Ping'an residents, the company, and the county government; in fact, most people typically did not distinguish between the
tourism company and the government and instead referred to them both
as a single entity. From the perspective of the Ping'an residents, the tourism company and the government were sharing the profits from the Longji
Scenic Area and leaving little for the village residents. The original agreement between the company, the government, and the village in 2001 was
that Ping'an would receive ¥150,000 a year to be divided among residents,
the county government would receive 6 percent of total profits, and the
remainder would go to the company and shareholders (Huang H. 2006,
70). Villagers in Ping'an realized quickly that ¥150,000 was quite a small
percentage of the total earnings from ticket sales, and a protest ensued in
2002 between the village and the company. Ping'an residents told me that
they felt "sold out" to the Guilin-based company, that they had had no
idea of the negotiations between the Longsheng tourism bureau, the local

company (which they perceived as essentially a for-profit extension of the tourism bureau), and the new investors. The result was that the amount allotted to Ping'an was raised to ¥350,000 in 2004. Another argument over profit-sharing erupted in 2005 between the villagers and the company, this time involving a blockade of the village entrance and, according to village accounts, the arrest of a few men who protested at the main entrance to the scenic area.

All of these arguments, from the perspective of village residents, revolved more fundamentally around the issue of the terraced fields, the primary attraction for tourists. Two viewpoints (*guanjing tai*) are located within the scenic spot, and flat viewing areas were built at these points on the slopes above the village itself, for tourists to gaze upon the terraced fields: viewpoint 1 looks down over the Nine Dragons and Five Tigers (Jiu Long Wu Hu) view and viewpoint 2 onto the view known as Seven Stars with Moon (Qi Xing Ban Yue). Both names refer to the shape of the fields, as seen from the respective viewpoints. Tourists come to the region, Ping'an residents argued, to see these terraced fields, but the labor villagers expended in maintaining the fields was grossly undercompensated by the company and the government. After all, most families in the village no longer relied upon cultivating the fields for their everyday consumption needs, but terraced fields require constant upkeep and maintenance, residents stressed to me, and only they knew how to take care of the land. In effect, the company, the local government, and outside entrepreneurs opening businesses in the village were making money as a result of the labor of the villagers. The villagers kept the terraces attractive as a worthy sightseeing destination, but the company, the local government, and outside entrepreneurs were not properly compensating the villagers for their work.

This emphasis on photographing the terraced fields as the primary tourist activity in Ping'an overlooked the villagers—the focus on landscape and photography in the village's tourism activities minimized the presence of the villagers who maintained the terraces every year. The terraced fields were considered most attractive when they were flooded with water in late spring. Dry fields (used for growing vegetables and other crops) were less attractive, photographically speaking, because they did not reflect light or provide visual contrast as dramatically as the flooded fields. As tourism became increasingly central to household economies, the village residents' actions reinforced the centrality of the terraces. Residents gradually focused their attention to the fields that were a part of the named views. The terraces not within the visual scope of the two main viewpoints were neglected, left uncultivated, and sometimes left to collapse. During the spring and early summers, when photography tours were most frequent because of the water in the terraces, residents typically first worked the fields within the two main viewpoints, only later turning to the remaining fields as needed.

In 2007, villagers told me that they were now demanding 7 percent of the total profits from ticket sales, but the tourism company would not agree to the increase. One resident who was also a Party cadre and had been involved in many of the conversations commented obliquely that the company should realize the villagers weren't stupid; they could do the arithmetic to figure out that ¥350,000 was a minuscule portion of the money earned from tickets. A manager within the company explained that the villagers didn't realize how much the company had originally invested in 2001; even with the ticket sales as high as they were, the manager told me, the company was still not earning enough to make up for the initial investments. There was some discussion among villagers in 2007 of the Longsheng government buying "back" the majority share, but these claims were unsubstantiated. By 2011, the company agreed to pay 7 percent of the ticket sales to Ping'an, but this was calculated based off of the discounted "group ticket" sale price of ¥40 a ticket rather than the individual price of ¥80, which meant that the village received ¥2.8 per ticket sold. This amount was further limited by the number of tickets/tourists counted at the entry gate to Ping'an, where tickets must be presented, so that tourists who did not visit Ping'an would not be included in the sum total of allocated funds to the village.

Within Ping'an, the company and government bureaus did not run the majority of village businesses, which consisted of guesthouses, restaurants, and shops. There were, however, a number of hotels and restaurants in Ping'an opened by individuals affiliated with the county government tourism bureau and other tourism business in Guilin, and these establishments were usually much bigger, more modern, and busier than locally owned ones. Indeed, it has been suggested that the role of government officials in private businesses in Ping'an lay at the root of many confrontations between the villagers and the government and company representatives, because the latter were perceived as not only earning money from the scenic area's ticket sales but also invested in profit-making enterprises in the village (Huang H. 2006, 70).

Officials who were aware early on of the plans to create the two viewpoints and paths through the village shared this knowledge with their friends and relatives. In turn, these individuals began negotiating for land-use rights at the most potentially valuable sections of the village based on their privileged knowledge of the plans before the viewpoints and paths were constructed. The construction of the platforms were planned to direct tourists toward viewpoint 2, overlooking the Seven Stars with Moon landscape, by building a wider walking path from the parking lot through the village to this viewpoint; some of the biggest and most modern hotels owned by nonlocals are along this path. Village residents came to believe that the slower development of the other sections of the village—namely, those closer to viewpoint 1—was a direct result of these same government individuals not wanting to create competition with their own businesses. One of the most successful and earliest large hotels in the village, Ping'an Hotel (Ping'an Jiu Dian), opened in 2002 and is located right alongside the path to viewpoint 2. Unlike the family-run guesthouses, this hotel was opened by a woman who had previously worked for the Longsheng Tourism Bureau, and it was the first to feature en suite bathrooms.

Despite increasing investments by outside individuals, the majority of guesthouses and restaurants in Ping'an are family-run, or family-owned, although these are significantly smaller in size and scale than those opened by nonvillage residents. Some villagers have also opened shops selling drinks, souvenirs, daily household goods (such as oil, crackers, rice, noodles, and sandals), and, more recently, fresh vegetables and meat brought in from wholesale markets in Longsheng and Guilin. The other work in tourism for village residents begins at the village parking lot near the ticket office, where all tourists are dropped off. Here, sedan chair carriers (two per chair and usually men) offer rides for tourists up to the viewpoints, and porters (usually but not always women) offer to carry luggage and supplies up to the hotels and restaurants. Men and women also offer to guide tourists to their hotels and restaurants or to take them on longer walks in and around the village. The guides, porters, and sedan chair carriers have been divided according to a system of three groups (loosely based on the units created during collectivization, which were themselves based on lineages) lettered A, B, and C, rotating every three days. Only those within a given group on their given day are allowed to wait at the parking lot and to solicit tourists (la ke).

In 2007, the system was further streamlined to enforce a strict numerical order within each group. This was developed after a group of village cadres went on a study tour to Zhangjiajie, a national forest park in Hunan, sponsored by the tourism company—Zhangjiajie was known for having very well-organized tourism and sedan chairs carriers. In May 2007, a new management office was opened at the entrance gate to Ping'an, opposite from the ticket booth. Staffed by representatives of the village leadership committee (cunweiyuan hui), this office oversaw the daily order of sedan chair carriers and porters at the parking lot. Sedan chair carriers and porters were individually numbered, and each set of chair carriers or each porter had to wait for their turn. Previously, villagers and management employees told me, people would be so frantic to solicit a customer that they would undercut each other's prices and fights often broke out between village residents. Official prices for luggage porters and sedan chairs were listed on a board at the parking lot, although bargaining was still commonplace.

Incomes in the village have increased alongside the growth in tourist visits; according to one study, prior to tourism (no specific year is given), annual household incomes were approximately ¥4,000; after tourism, most households earned between ¥10,000 and ¥30,000 annually (Huang H. 2006). Similar amounts are reported in the research of Sha Yao, Wu Zongjun, and Wang Xulian (2007); these authors found that 61.7 percent of those surveyed reported per capita annual incomes of ¥2,000 (or, in an average family of five to six, ¥10,000 to ¥12,000 a year).[57] In my survey of fifty households in Ping'an completed in 2007, reported average annual household incomes hovered between ¥10,000 and ¥20,000, but a number of households did report significantly greater net incomes (table 1.3). One young woman used a traditional Chinese saying to describe the rising incomes in Ping'an: one generation plants the trees in whose shade another generation rests (qian ren zai shu, hou dai qing liang). After all, their ancestors had built the terraced fields and now the current generation of villagers could live off the labor of their forefathers, through tourism of the terraced fields. Of course, many households were in debt to friends and relatives, as well as to local credit cooperatives, because they

TABLE 1.3. Annual household income in Ping'an as reported in 2007

Reported Annual Household Income (RMB)	Number of Households (50 total)
Less than 10,000	7
10,000–19,999	20
20,000–29,999	11
30,000–39,999	4
40,000–49,999	2
50,000–69,999	2
70,000–99,999	2
More than 100,000	2

Source: Household survey by author, 2007.

had borrowed money to build their guesthouses, so much of the money earned was used to pay back loans. The cost of building and equipping an average-sized hotel to sleep thirty to forty, with modern facilities (usually a mix of en suite and shared bathrooms), was estimated to be anywhere between ¥200,000 and ¥500,000 in 2007.

In terms of living standards and incomes, tourism to Ping'an had been unquestionably beneficial for villagers overall. Relatively few people migrated out to find work by the mid-2000s, and during busy tourism seasons, many families in Ping'an hired friends and relatives from other villages to help out both in the fields and in their businesses. New hotels and shops cropped up on a regular basis; in April 2007, Ping'an had eighty-two hotels, the majority owned and run by villagers, although as noted before, a number of large, more well-equipped hotels had been built by individuals from Guilin, Beijing, and even the United States. About half of the 180 households in Ping'an were directly engaged in the tourism businesses in their own homes, but there were many more individual villagers working as porters, sedan chair carriers, guides, and shopkeepers or simply earning rental income from the lease of their homes to others. Renovations on existing hotels occurred constantly as well, as families sought to "catch up" to the latest designs and tourists' requirements (which in this period meant providing en suite bathrooms and air-conditioning and heating units). Hotels in Ping'an were modernizing so quickly, however, that by 2010, many village residents told me that they no longer bothered to run their family guesthouses because, given the option of an en suite, climate-controlled room in a large, well-appointed hotel, the majority of tourists simply wouldn't stay in a village home. The number of non–locally run restaurants in the village also grew in the late 2000s; by 2012, many families rented out one floor of their homes as restaurant spaces for outside entrepreneurs to run.

To an extent, the situation in Ping'an exemplified and supported the idea that being successful in tourism is not being mobile; fewer and fewer residents felt pressured to migrate out of the village to earn an income. This belief in "staying put" as a marker of achievement permeated throughout development programs in rural China. However, the idea that successful tourism development can be equated to an opportunity to stay in one's home posits mobility in a negative light and correlates almost too neatly with the notion of migration-for-work as undesirable or dangerous to society. For all of its economic success, the problem of tourism in Ping'an boiled down to a changing relationship between the land and the people. Tourists came to look at and to photograph the terraced fields, but this landscape required the constant effort and work of village residents to remain attractive. Yet the land itself did not directly generate an income for the village residents; residents needed tourists to spend money in their guesthouses, shops, and restaurants to really profit from tourism.

Although villagers continued to plant and grow crops in their fields, for the families engaged in tourism businesses, these harvests only supplemented the food they purchased from local markets and vendors. Very few tourists were satisfied with the selection of locally grown produce, and to maintain a greater variety in their restaurants, most villagers either purchased their meats, vegetables, and rice directly from markets in Longsheng and Guilin or bought them from village residents who, in turn, shuttled between wholesale markets and the village with goods. With chicken, for instance, the vast majority of live chickens slaughtered in the village had not been raised in the village, although all restaurants advertised them as local chickens (*tuji*). The same "white lie" existed for many other dishes served as local specialties, including bamboo rice (*zhutong fan*: sticky rice, dried fruit, and smoked pork cooked in bamboo), which was introduced to the village after some residents noticed how popular it was with tourists at the Longsheng hot springs. That said, when asked about the invention of bamboo rice as a local, Zhuang specialty, village residents were quick to explain to me that they had always known how to cook bamboo rice—they had just never thought of selling it to tourists.

Ping'an residents have gone through an enormous psychological shift in the past thirty years. From being called poor and backward in the discourse of Chinese national development in the 1960s and 1970s, by the 1980s and 1990s, the village was celebrated for its authentic ethnic customs and pure natural environment, which became the base of its tourism industry (Xu Ganli 2005, 197–98). The very features of the village itself—from the terraced fields to the wooden houses to the bamboo forests—took on new, cultural values in tourism, and villagers learned to adopt and embrace these ideas. This was a double value—life in the village became valuable as an example of minority culture within mainstream China and as a product in the marketplace with a price tag. These changing standards were further reinforced by the continued influx of outsiders into the village, who also wanted to profit from Ping'an's success. But the rapid increase in tourist arrivals and residents in the village prompted new problems, such as with waste management, as Lao pointed out. Other ongoing concerns in the village included persistent water shortages during busy seasons that affected not only household use in hotels and restaurants but also the amount of water available for flooding the terraces; fires due to shoddy electrical wiring and the increasing number of propane tanks used with water heaters and gas stoves; disputes between residents and tour guides demanding commissions from local businesses; and ongoing debates over who would do the work of maintaining the terraced fields and how much the village would receive from ticket sales.[58]

Some residents suggested, as one possible solution, that Ping'an should turn itself into more of an ethnic tourism destination. To "ethnicize" tourism in the village meant that tourists would no longer just come to look at the terraces—an activity from which the village residents earned very little. Rather, tourists would come to enjoy the Zhuang, which could bring the *people* of Ping'an back into the picture. The trickle-down income from ticket sales was hardly lucrative for village residents, with families reporting to receive no more than 200 RMB per person per year as their share. One concrete move to increase the "ethnic-ness" of the village was to call the entire village area the Ping'an Zhuang Terraced Fields Scenic Spot, which was printed on a banner at the entrance gate. The potential effect of this renaming was to shift the emphasis of the village experience away from the land and onto the residents. "Ethnicizing" the terraces and the village was important for two reasons: first, some tourists didn't realize that Ping'an was a Zhuang village; and second, it would help maintain their competitiveness and attractiveness in relation to other villages in the Longji Scenic Area.

Before coming to Ping'an, many of the tour groups first stopped at Huangluo, an ethnic Yao village along the river, where they would watch a performance by Yao women. Many Yao women from Huangluo and neighboring Zhongliu village also came to Ping'an to sell souvenirs, wearing their ethnic dress (consisting of a black pleated skirt, pink or red embroidered wrap top, with their hair tied in a prominent topknot and covered with an embroidered black cloth square), which was distinct from what the Zhuang women in Ping'an wore. As a result, some tourists believed Ping'an was a Yao village, not Zhuang. Specifically *ethnic* tourism activities in Ping'an were therefore envisaged as a way to increase the range of income-generating opportunities in the village; many Ping'an residents thought they could do more folk dance performances to attract tourists (see Turner 2010). There was a group of women who could be hired for a folk performance (costing between ¥200 and ¥400), and in 2009 a Longsheng-based performance director brought his show to the village, although it was ultimately unsuccessful.[59] In 2012, competition intensified even further when Longji village, next to Ping'an, was officially opened to tourism and in the process of total transformation, complete with new roads, a museum of Zhuang folk culture, special exhibits and signage throughout the village, and, eventually, electric carts to shuttle tourists between sights (see Chio 2013).

Upper Jidao, Guizhou

In Guizhou, ethnicity was at the forefront of the plans for rural tourism development that had been introduced in the early 2000s, spurred on by the relative success of ethnic Miao tourism villages in the province. Upper Langde, for example, had been recognized by Guizhou provincial authorities in 1985 as an "open-air museum," and Nanhua had been developed into a tourism village with municipal funds from Kaili (a county-level city) in 1997 as a competitor to Upper Langde.[60] My field site, Upper Jidao village, is located along the same highway connecting Upper Langde (two kilometers away) and Nanhua (four kilometers away), in Guizhou's southeastern Qiandongnan Miao and Dong Autonomous Prefecture. Xijiang, another popular and well-known ethnic Miao tourism destination (redeveloped and reopened in 2008) is also close, about twenty kilometers from Upper Jidao. In the local context of these well-established and heavily promoted tourism villages, Upper Jidao was expected to benefit from the existing tourism market (see Cheung 1996, Oakes 1998, and Schein 2000) and to create something new and different for the marketplace, under the guidance of the Guizhou Tourism Bureau and with financial support from a World Bank project loan that was approved in 2009.

Upper Jidao is a natural village (*ziran cun*) and a part of the administrative village (*xingzheng cun*) of Jidao that includes the natural village of Lower Jidao.[61] The two are linked by a concrete road. In 2006, Upper and Lower Jidao together had a total of 243 households and 1,160 residents (Kaili Shi Fupin Kaifa Bangongshi 2006, 1). But Upper Jidao makes up less than half of the total population, with 105 households and just more than 400 people, although village residents said the actual number of people living in the village was usually between 250 and 300.[62] As a tourism destination, the village is often referred to as Jidao Miao Village (Jidao Miao Zhai), although as of this writing, all of the tourism developments and activities occur in Upper Jidao as a result of decisions made by government officials and consultants in the early 2000s to focus tourism on Upper Jidao and not Lower Jidao. To that end, there is often no mention of the difference, spatial or otherwise, between Upper and Lower Jidao in World Bank publications; in some documents what is referred to as simply "Jidao" is listed to have 403 residents (see World Bank 2008, 18), which can only be the population of Upper Jidao.[63]

Average reported incomes in Jidao (including migrant remittances) have hovered around ¥2,000 per household (World Bank 2008 and 2011), or, more precisely, the average annual per capita income for the majority of households in the mid-2000s was about ¥1,100 (Kaili Shi Fupin Kaifa Bangongshi 2006, 2). In my survey of forty-five households in Upper Jidao from 2006 to 2007, the majority of households reported an annual income of less than ¥3,000 (including remittances; table 1.4). The higher household incomes included those who received retirement salaries and

TABLE 1.4. Annual household income in
Upper Jidao as reported in 2006–2007

Annual Household Income (RMB)	Number of Households (45 Surveyed)
Less than 1,000	8
1,000–1,999	7
2,000–2,999	12
More than 3,000	17*
No response	1

Source: Author survey, 2006–2007.
*(Ten reported incomes were more than 7,000)

those with professional training (including a teacher, a village clinician, and individuals engaged in carpentry, livestock sales, and construction). Because of extensive out-migration, households in Upper Jidao were fairly small at the time, averaging around three to four people; in the mid-2000s, approximately 38 percent of the population in Upper Jidao had migrated out (World Bank 2008, 21). The stated goal in the village's 11th Five Year Plan was to raise average village per capita annual incomes to ¥3,500, with 40 percent of this income to be derived from tourism (Kaili Shi Fupin Kaifa Bangongshi 2006, 5). According to the project agreement document prepared by the International Bank for Reconstruction and Development (the World Bank unit involved in the loan project) and Guizhou provincial authorities, the target average per capita income for 2014 in Jidao (Upper or Lower is not specified) is ¥2,240 (World Bank 2009, 12).

Tourism development in Upper Jidao began in 2002, when the village was selected to be a part of the Bala River Demonstration Project for Rural Tourism, a provincial program for poverty alleviation through tourism development (figure 1.3). Tourism to the Bala River area was intended to capitalize on the ethnic minority customs and crafts of the region's Miao population through the development of handicrafts for sale, cultural performances, and general rural sightseeing. The Bala River project included seven villages, among them Nanhua and Upper Langde. Three of these villages fall within the administration of Kaili and four within neighboring Leishan county, a fact that complicated the execution of the program

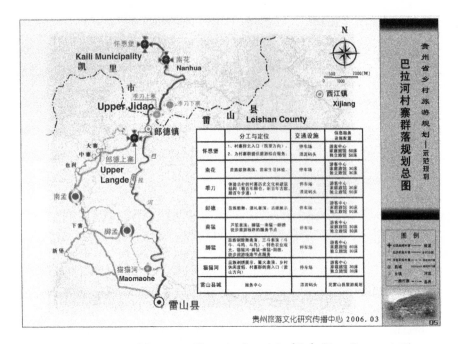

FIGURE 1.3. A map of the seven villages in the original Bala River Demonstration Project for Rural Tourism illustrates the idea for a tourism region. The chart on the right outlines the various tourism resources and attractions in each village, the transport infrastructure to be constructed, and plans for accommodation. The dotted line between Upper Jidao and Upper Langde indicates the administrative division separating Kaili from Leishan county. Adapted from map 5 in Guizhou Tourism Bureau, *Rural Tourism Plan, 2006–2020* (Guiyang: Guizhou Provincial Tourism Administration, 2006).

as local governments competed against each other for tourists and tourism profits.

Since 2002, the push to turn Upper Jidao into an ethnic tourism destination has involved a number of different organizations and companies, both international and domestic. My account of Upper Jidao's engagement with tourism development is culled from a number of sources, including publicly available World Bank publications, interviews with government officials and NGO directors, discussions with village leaders, published newspaper articles in the Chinese and international press, published conference proceedings, local government documents and reports, and information posted on the websites of relevant groups, funders, and organizations. The attention paid to tourism, ethnic cultural heritage, and rural development by the central Chinese state, provincial governments, and international development agencies has also motivated a wide range of Chinese academic research on such issues, especially in Guizhou.[64]

At a provincial level, the goal was (and continues to be) to expand upon the existing rural tourism industry to address problems of persistent rural poverty and concerns over heritage loss. With a seed grant of US$360,000 from the World Bank, the first project in 2002 aimed to produce a Tourism Development Master Plan for Guizhou and was implemented by the World Tourism Organization, a United Nations agency (UNWTO), and the Ireland International Tourism Company, who won the project bid. Together with the China National Tourism Administration (CNTA) and the Guizhou Tourism Bureau, these agencies invited tourism experts from around the world to help create a twenty-year tourism development scheme for the province. The Bala River Demonstration Project for Rural Tourism (see figure 1.3) was one outcome of this project. According to the UNWTO (2003), "It is believed that the development of the villages surrounding the river valley, will play an integral part in attracting tourists and improving the quality of life for the local inhabitants. . . . With a population of approximately 400–500 people in each of these villages and an estimated activity rate [or participation rate] within a single village to be of the order of 50 per cent or greater, it is expected that each village has at least 200 employment opportunities." The project acknowledged drawing on the experiences of existing tourism villages like Upper Langde and Nanhua. The other five villages included in this demonstration project were Huai'enbao (a former Qing dynasty fortress village originally built by Han migrants to the region), Upper Jidao, Jiaomeng, Nanmeng, and Maomaohe.[65]

With the seed funding, the Irish consultancy firm and provincial government officials evaluated the potential of rural tourism in the selected villages and developed a set of principal objectives. These included the development of tourism as a key economic growth sector, sustainability, increases to revenue and cash incomes, and more effective branding of Guizhou as a cultural and environmental tourism destination (UNWTO 2003). In October 2004 an international forum on rural tourism was held in Guiyang, the provincial capital, during which a number of invited consultants and experts went on an evaluation and study tour to some of the demonstration projects throughout the province, including the Bala River region (Yang S., ed. 2005). This initial evaluation program was further bolstered by a grant of NZ$500,000 from New Zealand's International Aid and Development Agency (NZAID) for a project titled "Community-Based Cultural Heritage Tourism Systems," which was executed by a New Zealand consultancy firm called Performance Excellence Ltd. (Zhang X. 2005), with the cooperation of the Guizhou Tourism Bureau. This project ran from March 2004 through April 2006 with the goal of implementing a community-centered, regional network of village-based tourism associations between the seven Bala River villages. Again, the focus was to create practical methods for diversifying tourism in the area and to alleviate rural poverty (Zhang X. 2005). The key individuals implementing the program in Guizhou included Bill Rout, a sociologist from New Zealand, and Zhang Xiaosong, who has held multiple positions as dean of the School of International Tourism and Culture at Guizhou Normal University, director of the Guizhou Provincial Center for Tourism Research and Public Outreach (established in 2004 as a unit of the Guizhou Tourism Bureau) and as a committee member of the Guizhou Political Consultative Conference. Zhang Xiaosong has played a significant role in mediating and directing tourism plans in the Bala River region, and in 2006, she established the Guizhou Rural Tourism Development Center.

According to reports written by Zhang Xiaosong (2005) and Li Zaiyong (2005), then the vice-governor of Qiandongnan prefecture, the 2004–06 community-based tourism development program sought to construct a management system for monitoring, controlling, and evaluating tourism at the village level. As one of the first parts of this training program, representatives from each village and a selection of government officials went on a study tour in spring 2004, traveling to other ethnic tourism sites in Guizhou as well as to Ping'an in Guangxi. Two residents of Upper Jidao and three from Lower Jidao went on this trip. The purpose of this tour was to allow villagers to experience rural tourism, to study rural tourism businesses such as family-run guesthouses, and to gain new perspectives on how to do the work of tourism.[66]

The NZAID-funded community-based tourism project developed a series of workshops to promote "self-enlightenment" (Zhang X. 2005, 17) among the villagers, who discussed their resources, opinions, and experiences to develop workable approaches to tourism management in their home villages. Tourism associations (*lüyou xiehui*) were created in each of the seven Bala River Demonstration Project villages, and women in particular were encouraged to create their own associations to solidify their role and participation in the tourism industries. Representatives from these associations held meetings with each other, where they were to share information about issues such as sanitation, cooperation, and leadership strategies. In a published report on these workshops, Zhang Xiaosong notes that the tourism association in Upper Jidao was particularly creative and efficient in using the ten tons of cement provided to each village as part of the program for the repair and construction of village paths by creating cobblestone walkways and a performance space. Through the ingenuity of the villagers in combining cement with the aesthetically more attractive stones, Zhang wrote, in Upper Jidao "an ancient yet civilized village was appearing before your eyes" (Zhang X. 2005, 18). The basic goal was to make the villagers the "owners" of their tourism industries. Other responsibilities, such as keeping statistics on the number of tourist visits and using transparent accounting methods for recording tourism incomes, were stressed.

The end of this funding program in 2006 marked the beginning of the economic and industry-building phase of rural tourism development in Guizhou, coinciding with the declaration of the China Rural Tourism year and the start of the 11th Five Year Plan, with the focus on building a New Socialist Countryside. By spring 2006, plans were well under way in Upper Jidao. Zhang Xiaosong, with the support of the Guizhou Tourism Bureau, negotiated an agreement for a private firm, the Guizhou Shan Li Tourism Development Company, to finance infrastructural improvements in the Bala River region and the Libo National Nature Reserve tourism region, another designated tourism development area.[67] One of Shan Li's projects would be the construction of high-end hotels in both regions, and Upper Jidao was selected as the location for the Bala River hotel.[68] The relationship between the Guizhou government, village associations, and Shan Li was viewed as a mutually beneficial arrangement, where Shan Li leased land use rights from the village for twenty years to build and start up the hotel.

According to a report by the general manager of Shan Li, Zhang Tan, 10 percent of annual profits would be split equally between the village tourism association and a "workstation" in the village for experts and researchers, and another 10 percent would go directly into cultural and environmental protection efforts in the village. It was anticipated in such an arrangement that the initial investment would be paid off in fifteen years, and after twenty years, the entire business would be given back to the village (Zhang T. 2008, 182). In Upper Jidao, land was selected for the hotel and initial contracts for land use rights were arranged. According to Zhang Xiaosong in 2006, she envisioned the hotel to primarily attract wealthy foreign tourists, with rooms priced around ¥200 or more a night.[69] She emphasized that the desire for a hotel in the village, instead of family guesthouses, had also been expressed by Upper Jidao residents, where male and female visitors stayed in separate rooms, if not separate homes, even if married. This cultural norm, they realized, would not suit tourists.

Activities around rural tourism promotion and development flourished at the national and provincial level in this period; another major international conference on rural tourism was held in Guiyang in September 2006, organized in conjunction with the World Bank and UNWTO, with another study tour arranged for conference participants. Unfortunately for Upper Jidao, although the original itinerary for this conference included a stop in their village, construction on a parking lot and other transport infrastructure had not yet begun, and the conference tour bypassed them for the more accessible village of Upper Langde. Foreign press coverage on rural tourism in Guizhou increased over this year and the next; an article about the Bala River region was published in the *Wall Street Journal* (Sesser and Fong 2006), and Upper Jidao was featured in a Reuters report on the New Socialist Countryside program (Blanchard 2007).[70] The Guizhou Tourism Board published a Guizhou Provincial Rural Tourism Development Plan in June 2006, which was approved by the CNTA (Guizhou Tourism Bureau 2006), in anticipation of a larger application for World Bank funding. In the 2006 Guizhou provincial plan, the original Bala River Demonstration Project from 2002 was renamed the Bala River Miao Minority Village Community, and Upper Jidao was again identified as a "demonstration village" (ibid., 40–41). The Guizhou provincial government eventually submitted an application to the World Bank for US$60 million to fund a broader project titled "Guizhou Cultural and Natural Heritage Protection and Development Program" (which was approved in May 2009).

A New Socialist Countryside development program for Jidao (both Upper and Lower villages) was concurrently produced by the regional governments of Kaili and Sankeshu township in May 2006; this program outlined a variety of infrastructure, construction, and sanitation projects to be undertaken during the 11th Five Year Plan, much of it directed at improving the village's prospects as a tourism destination. This included building a new bridge directly into Upper Jidao, creating a larger performance space, and constructing a cultural center in Upper Jidao (Kaili Shi Fupin Kaifa Bangongshi 2006). Allocated funds totaled more than ¥8 million, with nearly ¥4 million coming as aid from the wealthy eastern city of Ningbo. According to village leaders in Upper Jidao, Jidao as a whole would receive ¥500,000 a year for projects that they would be responsible for executing, such as paving roads and improving water lines. Of these funds, 80 percent (¥400,000) was allocated to tourism-related projects in Upper Jidao specifically, such as for building a cultural center, while Lower Jidao received less aid because, ostensibly, it was not considered a major part of tourism-related development that was intended to be the central project in the village.[71]

As part of the preparations for the larger, provincial World Bank loan application, a social assessment report on the state of Indigenous and local peoples included in the project was completed in 2008 by the Center for Ethnic and Folk Literature and Arts Development (a unit within the national Ministry of Culture) with the Guizhou Provincial Center for Tourism Research and Public Outreach (World Bank 2008). In this particular document, the authors address in detail the anticipated expenditures and components of the project. Upper Jidao is identified as a village for tourism development and cultural heritage preservation, focusing on the well-preserved songs, dances, and old houses (ibid., 40). Moreover, the process of making Upper Jidao into a tourism destination is noted to require not only infrastructure but also the creation of appropriate ethnic Miao song-and-dance performances. This model of tourism was precisely the idea of "the village as theme park" and had already been popularized in Upper Langde and Nanhua, which both offered choreographed shows for tourists.

Unlike in Ping'an, where the "content" of its tourism was primarily the landscape, from the beginning Upper Jidao was being developed as an *ethnic* tourism site. Thus village residents have continually needed to find ways to display their ethnicity. As early as 2004, plans for tourism in Upper Jidao included creating various groups that would each practice and prepare a particular Miao traditional performance. There was one group for singing traditional "love songs" (*qing ge*, typically a call-and-response performance between men and women, although they practiced separately out of propriety), a group of men who practiced playing the *lusheng*, a group of women who practiced *lusheng* dances, and a group of older men and women who practiced "ancient songs" (*gu ge*, also in the call-and-response style, retelling stories with a moral lesson). Group practices were originally scheduled to occur every other day, but in 2006, villagers said without many tourists to perform to, there was no reason to practice so frequently. Inspiration and influences for these performances were drawn from a range of sources. For example, the "love song" group watched locally produced video recordings of other Miao villagers performing the same genre for ideas on how to sing, what to sing about, and how to dress.[72] In 2007, the Kaili municipal government hired a professional dance troupe to teach the villagers a more professionalized song-and-dance performance.

The internal leadership structure and tourism organization in Upper Jidao was complex yet straightforward. As a result of the training sessions from 2004 to 2006, Upper Jidao, like the other six Bala River region villages, created a village tourism association that included two women's representatives (required by the program) and also Teacher Pan, who was not an elected village subcommittee member but had been involved with tourism projects from the beginning. The rest of the tourism association was comprised of the six or seven elected members of the village subcommittee members (*xiaozu*). When I inquired about this overlap between the elected village subcommittee and the tourism association, they simply said that there weren't enough people in the village to have two separate committees and that because the subcommittee members were already elected to be leaders, it made sense that they should also be in charge of tourism. This meant, however, that every year the subcommittee and the tourism association might change members, as new people were elected or others left the village. As a result, those who stayed in Upper Jidao bore the burden of carrying plans forward each year—namely, Teacher Pan and a woman named Qin. Both were educated, fluent speakers of standard Chinese (Mandarin), who also, as some villagers mentioned, had steady incomes, so neither Teacher Pan nor Qin needed to worry about making money and could instead give some of their time to the tourism association.[73] Teacher Pan received a monthly retirement stipend, having served for many years as the principal of the local middle school in Paile village; Qin was married to a schoolteacher from Upper Jidao who taught at the school in Nanhua. Qin ran the village clinic, which she regarded as her primary occupation even though the work carried no wage, only minimal compensation. She was also the village's unofficial tour guide and usually the first called upon by tour agencies and government officials to greet and host visiting groups.

Teacher Pan was a central figure in Upper Jidao's tourism plans, although he was never elected to the village subcommittee. Rather, local government officials, including Zhang Xiaosong, had approached him directly to assist with the tourism development in Upper Jidao because of his previous leadership experiences. In effect, he became the de facto director of tourism in the village, serving as the coordinator and negotiator for tour groups that wanted to visit (and hosting researchers like me in his home). Like Teacher Pan, Qin was more educated than her village peers, having completed postsecondary studies in nursing at a polytechnic school in Kaili. She spoke standard Chinese with ease, and she seemed to genuinely enjoy being involved in tourism development. All of the participation in tourism was strictly voluntary, although Teacher Pan was frequently chosen as the village representative for study tours (to Ping'an in 2004 and to Yunnan in 2007). Qin, along with ten other young adults from Upper Jidao, participated in a tourism training program at Guizhou University in the summer of 2006. Upon their return, however, most participants said it was not an especially interesting experience. Both Qin and Teacher Pan were frequently called upon to speak to media reporters and officials about the village, appearing on domestic television programs broadcast on Shanghai TV and on CCTV 9, the state-run English-language station. Tour guides and government representatives tended to engage with these two first when discussing tourism plans, thus bypassing the elected village leadership subcommittee members. When I asked them about their role in the village's affairs, both Teacher Pan and Qin agreed that they felt it was their obligation to help the village as best as they could. And yet, for Qin particularly, her responsibilities in tourism sometimes conflicted with her own aspirations to further her medical training.

Ongoing beautification projects in the village were initiated to make the place look more inviting and to look more like a rural ethnic tourism destination. Concrete and cement walls were covered with wooden planks, glass windows were covered with decorative wooden frames, trash cans were made out of straw baskets (later, ceramic pickling vats wrapped in straw were used as trash cans), and a large wooden gate was raised at the village entrance along the main highway passing through the Bala River region. Signs on the highway announced "Jidao Miao Village," indicating its status as a worthy tourist destination and marking the village as an ethnic minority community; large color posters advertising events were periodically raised next to the road (figure 1.4). A new parking lot was built in 2010 along the newly constructed highway, further announcing the village as a tourism destination (see figure 5.6).

Given all of the attention paid to tourism and the village from 2002 on, from the perspective of the residents of Upper Jidao, it seemed like everyone—locally, regionally, nationally, and internationally—wanted them to do tourism and to do it well. At first, enthusiasm for tourism was high, and a number of young adults who had migrated returned to the village around 2004 in the hopes of participating in the new industry. By the time of my research in 2006, though, the fever for tourism had waned somewhat. There simply weren't that many tourists coming to Upper Jidao; between the few tour groups that did pass through and a smattering of independent tourists, village leaders estimated approximately two thousand tourists in all of 2006. Part of the problem was infrastructure; without a wide, stable bridge and road that could support a large tour bus, many potential tourists and tour guides simply passed by without stopping. The seven Bala River region villages did not cooperate with each other as the NZAID-funded workshops had hoped. Instead, the villages viewed each other as competitors not collaborators.

A lack of coordination between the county-level governments in Kaili and Leishan meant that there was no single central clearinghouse for tourist information on the Bala River region; each government only assisted the villages in its own administrative region. Within Jidao village, the decision to focus on Upper Jidao for tourism was met with dismay from the residents of Lower Jidao. By the end of 2006, the Shan Li hotel project in Upper Jidao had stalled and was abandoned before construction even began. During a visit to Upper Jidao in December 2006, Zhang Xiaosong was asked directly by the members of the tourism association what had happened to Shan Li. Her response was simply that it was not the right

FIGURE 1.4. Signs along the old highway S308 attempt to capture the attention of passing tourists. The poster to the left advertises the "Kaili Ecological Minority Culture Festival–Bala River Summer Tourism Holiday." The wooden gate to the right reads, "Jidao Miao Village" (2007). Photo by the author.

project for this place. Later, Teacher Pan explained to me that the Jidao village Party Secretary, who was from Lower Jidao, had written a letter to a provincial-level official in 2006, complaining about the unequal allocation of development funds and resources in the village. This had caused enough of a stir at the provincial level, Teacher Pan surmised, to prompt the Guizhou Tourism Bureau and Shan Li to back off from their original plan to build a hotel in Upper Jidao.

But over time, despite the slow start, things did progress, albeit haltingly. Tour guides seeking new destinations started bringing tourists to the village in 2007. This was evidenced not only by the villagers' accounts but also by the increased presence of photographs of Upper Jidao on travel blogs and photo-sharing websites. Media publicity increased: Japan Airlines's in-flight magazine published a special issue on Guizhou in 2007 with a multipage color spread on Upper Jidao; the Chinese version of the fashion magazine *Marie Claire* published a long story on women's embroidery in Upper Jidao in December 2011. In July 2008, with the money from the New Socialist Countryside program, Upper Jidao built a new, larger performance space, a new cultural center (also used for meetings), and could now organize performances for tour groups (figure 1.5). All village residents could (and most would) dress in their festival attire before the arrival of a tour group and set up tables for welcoming tourists with rice liquor. Once the tourists entered the village, young men and women performed a series of songs, dances, and *lusheng* playing. The "ancient songs" group of older men and women were also part of the performance. They charged the visiting tour groups anywhere between ¥400 and ¥800 per reception-performance, depending on how well Teacher Pan negotiated. After deducting for the costs of alcohol and any food served to the tourists, those who performed and helped with the organization earned at most ¥5–¥7 each. The money was viewed not as a source of significant income, because it was practically negligible, but more as shared outcome to the years of preparation and organization.

After the Shan Li hotel plans fell through, another developer, introduced by the Kaili municipal government, came to Upper Jidao with plans to build a new hotel using funds obtained by the Guizhou Tourism Bureau directly from the CNTA. Again, land use rights were arranged, contracts were signed, and this time construction began. However, by summer 2008, the hotel's construction was at a standstill. In March 2010, the hotel's wooden frame was complete but lacked windows, fittings, and internal wiring; Teacher Pan said he had no idea when it would be finished. The developer had been evasive during their last conversation, Teacher Pan added.[74] Zhang Xiaosong's organization, Chain Reaction (founded as part of the Guizhou Rural Tourism Development Center), started a handicrafts training program in 2008 for the women's association of Upper Jidao to both preserve the craft and to create a new source of income.[75] Older women, with the skilled knowledge to embroider elaborate designs, were to teach embroidery to the younger women, many of whom had little experience with the craft. Qin was put in charge of the group, organizing nighttime meetings, managing the funds, and collecting finished pieces.

The women's association was provided with fabric, thread, and needles, and they were given color copies of embroidery designs taken from books that the development center's collaborators thought would be marketable.

FIGURE 1.5. Qin and Wu of the Upper Jidao Tourism Association organize village residents before a reception and performance for a tour group (2008). Photo by the author.

This project was largely funded through the personal efforts of Zhang Xiaosong and a Hong Kong–based philanthropist, who provided funding to purchase supplies.[76] In my conversations in 2008 with the women in Upper Jidao about this project, many said that the designs and embroidery styles they were given to practice were entirely new to them; some women were afraid of doing a bad job and thus reluctant to participate. Others were unhappy or disappointed when their works were not deemed good enough to sell or not selected for recognition; gradually some women stopped participating. The project did not cease entirely, however, and by 2012 the lower level of the village cultural center had been turned into a small exhibition space, holding some of the embroidered pieces and a copy of the 2011 *Marie Claire* issue, while the better works were framed and gifted by the organization to visiting dignitaries including, in 2010, the president of the World Bank, Robert Zoellick.[77] As I observed their meetings and spoke with Qin about this project, I realized that the village women were not practicing old forms of embroidery so much as learning new methods and designs for doing it. This seemed a fitting way of understanding tourism in Upper Jidao more generally: in the guise of cultural preservation and doing the work of tourism, the villagers spent the past decade learning new ways of how to be ethnic.

SIMILAR, WITH MINOR DIFFERENCES

Looking at these histories of tourism in Ping'an and Upper Jidao, there is an implicit tendency to compare the experiences of both villages. Their experiences could also be taken as different "stages" within a singular tourism development process, where Ping'an could serve as a mature example and Upper Jidao as a young, inexperienced newcomer. Indeed, village residents in both places often commented that they wanted to see other tourism villages in order to learn how other rural ethnic minority communities were doing tourism. But given the sometimes subtle, sometimes obvious differences in government participation, funding, local politics, social and cultural norms, and economic options available in Ping'an and Upper Jidao, what these villages were experiencing was simultaneously *familiar* to other rural ethnic tourism destinations and *unique* to their own circumstances. Teacher Pan assessed the situations in Ping'an and Upper Jidao with a Chinese saying: similar, with minor differences (*da tong xiao yi*). Having visited Ping'an before as part of the provincial-level study tour in 2004, and again in 2007 at my invitation, Teacher Pan did not see the need to differentiate between the two villages; rather, he suggested that I concentrate on their similarities.

Instead of focusing so intently on the differences between the villages and, by extension, the *classification* of each village's tourism as a stage of development, exploring the similarities illuminates the deeper and broader issues at stake in doing tourism while acknowledging the myriad contextual differences. Understanding the impetus for villagers in Ping'an and Upper Jidao to learn how to be more ethnic for the tourism market opens up the question of how they were also learning how to be rural in particularly touristic ways. For Ping'an and Upper Jidao, this meant producing (or reproducing) themselves as rural ethnic sites for tourist consumption. The national agenda for rural development encapsulated in the campaign to build a New Socialist Countryside explicitly called upon rural Chinese to learn to be rural and to modernize at the same time. For both villages, how they were expected to do so in practice also drew upon the recent history of tourism in postreform China as well as discourses about rural livelihoods and subjectivities in order to justify national policies and proposed changes.

农家乐

CHAPTER 2

PEASANT FAMILY HAPPINESS

A New Socialist Countryside

For a few years, the phrase *nong jia le* seemed to appear everywhere I went in China. In March 2006, on my first visit to Upper Jidao, a handful of houses had the three-character phrase printed on woven bamboo plates that were hung above doorways. Under each of the Chinese characters of *nong* 农, *jia* 家, and *le* 乐 was written "farm," "-er," and "inn" (figure 2.1). Ostensibly, I later learned from Teacher Pan, the families whose houses displayed these signs had agreed to, or at least expressed interest in, hosting tourists who came to the village. I only ever saw one of these households hosting any tourists, largely facilitated by the fact that their home was located directly above the parking lot, which was also the village basketball court. "Hosting," in Upper Jidao, meant providing a meal or even just a cup of tea and a place to sit down; at the time, there were no tourist facilities in the village. These efforts at *nong jia le* were modeled on nearby established tourism villages—in particular, Upper Langde (Oakes 2011, 29), where the Leishan county government had provided carved wooden plaques that read *Miao* 苗 *jia* 家 *le* 乐 (苗 is the character for the Miao ethnic group) for households engaged in providing rooms and meals to tourists.

In the following years, I stayed overnight at a *nong jia le* guesthouse in Jiankou village, Huairou county, north of Beijing; spent time with friends in Ping'an whose new guesthouse was called Nong Jia Le in Chinese and

FIGURE 2.1. In 2006, households in Upper Jidao that had indicated they were willing to receive tourists hung *nong jia le* signs above their doorways. By 2007, most of these signs had been removed or turned around, leaving the blank backs facing outward. Photo by the author.

Peasant Family Happy in English; spied small restaurants named Nong Jia Le in towns and cities across Guangxi and Guizhou; and enjoyed a postconference dinner at a three-story restaurant in Hefei, the capital of Anhui, also called Nong Jia Le.[1] During that particular evening in Hefei, I wondered what the people in Upper Jidao and Ping'an would have thought of this rural-themed restaurant. Would it have been *rural* enough for them? The interior was predictably decorated, with a few displays of wooden farm tools in the lobby, tables and chairs made of bamboo and woven reeds, and blue and white batiks serving as tablecloths and wall decorations. This was rural tourism, inside out—a taste of the country in the city. What Ping'an and Upper Jidao were striving for, however, was rural tourism that could bring the city to the countryside.

In addition to serving as the name of a family guesthouse or a restaurant, *nong jia le*, which I translate as "peasant family happiness," was the phrase used in both Ping'an and Upper Jidao by residents when they would describe the *business* of running guesthouses and restaurants.[2] The phrase was oftentimes used interchangeably with "doing tourism"—villagers would talk about doing *nong jia le* as a way of explaining what possibilities they saw for participating in tourism development. For the village residents, *nong jia le* simply meant they would establish and operate their own guesthouses and restaurants. At a broader, national level, *nong jia le* has become a catchphrase for any and all types of "rural" tourism experiences throughout China, typically focused around eating locally grown foods and participating in other agricultural activities that could take place in a village.

Throughout the 2000s, the growth of domestic tourism in China occurred alongside, and in conjunction with, multiple campaigns for rural socioeconomic development, civilized tourism, and the promotion of rural tourism under the moniker of *nong jia le*. All of these campaigns merged together in 2006 as part of the national policy to build a New Socialist Countryside—a key component of the 11th Five Year Plan (2006–10). The theming of 2006 as the year of China Rural Tourism indicated a renewed energy and attention from the national government on strengthening and promoting the relationship between rural development and rural tourism. But these campaigns were only the latest iterations of previous efforts, including the campaign to Open Up the West (Xibu Da Kaifa) begun in 2000, and rural ethnic tourism had already been promoted as an opportunity for socioeconomic development in rural ethnic regions, particularly in Guizhou and Yunnan, in the 1990s (Donaldson 2007, Oakes 1998, and Schein 2000).

The development of rural tourism in ethnic minority communities during the postreform era has drawn on a set of historical state policies and shared social discourses that continue to characterize the nation's rural ethnic minorities for tourists, government officials, and village resi-

TABLE 2.1. National per capita annual income, 2006–12

	Urban Disposable (RMB)	Rural Net (RMB)
2006	11,760	3,587
2007	13,786	4,140
2008	15,781	4,761
2009	17,175	5,153
2010	19,109	5,919
2011	21,809	6,977
2012	24,565	7,917

Source: All China Data Center 2012.

dents alike. Communist-era documentary and feature films about ethnic minorities established particular visual representations of peoples in ways that highlighted how ethnicity was to be known visually and that tied ethnic identity firmly to strategies of visual recognition and, by extension, to tourist imaginations that persist to this day. These ideas about ethnic identity and culture, further codified and communicated in official government reports, scholarly publications, and media representations, now exist in dialogue with the expectations and experiences of what it means to be ethnic and to do tourism in Ping'an and Upper Jidao. Moreover, the designation of Ping'an and Upper Jidao as *rural* ethnic minority communities intensifies justifications for the need to develop these places and renders the villages and landscapes even more exotic and interesting as sights within the nation. To that end, in the first decade of the twenty-first century, the Chinese state has again turned its attention to the growing income gap within the national population and the often violent eruptions of social unrest, which frequently (though not exclusively) occur in less-urbanized, less-developed regions of the country.

National statistics on average incomes in urban and rural regions in the 2000s reveal a widening economic chasm and are sometimes used as statistical evidence for why tourism should be promoted in rural areas as a means of poverty alleviation (table 2.1). Although these numbers offer a simplistic, binary view of the Chinese population divided upon only one axis (the rural-urban divide), they are useful in understanding how and

TABLE 2.2. Guangxi per capita annual income, 2006

	Urban Disposable (RMB)	Rural Net (RMB)
Guangxi	9,899	2,771
Guilin	11,220	3,391
Longsheng county	9,770	2,350

Source: Data compiled from Guangxi Statistical Bureau 2007 and the Guilin Statistical Committee 2007.

why development efforts have been targeted at "the countryside" and at speeding up processes of urbanization (*chengshi hua*) in rural areas. This has been achieved partly through the resettlement of rural communities in newly built, mixed-use housing complexes closer to main roads and transportation. Urban annual per capita incomes are calculated in terms of annual disposable income, meaning the total household income plus a subsidy for keeping a household diary minus income tax and personal contributions to social security. Rural annual per capita income is the net amount, meaning the total income plus the participation subsidy and gifts from nonrural relatives minus taxes and fees, household operating expenses, and depreciation of durable goods.[3]

More specifically, in the regions where Ping'an and Upper Jidao are located (including province, municipality, and/or county), the urban-rural income gap is notable in two respects: first, for the relatively lower incomes overall in Guangxi and Guizhou, as compared to 2006 national figures, and second, for the disparity between rural and urban incomes within each region. Table 2.2 provides 2006 data from Guangxi, Guilin municipality, and Longsheng county (where Ping'an village is located). Table 2.3 provides 2006 data from Guizhou, including provincial averages and statistics from Kaili municipality (where Upper Jidao village is located). While both urban and rural per capita annual incomes in Guangxi and Guizhou were below the national average in 2006, the *differences* between urban and rural incomes within Guangxi (¥7,128) and Guizhou (¥7,132) are relatively similar to the *difference* between national per capita urban and rural incomes (¥8,173).[4]

China's efforts in the mid-2000s to build a New Socialist Countryside where *nong jia le* could flourish indicated that tourism was not only seen as an economic force, but that these policies also harbored intentions and ambitions beyond the purely financial. In these years, domestic tourism

TABLE 2.3. Guizhou per capita annual income, 2006

	Urban Disposable (RMB)	Rural net (RMB)
Guizhou	9,117	1,985
Kaili	8,366	2,341

Source: Guizhou Statistical Bureau 2007.

numbers and revenue began to overshadow in-bound, international tourist figures; media reports predicted the Chinese domestic tourism market was the fastest growing such market in the world (Wang Yongchang 2006). In 2007, domestic tourism expenditures in China comprised about 70 percent of total tourism revenue. The rapid increase in numbers of Chinese tourists, both at home and abroad, prompted numerous popular mass media and online reports about the negative effects of tourism on domestic transport networks and on the environment. There were also well-publicized complaints about unseemly tourist behavior.

To address these concerns, tourism was transformed into social policy in a national campaign to create "civilized" tourism (*wenming lüyou*, see Chio 2010). While the campaign was intended as part of a larger "civilized behavior" promotion in the years before the 2008 Beijing Olympics and the 2010 Shanghai Expo, the impetus for the civilized tourism campaign was rooted in the increasing number of reports of "bad behavior" committed by Chinese tourists abroad.[5] This campaign drew specifically on the Chinese concept of *suzhi* (quality), which has been commonly represented by the contrast between rural migrant workers and the idealized middle-class urban individual. Tourism was specifically invoked as a viable means of promoting economic and social progress, the former for rural Chinese and the latter for both rural and urban Chinese. Thus the attention paid to domestic tourists and tourism in 2006 effectively directed the focus of tourism onto discourses of development and state contributions to strengthen national unity.[6]

Nevertheless, for the village communities that receive tourists, the distinction between domestic and foreign tourists matters relatively little. What is infinitely more important is how they can harness the potential of tourism and travel to improve upon their own life conditions and prospects. Doing tourism involves much more than being a tourist; it is a process of negotiation with politics, policies, and shared social practices. My anthropological analysis of tourism thus contends with preexisting understandings and structures of travel within China.[7] Tourism and mobility more broadly must be approached not only from the subject position of the tourist, but also through the various policies and changes that have affected the lives of those who are in the business of doing tourism.[8]

DOMESTIC TOURISM IN CHINA

Historically, travel for pleasure in China was limited to wealthy classes of the ruling elite, and for others, travel was typically for purposes of wage-earning in urban centers or religious pilgrimage (Gang Xu 1999). The latter was greatly limited, and essentially forbidden, on ideological grounds from the early 1950s to the mid-1970s, while wage migration was intentionally hindered through the establishment of the *hukou* (household registration) system in the late 1950s (ibid., 72–73). A complex bureaucratic system intended to concentrate development in urban areas while continuing the productivity of rural agricultural regions, the *hukou* system categorized individuals both by place of residence and means of production, categorized as either agricultural (*nongye*) or nonagricultural (*fei nongye*).[9] The net effect of the *hukou* system, coupled with the state-led sociopolitical mass movements of the Great Leap Forward (1958–60) and later the Cultural Revolution (1966–76), meant that leisure and pleasure travel were hardly imaginable, let alone feasible, for the vast majority of Chinese people.

While contemporary nostalgia for rurality has led to some depictions of the "sent-down" or "rusticated" youth movement (*zhishi qingnian*) from the late 1950s to mid-1970s as infused with a pretouristic golden glow of discovery and enjoyment, in the early years of reform and opening from the late 1970s into the 1980s, domestic tourism was openly discouraged in government policy.[10] According to Gang Xu (1999, 73), drawing on R. Tang (1990, 144), "in the early years of the 1980s, policymakers still squarely insisted . . . that 'it is temporarily not suitable to promote domestic tourism.' Obviously, the primary interest of the Chinese government in tourism promotion was to earn hard currency. Plagued by dozens of problems in the tourist supply system, especially the over-loaded transportation infrastructure, most tourism planners held that, for the sake of international tourism, domestic tourism should be controlled." This attention to international inbound tourists was led by the Chinese state's intention, beginning in the 1970s, to harness foreign tourism as a means of increasing foreign direct investments and foreign currency reserves, which served as the main incentive for including tourism in national economic development policies (Ghimire and Zhou 2001, 86–87; Gang Xu 1999, 18–22). One of the first Chinese cities to be opened to international tourism, in 1973, was Guilin, less than one hundred kilometers from Ping'an.

As a result, "domestic tourism in China was virtually induced by market demand" rather than by direct state intervention (Ghimire and Zhou 2001, 97), and early rural tourism developments were "spontaneous," emerging out of villages conveniently located near major sites of national significance and the implementation of the "household responsibility system" (*geti hu*) that allowed farmers to pursue nonagricultural, income-generative activities (Gao, Huang, and Huang 2009, 3). Tourism as an industry was first addressed in a 1984–85 policy document that set out an initial framework for private and state-run investments in tourism development and management, and in 1987, the "first national conference on domestic tourism" was held in Tianjin (Gang Xu 1999, 25 and 75). Tourism (here meaning both international arrivals and domestic travels) was formally identified as an industry in the 8th Five Year Plan, which prompted policy changes at a structural level. Nevertheless, the state prioritized international arrivals, although by the early 1990s, scholars began to take stock of the domestic tourism industry as more than an economically beneficial side-project to the supposedly more important international tourism market to China.[11]

Beginning in 1993, the central government took concrete steps toward the better regulation and management of domestic tourism, including the establishment of an "insurance deposit" by travel agencies to guard against potential complaints and claims, improving public security at major tourist sites, restructuring tourist prices, improvements to infrastructure and sanitation, and environmental protection measures (Ghimire and Zhou 2001, 97–98).[12] This increased attention to the business side of domestic tourism came about after June 1989, when international tourist arrivals to China dropped steeply after the student protests and violent government response on Tiananmen Square in Beijing, compelling "large state-owned travel services to engage actively in domestic tourism" (ibid., 96).

Local provincial governments quickly realized the potential of tourism as a part of national calls for rural poverty alleviation. Various efforts emerged to create policies to address poverty alleviation and modernization through rural tourism in the 1990s in Guizhou, Hebei, Sichuan, and Yunnan (Gao, Huang, and Huang 2009, 3; and Oakes 1998, 125–30). Nationally, additional structural reorganizations included the establishment of the five-day working week on May 1, 1995. The Chinese government deemed tourism a new key growth area of the economy in 1998 and introduced the Golden Weeks in October 1999 (Nyíri 2010, 61–62). The Golden Weeks were three week-long national holidays, encompassing one week each at Spring Festival (Lunar New Year), International Labor Day (May 1), and National Day (October 1). These weeks provided for three days of paid holiday or time off, and the remaining two working days of the week were rearranged to the weekends immediately before or after, to create five full nonwork days.

The Golden Weeks were essential for the success of tourism for Ping'an and Upper Jidao because of the villages' distance from major cities and transport hubs. Both Ping'an and Upper Jidao are a two- to three-hour drive from the nearest airport, in the cities of Guilin and Guiyang respectively; flights from Beijing or Shanghai to these airports take around two to three hours. Even with a flight and direct private transportation to the villages, travel takes at least half a day and can be quite expensive. Most domestic travelers I met preferred to visit these villages as part of a longer package tour of the region to make the most economical trip (typically by flying to the region and then traveling to a number of sites by tour bus for five to seven days). The Golden Weeks allowed more domestic tourists to undertake longer trips farther away from their places of residence, but because these holiday periods were national, they created enormous seasonal demands on transport systems (air, rail, and highways), hotels, and other related industries. In response, the state revised the Golden Week holidays in late 2007, and beginning in 2008, the May 1 holiday was shortened to just one day before or after a weekend, while the National Day and Spring Festival holiday weeks were left as before. To compensate, the national government established additional one-day holidays for the traditional Chinese festivals of Tomb-Sweeping Day (Qingming Jie, in the early spring), Dragon's Boat Festival (Duanwu Jie, in late spring/ early summer), and Mid-Autumn Festival (Zhongqiu Jie, in autumn). At the time, the impact of this change to the national holiday schedule on village tourism businesses was a matter of great concern for residents of Ping'an and Upper Jidao, whose businesses depended largely upon the ability and willingness of tourists from Beijing, Guangzhou, Shanghai, and other major cities to take a full week off for leisure travel.

Despite the revisions to the national holiday schedule, domestic tourism numbers continue to increase steadily. Statistically, domestic tourists now far outpace and outspend international tourists coming to China; in 2006, there were 124.94 million foreign tourist arrivals (including tourists from Hong Kong, Macau, and Taiwan), as compared to 1.394 billion domestic tourist trips. Similar to how the numbers of incoming foreign tourists are calculated based on arrival numbers at ports of entry (i.e., airports and land crossings), Chinese tourism authorities calculate the number of domestic tourists based on ticket sales at official tourism destinations or scenic areas (Nyíri 2010, 62). In 2008, just during the October 1 National Day Golden Week, the China National Tourism Administration (CNTA) estimated there were 178 million tourist trips taken, a 22 percent increase over the same period in the previous year (CNTA 2008c). As for tourism revenue, according to CNTA figures, foreign tourism revenue in 2006 was US$33.949 billion, compared to the domestic tourism revenue of ¥622.97 billion, or approximately US$78.8 billion. The dramatic growth and strength of domestic tourism in China over the 2006–10 period thus reflects and explains, in part, increased government attention to tourism and its effects, both positive and negative (table 2.4).

A closer look at the statistics on domestic tourism, however, illuminates the vastness and persistence of economic inequality in China in the 2000s. According to the National Bureau of Statistics of China (NBS), the total population of China at the end of 2006 was 1.314 billion, of which 582 million (44 percent) were registered urban residents and 731 million (56 percent) were rural residents (NBS 2011). The year 2006 was the first in which the number of domestic tourism trips taken exceeded the total population of the country; official statistics state that there were 1.394 billion domestic travel trips taken that year. This number increased to 1.610 billion domestic trips in 2007, or on average 1.2 trips per person. In practice, of course, this figure indicates that many people may have taken multiple tourist trips while others, presumably, may not have taken any at

TABLE 2.4. Comparison of domestic and overseas tourist numbers
and revenue, 2006–10

m = million; b = billion; t = trillion

	2006	2007	2008	2009	2010
Domestic tourists	1.394*b*	1.610*b*	1.712*b*	1.902*b*	2.103*b*
Domestic revenue (RMB)	622.97*b*	777.06*b*	874.93*b*	1.018*t*	1.258*t*
Overseas tourists*	124.94*m*	131.87*m*	130.03*m*	126.48*m*	133.76*m*
International revenue (USD)	33.949*b*	41.919*b*	40.843*b*	39.675*b*	45.814*b*

Source: NBS 2011.

*The category "Overseas tourists" includes those from Hong Kong, Macao, Taiwan, and all other international arrivals.

all. These figures should be regarded with some degree of critical distance; within the categories of urban and rural populations there are significant differences between income levels and travel habits. Rural populations in China can include peri-urban, or suburban, communities close to such major metropolitan commercial centers as Beijing or Guangzhou, where incomes may be substantially higher than in the largely nonindustrialized regions of Guizhou and Guangxi where I conducted fieldwork. These tourism statistics, taken from official sources, do not acknowledge the spectrum within each population group.

Table 2.5 disaggregates domestic tourism statistics from 2005 to 2010 for the country as a whole and according to urban/rural population categories as reported by the NBS.[13] For a clearer sense of these numbers in relation to total national population, table 2.6 provides an extract of the 2007 statistics on population, domestic tourism trips taken, and average per capita spending by tourists, defined as urban or rural in the reported figures. Urbanites outspent their rural counterparts by about ¥685, or three times more, per trip in 2007; indeed, urban tourists that year spent ¥131 more than the urban average from 2006 (¥766.4). Rural tourists, however, were much more frugal, spending on average a mere ¥0.6 more per trip in 2007 than in 2006. For further comparison, table 2.7 presents national and regional data on tourism visits between the country, Guangxi, and Guizhou. Guangxi receives far more tourists (both domestic and international) than Guizhou, largely because of Guangxi's earlier involvement in the tourism industry with the historically famous city of

TABLE 2.5. Major statistics of domestic tourism, 2005–10

	2005	2006	2007	2008	2009	2010
Domestic Tourists						
Total (percentages reflect the total number of tourist trips taken against China's total population in that year)	1.21 billion (92.7%)	1.394 billion (106.1%)	1.61 billion (122.5%)	1.712 billion (128.9%)	1.902 billion (142.5%)	2.103 billion (156.83%)
Urban	496 million	576 million	612 million	703 million	903 million	1.065 billion
Rural	716 million	818 million	998 million	1.009 billion	999 million	1.038 billion
Average Per Capita Expenditure						
Total (RMB)	436.1	446.9	482.6	511	535.4	598.2
Urban	737.1	766.4	906.9	849.4	801.1	883
Rural	227.6	221.9	222.5	275.3	295.3	306

Source: NBS 2011.

TABLE 2.6. Domestic tourism statistics, urban and rural comparison, 2007

	Urban	Rural
Population (by residence)	606,330,000	714,960,000
Number of tourist trips	612,000,000	998,000,000
Average expenditure per trip (RMB)	906.9	222.5

Source: CNTA 2008b and NBS 2011.

TABLE 2.7. Domestic and international tourist statistics for Guangxi, Guizhou, and China, 2006

	Guangxi	Guizhou	China
Domestic tourists	73,996,700	47,157,500	1,394,000,000
International tourists	1,707,729	321,400	124,942,100

Source: Data compiled from Guangxi Statistical Bureau 2007, Guizhou Statistical Bureau 2007, and CNTA 2007.

Guilin and later the popular "backpacker" destination, Yangshuo (Oakes 1998, 48–49).

Tourism statistics alone cannot reveal the myriad problems faced by rural communities, which by no means are all the same, but tables 2.5 and 2.6 show a continued economic divide between urban and rural populations in China in terms of tourist expenditures. Granted, in the 2000s, more and more rural and urban Chinese were taking more leisure trips. Yet the problem of rural poverty and the uneven pace of development in rural regions remained unresolved. In terms of income, the gulf between urban and rural Chinese was stark: in 2006, the per capita urban disposable income was ¥11,760, as compared to a per capita rural net income of just ¥3,587 (see table 2.1). Of course, within rural regions and even within villages (as my own data from Ping'an and Upper Jidao showed), there was a range of incomes and relative senses of wealth or need. These imbalances were meant to be addressed in 2006 through a multipronged effort to expand the possibilities of rural tourism as a contributor to socioeconomic growth, to enact further rural development policies, and to rebrand and promote rural areas as a valuable, worthy, and ultimately pleasurable part of the modern Chinese nation.

A NEW COUNTRYSIDE

The convergence of three national initiatives in 2006 marked tourism—domestic tourism in particular—as a recognized, valuable avenue for rural socioeconomic progress and development. Together with the growing popularity of *nong jia le* as a type of tourism experience, the nexus of concerns exhibited in CNTA's China Rural Tourism theme, the campaign to build a New Socialist Countryside, and the concomitant public campaign for civilized tourism all pointed toward changing ideas about leisure, imaginations of the future, and uses of the past in contemporary China. The social, political, and economic issues at stake, as suggested in these various programs, ranged from alleviating rural poverty to disciplining one's behaviors as a tourist to celebrating the pleasures of rural life. Plans for using tourism development as a means toward rural economic growth and modernization were under way well before 2006.[14] But significantly, the prominence of rural tourism in national campaigns in 2006 marked a particular moment of attention paid to the potential capacity of rural and ethnic minority communities to contribute to the nation's overall well-being. The push of rural development programs went far beyond material improvements to offer new discourses of rural subjectivity and ways of imagining and contributing to Chinese modernity.

The campaign to build a New Socialist Countryside, introduced in late 2005 and officially begun in spring 2006, had its precedents in recurring attempts by the Chinese government to address rural problems. This extends as far back as Mao Zedong's call for a Communist revolution in his 1927 report on conditions of rural life in Hunan (Mao Z. 1975). At the heart of these problems over the decades has been the question of rural subjectivity, or the significance of rural Chinese to modern Communist China's political, social, and economic narratives of nationhood and progress. Indeed, "the 'peasant' construction of the countryside built cultural and ideological legitimacy for Mao Zedong's political and organizational revolution" (Hayford 1998, 150–51). This effectively created the image of an older, undesirable society that had to be rejected and transformed through discourses of turning farmers into peasants, tradition into feudalism, and customs and religion into superstition (Cohen 1993, 154; see also Chu 2010, 63–69; and Kipnis 1995).[15] The vision and state-authorized classification of Chinese peasants (*nongmin*), who are seen as at odds with unforgiving nature and burdened by their unequal status in relation to landowning classes, justified the role of the Communist Party in the nation-state.[16] Similar to the Ethnic Classification Project, this vision provided a structure within which the government could do the work of governing its population.[17] The *hukou* system was one such national policy that created distinctions between populations, creating "a veritable paper barrier" between rural and urban areas and limiting the mobility and opportunities of state-classified peasants (Chu 2010, 64).[18]

In the postreform era, rural underdevelopment has been frequently glossed as the "three rural problems" (*san nong wenti*): agriculture (*nongye*), peasants (*nongmin*), and villages (*nongcun*).[19] As China's domestic and regional economies have diversified, however, rural residents are no longer bound to agricultural labor and engage in an increasingly wide range of income-generating activities, even while they may continue to hold land-use rights and produce food for their own consumption. Some may be large-scale farm owners or migrant farm laborers (Zhang and Donaldson 2010); others, such as the guesthouse owners and restaurateurs in Ping'an who are still classified as rural, may run their own businesses that are only tangentially related to agricultural labor but remain dependent upon certain administrative and historical conditions (such as inherited family land) to exist. Nevertheless, despite these realities, the category of the Chinese peasant persists to this day, particularly within contemporary development and modernization plans including rural tourism.[20]

The 2000 campaign Open Up the West (Xibu Da Kaifa) set the stage for many of the policies and programs that followed in 2006. According to David Goodman (2004, 3), "the stated goal was the development of the interior and western regions of the PRC, in distinct contrast to the emphasis of regional development policy since 1978 that had favored its eastern and southern parts." Both Guizhou and Guangxi were included, the rhetoric of which suggested that "the west" was bounded and characterized by "economic underdevelopment, a lack of economic infrastructure and large number of minority nationalities, as well as being in the far interior of the land mass" (ibid., 6). Guangxi, of course, actually has a southern coastline, and as Goodman points out, the sheer range of areas and situations covered by the general designation of "the West" discursively elides the many significant differences between these administrative units and cultural regions.[21] This campaign, like the New Socialist Countryside campaign to come later, had a basic double aim: to increase opportunities for rural residents in rural places (thereby ideally reversing the flow of internal migrants from the western interior regions to the eastern coastal cities) and to rewrite the discourse of "going West" in terms of contributing to a positive, desirable pioneering spirit and activist sensibility (ibid., 13).

The campaign to Open Up the West drew the attention of many Chinese scholars to the potential of tourism in rural western China as a means of socioeconomic development.[22] Rural tourism could address and solve the "three rural problems" of agriculture, the peasant, and the village by developing the "nonagricultural" possibilities in rural regions, including specialty products, service and hospitality, and small businesses—all in service of rural tourism (Yang and Hui 2005, 52). The region designated as "the West" in the campaign included all five ethnic autonomous regions—a designation that implicitly collapsed, to an extent, ethnic minority identity with socioeconomic underdevelopment.[23] Furthermore, ethnic minorities make up two-thirds of the total population of the western regions, and of the fifty-five officially recognized ethnic minority groups in China, forty-nine of these ethnic groups reside primarily in the region designed "the West." All of this corroborated a general perspective that rural tourism could be beneficial and viable in these areas by emphasizing folk ethnic traditions as tourism resources (ibid., 51).

The justification for promoting tourism in rural ethnic minority regions thus illuminated the assumption that tourism *as* development could perform a double duty in China by addressing a range of socioeconomic problems attributed to both rural and ethnic communities.[24] New economic opportunities could also combat the "small farmer mentality" by regulating and regularizing rural economies. The idea of a "small farmer mentality" was commonly associated with notions of subsistence, or semisubsistence, modes of production which were, as Tim Oakes (1998, 148) has written, "thought to prevent modernization as [the subsistence farmers] persist in their ways of self-sufficiency and *ad hoc* participation in local markets." Furthermore, this mentality was perceived to mean that "such peasants are not sufficiently entrepreneurial" (ibid.). Suggestions on how to use rural tourism in the development of western China as a new form of business opportunity therefore implicitly addressed not only economic underdevelopment but also a perceived social and psychological lack of progress.

Another parallel arena of state-promoted social development has been the public campaign to increase the "quality" (*suzhi*) of the Chinese population.[25] Contemporary discourses of *suzhi* were first linked to notions of population quality (*renkou suzhi*) from the early years of economic reforms in the mid- to late 1970s, which in turn were reevoked in the 1980s to spur development and progress at a national scale by changing population discourse from issues of quantity (manifest in birth restrictions) to quality (Anagnost 2004). Rural regions were specifically marked as "low quality" in an effort to explain poverty and the slow pace of modernization in these areas; gradually, however, ideas of population quality were taken up "more broadly as a general explanation for everything that held the Chinese nation back from achieving its rightful place in the world" (ibid., 190). Throughout the 1980s and early 1990s, in this era of rapid privatization and economic growth, *suzhi* became a positive attribute associated with the new ideal type of the rising middle-class, urban Chinese individual. From representing an apparent lack of progress in the body of the Chinese nation, *suzhi* was now taken as a personal characteristic of high-achieving individuals within Chinese society. *Suzhi* discourse gained common acceptance as a reflection of the relationship between "two figures: the body of the rural migrant, which exemplifies *suzhi* in its apparent absence, and the body of the urban, middle-class only child, which is fetishized as a site for the accumulation of the very dimensions of *suzhi* wanting in its 'other'" (ibid., 190).[26]

Within this context the campaign to build a New Socialist Countryside took shape as a key component of the 11th Five Year Plan from 2006 to 2010. Paired with two core concepts promoted in this plan—namely "scientific development" (*kexue fazhan*) and "harmonious society" (*hexie shehui*)—this campaign explicitly sought to address and improve social and economic aspects of rural lives through five areas: enhanced production, higher living standards, a healthy and stable lifestyle, neat and clean villages, and democratic town and village management (Su 2009, 121).[27] Notably, within these five areas, only two are directly targeted at *economic* goals—enhanced production and higher living standards. "Enhanced production" meant an increased focus on modernizing agricultural technologies to achieve higher yields and, importantly, greater food security for the nation as a whole.

Higher living standards were to be achieved through higher rural incomes, by increasing rural productivity and access to markets but also through increased social security programs and educational opportunities. In Upper Jidao, for example, throughout 2006 and 2007, villagers often mentioned to me the elimination of previously mandatory school fees at the primary level, the end of the rural agricultural tax, and the newly introduced cooperative rural health insurance scheme as beneficial recent changes. Of course, residents also noted local corruption, the lack of more modern infrastructure (in particular, outdated water and sewage systems in the village), and overall low incomes and resultant pressures to seek wage labor far away from home as ongoing struggles in their daily lives.

Less overtly discussed in the village, and yet widely present in public media discourse, were the remaining three areas of the campaign that focused on social development: a healthy and stable lifestyle, neat and clean villages, and democratic management. Indeed, the theme of cleaner and neater-looking rural places became a cornerstone of the visual representation of a New Socialist Countryside. As David Bray (2012) has shown, the planning and ostensible "urbanization" of one community in Jiangsu, Qinglong (an administrative village southeast of Nanjing), as part of the New Socialist Countryside program began with efforts to clean up and modernize the built environment in 2006. In Qinglong, village leadership implemented the "six clean-ups and six set-ups" (*liu qing liu jian*), which included cleaning up rubbish, manure, straw, waterways, industrial pollution, and chaotic construction practices. By mid-2007, "Qinglong leaders were able to report . . . [that] the former 'dirty, chaotic, and backward' local environment had been given a 'new look'" (ibid., 12). Many villages underwent extensive rebuilding and reconstruction efforts, tearing down existing residences and buildings to construct new units that looked more modern (Lora-Wainwright 2012 and Oakes 2011), and entire village communities were moved into newly planned residential areas (Bray 2012 and Guo Henqi dir. 2010). Many of these developments were perceived as mere vanity projects, however, and duly criticized by government officials as such (Wu N. 2007).[28] The implementation of a new urban-rural planning law in 2008 thus aimed to increase rural urbanization and to better oversee the ways in which rural buildings and spaces were being transformed, physically, under the guise of development.[29]

Tourism, conceived as a means of development, provided villages and government offices with a ready-made agenda that could encompass the three goals of income generation, "tidying up" village spaces, and social progress. But as Oakes (2011, 28) has pointed out in an overview of the New Socialist Countryside transformations in Guizhou, "village based beautification assumes an urban-based aesthetic eye," and, as a result, "the problem lies in an urban aesthetic that reinvents the villages as a repository of soon-to-be-lost heritage" and not necessarily as a *productive* space for wage-earning, let alone farming or food-raising.[30] The conceptual connection between space and subjectivity is apparent: cleaner, neater, and more modern living spaces could create civilized, higher-quality people. Upper Jidao was "planned" for tourism by various government construction bureaus from the township (Sankeshu), to the municipality (Kaili), to the province (Guizhou). Changes laid out in the 2006 New Socialist Countryside plans for Upper Jidao included building a new decorative "wind and rain" bridge (*fengyu qiao*) into the village, a common-use garbage incineration area, a bigger "song and dance" space (*tiao ge chang*), and a tourist reception office (*jie dai shi*).[31] In 2007, funds were provided to build single-purpose pens behind the village's central residential area to house pigs and oxen instead of raising them directly underneath a household's living space (something noted also in Bray 2012 in Jiangsu and in Oakes 2011 in another village in Guizhou), in the name of cleanliness and comfort. Ping'an had already implemented a similar rule in the early 2000s that required pigs and oxen to be kept in pens separate from houses. But in Upper Jidao this particular change was met with some resistance, as many older village residents were unhappy at having to carry heavy buckets of slop and bundles of hay across the village, multiple times a day, to feed their animals. While some of the new pens were eventually used, other families continued to raise animals underneath their homes.

A NEW (CIVILIZED) TOURISM

Travel and travel experiences were another component of the pursuit to create "high quality" Chinese subjects, even before the New Socialist Countryside campaign; as part of Open Up the West, for instance, "the rural population was encouraged to acquire new skills and a more modern mentality by migrating to cities" (Nyíri 2010, 84). Likewise, tourism was viewed as a positive contribution to improving *suzhi*; parents in the city of Kunming, Yunnan, invested in summer travel opportunities for their children in an explicit effort to raise the *suzhi* of their sons and daughters (Kuan 2008). The contribution of tourism to increasing collective national levels of *suzhi* was evoked further in other state plans and projects.

Analyzing the competing visions for development and nature tourism along the Altai Road, which crosses the China-Russia border, Pál Nyíri and Joana Breidenbach (2008) have argued that for China, nature tourism in this region fit into current discourses of travel, *suzhi*, and the general uplifting of China's "spiritual civilization." "The state-driven tourism boom has not only been a major tool of increasing domestic consumption," write Nyíri and Breidenbach, "it also fits into the Chinese state's use of tourism development as a tool of both 'material and spiritual civilization' that should strengthen national pride and 'raise the quality' of the rural population and especially of ethnic minorities" (ibid., 131). The appeal of tourism to the Chinese state and Chinese tourists in the postreform era echoes what Anne Gorsuch (2003) has called a "ritual of reassurance" in the context of the late–Stalinist era tourism in the Soviet Union.[32] There, tourism "offered a means of producing socialist-minded citizens focused internally on the advantages of the Soviet system. It may also have been a ritual of reassurance for Soviet citizens in so far as tourism offered hope that life post-war would be an improvement on what they had thus far endured" (ibid., 785). Certainly for many domestic Chinese tourists I met, as well as for the villagers in Ping'an and Upper Jidao, the new opportunities for tourism and leisure were seen as proof that life conditions were much improved now as compared to thirty or even twenty years ago.

Increased mobility across the nation also has brought more and more diverse communities in contact with one another, and yet migrant workers continue to be regarded frequently as "low quality," despite the supposed modernizing influence of mobility and travel. But the emergence in the early 2000s of reports and stories of the "ugly Chinese tourist" both domestically and abroad put a damper on this new positive association between travel, individual quality, and potential (Chio 2010). The China Central Spiritual Civilization Steering Committee[33] took this matter of unattractive tourist behaviors very seriously, issuing a document in August 2006 entitled, "Plan to Raise the Civilized Tourism Quality of Chinese Tourists" ("Tisheng Zhongguo gongmin lüyou wenming suzhi xingdong jihua") (CNTA and Zhongguo Wenming Xie 2006). Further-more, the Spiritual Civilization Steering Committee and the CNTA jointly issued a call for stories and submissions on "uncivilized tourist behavior" (the article subtitle read: "Zhongguo gongmin lüyou bu wen-ming xingwei biaoxian") and "suggestions for quality tourist behavior" ("Tisheng Zhongguo gongmin lüyou wenming suzhi jianyi"); by September, they reported having received more than thirty thousand entries and three million hits (Zhongguo Wenming Wang 2006c).

An article from the *Beijing Youth Daily* newspaper, published in September 2006, ran the headline "How Do Foreigners View Chinese Tourists?" and recounted the unbecoming antics of Chinese tourists as reported in Thai, Malaysian, and American media outlets (Zhongguo Wenming Wang 2006a). Amid much publicity and attention from both domestic and international news outlets (Macartney 2006, Xinhua News 2006a and 2006b, and Zhang R. 2006), specific guidelines for tourist behavior were published as booklets and posters. These guidelines were made public on October 2, 2006, during the October 1 National Day Golden Week holiday. One set addressed issues for outbound Chinese tourists (traveling internationally) and another set of guidelines was directed at domestic Chinese tourists.[34] Travel agencies were responsible for giving each of their tourists the appropriate guidelines before commencing a tour, and posters with the guidelines were displayed as late as 2008 in airports, airline ticketing offices, and other relevant travel industry locations.

According to the guidelines, civilized quality improvements in tourists could be made through small changes to everyday behaviors; among other regulations, outbound Chinese tourists were reminded to "be polite and respectful," "wear appropriate clothes and don't spit," "let women and the elderly go first," and to "be quiet while eating" (Zhongguo Wenming Wang 2006b). For domestic tourists, the guidelines included an emphasis on environmental protection and admonishments against littering and spitting, as well as reminders to protect ancient heritage objects, respect religious traditions, and not to insist on taking pictures with foreign tourists (ibid.). According to an article in a Beijing newspaper, tourism—and by extension the "quality" of Chinese tourists—was matter of image management and represented the quality of individuals and of the nation as a whole. Therefore, only when domestic tourists were civilized would outbound tourists also be civilized (Xin Jing Bao 2006).

This push to civilize the *tourist* thus coincided with the deployment of tourism to civilize *the toured* in China following the joint proclamation of the China Rural Tourism year and the beginning of the national New Socialist Countryside campaign. The theme of China Rural Tourism was to establish, according to its slogan, "new villages, new tourism, new experiences, new customs" (*xin nongcun, xin lüyou, xin tiyan, xin fengxiang*). Numerous reports and scholarly articles published around this time proclaimed with great insistence the positive role of rural tourism within the larger challenge to build a New Socialist Countryside.[35] In a widely circulated article written by the CNTA director Shao Qiwei, the relationship between the year of China Rural Tourism and the national campaign to build a New Socialist Countryside is extolled for its multiple advantages for both tourists and rural people (Shao 2007).[36] Titled "Develop Rural Tourism, Promote Building a New Countryside," Shao makes explicit in his argument that the role of rural tourism development is not only to increase the types of work and income-generating activities possible in rural areas, but also to contribute to the improvement of rural *suzhi*. The key strategy behind rural tourism and rural development, Shao writes, is to "use tourism to help peasants" (*yi you zhu nong*). He lists five specific ways in which rural tourism contributes to positive development. Besides assisting in the creation of rural products for sale and the improvement of rural livelihoods, Shao explains in his third point that rural tourism "benefits the raising of rural people's quality and countryside civilization." Increasing "civilization" in the countryside, Shao continues, includes the introduction of new ideas and concepts from the city, better education, learning to speak standard Chinese and foreign languages, and learning to use computers. All of these specific features of "civilization," Shao concludes, will benefit the *suzhi* of rural residents.

Shao (ibid.) also stresses the need for local governments to incorporate rural tourism development directly into their own programs and the importance of increasing opportunities for rural residents in rural areas, evoking the Chinese slogan "leave the fields without leaving the countryside" (*li tu bu li xiang*). To make the shift from agriculture and subsistence farming to enterprise, rural people must incorporate the charm and soul of rural traditions and livelihoods into their tourism efforts, Shao writes. Although rural tourism can be a part of the new countryside, he continues, it should not "be that as a result of development, the new villages are built without agriculture, vernacular architecture, peasants, or (other) unique characteristics" (ibid.). He emphasizes the necessity of adequate governing structures in rural tourism and of paying attention to local opinions; while community participation should be encouraged, rural residents cannot be forced to do tourism, he notes.

PEASANT FAMILY HAPPINESS

How, exactly, were rural communities supposed to do tourism in this case? The business model called *nong jia le* is generally associated with spending leisure time in a village household, usually a family home or guesthouse, eating locally produced "simple" foods, possibly engaging in agricultural activities such as harvesting fruit, and perhaps staying overnight. By one account, *nong jia le* first emerged in 1987 in the village of Long Quan Feng outside Chengdu, Sichuan, although the phrase has also been used for holiday villages near Beijing, Shanghai, and other larger cities (Yang Y. 2007, 1). In ethnic minority regions, the first character, *nong*, is often changed to the ethnic name of the particular community.[37] The capacity of the phrase to be rewritten or revised to accommodate different ethnic names points to the centrality of the body of a rural, and/or ethnic, person as the provider of the experience for tourists. It is therefore critical to acknowledge that *nong jia le*, as it has been envisioned to take place in rural villages in China, anticipates and indeed demands the participation of rural people in this touristic encounter.

The emphasis of *nong jia le* tourism is on the experience of rural life: through enjoying the proverbial fruits of farm labor and through the provision of the romantically uncomplicated, unassuming pleasures of the idealized countryside. In this way, *nong jia le* tourism relies upon the discursive category of the Chinese peasant, which operates here in a cultural mode as the ultimate "Other" to the modern Chinese citizen.[38] Beyond the commercialized desirability of a rural experience for potential tourists in contemporary postreform China, as a concept and a commodity, *nong jia le* also deliberately and self-consciously ignores the increasing diversification of rural livelihoods and economies in favor of a timeless, stable rural folksiness that exists in contrast to the existential whirlwind of the city (Williams 1975).[39] *Nong jia le* thus promises an experience of the happiness of peasant family life, and this experience dominates *nong jia le* advertisements and promotions. For village residents, however, the intersection of peasant discourse with *nong jia le* tourism opportunities has resulted in "tourism entrepreneurship [becoming] an entanglement of a moral and a capitalist economy," as Hazel Tucker (2010, 928) has shown for "peasant-entrepreneurs" in a Turkish destination.

As a business model for private enterprise, *nong jia le* arguably could be integrated into the policy of "using tourism to help peasants"; the national agricultural bureau published a handbook on how to run a *nong jia le* business, which gave detailed instructions on the elements of such endeavors, such as how to set prices, how to publicize businesses, and how to be proper hosts (Yang Y. 2007). According to the handbook, *nong jia le* businesses are characterized by low overhead costs and rapid returns on investments. The model emphasizes participation (from both village residents and tourists) and celebrates the rural, agricultural, and traditional cultures. In chapter 1 of the manual, the character *nong* is discussed in relation to its role in *nong jia le* businesses. The book explains that *nong jia le* is based on agriculture, village and rural materials, and rural sightseeing, in which the village itself provides the resources for tourism development (ibid., 3). But perhaps even more important than a village's rural environment is the role of rural familial *affect* (*nongjia qinqing*) in building successful rural tourism (ibid., 4). The invocation of affect, and kin affect no less, serves to acknowledge the significance of rural people in China's development and utilizes the category of "the rural" to justify particular policies and programs, shifting the significance of what is rural from the economy (and modes of production) to the realm of sociality and interpersonal relations. Indeed, the true goal of *nong jia le* is "to make the guest a family relation" (*ba keren dang qinren*) by stressing that even though the tourist is a consumer, the service provided should be at the level of the familial. This is how rural people are to participate in the modernizing effects of tourism—namely, by sharing their social identities as peasants in ways that bring tourists into the fold; the guide emphasizes that through "personable, familial service, guests will experience a feeling of 'coming home'" (ibid., 4).

Chapter 2 of the manual details the concepts and methods related to the development of tourism resources, first by outlining the different types of cultural tourism resources that exist, including landscape, water, animals, architectural/historic, relaxation/activity-based, and shopping experiences (ibid., 18). Opening the market for tourism requires a comprehensive understanding of the tourist desires and the available resources, and for *nong jia le* businesses, the manual stresses that potential owners must consider such factors as safety, low overhead, environmental protection, and the potential for tourist participation. After all, the handbook instructs, "*nong jia le* tourism products should consider the ability for tourists to experience, to see with their own eyes, to use their own hands, to both play and work" (ibid., 29). As an experiential trope, the idea of participation thus creates the opportunity for rural communities to contribute to national development and for (presumably) urban tourists to cope with the stresses of modernity. Both groups, of course, would in turn raise their respective *suzhi* levels as productive Chinese citizens.

In an article entitled "Philosophical Thoughts on the Era of *Nong Jia Le*," Lin Hesheng (2007) muses over the potential negative effects of *nong jia le* enterprises on rural people. Recalling an anecdote about a seeing a *nong jia le* business owner who grew organic produce only for consumption by his family and served chemically fertilized vegetables to tourists, Lin asks, rhetorically, if this state of affairs had been brought about by the city tourists or by the corruption of rural peasants (ibid., 89). Using *nong jia le* as a conceptual fulcrum to consider the social and psychological effects of modernization and development, Lin nevertheless voices his support for the positive potential of this industry but concludes with a call for a "postmodern" form of *nong jia le*—one where the urban tourists can enjoy the countryside, but the rural hosts participate not only for economic profit but also out of their own enjoyment of this type of business and lifestyle (ibid., 90), thus rendering the subjectivity of the rural hosts completely in line with modern, developed, and effectively *urban* perspectives on labor, leisure, and mobility. Indeed, national government plans for rural tourism extended well beyond the year of China Rural Tourism, presumably in pursuit of precisely such goals for the social development of rural people. In 2007, the CNTA signed an agreement with the Ministry of Agriculture "to jointly promote rural tourism development and the construction of new socialist rural communities" (Gao, Huang, and Huang 2009, 443).

Such policies aimed at rural communities were never to be just about the money: tourism in China was bound tightly with explicit attempts to construct a new Chinese countryside, a new Chinese tourist, and a new rural Chinese subject. In this way, contemporary tourism in rural China has made claims on the rural as a social identity, whether by commercializing a shared nostalgia for rural lifeways or, in many regions, by highlighting ethnic minority traditions as a valuable resource in creating and sustaining the appeal of tourism to these areas. Tourism should be able to perform a double duty: as an effort to increase rural incomes and also to raise the *suzhi* of ethnic minorities by modernizing them through tourism as development.

To participate in these efforts, however, residents of tourism villages like Upper Jidao and Ping'an were expected to look, perform, and behave *like* their counterparts in urban ethnic theme parks, only in a rural setting that would, in theory, make the experience of meeting an ethnic minority and watching an ethnic performance even more authentic. For both villages, rurality and ethnicity were equally promoted as attractions. Nevertheless, most residents I spoke with emphasized that their less-developed socioeconomic status as compared with the domestic and foreign tourists they encountered was a result of their rural location in relation to China's rapid growth in urban centers along the southern and eastern coasts, and not a consequence of their ethnicity. Upper Jidao and Ping'an residents were proud of their ethnic identities and cultural traditions, even or perhaps especially in the contemporary Chinese marketplace that encourages certain ways of appropriately producing and consuming ethnic difference (McCarthy 2009). In the case of these two villages, because they were promoted as ethnic and rural tourism destinations, village residents felt a particularly strong connection to making tourism succeed since they were literally being asked to sell themselves in the postreform tourism marketplace. Therefore, residents had to reconcile with the current benefits and disadvantages of being different, ethnically and rurally, or as Sara Friedman (2006) has dubbed it in her study of the "Hui'an woman" in rural Fujian, the "power of difference." Understanding the power of difference in China is crucial for unpacking how tourism as development has become meaningful for village residents, and the history and conditions of *difference* in China, between ethnic minorities and the majority, between rural and urban, have affected not only *how* Chinese travel but also *why* and *who* travels at all.

The synergistic effects of national policies on and mainstream discourses of the rural and the ethnic in contemporary China informed the everyday experiences of communities and individuals living in rural ethnic tourism destinations and shaped the ways in which village residents could envision their own roles and participation in doing tourism. A select number of residents in Upper Jidao learned what tourism meant partially by attending internationally funded training workshops on tourism and heritage preservation and hosting visiting World Bank consultants and experts. Villagers in Ping'an reacted and responded to changing demands and expectations from tourists, as well as to the influx of outside entrepreneurs, government officials, and investors. Yet at a more immediate, personal level of experience and reflection, residents in both Upper Jidao and Ping'an increasingly drew upon their own travel experiences and their opinions about tourism as gleaned from media sources and personal encounters. For most villagers, their previous travels were undertaken as migrant laborers, in search of income and wages by working as laborers in factories, farms, and construction sites around the country. Their stories, told in chapter 3, thus mapped the myriad paths, opportunities, and desires over time and for diverse reasons of a landscape of travel that influenced why tourism was significant, what they envisioned they could *do* in tourism, and perhaps most important, what tourism might eventually do for them.

离土不离乡

LEAVE THE FIELDS
WITHOUT LEAVING THE COUNTRYSIDE

The Orders of Mobility

In February 2007, I was roaming the paths of Upper Jidao to complete a household survey in the village. By this time, I had lived there for more than five months, and I thought most everyone knew who I was, given the small size of the village. But starting in November of the previous year, the population of Upper Jidao had suddenly "boomed." Over the course of a few weeks, people began returning to the village to celebrate Miao New Year (held the middle of the tenth month of the lunar calendar). Mostly adults between the ages of eighteen and forty, they came back from manufacturing districts in Guangdong and Zhejiang in the south and east but also from as far north as Heilongjiang, bordering Russia.

While I walked around the village on this particular day, I heard voices from a house I had not yet approached. I knocked on the door and began my customary introduction, shouting, "Is anyone there? (*you ren ma?*)" Some children peered out over the second-floor railing, and after recognizing me, said to come upstairs; they were watching television. Once inside, I asked if the head of the household was available, and a teenager sauntered into a back room and came back with a middle-aged man whom he said was his uncle. The uncle seemed reluctant at first to talk; it was only after he realized that the children already knew me that he agreed to answer my questions. By this point in my fieldwork, the man's hesitation no longer surprised me—every year, researchers from prefectural, provincial, and national government offices came to Upper Jidao to collect data on rural livelihoods by interviewing village residents. Internationally prominent organizations such as Oxfam and (the now defunct) China Development Brief had also previously sent people to gather information about rural life in Upper Jidao. It was clear that some residents were tired of being studied.[1]

The man spoke slowly and carefully as I asked questions about his educational background, his opinions on tourism development, and his annual income. In his fifties, he was an example of why the well-intentioned tourism development plans for Upper Jidao simply might not work out—he was neither keen to participate in tourism nor particularly enthusiastic about the idea of having tourists in his home village. He had been working outside of Upper Jidao on and off for about fifteen years, once going as far as Xinjiang to work on a tomato farm. To get to Xinjiang, the man said, he had traveled with a group of migrant laborers through the cities of Chongqing, Chengdu, and Urumqi. Before that trip, he had worked in construction in Guangdong. Now he was working nearby in Kaili, also doing construction. The wages he earned went toward the costs of his sons' schooling—from room and board to supplies and other necessities. As we reached the end of the survey, I commented that he had traveled quite a lot. I concluded with my final question: Where might he like to go next if he had the chance to be a tourist? To this he replied, with no small degree of exasperation, "You can go anywhere as a migrant worker, but as a tourist you need money!"

In his statement lay the crux of this chapter's analysis: how travel and the idea of mobility can become valued in terms such as "freedom" and "lack." By "mobility," I am referring to both the ability to travel and to all of the attendant desires and notions of agency associated with this capacity to envision travel as a socially significant element of one's subjectivity and life experiences. What do these qualities that are so frequently attributed to mobility reveal about conditions in contemporary, modernizing rural ethnic China? This man's cogent assessment of his own travels prompted me to reconsider the consequences of mobility for tourism, development, and rural socioeconomic livelihoods. His exclamation hinted toward an approach to mobility that could capture the social, economic, and political potentialities at work and at stake in China today. By making the distinction between the mobility of migrants and tourists in terms of possibility (going anywhere) and economy (needing money), he highlighted precisely how travel and movement are integrated into emerging forms of imagination, opportunity, and modern subjectivities.

For many returned migrants in tourism villages, tourism and migration have become interlocking ways of envisioning identity and mediating their current economic and social circumstances. After all, in both Upper Jidao and Ping'an, migrant workers were returning to find their homes in the process of becoming tourist destinations for urbanites from some of the places the migrant workers had just left. In the ways that returned migrants recounted their own travels, it thus becomes possible to understand how villagers see, and one might say assert, themselves and their village in rural ethnic tourism. Moreover, from these individual stories of travel, potential, current, and former migrants were making sense of contemporary conditions. Travel was doubly positioned as a personal experience of growth and as a shared potential chance for an entire community to enter into modernization processes through tourism.

The case of tourism in rural China has much to contribute to analyzing the orders of mobility, or how different types of mobility come to be resignified in times of immense social change and the consequences of these symbolic shifts on local understandings of ethnic identity and rural livelihoods. In this chapter I draw attention to how mobility and immobility together generate the conditions of possibility for understanding economic opportunity, identity, and inequality in rural ethnic tourism villages. I do so by examining how mobility orders social relationships and how certain forms, such as tourism or migration, become valued in relation to each other. These understandings of mobility were ordered by residents in such a way as to provide the social structure within which individuals negotiated their situations and identities, even for those who did not, or could not, actually travel.

As I discovered during the winter in Upper Jidao, there were a lot of people from the village who no longer lived there on a regular basis. But in the weeks immediately prior to Miao New Year, as the village filled up with people, I wondered what kinds of stories they would tell about the city and what kinds of stories they would tell about their home. What did a familiarity with "the urban" contribute to ethnic minority people and rural places, especially when what constituted "the rural" was being re-presented and rewritten for tourism? As they spoke about their experiences elsewhere and returning to the village, their comments hinted at a developing sense of "traveler's knowledge," or a tourist's subjectivity, which could be employed and integrated with the plans for rural tourism development. How did they formulate a tourist's subjectivity toward understanding tourism development that was based, in part, on their own travel experiences? Their travels as migrants provided a mirror, albeit asymmetrical and imbalanced, for these individuals to reflect upon why and how travel as tourists could be desirable and enjoyable. In trying to promote tourism in their villages, the main question facing residents was, "What do tourists want?" What could village residents rely on to formulate an idea of what urban tourists might want from a rural village?

Memories of travel among residents of Upper Jidao of course predated the most recent phase of rural-to-urban migration. During the Great Leap Forward in the late 1950s, for example, some young men had been sent from Upper Jidao to work in factories in urban areas near Guiyang but also as far as Chongqing, then part of Sichuan. Other culturally specific patterns of travel include patrilocal marriage practices in Miao communities around Upper Jidao, in which the bride moves into the groom's family home, often in a nearby village. More recently, given increased transport links and opportunities to meet new people through school or work, the distances traveled by young women for marriage have been increasing; in Upper Jidao, I met young wives who were not ethnically Miao from other areas of Guizhou. In Ping'an, where it is common (though not universal) for a husband to join his wife's family after marriage, I encountered young men from all corners of Guangxi who had met their brides in vocational school or while working in Guilin. But, overall, the increasing distances traveled by residents of Upper Jidao and Ping'an were largely the result of labor migration—village residents had left to seek paid work and now returned with their new lives and new opportunities (made possible through their mobility) in tow.

LEAVING THE FIELDS, AND THE COUNTRYSIDE

By examining what "travel" means to village residents, it is possible to explore how domestic and global networks of labor and leisure are changing rural Chinese society and individual senses of possibility. Travel, for many villagers, was defined by its practical purpose to earn money, hence the interviewee's comment that while migrant workers may have the apparent "freedom" to travel anywhere, tourists are "limited" by the possession or lack of money. Although it would be a denial of the very real existing inequalities, structural biases, and social stratifications in China to suggest that by traveling as migrant laborers, rural people were also somehow the same as tourists, travel as migration could be, and indeed was, integrated into understandings of travel as tourism. The ability to make sense of travel was especially significant for residents of rural tourism villages, who by necessity had to contend with the mobility of tourists in order to make tourism profitable and worthwhile for themselves.

At the same time, discourses of rural "peasants" rooted in the land continued to shape policies promoting rural tourism, despite the parallel concern by the state to use tourism development as a means of social, economic, and cultural modernization. Indeed, from the perspective of tourism development, the assumption seemed to be that residents of Upper Jidao and Ping'an would simply be at home, ready and willing to participate in tourism.[2] In the dominant framework of tourism, development, and Chinese modernity, urbanites were expected to want to travel, to obtain release from the pressures of city life; rural people were expected to want to stay home, to develop ways to *not* have to migrate as laborers. The different expectations of mobility for different groups thus make it critical to explore the orders of mobility, or how mobility comes to shape social experiences and identities, by beginning with an exploration of how migration functions in the lives of village residents. Only in this way is it possible to situate the experiences of tourism village residents within a larger landscape of travel in contemporary China.

The dramatic and massive phenomenon of internal migration in the postreform years has had enormous consequences for the country and its growth.[3] Official statistics report that there were 242 million migrant workers nationwide in 2010 (Zhongguo Wang 2011). Analyzing the experiences and reasons for migration necessitates a variety of perspectives on the social, economic, and political aspects of migrant labor in order to understand the impact of migration on rural socialities and subjectivities.[4] Coupled with the explosion in internal migration has been a significant increase in international migration, bolstering national discourses on the significance of Chinese diasporic communities in constructing and maintaining a contemporary Chinese identity around the world. Xin

Liu (1997, 96), writing about perceptions of space and power by Chinese rural villagers and overseas scholars, outlines a structure of "social-spatial hierarchies" in China within which particular strategies of spatial meaning-making emerge. This hierarchical structuring of space/place through access to mobility characterizes everyday imaginings of social difference, and "travel and movement have reordered the power relations between different groups of people, and their identities are reworked according to the shifting images of various kind of selves and others" (ibid., 110).

Pál Nyíri (2006, 99), in assessing Xin Liu's argument, points out how the modern "Chinese subject was linked to mobility" through national discourses of being "'advanced' (*xianjin*), 'civilized' (*wenming*), 'cultured' (*you wenhua*), or 'high-quality' (*you suzhi*)," resulting in notions that "[overseas] migrants are symbolic figures because they represent the vanguard of modernity, not only by virtue of their connection to more 'advanced' nations, but also by the very fact of their mobility." Here, discourses of the "new migrant" in China, celebrated as a modern Chinese figure who successfully "makes it" overseas (Nyíri 2001, 2003, 2005a, and 2006), run parallel to the situation in villages where returned migrants are also considered to be a positive contribution to the community and its future. That international migration is so broadly celebrated while internal migration is largely presented as a problem in need of solution only further emphasizes the imbalances of mobility, particularly as a problem of socioeconomic class in China. It also mirrors, in a reversed way, the explosion of domestic tourism and the relatively more cautious approach of the Chinese government to international outbound tourism (see Arlt 2006).

These varying frameworks of mobility in postreform China illuminate how mobility can be ordered in ways that reveal particular desires, inequalities, and power relations. While overseas migrants may be perceived as vanguards of modernity, some forms of mobility are negatively assessed in development and modernization projects. In a 1983 study on rural development interventions undertaken between the governments of developing nations and international and national aid organizations and donors like the World Bank, Richard Rhoda (1983, 34–35) set out to examine the "common belief that improved conditions in rural areas will reduce rural-urban migration and consequently reduce the growth of urban poverty." Implicit in this belief is the idea that rural-to-urban migration is undesirable and potentially harmful to urban economies and living conditions. This type of mobility is seen as a social ailment in need of treatment, ideally by eliminating the mobility of rural people into urban spaces. Rhoda (ibid., 60) concludes that rural-urban migration appears inevitable, however, and that policy changes ought to focus on urban conditions rather than continuing to target rural areas as the only places in need of development.

A similar desire to keep the rural "in place" is present in the Chinese slogan "leave the fields without leaving the countryside" (*li tu bu li xiang*), in which there is an attempt to conceive of modernity without mobility—in other words, an immobile modernity. This linguistic sleight of hand suggests that rural people ought to move "away" from the unmodern (the fields) but simultaneously reinforces the idea that rural people are best left unmoving (not leaving the countryside). While modern development is apparently available to all, mobility and immobility are rendered absolute, paired to map neatly onto an urban-rural binary. This idea has been further reinforced for rural ethnic minority communities, where women in particular are seen as doubly bound to the land within a set of discursive practices Louisa Schein (2000, 100–31) has called "internal orientalism" (see also Gladney 1994), in which class and gender are asymmetrically structured in commonplace representations of ethnic minorities as rural women and majority Han as urban men.

The notion of travel as a social force is indeed so pertinent and so obvious that it is perhaps, as Schein (2006, 213) has argued, "a banal commonplace to note that people in China are on the move." More attention is needed to the particularities of movement—the questions of when, where, why, and what for—as well as the specific forms of travel engendered by rapid economic development at a national level and in response to China's increasing political economic links with the global marketplace. In this way, mobility must be understood as a scalar practice "in which the 'local' is positioned in relation to urban, provincial, national, and global scales" (ibid., 214). Schein discusses the experiences of Miao women who were "jumping scales" by living in Beijing as purveyors of Miao handicrafts for an urban market, by opening modern beauty salons offering urban styles in rural Miao villages, and by "marrying up" the scale from an ethnic minority village to a Han (more mainstream) location. But rather than abandoning the "lower scale" through their mobile transgressions, these women actually demonstrated an increased sense of the "local" (or ethnically Miao and gendered female) as they simultaneously courted the mainstream, male, non-Miao "Other" (ibid., 233–35). Subsequently, translocal Miao women not only moved up and out of certain political "scales," they also fostered new lateral connections between scales as they themselves embodied multiple social positions. How individuals understand social stratification, hierarchy, and change in the forms of migration and tourism is a key to conceptualizing the symbolic and social import of travel in contemporary China.

MIGRANTS AND TOURISTS

A critical approach to tourism and migration is an intervention toward breaking apart the persistent, commonplace expectation of rural communities and people as ideally immobile and, by extension, as relatively unmodern. This is a move toward unpacking how mobility is resignified in processes of modernization. As modernity and mobility are increasingly equated with one another, the converse has dominated policy perspectives on rural development. But even if rural villagers were to leave the fields without leaving the countryside, what would they draw on to formulate their new modern subjectivities?[5] The emphasis on civilized behavior, high-quality individuals, and "neat and clean" villages encompassed in the campaign to build a New Socialist Countryside attempted to provide precisely these shared social and cultural meanings in addition to increasing rural incomes and economic productivity.

By addressing mobility as variously constructed through the particular "desires and emotions that drive migration and tourism" (Lindquist 2009, 150), the stories of travel told by returned migrants in Ping'an and Upper Jidao reveal how village residents learned to be touristic to better adapt their village-based tourism industries to potential visitors. To consider migrants and tourists together means attending to mobility's failures and its productive qualities, particularly in such contexts as contemporary rural China, where the socioeconomic conditions between tourists and local villagers are often quite unequal and many village residents have not (yet) had many opportunities to travel for leisure. In some cases around the world, migrant laborers have sought out work in tourism destinations, and in turn, their labor experiences in the tourism industries have engaged them in direct, face-to-face contact with tourist desires for education, relaxation, adventure, or enlightenment.[6] This type of contact with tourism and tourists has the potential to change the values and meanings of migration and tourism.[7] Travel becomes a practical way of finding employment by migrating and a discourse necessary to comprehend when developing tourism activities.

Whether labor or leisure, the act of travel comes to signify new conceptualizations of belonging, aspirations, and identity. For certain classes of wealthy individuals, tourism labor has become a way for them to seek employment as migrant laborers while enjoying the benefits of being in a tourist/leisure environment.[8] Instances of "privileged travel and movement" (Amit 2007), perhaps best embodied by the figure of the contemporary expatriate, point to the social and class asymmetries unveiled in mobility. What is analytically important, however, is to resist elevating these privileged travelers to the level of symbolizing modern existential themes of displacement (following Clifford 1997, 2), because "what links various forms of contemporary travel are not global convergences but a host of asymmetries" (Amit 2007, 8). Likewise, the imbalances revealed by a "grounded" analysis of mobility at the specific places where tourism happens also shed light on how tourist village residents in less-developed places contend with migration and tourism as equal opportunity partners in their livelihoods and life chances.

The "asymmetry of tourism" as mobility is not only limited to the differences between tourists and migrants in a tourism destination; it also extends to the social relations between local residents, where individual mobilities affect community relations precisely because of the values associated with travel experiences. Hazel Tucker (2003 and 2010), who has conducted long-term research on tourism in Göreme (near the UNESCO World Heritage site of Göreme National Park and the Rock Sites of Cappadocia in central Turkey), notes that in many ways migration buttresses Göreme's tourism enterprises and development. With the rise of tourism, some returned migrant workers found their economic and social places in the village bolstered by their familiarity with the cultures and societies of the non-Turkish tourists. "[Migration] has blurred the boundaries demarcating the Göremeli community [and the tourists], and it has concurrently forced the villagers to reconsider their place in the world and to open their lives to 'other' possibilities" (Tucker 2003, 89). But locally the consequences of out-migration in Göreme include great variations in wealth, leading migrants to disparage or "look down" on those who have stayed and prompting some of those who have not left the community to view migrants with bitterness as sellouts (ibid., 88).

STORIES OF TRAVEL

In the landscape of travel for Upper Jidao and Ping'an, the two forms of mobility of greatest concern for villagers were tourism and migration, linked by the expectation that through successful tourism development, more tourists from urban centers would arrive and village residents could (and would) stop being migrants. Networks of travel, migration, and leisure tourism thus shaped the lives of these villagers through the efforts to construct rural China as a tourist destination. As international and domestic tourist flows intersected with the socioeconomics of rural livelihoods, mobility became a crucial concept to integrate into understandings of contemporary conditions. Both migration and tourism suggest the limits of possibility for rural villagers. And both restructure individual notions of self and identity (to be a migrant or to be a tourist "object"), especially in these villages that had to capitalize on the ethnic minority heritage of the residents to sufficiently attract tourists.

Some migrant workers returned home knowing what it was like to visit someplace else, knowing what was famous or which scenic spots existed in other parts of the country, and intrinsically drew comparisons between what they have by way of tourism resources at home and what other places are offering. This may be quite practical; Tim Oakes (2006b, 167) has described a case from the mid-1990s in Hainan, where two ethnic Li villages were transformed into "village theme parks" for tourists; the founder of the company managing these villages was himself a local who "had traveled extensively throughout China and had been impressed by the tourists sites in the urban centers of Beijing and Guangzhou. He had modeled his villages on these tourist displays. Displaying village traditions was, perhaps, one way of making villagers seem more modern." To do the work of tourism properly, villagers participated in mainstream models of what tourism, leisure, and rural ethnic identities entailed—and by seeing it firsthand elsewhere, as the man from Hainan did, he could literally bring tourism back to his village. Returned migrants also brought back ideas about who is a tourist, or what is needed to be a tourist versus another kind of mobile subjectivity—such as the assessment that migrant workers could go anywhere, because they were looking for money, whereas tourists needed to *have* money at the outset to go somewhere. This kind of experiential knowledge often was perceived as a form of social capital; in interviews, migration was always retrospectively considered for its potential benefits, despite the hardships that might have prompted the decision to migrate and the difficulties endured during the migration experience.

Four recurring themes emerged in my interviews with returned migrants: first, the advantageous notion of "experiencing the world" (typically expressed in the phrase *jian shi mian*, literally "to meet the face of the world"); second, the ability to articulate an opinion on what tourists want from a rural ethnic tourism experience; third, a confidence in one's own entrepreneurship and business savvy (often described as "business brains," *jingji tounao*); and fourth, a sense of dissatisfaction with the "way things are" in rural China and other difficulties in reintegration to village life. Of course, discussions about these four themes were not only limited to the experiences of returned migrants; however, their travel experiences contributed significantly to a new sociality in rural tourism villages, one that centralized the role of travel in assessments of individual identity, leadership, and ability.

These individual travel experiences were often first mentioned to me during the course of a household survey. In total, I video-recorded interviews with twelve individuals specifically about their travels. From these recordings, I selected five representative interviews for closer analysis—the stories of Ze, Fa, and Hua from Upper Jidao, and those of Mei and Feng from Ping'an (table 3.1). Of these individuals, Ze and Fa are male, both in their early forties; Hua, Mei, and Feng are female, and Hua is in her early forties while Mei and Feng are in their early thirties. All interviews lasted about an hour and were conducted in standard Chinese (Mandarin), a language skill that is explored in the following analysis. I began each interview by asking the individuals to tell their story, from beginning to end, and I posed clarification questions throughout.

Between them, their travels had taken them to the following cities and provinces of China: Beijing, Guangdong, Hainan, Heilongjiang, Shandong, Shenzhen, and Yunnan. Spanning from the very northern reaches of the country to the southern tropics, the travels of these individuals rep-

TABLE 3.1. Details on returned migrants interviewed in Upper Jidao and Ping'an

Name, Gender	Age	Village	Interview Date	Places Traveled	Occupations
Fa, male	Early forties	Upper Jidao	December 18, 2006	Guangdong, Hainan	Factory worker; orchid farm worker
Hua, female	Early forties	Upper Jidao	December 1, 2006	Heilongjiang	Agricultural farm worker
Ze, male	Early forties	Upper Jidao	December 22, 2006	Beijing, Shandong, Guangdong	Quarry, construction worker; farm worker
Feng, female	Early thirties	Ping'an	March 2, 2007	Guangdong, Shenzhen, Zhongshan, Guilin	Factory seamstress; shopkeeper; beautician
Mei, female	Early thirties	Ping'an	March 3, 2007	Guangdong, Shenzhen, Yunnan, Zhejiang, Beijing	Office clerk; lumber salesperson; factory worker; live-in caretaker

Source: Author interviews, 2006–7.

resent the vast distances and differences traversed these days by rural Chinese. Some worked in cities, such as Ze, who was a construction worker on the Beijing West Railway station; Mei, who worked as a live-in helper for an elderly Beijing couple; and Feng, who sewed suits and undergarments at a factory of six thousand workers in Shenzhen. Others had left their rural villages for agricultural areas elsewhere, such as Fa, who worked at an orchid farm in Hainan, and Hua, who did seasonal farm labor in Heilongjiang. Most people I spoke with had years of experience as migrant laborers, and many had done a combination of all types of work—in a factory assembly line, in industrial agriculture or forestry, or in the service sector, such as working as a nanny or in a salon. Some said they were back for good; others left the village shortly after the interview in pursuit of further opportunities and incomes.

The five stories, while unique in their own terms, intersected in meaningful ways to suggest a movement of ideas and impulses that contributes to the driving forces in rural ethnic village tourism today. Their stories shed light on some of the problems these communities are facing. In all of the interviews, the common thread linking migration and tourism was opportunity—for Fa, Feng, Hua, Mei, and Ze, migration meant opportunities for addressing immediate economic needs. As tourism development became further entrenched in the villages, migration was also an opportunity to understand what tourism was all about and how to be more successful in the industry. Of course, the interviews were premised on my interest in their travels, but each person's assessment of his or her experiences and histories revealed how mobility factored in their life choices, social identities, and future opportunities. Their mobilities were tempered by the social significance associated with differing forms of travel—from the compulsion to migrate as a means to meet family obligations to returning for a chance at success in village tourism.

TO MEET THE FACE OF THE WORLD (*JIAN SHI MIAN*)

A slogan painted on a wall about a mile away from Upper Jidao plainly announced that rural villagers should prioritize continued education at home over migration (figure 3.1). However, the slogan could also be read in a different light—if it was precisely the urban familiarity, an urban perspective in other words, that was valued in migration, then able-bodied

FIGURE 3.1. A slogan painted on a wall in another village about a mile away from Upper Jidao reads, "Not pursuing an education is really bad; migrant workers, come back home" (2006). Photo by the author.

rural residents could give precedence to "an education in the city" before coming home. The educational opportunities afforded by out-migration were emphasized in a number of interviews I conducted; the ones who leave, people said, return with a better understanding of the world (in Chinese they used the phrase *jian shi mian*, which generally referred to having experienced life in the world outside of the village). Every interviewee mentioned the idea of having experienced the world when speaking of the positive advantages gained from migration. Other villagers would occasionally use a negated version of the phrase (*mei jian shi mian,* not having experienced the world, or not having seen the world) to describe people who were perceived as being less educated or having less common sense and worldliness.

For example, in Upper Jidao, Fa was widely regarded as one of the more capable men in the village. I interviewed him in late 2006, when he and his wife had just returned from Guangdong. Other villagers had repeatedly suggested I talk to Fa about the village's tourism plans, because he had been a part of the village leadership subcommittee (*xiao zu*) in 2002, when the provincial government obtained the initial seed grant from the World Bank and consultancy services from the World Tourism Organization (UNWTO). Invited experts and planners from all over the world had come to assess the tourism potential of Upper Jidao, and as a part of his leadership position, Fa attended most of the training courses and went on the study tour to regional rural tourism destinations, including Ping'an, which was organized by the provincial government. When I arrived in Upper Jidao in 2006, Fa and his wife were in Guangdong, having left the village in 2005.

Years before, Fa had worked on an orchid farm in Hainan in the late 1990s; he returned to Upper Jidao in the early 2000s, when tourism development plans were in the beginning stages, participated a bit in village affairs since he had been elected to be a village leader, but he left again in 2005 to find work in Guangdong. Despite government plans, he said, there just wasn't any money to be earned in the village from tourism yet. For him, the advantages to be gained from experiences away from the village were less of a pull factor; rather, the push factor of very few opportunities to earn an income in Upper Jidao prompted his second migration. Coming back in 2006 was a big deal for him and for the other villagers; Fa was banking on tourism really being something soon. After our interview in December 2006, village residents again, in January 2007, elected him to lead the Upper Jidao subcommittee. But by June 2007, I was told Fa had left again for Guangdong. The reason was simple: he had a wife, children, and parents to take care of, and there was little money to be earned by serving in the village leadership. Fa returned to Upper Jidao in 2009, working again as a member of the village subcommittee as the accountant, keeping track of the village's burgeoning tourism income. He kept being elected to the village committee because to the other villagers Fa had "seen the world" and knew what to do—they saw him as someone who could go between places, literally and symbolically.

Here migration and tourism coincided in conflicting ways. Fa felt pushed out of the village because of increasing financial obligations to his family; the village residents, by reelecting him to the leadership committee, tried to pull him back in because of his proven experience and ability to walk the line between urban and rural environments, perspectives, and even languages. For Fa, travel was thoroughly woven into the fabric, the expectations and possibilities, of his livelihood. He acknowledged the contradictions inherent in trying to develop tourism in Upper Jidao; the problem, he told me, was that overall in the village, residents' education levels were too low. Too few people had experienced the world enough to understand what would make tourism successful and what wouldn't. The conundrum was obvious: without enough education and experience in the world, the village residents would never get tourism off the ground. Without steady sources of income in the village, those who had more responsibilities and family pressures would leave. Without people in the village, there would be no one to do the tourism work. Thus, in Fa's formulation, leaving was beneficial—if you eventually came back.

In Ping'an, Mei expressed the educative value of migration in more personal terms. I asked her about how she had found work during her years in south China and Beijing. "From 1999 onwards," she said, "I just went looking around to see if there was any suitable work; I just looked around—it was like doing research, researching myself." Unlike most of the others I met, who tended to travel in groups with relatives and friends from their home villages or regions when they migrated, Mei had struck out on her own. She had worked a number of jobs, from selling lumber to taking care of an elderly couple. In retrospect, she assessed each job as a chance to develop her skills, to see what she was good at and what she liked to do.

Villagers often pointed out certain practical skills and behaviors gained from experiencing the world. First and foremost, those who had migrated to other parts of China learned to speak standard Chinese. Being able to speak standard Chinese is critical for doing tourism; it is the first step to simply being able to communicate with tourists and other nonlocals, such as consultants, government officials, and potential investors. In Upper Jidao, for instance, much of the tourism work fell upon the shoulders of Qin, Teacher Pan, and Fa, when he was around—all of whom were well spoken in standard Chinese and therefore considered good candidates for interfacing with the outside world. Speaking standard Chinese comfortably was also a social distinction that was made immediately apparent to me as I conducted my household survey in both villages. As an outsider in Upper Jidao and Ping'an, standard Chinese was the lingua franca between myself and the villagers; it was taken for granted that I would not be able to understand, let alone speak, regional dialects and minority languages. As a result, the first people in each place whom I met were those who spoke standard Chinese. It wasn't until I was able to understand the regional Chinese dialects in each place that my networks expanded in a more meaningful way beyond those individuals who spoke standard Chinese because of their education or experience in other parts of China.

When asked what she had learned while being a migrant worker, Feng, who ran a shop and family guesthouse in Ping'an, replied: "I learned some sewing, standard Chinese, Cantonese, and a little bit about the outside world." She had even purchased tapes and books to teach herself Cantonese when she first went to Guangdong; in the mid-1990s, when she was there, many factories required their workers to speak or at least understand some Cantonese. She attributed her relatively good job in Shenzhen partly to her ability, upon hiring, to speak Cantonese; the factory manager was a Cantonese-speaking woman from Hong Kong who had taken a liking to Feng. Now, back in Ping'an, Feng said that Cantonese was sometimes useful as the village did receive a lot of tourists from Guangdong. However, she added, nowadays "most young people from Guangdong speak standard Chinese anyway."

Experiencing the world, and learning how to negotiate it, was crucial for these individuals, and the relevance of this education to working in tourism was not overlooked. Fa and Mei were both considered two of the more capable people in their respective villages: Fa's election to the village subcommittee was proof enough of the village's opinion. Mei, whose time out of the village she considered as personal research, was approached in mid-2008 by a representative of the Guilin municipal government about possibly becoming a Party cadre and serving in the local village and township government administration. When she asked this representative how he had heard of her, he replied that the other villagers had mentioned her.

WHAT DO TOURISTS WANT?

Upper Jidao residents were extremely concerned with making sure they could appropriately and adequately address the perceived needs of tourists—this was the focus of many training sessions organized by the Guizhou provincial government as well as a frequent topic of conversation between myself and residents. Since most villagers said they had never actually been tourists before, they referred to media representations of tourism from television and magazines, as well as to firsthand encounters with tourists, tour guides, and government tourism bureau officials in the village, to frame their understanding of what tourists want. In Ping'an, because tourism had become a steady industry and source of income in the 1990s, village residents generally expressed a fairly confident grasp of tourist desires and needs. However, in both villages I noted that many of these opinions and perspectives had been developed from the personal experiences of returned migrants, who had come back with their own stories about visiting scenic spots, having seen something different while outside of the village, or perhaps having befriended (or at least interacted with) urban middle-class Chinese while working in cities.

Hua, in her mid-forties, was unusual because she exuded a boisterous, contagious personality even when speaking standard Chinese, which she had learned only by virtue of having gone to Heilongjiang to work on a large farm. She had left Upper Jidao just as the government tourism plans were getting under way in late 2002, so she had not had much firsthand exposure to tourism in the village. While in Heilongjiang, Hua said she would occasionally see television programs about Guizhou and ethnic tourism in Miao villages in particular; she thus came to equate ethnic identity with tourism in a one-to-one correspondence based on the lack of tourism she had seen in rural Heilongjiang, which was largely Han. "Once you come to our Miao home," she explained to me, "there is tourism; the Han don't have tourism." She continued, describing how one evening "on television there were our Guizhou [people] wearing Miao clothes; they were dancing, and the northeastern people [*dongbei ren*] said, 'Oh, this is Guizhou; it says so on TV. Wow, they are wearing such beautiful clothes. Is that your home?' And I said, 'It is.'"

Later, Hua recalled, the others asked her to bring some of her own Miao festival clothes back to Heilongjiang sometime: "They said, 'you bring the clothes and we'll try them on and take a picture!'" Hearing about the changes in Upper Jidao from her daughter who had remained in the village to attend the local middle school, seeing ethnic Miao visually represented on television, and being the ethnic "Other" herself in another part of China (rural Heilongjiang) taught Hua some of the things that potential tourists might enjoy or want in Upper Jidao. Her understanding of tourism was highly visual and based largely on what she had seen on television and the reactions people had to these images.[9]

Hua experienced tourism through television representations, where she literally became identified as the ethnic "Other" to her friends and neighbors in Heilongjiang. Other migrant workers occasionally had the chance to be tourists while away from home. Ze was one of a few individuals in Upper Jidao who had been to Beijing. He had gone in the mid-1990s, and when he mentioned his experience as a migrant worker there during my household survey, I told him that I was interested in hearing about his time there. Only many weeks after the survey did I manage to find Ze with a bit of time to sit down and talk about his experiences in Beijing (and in many other parts of China as well). He began by saying that the trip had happened a long time ago and he didn't remember much, but as soon as I began recording with my video camera, Ze recalled fluidly, "It was nighttime when we got on the train [bound for Beijing]. It wasn't as easy back then. We didn't have much luggage, there were a couple of us men from the nearby villages traveling together, we climbed through the windows of the train to get inside the carriages."

At first, Ze worked in a quarry outside of Beijing; after a year, one of his traveling companions returned to Guizhou, but he and another decided to go into the city to search for new jobs. They found some temporary construction labor—one of the biggest projects he worked on during that time was the construction of the Beijing West Railway station. On the rare off days that they had (and these might have numbered one or two a month at most, he said), or in between jobs, they went sightseeing. Ze visited the Great Wall, the Ming Tombs, the Fragrant Hills, the Temple of Heaven, the Temple of the Earth, and the Beijing Zoo. When I asked him about what he thought of his village's tourism prospects in light of his own tourist experiences, Ze thought for a moment and then said there could be some sightseeing—"like here, at our place it's to see the scenery [*fengjing*], to get up in the mountains and see the scenery." He compared it to going to the Fragrant Hills just outside of Beijing in the autumn to see the red foliage; it's what you *do* in the autumn in Beijing. He understood what the tourists who come to Upper Jidao village are looking for; like sightseeing in Beijing, where you go specifically to see a particular site (the Forbidden City, the Temple of Heaven), tourists come looking for something in Upper Jidao—namely, the rural landscape, a small village, a glimpse of the subsistence farming lifestyle of ethnic Miao people. Ze had a tourist's eye for Upper Jidao.[10] All of this, he said, would need to be consolidated, signed, and marked to facilitate the tourist's encounter, much like the famous sites of Beijing, where the significance of the sights is promoted, named, and explained. Ze's take on Upper Jidao's tourism prospects was informed by his own experiences visiting tourist sites outside of the village, which had provided him with firsthand knowledge of where tourists come from and what tourists do.

Besides sightseeing, experiences with different places, lifeways, and (more often joked about) foodways—such as eating rice versus eating bread/wheat products or salty versus spicy flavors—were considered a part of the necessary knowledge required to do rural tourism properly.[11] Like Ze's knowledge of tourist activities, such as sightseeing, a familiarity with mainstream appetites and tastes was also considered vital for tourism success. Some villagers in Upper Jidao had taken part in a training program organized by the Guizhou Tourism Bureau in the summer of 2006. A portion of their training, they said, was to learn how to cook for Han tourists, who, they were told, preferred to eat stir-fried foods rather than hot-pot style (where all vegetables and meats are cooked together in a broth at the table), which was the common way of eating in both Ping'an and Upper Jidao villages. Being able to cook other types of food besides their own cuisine could also be learned from experiences as a migrant worker; one evening, for example, I was invited to a friend's home for dinner in Upper Jidao, where her husband prepared Sichuanese dishes for me. Some Sichuanese migrant workers he had befriended in Guangdong had taught him, he explained.[12]

In Ping'an, guesthouses and restaurants hosted tourists from all over the country and the world, and being able to offer a diversity of food choices was a crucial part of each establishment's advantage in the village's competitive tourism industry. Feng said that her experiences in Guangdong and Shenzhen had helped a little in running her family business because she recognized the names of dishes and foods that tourists might sometimes want to order. Otherwise, she added, "some of the tourists come and order certain dishes that local people don't know, or that local people can't understand what they are. Local people don't know these dishes; they stay at home and are rigid [in their ways; *si ban*, literally 'dead wood']."

ENTREPRENEURSHIP AND BUSINESS SAVVY

Innovation was a critical component of being successful in tourism, and many ideas developed out of the personal experiences of individuals who had left the village for some time. In Ping'an, as competition increased, some residents created their own opportunities to improve how they could do tourism. The need and desire for this kind of knowledge was firmly integrated into understandings of how to run a successful business. In one instance, Lao's family, who operated three very successful guesthouses particularly popular with European and American tour groups, went for a time to Yangshuo, a popular tourist destination south of Guilin famous for its "West Street" lined with restaurants catering to foreign travelers. There, they said, they worked in the kitchen of a café, learning how to cook Western foods and eventually returned to Ping'an with a new menu and new food suppliers, from whom they bought items such as processed cheese, hamburger buns, frozen chicken cutlets, and frozen deep fried pork to expand their menu and offerings.

Creative business ideas extended beyond food. Mei, who had done "research" on her own skills and abilities during her time outside of Ping'an, was entrepreneurial through and through. Her mother, who was from Ping'an, married Mei's father, who was from Guangdong, and the family lived in Guangdong for a while when Mei was a child. She returned to Ping'an at the age of eleven when her mother passed away. From that time on, she was raised by her maternal grandparents in the village until she graduated from middle school at age sixteen. Mei joked to me that she was like her grandmother, who had a real head for business (*jingji tou-nao*)—once, Mei said, her grandmother noticed that billiards was popular with kids in the village. She promptly purchased two billiards tables and had them delivered up the mountainside to the village where she charged local kids a few *mao* (cents) a game. Mei's middle school teachers recognized her academic potential, and through a complex web of personal networks, they managed to find her a family in the city of Liuzhou, in Guangxi, who provided her with room and board while she attended a vocational school for two years.

At the suggestion of another teacher, Mei left Liuzhou in 1999 for Guangzhou, where she worked as an assistant to a factory manager for a few months. Over the next three years, she traveled from Guangzhou to Kunming and around Yunnan (where she tried to start a business buying and selling lumber), Zhejiang, and eventually to Beijing in 2000.[13] Mei explained that a factory owner in Zhejiang had recruited her and some other young migrant laborers to go to Beijing with him to work in his company. Mei said they were taken to Beijing's Zhejiang village (Zhejiangcun), a migrant neighborhood in Beijing composed of mainly laborers and small business entrepreneurs from Zhejiang (L. Zhang 2001). She described the community as extremely corrupt and disreputable (*hei*). Mei left Zhejiang village with one of the other recruited migrant laborers after a few months, but they only managed to leave after they twice phoned the police and convinced an officer to demand that their ID cards, which the company owners had kept, be returned to them.

Mei stayed in Beijing for two years; her second job there was as a personal assistant/live-in caretaker for an elderly couple who ran a small business. Because their children had all moved away, Mei served as a stand-in filial daughter—cooking, cleaning, and generally caring for the couple at home and at work. During these years, Mei said, she kept in touch with her relatives in Ping'an through letters and occasional phone calls; in 2001, her uncle in Ping'an began sending her newspaper clippings on the rapid tourism development in the village. They wanted her to return, with her knowledge of business and her good command of standard Chinese, to open a guesthouse. Mei admitted that she was hesitant to return; although her job in Beijing was not particularly exciting, it was stable and well-paid. Her uncle insisted, and in 2002, Mei went back to Ping'an, where she immediately opened a souvenir shop at the parking lot and applied for permission from the local postal bureau to sell stamps. Hers was the first shop to officially sell stamps and mail postcards, bringing in quite a lot of new business and garnering the envy of many residents, who, Mei said, simply hadn't thought to offer this kind of service. Not much later, other families applied for postage licenses and, according to Mei, because the local county postal bureau did not want to foment anger in the village, every applicant was granted permission to sell stamps, thus diluting Mei's advantage of being the first (and for a time only) seller of stamps.

Mei never described her travels through China as tourism, yet her experiences outside of Ping'an clearly shaped her ways of thinking about tourism and business. More than the other village residents I knew, Mei regularly invited outside entrepreneurs (some of whom lived part-time in Ping'an) over to her house for dinner and attempted more collaborative projects with them. In 2007, she started building a new hotel in a joint-ownership agreement with a travel agency manager from Shenzhen, who invested in the construction materials and labor costs while Mei was to be in charge of design and management. Mei and her husband had already built one guesthouse in 2002, but rapid growth of hotels in Ping'an meant that this first one, with its shared toilets and simple rooms, was no longer competitive. She made it a point to meet as many researchers and scholars, including myself, as she could; she actively sought out information about other rural tourism destinations in China and even subscribed to the official newspaper of the China National Tourism Administration (CNTA). Of course, other individuals in Ping'an also demonstrated business savvy, often through their connections with domestic and international tour agencies. The guesthouse owners who had learned how to cook Western foods in Yangshuo worked closely with major travel agency operators and tour companies from across China and western Europe, using these connections to increase their own profits and ensure a steady business.

Being a migrant worker did not necessarily require one to be entrepreneurial, but for Mei, in retrospect, it gave her the chance to think outside of her known ways.[14] She saw herself as a businesswoman, able to engage in any type of enterprise. Having been exposed to life in the cities, Mei felt that she understood what tourists wanted in a rural destination—namely, the convenience of the city (such as being able to buy stamps for postcards) and the rustic "feel" of the countryside. Her new guesthouse, for example, was one of the first in the village to feature individual balconies off each of the rooms. Likewise, in Ping'an, Feng said she'd opened a shop selling drinks, snacks, cigarettes, and soap next to her family's guesthouse because she had had some experience in shop-keeping while working in Guilin for a few years between stints in Shenzhen and elsewhere in Guangdong. For these women, migrating had meant not only *working in* industry but *learning about* industry. When they returned to live in the village, they brought some of this industrial "spirit" into their work in the tourism businesses.

RETURN AND REINTEGRATION

While returning to the village was almost always considered positive by other villagers and in public discourse—largely because the returnees could bring back their newfound knowledge, experiences, and (ideally) savings— it was not without problems as well. In Upper Jidao, returned migrants faced the difficulty that there simply wasn't enough to be earned from tourism yet. By 2008, tour groups visited Upper Jidao with some regularity, but

Teacher Pan lamented that there weren't enough young people to do the performances properly. School-age children were not allowed to perform, he said; they had to attend school and could only participate if tour groups arrived on weekends or during school holidays. As a result, performances for tour groups in Upper Jidao included three segments featuring the village's elderly men and women. They took some pride in being different in this way, saying that by incorporating older songs and dances (and people) into their performances, Upper Jidao offered something that the other nearby tourist villages did not. Nevertheless, the other parts of the performances did not necessarily achieve the exuberance or scale of similar shows in nearby villages such as Upper Langde, where performances were often staffed by a professional dance troupe from regional towns.

As far as remaining in the village, Fa felt pushed and pulled between serving the village in a leadership capacity and seeking further income for his family. He opted for the latter, left Upper Jidao in late 2007, but returned in 2009; by 2012, however, although Fa was living in the village, he was no longer involved with the tourism plans, choosing instead to raise and sell vegetables. Hua left Upper Jidao in early 2007, fewer than three months after she'd returned from Heilongjiang, and had not returned on a more permanent basis by 2012. Ze, because of health problems, said he wasn't planning to leave Upper Jidao anymore, but if he were able to, he would; he did not, however, participate in the village's tourism activities.

In Ping'an, competition rankled relations between some locals and some returned migrants. For Mei, her lengthy time away from the village community limited her belonging in Ping'an, partly because she was more determined than most in attempting and succeeding at new business ventures. She occupied a peculiar social place because of her relatively recent "reintegration" into the village, and she was often derided by other village residents as not "really" from Ping'an—despite the fact that she spoke and understood Zhuang, was related on her mother's side to families in Ping'an, and married to another local Ping'an resident. Mei's education, her experiences outside of the village, and her entrepreneurial spirit set her apart from many of the other village women of her generation who had grown up in Ping'an with the tourism development and did not necessarily question the status quo. The knowledge and opinions Mei gained while traveling as a migrant were thus considered an advantage *and* a detriment. Some villagers scoffed when I mentioned I would be interviewing Mei about tourism in Ping'an: "What does she know?" one man asked bitterly, adding, "She's not even *from* here."[15]

Mei's first business innovation (selling stamps), along with her absence from the village during the early years of the tourism boom, marked her as an outsider to many local residents. To the villagers who started organized ticket sales and tours in 1996, Mei's entrepreneurial attitude was not very different from any other outsider coming into Ping'an around 2001 to do business, when the investments by the private management company radically increased tourism to the village. As these outsiders raised the bar for service and accommodations in Ping'an, village families, with their limited resources, struggled to compete. Copying Mei's innovations was seen as simply the next step in running a business in Ping'an. In small rural communities, copying can be a means of social and economic equalization; it "is another tactic in business competition, tending to ensure that one's business will at least remain equal with the others, even if it does not manage to achieve a higher level of success" (Tucker 2003, 111). Perhaps this is also what the local postal bureau considered when deciding to offer anyone in Ping'an a permit to sell stamps; the effect, from Mei's perspective at least, was to admonish her for being creative.

The key problem facing younger returned migrants and young people in the villages more generally was the problem of being a peasant in the *nong jia le* rural tourism formula, while the countryside was, discursively, still the "emaciated other" to the modern city in China (Yan 2008, 44). This was especially contentious in Ping'an, where the terraced fields required constant labor in order to be maintained. Because the fields were advertised as having particular aesthetic looks in each season, they had to be used and worked as *fields*, with crops that required plowing, seeding, planting, and watering. Someone had to do the agricultural labor to keep tourism afloat. To this, Feng, in her straightforward manner, said simply: "If I had the chance, I would go back to the city because I don't want to plow fields!" Most young people felt the same way. She added, "Nowadays, everyone is afraid of having to plow fields; they want to go out and see the world. Young people want to go with the modern world" and not be forced to stay and be farmers. If staying in the village means having to live a farming lifestyle, taking care of pigs, and waking early to go to the fields, Feng concluded, then "if I had the chance to live in the city, I would absolutely be willing [to do so]."

THE MONEY TO BE A TOURIST

Rural ethnic tourism, particularly in the model of *nong jia le*, cannot occur without someone in the role of the peasant, but it was precisely the rural Chinese person, as the "peasant," who was intended for change through development. To grasp at what rural tourism *as* development meant to the communities involved, these stories of travel provide necessary analytical and contextual depth to the experiences and imaginaries that influence and shape how tourism develops in a village community. Encounters with other, sometimes urban, places became stories told by village residents as they participated in national development and modernization programs like the New Socialist Countryside and efforts to create tourism businesses in their village. In all these stories of travel, the common thread linking migration and tourism was opportunity. For Fa, Feng, Hua, Mei and Ze, migration meant opportunities for addressing immediate economic needs, but also, as tourism became further entrenched in Upper Jidao and Ping'an, migration was an opportunity to understand what tourism was all about and to be more successful in this business.

Moreover, the *nong jia le* model of rural tourism emphasized the idea of home and the family, paralleling the idea promulgated by the national government that migrant workers ought to either return home or perhaps be able to establish a home where they now are.[16] More important, in the case of rural tourism, it is the idea that rural homes are worth returning to and worth visiting that is nicely packaged in the idea of celebrating the happiness of peasant life through leisure travel. This is a way of envisioning rural life that is distinctly urban. Rural residents thus come home to see their villages through "urbanized" eyes, to see their homes as a destination, rather than as a starting point. In part, this is the result of the villagers' own exposure to seeing tourism (perhaps best exemplified by Hua watching Miao people on television while working in Heilongjiang) and their experiences as tourists and sightseers as well.

How Fa, Feng, Hua, Mei, and Ze came to talk about their experiences away from home exemplifies what is happening to rural places in China that are being drawn into national and global tourism industries. Rural tourism relies upon the distinction and juxtaposition between the urban and the rural in order to succeed. Rural village tourism necessarily writes this difference upon the bodies of the rural villagers; unlike a historical site, such as the Forbidden City, tourism in Upper Jidao and Ping'an demands that there are people living in the village to make it succeed and "worth visiting." This, in turn, is reinforced when villagers look to returned migrants as a resource and as valuable, necessary assets to successful tourism development. In Ping'an, a newer, younger generation of adults is poised to change the social, economic, and political conditions in the village. This next generation of guesthouse owners is comprised of the twenty or so college-educated young adults—many of whom are returning to Ping'an after finishing university (or during holidays) to help out with the family business. Increasingly, they are setting out new hotel and business plans for their families. Some of these younger residents, familiar and comfortable with computers and the Internet, have taken to advertising their hotels in local chat rooms and with dedicated websites, and the effects of this group of individuals on tourism in Ping'an should be observed, as they bring new methods, expectations, and interests to the fabric of village life.

As the younger village residents traveled for education, in recent years a group of older residents in Ping'an hired a local travel agency to organize group tours to Beijing in 2006 and to Shanghai in 2007 (figure 3.2). The cost of the trips was relatively affordable, about ¥1,300 per person all-inclusive for five days and four nights. For the participants and their families, this represented a significant step forward—finally, they were not only the toured but the tourists as well. Of course, this was not the first time that these individuals had left the village; some had been labor migrants in the past, and many still traveled to Guilin regularly to buy goods, visit relatives, and conduct business. But these trips were distinctly, and strictly, organized leisure. They were proper holidays with tour buses, photographers, and even a videographer who recorded the entire trip and then presented each participant with a set of video recordings once they had returned to Ping'an. It was not just the travel that was so exciting, although admittedly many people told me they did enjoy the flight, which was the first for most of them. The social distinction of being able to be a tourist, after two decades of being visited and seen by tourists, was equally memorable. Of course, only those families who were doing well enough in Ping'an's tourism business had the extra money to send their grandmothers and grandfathers on vacation. It is perhaps only mildly ironic then that these same rural communities relied on the tourism industries to make the money needed to be a tourist.

FIGURE 3.2. A souvenir group photo of Ping'an residents who visited Shanghai hangs on the wall of a house in the village (2007). Photo by the author.

Returned migrants influenced tourism developments in their home villages by bringing their personal experiences in travel to bear on the future of their village tourism industries. Within this landscape of travel, mobility played a formative role in giving order and meaning to the identities and economic possibilities available. Through the stories of travel of five individuals, it is clear that the topics of experiencing the world, knowing what tourists want, entrepreneurship, and reintegration were all pertinent to the ways in which tourism was perceived as a livelihood and opportunity, much as out-migration was also already so understood. It is by tracing these changes in mobility that a more nuanced understanding of social transformation and modernization programs in rural tourism villages can be pieced together, thereby allowing for a closer examination of how both discourses of and experiences in travel operate in conjunction and in competition with each other.

ORDERING MOBILITY

By examining how mobility orders social relationships and how certain forms of mobility, such as tourism or migration, come to be valued in relation to each other, I have drawn attention to how mobility and immobility are integrated into how individuals make sense of economic opportunity, identity, and inequality in rural ethnic tourism villages. This "differentiated mobility" (Massey 1993), understood as "the uneven and unequal position of different groups and persons in relation to various flows and movements" (Chu 2006, 401), uses travel experiences and discourses to understand social relations and subjectivities. But as the stories reveal, different forms of mobility are not necessarily perceived as independent of each other; rather, tourism and migration as well as other travels are structurally ordered in meaningful ways, each informing the other and gaining greater significance as a result of their relationships. Such an approach to mobility studies is what John Urry (2007, 46) has dubbed the "mobilities paradigm"—a conceptual framework in which using mobility as an analytic and social process thus acknowledges that "all social relationships should be seen as involving diverse 'connections' that are more or less 'at a distance.'" The mobilities paradigm "forces us to attend to this economic, social and cultural organization of distance, and not just to the physical aspects of movement" (ibid., 54) because, after all, global "scapes and flows [or, the mobilities of people and things] create new inequalities of access" (Urry 2003, 5).[17]

Anthropological attention to the social formation of mobility can illuminate how different types of mobility and immobility are variously valued in relation to one another, the differences of these values for different social groups, and what the consequences of these values might be on lived experiences and social relationships. Urry (2002a, 264) has explained that "for many social groups it is the lack of mobility that is the real problem, and they will seek to enhance their social capital through access to *greater* mobility"; yet in rural China, mobility and immobility are understood in conflicting, though nonetheless desirable, ways. To start, rural ethnic tourism required village residents to be immobile. To that end, returning was highly regarded in tourism villages, but at the same time, experience *outside* of the village was considered imperative to doing tourism. Once tourism was successful enough for families and households, a new form of mobility was desired—travel as tourists. As such, mobility was ordered, and it was through these orders that returned migrants in tourism villages made sense of their past travels, anticipated the future arrival of tourists, and envisioned their place in present-day village life.[18]

In discourses of mobility, some subjectivities appear to be considered as more amenable to being mobile while others are viewed in terms of stasis and immobility. Immobility is not always discursively constructed negatively; in some instances, a "sedantarist metaphysics" works in relation to nationalistic discourses of refugee populations, where "in the national order of things, the rooting of people is not only normal; it is also perceived as a moral and spiritual need" (Malkki 1992, 30). The same claim for the moral need fulfilled by immobility may be applied to the development of rural regions as tourism destinations for domestic national and international tourists, who seek their own moral uplifting through the experience of the immobility of rural peoples and communities. If the tourist is a model of "modern-man-in-general" (MacCannell 1999 [1976], 1) partially by virtue of her or his mobility as a tourist, then the rural tourism village resident seems clearly positioned as the ideal unmodern-man-in-general. What links these notions of modernity and mobility together, then, is the particular order of mobility that allows for and encompasses a socially meaningful way of making sense of the inequalities produced by differing forms of mobility. Within this order, migrants and tourists each come to play a part in maintaining social stability, although differences of power, access, and perceived value still persist.

As the stories of travel reveal, there are important inequalities inherent in different forms of mobility. To consider the ordering of mobility is to acknowledge that choices about mobility, such as whether to migrate or to stay, hold consequences that extend beyond the economic or strictly functional but rather double back onto the very identities and social subjectivities of the individuals and communities themselves. Any ordering of mobility is always based on inequalities and certain inaccessibilities. Tim Cresswell (2006, 177) has argued, in examining migration policies and histories in the United States, that "the ways in which mobility is given meaning and then enacted is intimately tied to notions of sameness and difference." This creates the unavoidable entanglement of the politics of mobility and the politics of difference, encapsulated in the orders of mobility, which holds very real consequences for the persons who must negotiate these conditions. From the four common themes raised in the migrants' stories, the landscape of travel in which these individuals consider, deliberate, and make decisions can be seen as one in which mobility is simultaneously considered as an expression of potential, an assertion of place in the process of modernization, and as constitutive of unexpected inequalities. One's mobility can be an asset and a skill toward participating in new tourism industries, while remaining a threatening possibility vis-à-vis leaving the village community entirely.

In rural China, modernization plans are rendering ever more apparent the intrinsic contradictions of mobility by implicating subjectivities such as tourist/migrant within the lived experience of tourism *as* development. However, the aversion within tourism planning, as a modern phenomenon, to acknowledging the consequences of mobility (exemplified in noting that a highway in rural Guizhou could detract from the region's visual amenity), is similar to the impossible notion of "leaving the fields without leaving the countryside." It is a failed attempt to pretend that mobility is not somehow inherently shaped by differences, inequalities, and social distances. In taking up mobility as a conceptual framework, there must be a commitment to acknowledging and exploring reverse flows and stopped traffic—the problems created by mobility. This means taking seriously how migration can be both liberating and constraining in rural China, in this instance; how returning to the village can create new conflicts as well as provide for novel innovations toward solving old problems; and recognizing that sometimes some people may want to leave both the fields and the countryside, all in the name of being (and becoming) modern. Within the villages, however, ideas about tourism were often debated in terms of "the look" of the village and how residents negotiated the visual expediencies of tourism, which were changing personal opinions on tourism and altering the very appearance of each place. By tracing these changes, both experiential and visible, a more nuanced understanding of social transformation in rural ethnic tourism villages can be pieced together.

跟我们合影

CHAPTER 4

"TAKE A PICTURE WITH US"

The Politics of Appearance

One day in late September 2007, I left Upper Jidao with Qin, the village clinician and frequent de facto tour guide, and Wang Xiaomei, a journalist at the *Guizhou People's Daily*. Xiaomei had recently completed a master's thesis for which she conducted a comparative study of tourism development in Upper Jidao and its more well-established, well-known, and well-touristed neighbor, Upper Langde (Wang X. 2007).[1] Xiaomei and I were headed back to Guiyang, via Kaili, after spending a few days together in Upper Jidao sharing notes and ideas. Qin was on her way to attend a medical training workshop in Kaili. The three of us walked toward the highway that linked the village to the city. Unusually, no buses passed us as we strolled along the road, which hugged the winding Bala River, and we continued about a kilometer to Paile village before we stopped to wait. Eventually a bus came careening by, and Qin, Xiaomei, and I scrambled on board as the driver hustled us to sit down.

As the bus zipped into the township of Sankeshu twenty minutes later, I saw that the town's formerly drab concrete and tile three-story shop fronts were now encased in bamboo scaffolding. Fresh planks of wood were piled high along the sidewalks. New tiled roofs with decorative features had been carefully set upon the previously flat tops of the buildings, and the wood planks were in the process of being nailed to the façade of the buildings. The remodeling project in Sankeshu had started during the summer, but I hadn't noticed it as closely on my way to Upper Jidao a few weeks earlier. "What's going on here?" I asked Qin. She replied that the Kaili municipal government had given some money to Sankeshu, in a cost-sharing agreement, to renovate the buildings. Sankeshu was to become the "gateway town" to the Bala River tourism area, and to achieve this, it needed to look the part. Qin used a four-character Chinese phrase to describe the changes: *chuan yi dai mao*, which translates as "to get dressed and put on a hat." In short, the town was wearing new clothes.

VISUAL EXPEDIENCIES

All over Guizhou, and indeed across China, villages and towns have been getting dressed. In Sankeshu, this latest phase of renovations was part of a regional response to the directives of the campaign to build a New Socialist Countryside, which explicitly promoted building renovations in achieving a "neat and clean" appearance. As domestic tourism in China has become integrated into economic development plans, efforts by local governments, village leaders, business entrepreneurs, and media producers to create or at least improve "the look" of a village or town were, and continue to be, considered an absolutely critical component of tourism success. Around Kaili and Sankeshu, located in the Qiandongnan Miao and Dong Autonomous Prefecture in Guizhou, ethnicity was being carved into the visible, physical environment—from wooden houses to bus stops and sports stadiums. This overriding concern with improving the visual appearance of rural places and people revealed a range of complex and contradictory impulses, illuminating the politics of appearance in contemporary China. It was precisely the critical importance of visual appearances in tourism—whether of buildings, landscapes, or people—that rendered the visual *work* of tourism so expedient to tourism success.

The expected visual experience of tourism *for tourists* is thus integral to how host communities and governments grapple with the visual expediencies of tourism. Given that the act of sightseeing in tourism is an established cornerstone of the modern tourist experience, it is crucial to examine how Upper Jidao and Ping'an have been planned, built, and maintained as rural and ethnic sights/sites.[2] Critically engaging with the visual world of the villages as it was being debated and created is central to understanding how sightseeing is anticipated, directed, and turned into a category of knowledge through the manipulation and representation of the environment (built and natural) by tourism bureaus, village residents, and media.[3] Tourists are expected to approach their experience in Upper Jidao and Ping'an visually and to leave the villages with images (including postcards, photographs, or videos) as evidence of their encounter. Stakeholders in the tourism endeavor therefore have to know how to *do* tourism in a way that can fulfill these expectations.

Knowing what tourists expect to see constitutes the visuality of tourism, but this visuality must be rendered into material, physical forms. Renovations, such as the new shop fronts and façades in Sankeshu, are both pragmatic and symbolic. Such visualizations of rural ethnic lives and identities are not simply fake or inauthentic; rather, these visual appearances are central to the process of creating knowledge about the self and the other that is inherent in and vital to doing tourism. Renovations play a central part in China's efforts to develop and modernize rural ethnic regions. There are political and social ramifications to *having a look*—the ways of using the visual to determine and define the meaning of a place and a people. After all, "appearance *is* knowledge, of a kind. . . . Visual knowledge (as well as other forms of sensory knowledge) provides one of our primary means of comprehending the experience of other people" (MacDougall 2006, 5; italics in the original). How residents of Upper Jidao and Ping'an worked to make their villages "look good" for tourists thus demonstrates how knowledge of and about rural ethnic China is being formed under the guise of tourism. Through the implementation of preservation programs, exterior building codes, and other mechanisms to consciously control the visible surface of tourism villages, residents were learning how to understand both tourism and themselves through these changes.

Renovating the architectural style and physical appearance of a tourism destination is frequently justified under the guise of "preserving" traditional environments, styles of vernacular architecture, and indigenous methods of construction (AlSayyad 2001). The popular tourism destination of Lijiang Old Town, in the center of Lijiang city in Yunnan, provides a case in point.[4] After a devastating earthquake hit the region in 1996, a massive rebuilding project was undertaken to recreate the atmosphere and appearance of the old town district. Following that, with the old town's inscription on the UNESCO World Heritage Sites list in 1997, locals rushed to renovate their homes into homestay guesthouses (Yu Wang 2007, 792). This required major, and expensive, physical changes to the structure of existing homes in order to maintain the "traditional" exteriors while installing flush toilets, bathtubs, TVs, telephones, and soundproof walls. Tourist desires guided these efforts; many households built "big windows in the guest rooms even in a break from Naxi traditional houses in which no windows were allowed in the middle room (the living room for a Naxi family)" (ibid., 793). Beyond the immediate impact of these changes for the local residents, the visual presence of objects like televisions and toilets marked these guesthouses as comfortable and suitable for tourists. After all, for most tourists, flush toilets are considered a wholly practical amenity. The overall visual effect of these renovations also held social and subjective ramifications for locals, who had to learn, understand, and be able to negotiate the physical and visual changes in their living environments. More broadly stated, and in line with the New Socialist Countryside promotion of "neat and clean villages," as lives changed on the outside, in terms of the built environment, residents were expected to transform (or be transformed) on the inside.

The politics of appearance embedded in architectural renovations are not limited to rural regions, of course; in urban environments, the trend in constructing self-consciously *visual* sites as a statement of presence, potential, and profits is encapsulated in the rise of "starchitecture"—brand name, mega-architectural projects by internationally famous architects that take on iconic status as emblems of modernity, wealth, and progress.[5] Pre-2008 Beijing Olympics building projects, such as the National Theatre, the Water Cube, and the Bird's Nest stadium, were part of the city's, and the country's, desire to assert itself as a formidable emerging world power that would not be ignored or overlooked (Broudehoux 2007, 385). These buildings were intended to be viewed not by human eyes from below, but from above, through the mediated perspective of a machine— as Anne-Marie Broudehoux has noted: "This global-scale architecture, meant to be seen from a helicopter, and experienced on large television screens, is symptomatic of the media-based economy of the new entrepreneurial city, and is entirely at the service of the spectacle" (ibid., 385). Creating an experience best enjoyed through modern visual technologies such as cameras and televisions suggests that the camera is no longer an intrusion or a thing to be merely tolerated. Instead, the camera itself becomes the primary reason for building, changing, or maintaining the landscape, urban or rural. It becomes the main justification for *looking at* a place or even a person.

Landscapes are made to be seen, and the ability to be seen is a crucial part of the visuality of tourism; determining what becomes valued as a sight constitutes the visual expediencies of doing tourism. Constructing or finding a way to be worth looking at, therefore, was one of the greatest challenges; villages, towns, and cities had to "change their clothes" so as to attract more attention and, by extension, additional investments and potential profits. In Upper Jidao and Ping'an, looking rural and looking different has become increasingly important because it is their look that enables these communities to pursue status and success in the booming Chinese tourism industry and national rural development efforts. Emphasizing "rural-ness" and "ethnic-ness" is a part of visually increasing the exotic "otherness" factor so often expected in tourism and represented in travel media. In some cases, the features and characteristics constituting "otherness" have been drawn from existing models, such as ethnic theme parks, which have codified the experience of ethnic performance and display.

Accordingly, tourism villages have attempted to rebuild, repackage, and renovate themselves by referencing already present typologies of otherness. In this way, in order to succeed, rural ethnic Chinese communities must necessarily engage with national mainstream discourses of modernity and development. As Tim Oakes (2006b, 167–68; emphasis in the original) has written:

> Such [ethnic tourism] villages replicated (or *hope* to replicate) across space the urban theme park model of what is often regarded in China as advanced or modern tourism. In doing so, they have become places where the newly acquired mechanisms of tourist display have generated a self-consciousness about identity conditioned by the broader networks of travel to which locals are now linked. Travel, in other words, fundamentally shapes the ways places are made and remade by encouraging villagers not just to welcome and perform for paying visitors but to *replicate* themselves in newly self-conscious ways.

Indeed, as demonstrated in their own stories, villagers' travels, whether as migrant workers or as tourists, influenced how they understood tourism and how they perceived the value of being rural and ethnic. Village residents were learning to "be themselves" for tourists (to paraphrase Stanley 1998) and to be more like themselves than ever before (Bunten 2010). The visual environment in which they negotiated and managed these identities played a critical role in making the practice of doing tourism meaningful for village residents. In some instances, this resulted in a straightforward application of visual, touristic motifs within a village setting, by bringing in ideas of theme park displays and stylized performance choreography. In other cases, visuality was comprehended more obliquely—for example, by conceptualizing the "scenery" of one's home village as potentially desirable to tourists. Overall, however, a significant part of the process of replication in ethnic tourism villages included a renewed emphasis on belonging by residents.

In a study of an ethnic Dai village park in Xishuangbanna, Yunnan, Sun Jiuxia and Bao Jigang (2007b, 33) describe how the women who hosted tourists deliberately stressed their personal connections to what tourists saw: the house tourists visited became "my home," the people in the house were "my family," and of course, all the products for sale were "locally made." But the initial step in foregrounding one's place in a village community, for the purposes of increasing profits and profitability, was for residents to learn how to visually assert themselves. The concrete ways in which this process of visualization unfolded thus illuminate the visual expediencies of tourism and the attendant politics of appearance. Power and knowledge intersect and interact in highly charged contests over who and what may constitute the appropriate and desired *look* of a place. In the remainder of this chapter, I analyze the creation and promotion of Upper Jidao as a village of wooden houses for tourism and for visual media (including films and advertising). Next I examine, ethnographically, the contentious maintenance of the terraced fields for photography and the role of "minority models" in the tourism business in Ping'an. Visual knowledge and visuality are embedded in the experience of tourism, for both tourists and village residents, and the move toward visual coherence in rural ethnic tourism villages has spurred unintended social and economic consequences.

BUILDING THE LOOK:
THE WOODEN HOUSE PHENOMENON

As described in chapter 1, the efforts from 2002 on for tourism development in Guizhou were led by the provincial government, which, after many years of planning and consultation, in 2009 successfully obtained a US$60 million project loan from the World Bank to fund a project titled Guizhou Cultural and Natural Heritage Protection and Development. The provincial government's involvement in rural tourism development was meant to limit the potential negative effects of commercial tourism development on ethnic cultural heritage practices and environments by mandating community-led tourism development and local input. Other regional government administrations embarked on related tourism development projects at the same time, driven by parallel desires for economic growth and political prominence in these years of national attention to rural tourism and rural development.

The renovations in Sankeshu township were funded, in part, by government units in Kaili, the prefectural capital. As a part of Kaili's own transformation, the city built some of the nicest looking bus stops anywhere in China. These structures carried a visual theme of Miao-ethnic-minority-ness, with plinths and decorative elements that mimicked the silver-horned headdresses and necklaces worn by the region's Miao women during festivals (figures 4.1 and 4.2). A new sports stadium, bus station, and the municipal administration offices all "put on hats" in the shape of ethnic Dong drum towers. These structures in Kaili served as a visual reminder of the prefecture's claim to fame as the homeland and spiritual heart of the Miao and Dong ethnic minority groups in China. The horn-shaped adornments, curvy tiled roofs, and, most important, wooden buildings (or wooden-looking buildings) alluded to the rural aesthetic of local village life. As I noticed passing through Sankeshu that day, one of the most pressing tasks was to cover the concrete walls of the shop fronts and buildings with wood planks in an effort to symbolize ruralness through the use of natural materials.

These types of exterior renovations are typical of tourism development plans; the World Bank's 2007 "Strategic Environmental Assessment Study" for Guizhou, prepared before the approval of the project loan, addressed a number of issues facing the region, such as biodiversity, environmental

FIGURE 4.1. Women wear their Miao festival clothes and headdresses (*sheng zhuang*) when performing for tour groups in Upper Jidao (2008). Photo by the author.

protection, and the question of what landscape architects and tourism consultants call "visual impact" (Landscape Institute 2002). According to the assessment study, "tourism development may also cause direct and indirect landscape and visual impacts. . . . [T]ourism development demands amenity infrastructure such as hotels, shops and recreational facilities that may result in landscape and visual impacts where their siting, architectural style or colour are inconsistent with the surrounding environment. This impact will become particularly significant for heritage-based tourism development, if new constructions are not compatible to host environment and cultural costumes" (World Bank 2007, 47). The authors recommend that visual impact be taken into account at a state or provincial level in all further environmental impact assessments, as their research revealed a lack of communication between various government departments involved in the promotion and management of scenic tourism areas, in addition to a total lack of regulations in parts of the province

FIGURE 4.2. Bus stops in Kaili are visually themed to resemble Miao headdresses (2007). Photo by the author.

not specifically deemed scenic tourism areas (ibid., 48). The gradual visual transformations in Sankeshu and Kaili clearly aimed at constructing and standardizing the "visual impact" of the prefecture for tourism.

The assessment study offers few details about village architecture, however, simply suggesting that villagers should follow "traditional architectural style," using "local style and local materials to minimise potential negative visual impact" (ibid., 47–48). Upper Jidao had been slowly taking steps toward a total makeover ever since it had been formally selected to be a part of the province's new tourism project. The ideal vision for Upper Jidao was a village of "wooden houses," but from the very beginning, conflicts arose about how to actually do this. This image of wooden houses stemmed from the fact that, as village residents repeatedly stressed to me, the appearance of their village was the reason why Upper Jidao and not Lower Jidao (only a few hundred meters away) had been chosen for tourism development. The excess use of concrete in Lower Jidao, both for village paths and houses, was often cited as part of its unsuitability for tourism; village paths in Upper Jidao had been made of river stones set in concrete. When it came to determining the tourism resources within Upper Jidao to be promoted and marked with signs, the village's "hundred year houses" (*bainian guwu*) and the "hundred year granaries" (*bainian liangcang*), had been selected as features, so these structures took priority when it came to figuring out how to make the village into an attractive tourist destination.[6]

One household in Upper Jidao found itself at odds with both the village subcommittee leaders and government officials from the provincial tourism bureau precisely because of the look of their house. During my first stay in the village in 2006, after learning that I'd met with Zhang Xiaosong of the provincial tourism bureau, the two adult brothers of the household implored me to carry a message back to her. It took some convincing to explain that I was not directly working for the provincial government and therefore had little influence on the provincial-level plans. Nevertheless, the brothers described how they had been criticized and later verbally threatened for beginning to build a block of three concrete rooms directly in front of their house, which was right on the riverbank and which could be seen from the highway on the other side of the Bala River.

At first, the brothers explained, the rooms were meant to be akin to tearooms in the city, where tourists could play cards and relax while gazing at the river and surrounding scenery. This was how they had envisioned tourism in Upper Jidao, basing it on models of leisure popular in cities and bringing it to the countryside. It wasn't "rural ethnic tourism" in the mode of the ethnic theme park and, unfortunately for this household, it was not exactly the *nong jia le* model of tourism championed at the time by the tourism bureau or international consultants engaged in the development plans because it did not involve any specifically rural or ethnic Miao elements. But because tourism had not taken off as quickly as they had hoped, the brothers said the rooms would now be used as pigsties and a new toilet for the household. Whatever the intended purpose of the rooms, the Kaili tourism bureau demanded they stop construction, and village leaders put pressure on the brothers to remove the offending cinderblock and concrete walls. The concrete was ugly, they were told, and it didn't fit the image of a rural ethnic village, where wooden houses should be the norm.[7]

Wood was designated the visual key to making Upper Jidao a more traditional village for tourism. Every building had to be made of wood, or made to look like it was made of wood.[8] In 2005, the Kaili municipal government used wooden planks to cover up all concrete sides of the houses that could be seen either from the highway or from the main walking paths in Upper Jidao. Most village homes, if not all, were built around a wooden frame with wooden planks fitted as interior and exterior walls and sometimes floors. However, cinder blocks and concrete were commonly used for the foundation; as walls for ground-level storage and animal pens; in and around the kitchen; for building flat roofs and outdoor spaces for drying unhusked rice and beans; and for general work areas inside a home. Fire prevention made concrete desirable; the threat of fire is imminent in such a densely populated village, where many families divide a single house into two by using wooden planks to create new rooms and a new kitchen area when households split (*fen jia*).[9] With the introduction of electricity, gas stoves (usually using propane tanks or biomethane), and other modern accoutrements, concrete was also practical and safer. But concrete was not considered an appropriate material for looking good in tourism; when asked about the further developments desired for Upper Jidao's tourism to succeed, one man, a migrant laborer in Shenzhen who had returned to the village for a short stay, said that of the changes he wanted, one was "to finish up the village appearance, the outside appearance."

When asked about the boarding up of concrete walls, residents' responses were always pragmatic—most said that they didn't mind since the government had paid for it, and in fact, many of the families whose houses were covered up weren't even home when it happened. Another man I interviewed in late 2006 said he was frequently away from Upper Jidao as a bridge engineer; when people began covering up the concrete and brick walls in 2005, he had no idea they were working on his house. "I didn't do it. I wasn't at home," he explained, but he thought the final result was beautiful. "And the wood benefits me," he added. "It blocks out [more] wind and rain and protects the house; I'm not opposed to it." However, he added one caveat: "There have been a lot of changes, and I think they're all very good, but I don't have time to participate in it, they [have to] do it." Villagers worried that they would later be asked to spend their own money on wood planks or on the upkeep of these covered walls. The initial "clothing" had been a fairly haphazard effort, and within a year of being put up, some planks had warped in the wind and rain and fallen off of the walls of many houses, exposing the concrete beneath (figure 4.3).

FIGURE 4.3. Wooden planks were used to cover up brick and concrete walls in Upper Jidao, but over time they warped and fell off (2006). Photo by the author.

Keeping up appearances did not stop at just the wood planks. In the words of Wang Qiao, Party Secretary of the Kaili Tourism Bureau in 2006, Upper Jidao needed "new packaging" to promote its local, folk-ethnic look. During a weekend trip through the prefecture with five members of the Kaili Tourism Bureau in December of that year, people commented repeatedly on the concrete that had been used to build new houses and shops in many villages we passed; these places, they said, would never make it as tourism destinations because they looked too modern, despite the spectacular surrounding scenery of mountains, valleys, and rivers. In Upper Jidao, every building was "getting dressed" in wood, and the vast majority of the changes to the village's appearance were being paid for by local and provincial government units as a part of the tourism preparations in line with the New Socialist Countryside plans. This included boarding up the houses, and in 2007, it extended to adding decorative window frames to the houses closest to the new cultural center and performance space. Further efforts to beautify the village by making it more wooden included more carved wooden frames for all windows, two wood pagodas designed like wind-and-rain bridges (*fengyu qiao*), and in 2012, the existing "hundred year granaries" were dismantled and being rebuilt with new wood as part of their preservation. Of course, in the schematic plans for the village, "dressing up" wasn't just for the buildings; when tourists would come to Upper Jidao, every *body* would get dressed too. Part of the tourism program for the village included, predictably, song-and-dance performances by the villagers themselves. The village houses changed their clothes, as would the village residents—all in the name of doing tourism.

AN EXCEPTIONAL PLACE: FILMING UPPER JIDAO

The process of how Upper Jidao became a wooden village illustrates how the visual experience of tourism was expedient for village residents, especially as they grappled with competing ideas of what tourism could, or should, entail. The visual side of tourism had to be created and anticipated; village residents were preparing themselves to be seen. It began with the physical built environment (such as houses and paths) and extended to the physical body (changing clothes to suit the audience), as these elements became a part of one's understanding of how to *do* tourism. One's knowledge of what looked rural, what looked ethnically Miao, and ultimately what looked correct became tangibly and materially visualized in the choices made about the appearance of the place and the people. In tourism, these visual differences were expected to be communicated and consumed through visual media, such as photography and film.

Knowing how to make a place and a people visually coherent with the expectations of tourists, government officials, anthropologists, and consultants is critically important, but this knowledge is also rife with competing power relations and ambitions. Qin, the village clinician, and I often joked that it would be a lie to keep promoting images in the media of Miao women in their traditional festival dress (*sheng zhuang*), complete with the large silver horn-shaped headdresses, because tourists would come to expect to see this when they actually visited the village. In reality, other than during the days of Miao New Year when there was *lusheng* playing and dancing, tourists had to prearrange or otherwise specifically request to see women in festival clothes. This little white lie of Miao women always in exquisitely embroidered and silver-adorned festival clothing was amusing for us to discuss in theory, but it was a very real issue for Upper Jidao.

Tour guides frequently asked Qin and other women at short notice to put on their festival clothes, including the full headdress, so that tourists could take pictures. While most women obliged, the process of dressing in festival attire was time-consuming. Moreover, since the vast majority of women only owned one complete set of festival clothes, they were very concerned about damaging the fabric, especially the embroidered sleeves and trim, through overuse and general wear. Over the years, Teacher Pan, the retired school teacher who often served as the first point of contact for tour guides, began preemptively asking guides if their tourists would like to photograph a woman in festival dress, and if so, one or two women would appear at the appointed time. The fee, Teacher Pan said, was about ¥10 to ¥20, depending largely on what the tourist was willing to pay.

Looking different, or at least distinctive, in visual representations was imperative, at all levels of the tourism experience. Ms. Chen, a host from the China Central Television program "Travelogue" (broadcast on the English-language station CCTV 9, now CCTV International), said that once in 2007 when she and her crew went to an ethnic Tujia village in Guizhou, "the entire time we went to film, we didn't see anyone in a local costume. No one's going to go there if they don't see anything different." Having recently returned from the province, where she filmed part of a series about China's ethnic minorities, Ms. Chen said she had found Guizhou attractive because of the "combination of ethnic minorities and location," implying the visual effect of the people and the landscape.[10] From the perspective of media producers and tourists, as outsiders, differences in the built environment arguably included expectations of differences in the people. I once observed a group of people from Kaili who had come with a few women dressed in Miao festival clothes, but not from Upper Jidao, who then proceeded to use Upper Jidao village as the backdrop for photographs for a record album. The production and subsequent circulation of such imagery meant that tourists and other outsiders often expected to see people in visibly distinctive, Miao ethnic clothing inside the perfectly preserved "wooden" village houses as part of the scenery.[11]

Upper Jidao was being imaged ever more frequently in national media projects. In 2005, a young graduate of the prestigious Beijing Film Academy, Chou Chou, used Upper Jidao for on-location shooting for her first feature film, *Anayi* (released in 2006). Almost all of *Anayi* was shot in villages throughout Qiandongnan, Chou Chou's home region and where she'd spent her childhood, and she was proud of her accomplishment in using these places as a backdrop for a love story about a young Miao woman and a young Dong man. When I interviewed her in 2007 about the film and her time in Upper Jidao, she said she'd found Upper Jidao to be very natural and very original (*yuan shengtai*)—but in some places there were too many walls made of concrete, she thought, and her team had had to find bark planks and such to cover them up. In the film itself, Upper Jidao was mostly used for long establishing shots and a few close-ups of houses.

Qin was the first person to tell me about the film *Anayi*. Because she was comfortable speaking in standard Chinese, Qin was frequently the spokeswoman for the village when media reporters or government officials came. In 2007, when she was about to be interviewed on camera by a Reuters television reporter, Qin rushed off to change her clothes, but not before asking me if I thought she should do so. I hesitated, trying to defer my reply, and Qin hurried back to her house anyway; when she returned wearing a black velvet shirt featuring an embroidered flower in the middle, a side bias seam, knotted buttons, and her hair twisted up into a topknot (*jiujiu*) with a large fabric flower pinned to the front, she said it was more "representative" (*daibiaoxing*, literally, "it had more 'representative-ness'") that way. Local women often referred to this kind of outfit simply as Miao clothes (*Miao yifu*), as opposed to the full festival dress (*sheng zhuang*): a thick jacket of shiny blue fabric with embroidered pieces on the sleeves and around the entire body, a black skirt, another skirt worn on top made up of multiple long, embroidered pieces sewn into a waistband, large silver necklaces, and a silver headdress with horns (see figure 4.1).

Full festival dress was limited to use during Miao New Year and, increasingly, for tourism purposes, and these clothes held deep significance because some of the embroidered pieces (particularly the dragons on the sleeves) would be hand-embroidered by one's mother or other female relations. Miao clothes were worn at more everyday gatherings, such as celebrations for the birth of a baby, a family wedding, or when going to public markets in the nearby village of Paile or in Kaili. Younger women, like Qin, tended to wear Miao clothes and festival dress made out of synthetic materials bought from specialty tailors and traders; much of the embroidery on the festival skirts as well as on the frontispieces for Miao clothes was machine-sewn. Older women in the village, when dressing up for tourism receptions or Miao New Year celebrations, more often wore festival clothing they had received years earlier, in their home villages, which tended to include more handmade components, including hand-woven cloth and hand-embroidered trim. As far as I could tell, however, women in the village did not place different values on whether festival dress was "old" or "new," although there was a collective appreciation of the time and effort that went into hand-embroidery.

Gendered expectations also played a role in who would (and who would not) put on festival or markedly ethnic dress for tourists. Interestingly, though perhaps not surprisingly, when the same Reuters reporter interviewed the 2007 village subcommittee leader, Fu, he did not make any move to change out of his jeans and leather jacket—but that interview did not end up being used in the final Reuters story package sold through the news agency's service, whereas Qin's interview did. Perhaps Qin's sound bite was better suited to the report than Fu's, but in conversations with television producers from China Central Television and the Beijing bureau of the American network CBS, they all stressed the utmost importance of finding something that "looks good" for TV. For the report by Reuters TV, what "looked good" included a "dressed up" Qin but not the male village leader in everyday, un-ethnically distinct clothing. Later that month, a photographer from Reuters came to Upper Jidao to shoot pictures to accompany the written news report (Blanchard 2007). He had a number of places to go and quickly grew frustrated at how "uninteresting" his pictures of Upper Jidao were. No one had expected his arrival, so villagers were wearing their everyday work clothes, and no effort had been made on this particular day to "dress up." In the end, to get more pictures, the photographer went down the road to Upper Langde, which, as a popular, well-known tourism village, offered daily song-and-dance performances.

Tourists expect, and are expected, to recognize what is rural and what is ethnic first by looking. The contradictions, criticisms, and controversies that emerge—such as the case with the half-finished concrete rooms—point to the symbolic fissures between what a place *is* and what it is *supposed* to look like. The same goes for the people, and the implications are manifold—if rural places and people are not supposed to look like modern urbanites, can they still enjoy the creature comforts of modernization such as flushing toilets, Internet access, and other amenities that are desired by today's tourists?[12] As tourism demanded a certain visual look to a place, the consequences of such demands were located in the ways different stakeholders came to understand what was appealing and attractive about that site, and eventually where and how money was spent. It was also about how village residents, like Qin, came to see themselves as needing to be a little more, or less, "representative"; how photographers came looking for something "interesting"; and how government tourism bureaus decided when and where to pressure village residents to build their homes in a certain way—in effect, molding the expectations and desires of the residents. Together, these decisions, made at both local rural and national levels, came to shape what would be known about rural ethnic places like Upper Jidao through their tourism.

TAKING CARE OF TERRACED FIELDS

Similar debates occurred in Ping'an, which was and remains the most heavily visited village within the Longji Scenic Area. In Ping'an, residents had similar troubles and arguments over the building of "wooden" houses that could also function as hotels, and in 2007 the county government opened a new office called the Longji Construction Bureau to oversee village building projects. According to villagers, however, the building codes changed almost every year, and any rule could be bent or simply dismissed with enough financial leverage. Because tourism revenue for the residents of Ping'an depended largely upon their earnings from family-run guesthouses and restaurants, with income from carrying sedans and luggage only supplemental, most families with enough money expanded or rebuilt their homes to feature larger dining areas, a bigger kitchen, and better appointed guestrooms. The general rule of thumb regarding construction and architectural style was that houses in Ping'an must be made of wood or look so—a widely accepted guideline was that building an "old house" (*lao fang*), which meant no more than two stories tall and completely made of wood, did not require permission from the construction office.[13] But to build a guesthouse or hotel with modern conveniences such as flushing toilets, on-demand hot water, en suite bathrooms, and heating and cooling units required concrete and lots of it. The completed building had to adhere to certain height restrictions (generally said to be three stories, but there were a handful of buildings with five stories by 2007, and by 2012 many more large hotels were under construction). Furthermore, the building must, in the end, be covered in wood. The goal was to maintain the look of the village, while at the same time allowing for increases in business. The enforcement of these rules waxed and waned over the years, causing much anger and resentment among the villagers. Many families simply ignored the rules or the complicated permissions system, figuring that it would be difficult for the government bureau to take down an already built house, but it would be very easy to lose an argument about a house that had not yet been built.

As the number of tourists and competition intensified, however, it became clear that the busiest, most successful accommodations were always the newer, more recently renovated hotels with en suite bathrooms, enough height for a good view of the terraces, and screened-in windows to keep out mosquitoes and other creatures. The view of terraced fields was central; after all, Zhuang minority architecture was merely an added bonus in a visit to Ping'an. Tourists came to the Longji Scenic Area to see the fields, and the terraces encapsulated yet another instance in which the visual expediency of tourism determined the decisions and choices made available to village residents. Many tourists were openly, and loudly, disappointed when the terraces did not look good. "Good" meant the fields had to resemble the dramatic images widely circulated in the mainstream media—from television advertisements to glossy photo books. Because of existing imagery and marketing campaigns, there were very specific looks for the terraces in each season (snowy white in winter, sparkling silver in spring, lush green in summer, and golden in autumn), which the villagers were expected to re-create by keeping up an annual cycle of rice planting and harvesting. When the terraces did not look like these images, such as in the late autumn or early spring when they were dry and mostly bare, many tourists complained that there was nothing to see.

A large segment of tourist arrivals in Ping'an is comprised of amateur photographers who often come as part of package tours during the most "photographable" seasons of the year—the late spring and early summer flooding of the fields and then the autumn "golden" fields of ripening rice just before harvest. According to the history of tourism in Ping'an, as written by village elder Lao for me, the first tourists to Ping'an were photographers, and the links between Ping'an and photography run deep. One local guesthouse owner told me that her main customers were photography groups from Guangzhou, and through these various connections her husband had even worked for a while with a China Central Television crew whom the couple had met in the village. Her business centered on catering to photographers; inside her hotel, the walls were covered with poster-size photographs of the terraces and pictures of the guesthouse owner herself taken by photographers who had hired her as a guide and model. She had hung up a sign on her hotel that read: "friends of photography" (*she ying zhi you*). Although photographers are not good tourists, many villagers told me, because they tended not to buy much in the way of souvenirs, they were good for business: they kept the image of the terraced fields in circulation, especially online. Their pictures attracted more tourists to Ping'an, village residents believed, and many photographers came year after year in search of that perfect shot.

Thus, according to the local logic, without the terraced fields there would be no photographers or other tourists in Ping'an. But terraced fields require constant upkeep—they have to be maintained annually, with the earth and stone walls regularly repaired, and they have to sustain wet-rice cultivation practices to match existing images. Village residents complained that they did not have enough time to do both agricultural work and tourism work; some families hired day laborers (from inside and outside the village) to do the plowing and planting for them, and other families, such as the one I lived with, tended to only maintain their fields that were within sight of the two major viewpoints (also reported in Xu Ganli 2005). A lot of physical and mental effort went into maintaining how the village and the terraces looked—and many of the struggles over control of the tourism profits, distribution of employment opportunities, and political leadership responsibilities were explained to me in terms of "we the villagers work the fields, but it is the outside entrepreneurs and government officials who earn all of the money from tourism."

Many villagers perceived themselves as being overlooked in the local political economy of tourism, with all the care and attention paid only to the terraced fields. But underlying these expressions of discontent, there was the agreed-upon reality that without terraced fields that are worth being seen, no one (or very few) would care about, let alone come to and spend money in, Ping'an. In an interview with a young woman who was a popular guide in the village, I asked what kind of photograph of the terraces she thought photographers should take, expecting a response about lighting, seasons, or other landscape features. Instead, she replied: "Photographs with people in them." When I asked her to elaborate, she explained that if there were people in the pictures of the terraced fields, tourists would know that people made these terraces and that terraced fields aren't naturally occurring. This latter point was a common misconception. Some tourists, she said, would even ask if the terraces "had always been there," ignorant of the labor involved. The tourists' desire for beautiful photographs of the terraced fields meant that tourists often perceived of the terraces as static and natural. But terraced fields require continuous human effort. Keeping the people in the picture was this guide's way of addressing the politics of appearance in Ping'an today.

THE PEOPLE IN THE PICTURES: PHOTOGRAPHING MINORITY MODELS

There were some people in Ping'an whose explicit job was to be in the picture. As tourist arrivals increased throughout the 2000s, a number of souvenir photography businesses sprung up along the heavily used path to viewpoint 2, which looked down upon the Seven Stars with Moon landscape. These businesses were made by building a concrete or wooden platform extension that commanded an expansive view of the terraced fields below, allowing tourists to stop and look at the fields without blocking the narrow walkway that led to the viewpoint. Because of their location and perspective, tourists posing on the platforms could have their picture taken with the full view of the fields behind them. Tourists could also pay to pose with "minority models": attractive young women dressed in a variety of stylized ethnic minority costumes specifically designed for performances and display (figure 4.4).[14] The outfits worn by the minority models were visually brasher and more ostentatious than the ethnic Zhuang

FIGURE 4.4. This photograph cost the tourist ¥30 in total: ¥10 to each of the two models, plus an additional ¥10 for the printed and laminated souvenir photograph (2007). Photo by the author.

clothes worn by women in Ping'an (see figure 4.6), and they were specifically manufactured and purchased as costumes to be worn for tourism performances or shows, including national ethnic minority dance performances.[15] The ethnic minority costumes worn by the models were also the same types provided to tourists who wanted to dress up in costumes for a fee, so they were designed to be easily slipped on over one's clothing. Conversely, the festival attire worn by women in Upper Jidao and the ethnic clothes worn by women in Ping'an were used both in nontouristic contexts *as well as* repurposed for tourism over the years.

The work of the minority models involved beckoning tourists to take a picture with them.[16] As tourism, and domestic tourism especially, was embraced as a sign of modernity and progress, these models were a part of the particular configuration of power, photography, ethnicity, and economy permeating China's rural ethnic villages. Put simply, their job was to wear ethnic minority costumes and to pose with tourists for souvenir pictures. The models used their visual appearances and their skills at creating interpersonal relations to become meaningfully ethnic and economically successful during their encounters with tourists. This encounter was a moment of image-in-the-making, mediated by photography as a social act in which the misconceptions, incongruities, and deliberate deceptions involved in processes of producing visual representations highlight just how political appearances can be.[17] To understand their work and the ramifications of "looking ethnic," it is thus important to tease out the ways in which knowledge of and about rural ethnic China was visually formulated and constituted in the encounter between models and tourists.

Practices and processes of visuality are vital to doing tourism, and the microlevels of interactions, assumptions, expectations, and payments involved in souvenir tourist photography reveal the contours of the politics of appearance that emerge between the moments of what is actually seen (before a photograph is taken) and what is shown in the resulting picture. Of course, power relations in photography are complex, and to that end, by drawing on the work of Sandra Hyde (2007), I consider the work of modeling and of being photographed in Ping'an as "transactional."[18] The work involves a monetary transaction of payment between the models themselves and tourists, and for this to take place, the transaction invokes the subjectivities of the tourist, the model, and the "uneven relations of power structuring the possibilities of such an exchange" (ibid., 129).[19] A transactional perspective integrates subjective identities and experiences into broader discourses and desires. Being, or looking like, an ethnic minority woman can be advantageous in certain situations; during her research in Jinghong, Yunnan, Hyde learned that most sex workers were ethnic Han women migrant workers dressed in ethnic Dai clothes for the purposes of attracting customers by playing off the stereotype of ethnic minority women as sexually promiscuous. Here, ethnicity was made meaningful in its display and subsequent consumption via sex—a process that in itself became a sign of personal progress.[20] In such a context, being ethnic "entails performing specific bodily signs rather than being specific bodies" (ibid., 119).[21] Ethnicity becomes simplified, reduced to a few key items of clothing, a linguistic inflection, or isolated physiological features.

Simultaneously, ethnicity is also made more visible as a mechanism to promote a particular vision of multicultural, multiethnic modernity that can assuage concerns over national unity. To domestic tourists, the models in Ping'an were familiarly, even reassuringly, "other"; they looked like the popular images of stylized ethnic minorities frequently seen in mainstream media and in ethnic theme parks. The actual encounter between models and tourists therefore relied upon a mixture of duplicity and complicity that functioned because of existing potent discourses of uneven power relations between ethnic minority women and mainstream Han men. This "internal orientalism," as Louisa Schein (2000, 101) has argued, "denotes a set of practices that occur *within* China, and that in this case [ethnic tourism among the Miao of Guizhou] involved, not international tourism, but the fascination of a more cosmopolitan-identified Chinese with 'exotic' minority cultures in an array of polychromatic and titillating forms. This intense fascination spawned encounters and images that were most commonly structured by a class/gender asymmetry in which minorities were represented chiefly by rural women, while Han observers appeared characteristically as male urban sophisticates." In Ping'an, models were ethnic in certain familiar ways that emphasized inequality in order to fulfill mainstream stereotypes, and tourists complied by paying for the experience of meeting, and being photographed with, a "real" ethnic minority woman.

The presumed unbalanced nature of the social positions held by each party in the photographic encounter was negotiated and exploited by both the models and the tourists through tactics of "sweet talk." The models' sweet talk lured tourists into a world of appearances that reaffirmed existing power asymmetries and that was tinged with a particularly modern desire for the commoditization and consumption of ethnic minority identity in China. The payment received by the models symbolically redressed this social inequality through economics, achieving a momentary balance of a kind. All of this occurred within known national narratives of ethnic unity and harmony promoted by the Chinese state, but the economy of ethnicity in minority model photography also affected social relations within the village. The models were, by and large, migrant laborers from other villages who had entered the economic sphere of Ping'an in search of work and wages, competing with the villagers themselves.

"There Is Nothing Special about It"

The appearance of the minority models in Ping'an referenced a web of preexisting expectations, images, and idealizations of ethnic minorities. Images of performers wearing highly stylized ethnic minority costumes are common in contemporary Chinese media and popular culture, including at ethnic theme parks, and the presence of women in such dress is nearly ubiquitous with China's ethnic tourism. Watching performers in ethnic costume has arguably become constitutive of how to appreciate China's ethnic diversity. Nowadays, ethnicity is consumed and made meaningful, first and foremost, through visual means in domestic tourism and high-profile national celebrations. Indeed, a minor scandal erupted during the 2008 Beijing Olympics, when it was revealed in foreign press reports that the children wearing stylized ethnic costumes in the opening ceremony were mostly, if not all, *not* ethnic minorities, and by no means were these children members of the ethnic minority group whose costume they were wearing.

The Western press leaped to attention—the "fakery" was reported by Reuters, the AP, and in the *Wall Street Journal*. But when asked about the apparently "fake" ethnic children, Games vice president Wang Wei explained that "there is nothing special about it. . . . [Performers] will wear different apparel to signify people are friendly and happy together" (quoted in Goldsmith 2008). The children in costume were not faking their individual identities, Wang's response implied. Rather, the viewing audience was supposed to understand that they were *really* signifying Chinese ethnic and national unity in a familiar visual way. Jianbin Guo, who has written on television viewing in a rural ethnic Dulong village in Yunnan, reported that when the children in ethnic costume appeared on the television broadcast of the Olympics opening ceremony, the Dulong audience in his research village began looking for a performer in Dulong costume. Even though "villagers were unable to find the child as they watched the broadcast[,] . . . they still believed that it was a special moment when they felt a connection to the four-hour ceremony" (Guo 2012, 99). For an audience cognizant of Chinese national visual discourses of ethnic identity, seeing the children in costume was very meaningful indeed.

The Olympics scandal raises two important analytical points about the meaning of ethnic identity and visual appearances in China. First, the wearing of stylized ethnic minority costumes by performers or other public figures is not necessarily unusual or unexpected for mainstream Chinese audiences. To follow the logic of Vice President Wang, there is nothing special about it. Second, as he implied, what really matters in a situation like this is the fact that the performers are wearing these costumes in a highly public venue *to be seen*. The children wearing different ethnic minority dress were intended to visually signify that people in China are friendly and happy together. Thus, having the right *look* can be infinitely important when being seen in an ethnic costume is meant to carry certain shared, social understandings and meanings about the nation and its people.

An Economy of Ethnicity: Duplicitous and Complicit

Just wearing an ethnic costume was not a business in and of itself, however; basic infrastructure and capital investments were required to run a profitable photography booth where the owners could make money by selling souvenir photographs and the models could earn a wage. First, photo booth owners had to obtain the land-use rights, either through personal connections or by leasing the land from a local family, for the fields alongside the path to the viewpoint that offered the best views of the terraces below. In the case of the photo booth discussed here, the owners were local Ping'an residents, so they built their platform on land that belonged to their relatives. Once a platform was built, owners purchased computers, cameras, printers, ink, and a laminating machine, as well as a selection of ethnic minority costumes either to lend to models to wear and/or for tourists to dress up in themselves. Models said they were usually recruited from nearby cities and tourism destinations—some had been approached somewhat randomly on the street, while others had been offered jobs in Ping'an while working as minority models at other booths. This configuration created a literal and symbolic economy of ethnicity, in which people who could "look ethnic" circulated for the purposes of creating a commodity that was both experiential and material: the souvenir photograph. For the multiple stakeholders involved in making a profit from the production of and trade in images of ethnic "Others," there was nothing fake about this work.

As migrants into Ping'an, the models were considered outsiders (*waidi ren*), a category whose increasing numbers included hotel and restaurant owners who leased local homes for their businesses and the owners of most, but not all, photo booths. The success of Ping'an as a tourism destination had inverted its history of out-migration into a contemporary practice of in-migration, as more and more people sought to benefit from the tourism boom. The models described their work as *dagong*, employing the same term that is commonly used to describe the work of migrant factory laborers (see Pun 2005). By describing their work in this way, the women implicitly acknowledged that they were not local, and in practice, the models were double outsiders—they were ethnic minorities to the tourists, the majority of whom were Han, and they were nonlocal, often non-Zhuang, outsiders to the ethnically Zhuang Ping'an residents. I knew of one exception, a young woman from Ping'an who modeled for a short period, but of the six models I became acquainted with and interviewed, she was the first to leave the job and, soon after, the village. The other five models were not from Ping'an, although one was from a neighboring Zhuang village within the Longji Scenic Area. All six women did self-identify as ethnic minorities, although only two were Zhuang. The other four were ethnically Dong or Yao. They were all between the ages of fifteen and twenty; some had completed some high school, but others had stopped their formal education after finishing the compulsory middle-school level.

In 2007, it cost ¥10 to pose for a picture with a model (or to simply take the model's picture), with the money paid directly to her (figure 4.5). Tourists could pay to dress up in an ethnic costume for an additional ¥10. A printed, laminated souvenir photograph cost another ¥10. Depending on whether the model owned her own costume, she earned a percentage of the ¥10 charge levied for posing. A costume, purchased from a specialty ethnic costume tailor or shop, typically cost anywhere from ¥200 to ¥500 depending on its complexity and accessories. Each costume represented a different ethnic group, although the models I knew would often swap headdresses just for fun.[22] If a model owned her costume, at the particular booth I observed, she paid the owners ¥25 a day as an overhead fee. If not, she paid a percentage (50 percent to 70 percent) of her daily earnings to the photo booth owners to cover the use of the costume plus overhead. In a very good month, models said they could earn as much as ¥1,500, but more average earnings hovered around ¥500 to ¥700 per month.[23] As part of the employment agreement, the owner provided accommodation in a

FIGURE 4.5. The minority models are paid directly by tourists who want to photograph or pose with them. At the end of each day, the models pay the photo booth owners a percentage for overhead costs (2007). Photo by the author.

shared house and two meals a day to the models—a relatively customary arrangement in China for migrant workers.

The models were less focused on the actual moment of posing with, or for, a tourist, and more involved in engaging with tourists *before* a potential transaction to secure business. This encounter between the models and tourists was duplicitous because the models knew it was important to come across as "ethnic" and even "local," and the tourists who were willing to pay for photographs knew that these women were wearing costumes, regardless of whether they identified as ethnic minorities. This duplicity was made clear in the signs stating the prices for posing with a model and for purchasing a souvenir photograph, which reminded the tourists of the economic foundations of the encounter. However, the entire exchange—from the models approaching the tourists who walked by to the tourist's final payment—was tinged with complicity because for this type of commercial photography to function, all parties on both sides of the camera had to understand how to exploit, for personal gain, the pre-existing ideas and expectations attributed to "being ethnic" in rural China today. Tourists participated in these duplicities and complicities by being tourists who were willing to do what tourists are expected to do: take photographs and spend money.

The models always stated that their best customers were male domestic Chinese tourists, reinforcing the pervasiveness of China's "internal orientalism" in rural ethnic tourism. Female Chinese tourists typically wanted to dress up themselves in costumes rented from the photo booth, thus leaving the models with nothing to earn.[24] Foreign tourists were more difficult to convince because the models lacked enough English skills to approach them, and furthermore, most foreign tourists were not well-versed enough in mainstream Chinese discourses of ethnic tourism, let alone ethnic minorities, to participate fully in the encounter. Some tourists balked when informed that they would have to pay to photograph a model; these tourists did not understand the situation, the models complained. They were either entirely duped into believing the models really were "just" friendly ethnic women, or they were ignorant of the appropriate role of tourists in a village destination, where tourists were expected to comply with the locals' need for income generation through tourism. Although the models felt they could understand the tourists' desires and demands (for beautiful, obliging, young ethnic women to photograph) and they were quite willing to comply with national narratives of ethnic harmony and gendered expectations of ethnic identity for the right price, at the question of economics, some tourists did not live up to their end of the equation by attempting to photograph the models surreptitiously.

One such encounter took place between the models and tourists in early summer 2007, the season for flooding the terraced fields with water for rice cultivation, which was generally considered the best condition for photographing the terraces. Many photographers came as part of group tours during these months, stopping for a night or two in Ping'an before going to other villages in the Longji Scenic Area. One morning, a small group of domestic and overseas Chinese tourists walked up to the photography booth with their tripods, SLR digital cameras, and telephoto lenses in tow. They set up their gear on the concrete platform at the photo booth, effectively blocking the view of the terraces for other passing tourists. Usually the photo booth owners would discourage the more serious photographers from lingering too long, since the owners had built the concrete viewing platform for *their* own photography business. Despite this, since it was overcast and not very busy yet this day, the models and the owners did not object even though these photographers were technically hindering the booth's business by obscuring the view of the terraces with their equipment.

The photographers largely ignored the models' initial requests, concentrating their lenses on the terraced fields below. Seeing that this group was uninterested in hiring them to pose, four models climbed the hillside behind the viewing platform and sat together, chatting and giggling, behind a thin patch of knee-high foliage. The models were savvy to the photographers' intentions and knew that some might nevertheless try to take their picture without paying. Therefore, while they sat on the hill behind the photographers, they used colored paper umbrellas to visually shield themselves. As I began recording the scene with my video camera, some of the models called out to me: "Jenny! Hello! Over here!" Hearing their voices, and seeing me with my video camera, two male photographers in the group pivoted around to shoot the models, who continued to hide behind their umbrellas. Half joking, but with noticeable exasperation, one photographer exclaimed: "You're worth a lot of money if I take your photo, I'm telling you. Don't block the photo."

From his outburst, this photographer deftly expressed his opinion—the models were acting inappropriately because if he took their photo, they would be "worth a lot of money" as visual images. Tellingly, he did not say that the photographs themselves would be valuable, but he directly attributed the potential value of these images to the models themselves, as visual objects. For the models behind the umbrellas, however, this situation was worthless to them because the photographers were not willing to pay for the production of these potentially valuable images. Ideally, minority model photography in Ping'an operated by maintaining an asymmetrical equilibrium between these two parties. These models worked firmly within certain expected, popular notions of social inequality and power imbalances in order to engage tourists in a deliberately lopsided encounter until payment was made, which then "equalized" the experience. When arguments erupted over cost and payment, or when photographers simply refused to pay, the fissures in the dominant discourses of ethnicity, rural livelihoods, gender, and social power were made most apparent. Without payment, the encounter was too unbalanced for it to be "worth it" to the models to allow these photographers to take their picture. In this case, the photographic act failed to sufficiently redress the inequalities between the tourists and the models because the ethnic appearance of the models, while acknowledged as desirable and of worth by the photographer, was not linked to an economic value that would, in effect, balance out the situation for the models.

Sweet Talk: The "Commodified Persona"

Referencing the social inequalities associated with ethnic minorities and ethnic women in particular was a part of the "commodified persona" (Bunten 2008) presented by the models as a means of luring in tourists. The "commodified persona," a concept developed by Alexis Celeste Bunten (ibid., 381), is an analytical perspective on processes of self-commoditization that takes into account the limits of cross-cultural models and, as such, suggests that this persona is a productive space in which "emotional labor, identity construction, and the politics of representation" converge. This process goes beyond "identity management" because it implicitly involves value adjustments, and, in Bunten's research based in Sitka, Alaska, it also referenced specific political expressions of identity and resistance to hegemonic, normative expectations associated with Native peoples in the United States. The converse was at work in Ping'an; here, the models constructed a deliberately depoliticized, almost generic image of the ethnic "Other" in their work, which was reflected in the stylized costumes they wore. For these models, their commodified persona was different, but not necessarily alienated, from their ethnic identities (e.g., one Zhuang woman typically wore a Miao ethnic costume on most days for no other given reason than that she liked it and she found this costume was quite popular with tourists). When it came to doing tourism in this way, these women were to be what they looked like—thoroughly modernized, stylish, and reassuringly familiar ethnics who spoke standard Chinese without hesitation and knew what tourists wanted. Their self-commoditization was a modern practice, and their commodified persona as modern ethnics was already known to Chinese tourists through mass media imagery. This persona entailed being a playful, entertaining ethnic "Other" in ways familiar to contemporary Chinese discourses—perhaps being like the ethnically attired performers at the opening ceremony of the 2008 Olympics who symbolized happiness and friendliness, if they came to life as their costumed selves.

The models' immediate task was to lure tourists into posing with them for a souvenir photo, thus bringing business both to themselves and to the photo booth owners. Sometimes the models asked tourists directly if they wanted to have a photograph taken together, but frequently the models would simply wait in plain view. In conversations with tourists, the models would present the encounter as a serendipitous, "once-in-a-lifetime" chance that created the "tourist moment" (Hom Cary 2004). The inequalities between the female models and the male tourists were most open for exploitation through "sweet talk" (*tian zui*, literally "sweet mouth"). Sweet talk typically involved flirty joking that directly referenced the perceived social inequalities attributed to gender, wealth, and ethnic minority identity. From the outset, the models referred to themselves as *a'mei*, a generic form of address for a young girl containing the character for "younger sister," thereby creating room for a feeling of kinship between the speakers. They typically called male tourists "boss" (*laoban*) or "Mister" (*xiansheng*), setting the stage as a conversation between unequals.[25] When asked why there weren't any men working as models at the photo booth, the models explained that men weren't as good at sweet talk, although they said that in some places there were occasionally male models, referred to as *a'ge* (or "elder brother").

From the models' perspective, "sweet talk" meant putting forth a willing, obliging persona when responding to questions and curious inquiries—the models who were impatient or uninterested in chatting with tourists were generally ineffective at this line of work. From the perspective of male tourists, sweet talk typically revolved around mildly sexual comments (usually jokes about being married to a model after being photographed together), tying marriage into conditions of rural underdevelopment (by suggesting that these women had no prospects and were just waiting to get married), and references to the general lack of socioeconomic opportunities for rural women.[26] Sweet talk negotiations could also involve the models not saying anything at all, but rather condoning jokes and comments through smiles and silence to build an atmosphere amenable to getting the tourists to agree to a photograph. The models' silence contributed to preexisting stereotypes of ethnic minority women as obliging, socially disadvantaged, and willing to defer to the economic power of the urban male tourist.

By paying to pose with a model, the tourist thus has the power to equalize this otherwise unbalanced relationship. That said, this end result is only possible through each model's physical appearance in costume and her command of sweet talk to lure tourists into a social relationship. When one side of the equation refuses to participate in the equalization of this encounter, the fine balance of the unequal status quo is upset, as was the case with the photographers who attempted to take the models' picture after they deliberately hid behind umbrellas. Photography, and the photographic act, is the fulcrum for all of these exchanges, which pivots on the open, joking recognition of social inequality.

A House of Pigs

In another exchange I video-recorded, one model, Yuan, successfully negotiated a brief period of sweet talk with a couple of male tourists through joking about rural lives, life chances, and marriage. Yuan was acknowledged by all of the other models as the best at the job; she was bold and knew when to speak and when to stay silent for the greatest effect. The two middle-aged Chinese men, whom I'll call Hei and Bai, paused at the platform one afternoon to catch their breath and wait for their friends who were still climbing the steep stairs up the hillside. Yuan saw Hei waiting by the platform railing and went to stand near him, without speaking.

Hei noticed Yuan and turning to her, he asked (in standard Chinese), "You all speak Zhuang [minority language]?" Yuan responded simply, "Yes." Hei repeated, "You can speak Zhuang?" Yuan said again, "Yes." She paused and added, "Take a picture with us." Hei, looking a bit flustered but smiling, said, "A picture with you? Then you're engaged to me?" Yuan looked down. With a small smile she murmured, "Um . . . no." "No? You're not engaged then?" Hei asked, jokingly.

At this point, Bai sauntered over to Hei and Yuan. Yuan repeated her suggestion to "take a picture with us," and Hei walked off a bit to join his companions, saying, "There's no need," while waving Yuan away. Yuan next turned to Bai, who was chewing on a leaf. Pointing, she exclaimed, "Mister! What are you eating?" Without replying to her question, Bai asked Yuan how much a photo would be. She responded, "Ten RMB," but quickly corrected herself, "Ten for the *a'mei*; ten for the souvenir photograph. It's twenty all together." Bai agreed to this price, and Yuan immediately called out to the photo booth owner, who hurried over with a digital camera. Yuan struck a pose next to Bai, gathering up a corner of her long skirt in her left hand and placing her right hand on the small of her back. This particular pose was used by many of the models when posing with men to ward off the possibility of any "wandering" hands while being photographed together, which was one of the potential problems they faced on the job.

As Bai and Yuan posed, Yuan motioned to Bai's friends, saying, "You can use your camera too." Bai called Hei and his friends back over. Camera in hand, Hei said to Bai, "I'll take your picture; now you're married." Then Hei laughed, exclaiming, "*A'mei* wants two pigs, you know! Here they want pigs!"[27] Bai retorted, "I'll give her pigs and cows!" At this, Yuan dipped her head a bit, smiled, and said nothing. Soon thereafter, Bai paid Yuan her fee and went to look at the printed souvenir photograph. The exchange was a success for both parties in this instance: by condoning the stereotypes evoked by Hei, Yuan positioned herself as a willing ethnic woman with "something to offer" to the male tourists, and Bai received a souvenir of his ethnic encounter. Concurrently, Yuan never directly contradicted herself, nor did she have to pretend to be anything except for what Hei and Bai saw—a young woman in ethnic costume, waiting for an opportunity to present itself.

Both the *work* of being a minority model and the social relationships created and reinforced between the tourist and the model were contingent on the mutually agreed upon importance of the photograph as a souvenir that documented the encounter of the tourist with the ethnic minority. The knowledge produced by this encounter was visually embodied in the photograph, but despite the fact that Yuan clearly stated the price she expected for posing and that Bai immediately complied, the range of associations elicited remained duplicitous, framed by joking and sweet talk. Likewise in the earlier example, by hiding behind umbrellas, the models made known their expectation to get paid in exchange for being photographed, although they never explicitly said so to the photographer who grew exasperated at their duplicity.

In the very moment of any encounter mediated by photography, a relationship is forged between the individuals involved, even if a photograph is not taken (or taken without express permission).[28] For the minority models, this relationship undulates between economics and ethnicity. Technically, the encounter between models and tourists is built upon a simple, straightforward economic exchange of money for a picture. This is not unique to Chinese tourism, of course. As Erik Cohen, Yeshayahu Nir, and Uri Almagor (1992, 224–25) have written of women dressed in ethnic minority or classical Thai costumes in Thailand who pose with tourists, "the commercialization of picture taking reaches it peak with the emergence of posing as a full time occupation. . . . A relationship started in a chance and often mistrustful encounter evolves into a routinized and obliging commercialized service." However, even when photography is transformed into a commercialized, routinized service, the contours of this act remain potentially ambiguous, shaped by a politics of appearance that is rooted in shared social expectations. In fact, it was precisely the commercialization of ethnicity, and of photography, that irritated the photographer who tried to take the models' picture without paying them. After all, "the role of the routinized tourist is generally understood to include the 'right' to take photos at liberty" (ibid., 226). But if the models' work is routinized as a economic transaction in tourism, can tourist photography still be considered a "right" without due consequence? What happened before the picture was taken—namely, the social relationships established and stereotypes evoked before the snap of the shutter—thus infused the material picture with the densely layered realities of gender, ethnicity, and inequality in China today.

MIGRANTS AND MODELS

Photography in Ping'an is full of contested values—value to the tourists, value to local villagers, and value to the migrants who come to Ping'an in search of employment and profit from the village's tourism industry. For the models discussed in this chapter, their work was entangled in broader social values that shaped their knowledge of when to speak sweetly and when to simply smile. This knowledge translated directly into symbolic interactions of power and social status between the models and the tourists, but in this relationship built around the act of photography, the models retained a measure of control and understanding over what the tourists wanted and how they, the models, would provide or withhold it. To the photographers unwilling to pay, the models simply physically removed themselves from the camera's frame of vision. To the male tourists who were game for a bit of joking and play, Yuan needed only to create the illusion of agreement for the transaction to be completed as she desired.

Whereas the relationship between models and tourists fluctuated around conditions of duplicity and complicity, the models' relationships to other village residents also played a part in the village's economy of ethnicity. This context of models, local women, and tourists in Ping'an outlines the complicated, multifaceted networks of labor and leisure shaping rural tourism in ethnic minority China. Images of the terraced fields around Ping'an circulate widely in domestic and international mass media, and after nearly thirty years of engagement in China's contemporary tourism industry, village residents know that they are being photographed, and they know that their images are used to sell other products (figure 4.6).[29] As such, village residents are highly cognizant of the potential value of allowing themselves to be photographed.

The ethnic Zhuang clothes worn by the women in figure 4.6 are much less stylized than those worn by the models who worked at the photo booth. Local women consciously wore these ethnic Zhuang outfits and terry-cloth headdresses when engaged in tourism activities that would have them in direct engagement with tourists, such as guiding or carrying luggage up from the parking lot. There was a shared knowledge among women in Ping'an that this Zhuang attire was suited for tourism work, and even non-Zhuang women who lived in Ping'an and worked at local guesthouses would wear these outfits. However, local women, with the one exception mentioned earlier, did not work at the kind of modeling that involved sweet talk. Women from Ping'an offered to be models usually when they were also hired as guides for photographers, a role that emphasized and prioritized their local knowledge of the village and their belonging to the community. They would often be photographed in their homes or in the terraced fields, physically extending their claim to this village.[30]

The visible distinction between locals who modeled for photographers in the fields and the models who posed "for" tourists in more fanciful costumes all reinforced the models' outsider status in the village. The models were migrant laborers, outsiders who had come because tourism had turned Ping'an into a regional economic center with opportunities. The

FIGURE 4.6. Images of Ping'an circulate worldwide, including this one, which appears on the cover of an anthropology textbook (Conrad Kottak, *Anthropology: The Exploration of Human Diversity*, 12th edition [New York: McGraw Hill Higher Education, 2006]). See also Aaron Podolefsky, Peter Brown, and Scott Lacy, *Applying Cultural Anthropology: An Introductory Reader*, 8th edition (New York: McGraw Hill, 2008).

young models, however, could not rely on being local to earn an income, so they found work by drawing on nationally circulated representations of the sweet, willing, and harmonious ethnic minority.[31] Their brighter, more stylized costumes marked them even more pointedly as objects only to be looked at; these stylized outfits visually linked them to the highly choreographed and mass-circulated images of ethnic minorities seen on national television programs and variety shows in China (such as the Beijing Olympics opening ceremony).

These young women's work opportunities as models were made possible because of the particular configuration of China's rapid economic growth, rural development, ethnic classification policies, and tourism industries. As young, undereducated women in rural China, the models arguably were empowered by the availability of this job over, for instance, going to work in a factory. When I asked them about other jobs they had held or wanted to pursue, they justified their choice to be models, however temporarily, on the grounds that the work was easy. It didn't require long hours, tedious manual labor, or even much overtime.[32] They could chat during the day and spend the evenings hanging out with each other and sometimes with the other young people in the village. However, in gaining this power to choose modeling over other employment options, these young women were also entrenched in reiterating other unbalanced power relations based on gender, class, and social status. To make their business work, these models not only had to look like ethnic minorities in a recognizable way, but they had to participate in popular conceptualizations of what ethnic minority women *are* like. Similarly, as discussed in chapter 3, Ping'an resident Feng's remark (that although she had returned to the village, she did not want to plow fields) echoes the same conundrum: to do rural ethnic tourism successfully, one had to accept and embody being a *peasant*, just as the models had to *be* ethnic, in specific ways.

When tourists leave the photo booth, taking with them a printed, laminated souvenir of themselves posing with a model, they carry with the material photograph their visible evidence of having "been there" with the ethnic "Other." The copresence of the tourist and the model reinforces narratives of national unity and harmony across ethnic distinctions.[33] Nevertheless, this unity is only made possible by the existence of recognizable and familiar forms of ethnic difference worn on the models' bodies. What matters is not necessarily if the models "are" ethnic in a genetic, or corporeal sense, but rather if the models can successfully *be* visually and presentably ethnic. Photography thus becomes the occasion for creating a familiar and believable shared social relationship between ethnic minorities and mainstream citizens in present-day China by playing to expectations and stereotypes, which could reinforce national discourses of social harmony.

The models' ability to work thus depended on their capabilities in looking the part. New complexes of belonging emerge when ethnicity is mainstreamed into familiar types and categories that are reproduced in tourism marketing and promotions. When ethnic identity begins with the visual moment of apprehension and appearance, it is vital to take seriously the process by which visual knowledge is communicated and translated into ideas, stereotypes, and expectations. Approaching photography as a moment of encounter therefore sheds light on the ways in which knowledge is socially produced through visual means. This pushes beyond the politics of representation to consider a politics of appearance that takes seriously the potential significance of "looking the part" and that illuminates the efficacy of the visual in preempting, prompting, and promoting social relationships. Visual knowledge is created and reinforced every day in the economy of ethnicity; for the models working in Ping'an village, appearing ethnic was their primary means of being employed. Their other options as young, undereducated rural women in today's China were less attractive or desirable. Therefore, for these women, when it came to wearing stylized ethnic costumes and sweet-talking tourists, there was nothing special about it at all.

The economy of ethnicity in tourism demanded that all stakeholders in Ping'an village's tourism—including local residents, models, and government officials—needed to negotiate and control the image world they sought to present to tourists, including the houses, the terraced fields, and the people. Frequent arguments and ongoing debates in the village around issues of architectural coherence, cleanliness, and the maintenance of the terraced fields all contributed to the prioritization of the village's appearance, which needed to be, first and foremost, appropriate for photography. The expectations brought to bear by the visual expediencies of tourism were inscribed onto the visible surfaces of rural ethnic lives in both Ping'an and Upper Jidao. The minority models were perhaps the culmination of the tourist's search for visual difference, a concrete means of ensuring that in every picture, in every image, there would be something, or someone, different—so long as the tourist is willing to pay. These expectations thus created a value-laden framework of visuality, a scaffolding of good or bad looks, right or wrong clothing, correct or incorrect appearances. The extension of these values beyond the surface of rural ethnic livelihoods is clear: perhaps some places and people were simply better at being different than others. Beyond a single village, however, success at creating and showing difference also factored significantly in the relationships between local tourism villages and neighboring non–tourism villages. The differences between rural communities, and the ability to be different "correctly," has resulted in a number of unintended social, economic, and political consequences between villages as tourism has developed unevenly across rural China.

差异性

CHAPTER 5

THE ABILITY TO BE DIFFERENT

Socialities and Subjectivities

Doing tourism in Ping'an and Upper Jidao involved not only visible modifications, such as changing one's clothes or renovating houses to cater to perceived tourist desires, but also transformations in socialities and individual subjectivities of village residents, migrant or local. As the previous chapters have shown, rural ethnic tourism pivots around more than just the relationship between "hosts and guests" (Smith ed. 1989 [1977]) or "tourist-tourate" (Ness 2003), which are the binaries commonly evoked as analytical frames for understanding tourism. Rather, it is vital to map how tourism villages are embedded in intervillage and intravillage networks shaped by myriad connections of kinship, politics, shared histories, and economics. In both Ping'an and Upper Jidao, as tourism has become more and more entrenched in local experiences, a range of unintended social and political consequences has emerged that deeply affects local lives and livelihoods. These consequences have often been made known through instances of physical violence and frustration.

SABOTAGE STORY NO. 1: UPPER JIDAO, 2006

On the morning of October 2, 2006, around 7:30 A.M., Chun, the village subcommittee leader that year, made an announcement from his house, which shared a wall with Teacher Pan's home where I lived. Using a bullhorn,

Chun hollered: "Announcement! Announcement! (*Tongzhi! Tongzhi!*)" The announcements were always made in Miao, and I could only understand the few standard Chinese (Mandarin) terms occasionally interspersed within, such as "tourist (*youke*)." At breakfast later, I asked Teacher Pan what Chun had said, and he explained that the village had been preparing for a week to host an anticipated onslaught of tourists during the October 1 National Day Golden Week. There had been announcements nearly every day to remind the men in the *lusheng* performance group to practice in the evenings, to reiterate the importance of keeping the village clean and litter-free (which included not hanging laundry in view from the paths or laying it out on the riverbank, a common practice during the sunny and dry autumn), and generally to exhort villagers to maintain a positive, friendly, and accommodating outlook toward the expected visitors.[1] This morning's announcement was a reminder to village residents about tidiness and, Teacher Pan added, about clearing the road into Upper Jidao. Someone had piled a number of concrete cinder blocks and other materials on the road into Upper Jidao during the night, preventing any cars from entering village. The road leading into Lower Jidao had not been affected. Teacher Pan, in his usual no-nonsense way, made no suggestion as to who might have done this.

Two weeks later, while conducting a household survey with a fifty-five-year-old woman in Upper Jidao, I received a more candid assessment of these events. Three middle-school-aged girls from the village were present during the survey, and together the five of us shared a conversation on tourism in Upper Jidao. When I asked for their thoughts on the potential negative consequences of tourism development, one of the girls quickly responded, "Lower Jidao is against tourism; they came and ruined the road." "They," meaning people from Lower Jidao, the girls declared, had also slashed the sign on the main highway that advertised the 2006 China Kaili International Lusheng Festival that had taken place in July (figure 5.1).[2] The older woman concurred, saying that the "relationship was never very good [between Upper and Lower Jidao]" and that tourism development in Upper Jidao had exacerbated preexisting tensions. Teacher Pan's earlier diplomatic refusal to point a finger at individuals from Lower Jidao reflected the depth of the troubles between the two villages. These isolated cases of relatively minor but very pointed physical retaliation directed at tourism-related events demonstrated the degree to which someone nearby was not in agreement with Upper Jidao's development into a tourism destination. It

FIGURE 5.1. A poster advertising the 2006 International Lusheng Festival in Upper Jidao was slashed and damaged (2006). Photo by the author.

was only later, in 2007, that Teacher Pan eventually told me about the letter written by the Jidao village Party Secretary to the provincial government, which had effectively halted the original plans to build a hotel in Upper Jidao and signaled the ongoing tensions between the two communities.

SABOTAGE STORY NO. 2: PING'AN, 2007

While relations between the residents of Ping'an, the county government, and the management company of the Longji Scenic Area could only be described as mutually suspicious at the best of times, on occasion these tensions also manifested into material destruction. Many villagers told me of collective attempts in 2005 to stage public protests over the allocation of profits from ticket sales, which were managed by the company not the village. They first protested outside the ticket office on the road leading into the entire scenic area and later at the entrance to Ping'an, blocking the entry of any tourists into the village. The local government's response was unsurprising and swift. According to the villagers, government representatives turned away all journalists and arrested a handful of young men as an example of what might happen to other such "troublemakers." After that incident, protests by villagers against perceived inequalities and unfair conditions took a decidedly more surreptitious, though no less confrontational, form.

For example, throughout 2005 and 2006, villagers had begun constructing one-story shop fronts and restaurant stalls along the wide path leading from the parking lot into the central part of the village. Many of these spaces were then rented out to migrant entrepreneurs or run as second businesses by relatives; shopkeepers sold a familiar variety of mass-produced souvenirs, specialty teas, fruit, snacks, and sometimes products brought in from other markets (including, for a while, dried snakes and lizards supposedly bearing medicinal properties). As the buildings kept being constructed, some villagers told me they thought the rows of wooden shops along the path were ugly and distracting. Moreover, the buildings blocked the view of the lower terraced fields around the village, and, as one village resident remarked, the *view* was technically for everyone.

Apparently the management company also shared this village resident's opinion, and in late 2006, representatives from the company began putting pressure on villagers who had shops along the path to take down their buildings. Some residents believed that the company wanted to remove all structures in the village that were not either hotels, restaurants, residential homes, or constructed by the company (such as the toilets at the viewpoints). The stated goal was to improve upon the visual continuity of the scenic area. But this was impossible, residents said, because so many small shops were already up and the land-use rights were granted to individual households who could legally lease these rights to others. The management company didn't *own* the land, villagers stressed. Buildings continued to be constructed at an even more rapid rate, it seemed; one young shopkeeper said it was because villagers knew that if the buildings along the path were eventually banned, they would receive compensation for anything already constructed. Nonetheless, perhaps by way of making a point, the company sent in a couple of men to forcibly take down a few half-finished shops by the entrance ticket booth in early April 2007.[3]

The retaliation was equally quick. Overnight, the men's toilets at viewpoint number 1 were destroyed (figure 5.2). The choice of this particular

FIGURE 5.2. Urinals in the public toilet at viewpoint number 1, in Ping'an, were smashed as a retaliatory act against changes proposed by the management company (2007). Photo by the author.

site seemed deliberate: the toilets at the two village viewpoints had been built and paid for by the management company, but viewpoint number 1 was much less visited than viewpoint number 2 (where the more well-known view of Seven Stars with Moon could be seen), so the damage would have a lesser impact on tourists.[4] Inside the toilet facilities at viewpoint 1, the countertops, urinals, and tile floors were broken, apparently hit with a blunt, heavy object. I asked a number of individuals in Ping'an about this incident. Everyone remained silent about the perpetrators, but most concluded that it had happened because the company had taken down the shops along the path. One feeling going around the village, a shop-keeper told me, was that if the government or company wasn't happy with the way things were changing in Ping'an, they should just get out and let the villagers go back to selling the tickets and taking care of the business themselves as they had done in the past. It was clearer than ever before that the line had been drawn in Ping'an, and that the ongoing tit for tat between village residents, the government, and the management company was far from resolution.

WHERE THE LINE GETS DRAWN

These anecdotes from Upper Jidao and Ping'an serve as a poignant reminder of the complex motivations, demands, expectations, and desires involved in tourism development. At the scale of everyday life in a rural village, the impact of these isolated cases was arguably more prominent than perhaps it would have been in an urban context. The past three decades of economic reform, paired with national policies for rural development in China, were experienced by residents of Ping'an and Upper Jidao in ways that reveal the pervasive uneasiness and uncertainties plaguing contemporary rural livelihoods. Outbursts of anger coupled with frustration over the slow pace of becoming a "successful" ethnic tourism destination exposed the disjointed relationship between ethnicity and economy, particularly in a country governed by strict definitions of ethnic belonging. The intersection of physical distances, socioeconomic differences, and cultural distinctiveness invoked by, and inherent in, ethnic tourism practices thus provide a focal point for understanding just how village residents negotiated with the consequences of doing tourism. The two sabotage stories suggest that these acts of willful destruction must be considered as a part of examining how discourses of tourism and travel exert pressure on, and influence change within, destination communities. In Upper Jidao, the perpetrators were perceived, by village residents at least, to be people from Lower Jidao; Upper Jidao was targeted because it had been selected to get rich first, to use the famous quotation by Deng Xiaoping from the beginning of China's reform-era economic and social policies. In Ping'an, the perpetrators were village residents, and their anger was directed at the county government and management company, who were perceived as working together to stifle and strangle local tourism profits.

The stories point to the importance of examining intervillage and intravillage relationships in tourism development. While conflicts between policy makers and community members are often examined in studies of China's domestic tourism industry, critical tourism studies more broadly continues to be primarily framed around the relationship(s) between tourists and the toured.[5] The charge to decenter tourism studies from its underlying theories and concepts based on the wealthy Western tourist (as argued in Winter 2009, 317–18) should be coupled with a willingness to consider the possible blind spots of current tourism scholarship—including the division between tourism management studies research and tourism theory. In Upper Jidao, it was provincial policy that drove tourism to take on the role of a wedge, causing the Upper and Lower village communities to feel more distant from each other than ever before. The relative success of tourism in Ping'an meant that more and more parties, including regional government bureaus, were trying to find ways to profit from the industry, leading to conflicting opinions and regulations. Emotional expressions of jealousy, envy, and anger reveal the depth to which rural tourism development programs and China's plans for a New Socialist Countryside were opening old wounds and creating new disappointments while simultaneously aiming to bring these rural areas into the fold of national modernization goals.

The lines drawn between rival parties in tourism businesses and development cut across villages, counties, and provinces, as tourism was entangled in the range of imaginable possibilities for local residents. The sabotage stories from Upper Jidao and Ping'an map out the margins of the landscape of travel in which these villages are situated and how they are connected with national forces, provincial goals, and local aspirations. While domestic tourism in Ping'an and Upper Jidao was intended, in large part, to be "involved in a pacification of the relations between the center and the periphery," as Olivier Evrard and Prasit Leepreecha (2009, 245) have written about Thai domestic tourism to the northern city of Chiang Mai, there were also multiple consequences at a range of other, more local scales. The parallels between Northern Thailand and Southwest China are useful here. Drawing on scholarship about ethnic minority communities in China, Evrard and Leepreecha (ibid., 245) have argued that as a result of domestic Thai tourism to the north of Thailand, "the Northern Thai turned themselves into objects of desire for mobile urban dwellers and at the same time also enacted the same process towards their own margins, the so-called 'Hill Tribes' (cao khao)." The effects of tourism, they argue, thus changed relations in the North between the Northern Thai and the "Hill Tribes," as well as between the Northern Thai and their mainstream urban counterparts to the south.

Similarly, just as tourism villages like Ping'an and Upper Jidao had to

develop and maintain ways of looking different from mainstream majority urban Chinese and foreigners to appeal to these tourists, individuals in
each place also had to contend with transformations in their relationships
with other residents, migrants, nearby villages, and local government
and business entities. The landscape of travel, therefore, encompassed the
physical distances traveled by tourists and migrants, the socioeconomic
differences evoked as part of development programs or experienced
within a village, and the forms of cultural distinctiveness demanded of
tourism villages as a part of their potential success as destinations. All
of these, ultimately, contributed to undulating waves of connection and
separation at multiple scales—from the national center to the periphery,
between villages in a particular region, and among households and businesses in a village. The tensions resulting from tourism development thus
outline how communities and individuals are increasingly alienated (or
differentiated) from one another, but also how their lives and livelihoods
are evermore interconnected, interdependent, and lived in response to
each other. In these changing relationships, the *conceptual figure* of "the
tourist" plays an influential role in everyday village social relations.

At the scale of the local, conditions in Ping'an and Upper Jidao exemplified two differing dynamics that were set in motion by rural tourism
development. In Ping'an, more and more outsiders were drawn *to* the village, in a centripetal force, thereby challenging local claims to belonging,
profits, and knowledge. Conversely, in Upper Jidao, village leaders and
regional government officials were driven to construct more apparent and
more obvious differences between villages in the Bala River Demonstration Project, arguably creating a centrifugal effect in the region. Villages
in the area tried to create symbolic distances between each other to distinguish themselves from their neighbors and to satisfy a presumed tourist
need for recognizable, consumable differences, but not without negative
consequences as the case between Upper and Lower Jidao shows. Such
attempts are part of the "touristic cultures" of places where tourism is
everyday life, and these new systems of values and expectations are logi-
cal, functional, and meaningful on their own terms (e.g., Cohen 2001,
41–43; and Picard 1996).

At a national level, the goal of tourism *as* development has been to
decrease the economic differences between rural and urban populations,
but paradoxically at the local level, the unequal distribution of develop-

ment funds and different strategies of income generation have increased the socioeconomic distances between neighbors and villages. Thus what was transformed included not only the different products offered in tourism to satiate the supposedly ravenous appetite of tourists for something "other" than their quotidian lives, but also the ideas and discourses about the usefulness and meanings of things such as land, people, and ethnic identity. These shifting concepts created new connections and power relations, and the systems of meaning generated in Ping'an's and Upper Jidao's tourism illuminate the socialities and subjectivities that have become valued, and devalued, in contemporary China.

DISTANCES AND DIFFERENCES

Tourism does not merely create hard and fast differences in the name of diversifying tourist experiences; indeed, the differences (ethnic, economic, social, and political) so often invoked in understanding tourism might be better understood as distances, where the lines that are drawn (between Upper and Lower Jidao, for instance, or Ping'an and the Longji Scenic Area management company) symbolize increasing disparities as well as ongoing acknowledgments of mutual reliance and dependencies.[6] Situations or contexts that may be more easily brushed aside as simply "different" actually reveal more complicated truths when these circumstances are considered as distant from one another, but not altogether unrelated. After all, distances separate and connect, while differences are often perceived as absolute. In tourism studies, the importance of difference has been well studied.[7] For tourists, tourism is a contemporary practice that engages, maintains, and produces differences through promoting travel across great physical distances. It appeals to the discovery of societies that are temporally or culturally distinctive from the tourist, such as through the trope of the "primitive" (N. Wang 2001, vii).

In China, as elsewhere of course, even as tourism promotions emphasize the appeal of traveling to distant, far-flung destinations, with improved roads, new airports, and competing transport companies, people in China are moving closer to one another more frequently and meeting in more of what James Clifford (1997), drawing on the work of Mary Louise Pratt (2008 [1992]), has called "contact zones." For Clifford (1997, 192; italics in original), museums are contact zones because their organizing structure as collections reflect "an ongoing historical, political, moral *relationship*—a power-charged set of exchanges, of push and pull." Likewise, tourism villages can be considered as contact zones, highlighting the need to analyze the relationships enacted by the copresence, following Pratt (ibid., 6), of tourists, village residents, and other stakeholders in the tourism enterprise. Moreover, this framework enhances the understanding of the organizing structures and principles of tourism at work in contemporary China.

But while actual travel times have decreased in China because of advances in modern transport, the two sabotage stories make clear that some types of distance are increasing.[8] The experience of shortening physical distances as a result of modern transport can inversely prompt the expansion of perceived socioeconomic and cultural distances between groups and communities, as the exotic and different become known and categorized as such. This may be one consequence of what Arjun Appadurai (1996, 70–71) has called the "cultural economy of distance" created by spatio-temporal processes of seasonal consumption that emerge from "the driving force of merchants, trade, and commodities, especially of the luxury variety." Rural tourism development has been ideally conceived as equal parts leisure and labor, desired by urban and rural Chinese, respectively. It is possible, then, to conceive of the simultaneous expansion and shortening of distances in China as the result of ongoing processes of mobility as a consumption practice in which tourism allows some to consume more of the nation, while others seek to become consumers (and tourists) through their efforts in producing the consumed experience. Such consumption practices necessarily are intended to assert both belonging to a particular group and social distinction from others, but the real effects of mobility as a consumption practice are much more unequal and stratified.

In tourism villages like Ping'an and Upper Jidao, the figure of "the tourist" comes to assume the role of the consumer, and all village activities are ideally intended to satisfy the needs and wants of this particular subject. Who is the tourist, however, and how does she or he figure conceptually into village social relations and socialities? Although village residents in both Ping'an and Upper Jidao recognized differences in desires, preferences, and behaviors between domestic Chinese and foreign tourists, at certain practical levels, they also regarded all tourists as the same—

as potential consumers. It mattered less, in the big picture, whether the tourists who arrived were foreign or domestic and more simply that *the tourist* kept coming, day after day. The permanent presence of tourists, ultimately, was the sought-after goal, and in this way, the figure of the tourist is conceptually akin to the idea of "the stranger" as conceived by Georg Simmel (1950) in his oft-cited essay.[9] Simmel (ibid., 402) wrote that "the stranger is thus being discussed here, not in the sense often touched upon in the past, as the wanderer who comes today and goes tomorrow, but rather as the person who comes today and stays tomorrow."

From the individual tourist's perspective, she or he is more like the wanderer, coming one day and leaving the next. But from the perspective of tourism village residents and other stakeholders in the business of receiving tourists, Simmel's stranger is precisely the ideal archetype of the tourist as someone who comes and stays. The tourism industry is concerned with *the tourist*, counted and calculated in terms of arrivals. According to Sally Ann Ness (2003, 23): "From the industry's point of view, arrival is the single most important act of consumption, prerequisite for all subsequent acts. A tourist is generally classified as an 'arrival' in the discourse of the industry. A single person becomes a series of arrivals on a tour as he or she moves to new destinations in the matrix. The act disfigures the individual, in rhetoric if not in fact. The thing done displaces the being." Or, in other words, what matters in tourism is not necessarily who is on tour but simply that the tourist arrives. In this way, Simmel's conceptualization of the stranger as someone who comes today and stays tomorrow illuminates the notion of the tourist as an arrival; as a subject, the tourist comes to a place and with this arrival, the receiving location changes in expectation and anticipation of the continuous presence of these, and future, tourists.

The stranger, Simmel (1950, 403) suggested further, is both near and distant to the host society as a result of being placed in a restricted position limited to "intermediary trade . . . [or] pure finance." Fixed in his wandering to be purposeful only as an economic go-between, the stranger formalizes a relationship with the group as "being inorganically [unnaturally] appended to it . . . yet an organic [necessary] member of (it)" (ibid., 408). The economic value of the stranger also sheds light on the figure of the tourist. The stranger's mobility, the ability to be near and distant, creates a relationship of closeness and distance, or copresence, not just between the stranger and the host community but also in relationships between host community members, who may come to question their own closeness to each other. Simmel (ibid., 406) wrote: "The stranger is close to us, insofar as we feel between him and ourselves common features of national, social, occupational, or generally human nature. He is far from us, insofar as these common features extend beyond him or us, and connect us only because they connect a great many people." It is precisely these expectations and potentialities made possible by the simultaneous relationships of nearness and distance that characterize the socioeconomic, ethnic, and political differences so often evoked in tourism.

Three types of distance are at work in motivating, and mobilizing, tourists: distance in time (suggesting evolutionary, linear time and progress), distance in space (which is often apprehended visually in the built environment), and distance in culture (including categories of the exotic, the unusual, or even the unexpected) (N. Wang 2001, vii). These distances serve as hurdles for the tourist to overcome, to embrace, and to evoke, and they validate the experience of travel as something sufficiently different from the quotidian, as in effect a "sacred journey" (Graburn 1989 [1977]). The consequences of these types of distances for destination communities like Ping'an and Upper Jidao, however, is that village residents and other stakeholders must address, satisfy, and perpetuate these ideals. The "distancing work" demanded of tourism holds immense consequences for the relationships between residents, villages, and management or political bodies involved in tourism development. To fully comprehend the "economic, social and cultural organization of distance" (Urry 2007, 46) in tourism, it is necessary to understand the ethnographic, everyday substrate of distances—not only between the tourist and the host but also how host communities such as Ping'an and Upper Jidao are negotiating the new forms of closeness and nearness brought about by tourism. Who is present in the villages, and who is absent? What happens when tourists regularly visit one village but not another just down the road?

Intense local-local tensions in Upper Jidao and Ping'an are apparent in the two sabotage stories; these conflicts reflect ongoing social and economic transformations in these years of increased mobility for villagers and for (potential) tourists alike. The tourist, in the role of the bearer of economic growth, comes to figure in both stories as the harbinger of modernization and progress. And yet, the undesired, unintended consequences of tourism are equally a sign of the times. The distance from the potential riches of tourism felt by residents of Lower Jidao (expressed through small acts of rage and retaliation against Upper Jidao) exemplify the "distancing" effect of state policies and programs that target one, or just a handful, of villages in a given region. Conversely, the second sabotage story illustrates the uncomfortable nearness of the county government and the management company in the Longji Scenic Area as perceived by residents of Ping'an village. The prickly relations between the village and the government-company complex were made manifest in an outburst of destructive acts on company property, yet it was precisely Ping'an's success in tourism that created the centripetal force that drew more and more entrepreneurs to the village. Ultimately, by closely analyzing the distances and differences in Ping'an and Upper Jidao, it becomes possible, and necessary, to reconceptualize understandings of how doing tourism (as development, as leisure, and as work) not only brings individuals in contact with one another but also constructs, divides, and differentiates between communities in accordance with supposed tourist demands and actual economic realities.

PING'AN: COMPETITION IN CONTACT ZONES

Conflicts in Ping'an were rooted in complicated layers of social inequalities and corresponding feelings of envy and discontent, spurred by competition and changing resident perceptions of what constituted progress, wealth, or poverty. In general, the tensions described by Ping'an residents fell into three categories. First, there was the distance between tourists and local residents, which was economic but also sociopolitical in terms of education, access to resources, and status. Second, there was a perceived distance between neighboring households pitted in competition against one another and with incoming entrepreneurs from other cities and towns, major metropolitan areas, and even from the United States. Third, there were distances between the villages in the scenic area where tourism was unevenly distributed. Whereas there was relatively little that village residents could do about their status vis-à-vis tourists, they were actively worried about and engaged in trying to overcome the distances between themselves and their competitors in the village and the area more broadly.

At the core of these concerns was the fact that the net success of tourism in Ping'an was by and large centripetal, drawing potential competitors into the village, from minority models to hotel owners and restaurateurs from across the country and overseas. More and more tourists were coming to Ping'an as well, further thickening the "copresence" of these myriad stakeholders in tourism. The increased proximity of all these parties added to the unease, uncertainty, and dissatisfaction among village residents regarding the management and experience of tourism in Ping'an. Simultaneously, the entrenchment of local livelihoods into the tourism industry solidified the reliance of these households and businesses on the permanence of tourism and tourists. In the summer of 2008, when foreign and domestic tourist numbers to Ping'an dropped (as they did across the country because of the rippling effects of the May earthquake in Sichuan and the summer Olympic Games in Beijing), many Ping'an residents took advantage of the unexpectedly slow traffic in tourists to begin new construction projects for hotels, restaurants, and shops. Most residents I asked no longer considered it feasible not to be engaged in doing tourism.

In numerous household surveys, respondents pointed out that tourism had brought about the negative social consequence of greater wealth disparities between families in the village and that although the vast majority of residents did participate in some way in tourism, the distribution of wealth was highly unequal. Families who could afford to build hotels and guesthouses did so; families whose land was located farther from the viewpoints or designated paths or who did not have enough resources to obtain a loan to invest in materials and labor to construct bigger guesthouses were consigned to small sales, carrying luggage or sedan chairs, or working for wages as staff at another business. The thirty-year-old female owner of the hotel popular with photography groups from Guangzhou and, at the time, the head of a performance group, assessed the situation in plain terms, saying, "Now that there's tourism, everyone is in competition with each other, right?" Another twenty-eight-year-old man, who along with his wife ran one of the Li Qing guesthouses started by Lao, one of the village elders, explained it this way: "Some have gotten rich," he said, "and there's a bit of selfishness; it's very difficult to manage this—everyone thinks about themselves, and no one thinks about everyone." The inference was that the sense of community had been dispersed by a feeling of estrangement from each other because of competition in the tourism industry.

A younger local hotel owner, Bo, echoed these sentiments but went even further one evening over dinner. He said that the selfishness of villagers extended to their perspectives on management and control—village residents neither paid much attention to each other's concerns nor heeded the rules and regulations of the management company and government construction office. Bo had returned to Ping'an to open a guesthouse after studying English at Guangxi Normal University in Guilin, and he said he had tried to generate a communal effort toward improving village infrastructure. "I want to invest a little money [into village projects]," he explained, "but it can't be that I do something helpful and no one is there to support me, and in fact, [they] still talk about you behind your back." Bo added that "no one is willing to stand up" and discuss these problems openly. In fact, in 2008 he tried to organize some of the young adults in the village to create their own volunteer work group (*yiwu gongzuo fuwu dui*) to counteract what he saw as the inefficiencies of the official village leadership. He admitted that he had the time to organize this group because his hotel had burned to the ground that past winter, leaving only the concrete walls of the kitchen and bathrooms standing. Bo had been away when the fire happened and did not think it would be possible to find enough money to rebuild.

Mr. Chou, an investor from Shenzhen who was funding a new hotel in the village, was at dinner with Bo and me that evening. Hearing Bo's comment about the volunteer group, Mr. Chou opined that what really mattered in Ping'an was that the younger generation, like Bo, would continue to work the terraces, insinuating that Bo's idea for a village volunteer work group was ill-conceived. Good-looking terraced fields were arguably the foundation of future success for Mr. Chou and his hotel business. Bo retorted that others could be hired to do the manual agricultural labor of maintaining the terraced fields; what matter for him, as someone born and raised in the village (*tusheng tuzhang*), was the loss of village social unity and the protection of their tourism profits. Bo added that he had never worked the terraces anyway; his generation was the first to be raised almost entirely on profits from tourism, not agricultural labor. The line was drawn, clearly, in this conversation between Bo, a local Ping'an resident, and Mr. Chou, an outsider in Ping'an, each with a particular investment in the tourism industry and each with his own sense of purpose. Whereas Bo viewed himself as similar to Mr. Chou in his shared concern over tourism in Ping'an, Mr. Chou's comment suggested that from his perspective, the village residents were really not part of the tourism business in Ping'an; instead, they were mostly useful for keeping the attraction—namely, the terraced fields and the village itself—looking good.

Like Bo, other Ping'an residents framed their comments around the socioeconomic tensions that had an impact on their community, their opportunities, and their assessments of what constituted a good life. Mr. Chou was only one of the many investors who had come from other parts of China to profit from the tourism industry in Ping'an. The village of Ping'an was a social and economic hub; residents of other villages within the Longji Scenic Area came to Ping'an to work as agricultural laborers, shopkeepers, and hotel staff. Indeed, the village of Longji, just a half hour away on foot from Ping'an, served as a reminder to Ping'an residents of just how far they had come. Longji was linked by kinship to Ping'an through generations of intermarriage, but prior to 2011 the village had little in the way of tourism infrastructure, let alone tourists. According to residents in both Ping'an and Longji, the latter village had chosen not to give up its land for road construction in the mid-1990s; as a result, it remained less accessible and far less visited than Ping'an. As the scenic area developed during the 2000s, Longji became referred to as Longji Ancient Zhuang Village (Longji Gu Zhuang Zhai) in signs and in everyday speech—a fitting descriptor that emphasized the relative modernity of Ping'an next door. The rise of tourism in Ping'an had expanded the gulf between these two villages to the point whereby one village was by name relegated to the past, while its neighbor faced the new future of the Chinese countryside.

Despite their geographic proximity, the economic and material differences between Longji and Ping'an were stark; up until late 2011, there were no gift shops, no Internet cafes, and no substantial tourism jobs in Longji. Yuan, one of the minority models who posed with tourists in Ping'an, was from Longji village and had come to work in Ping'an after she had completed her compulsory education through middle school. Yuan's mother also worked in Ping'an at a family guesthouse. While differences and disparities in incomes and wealth jarred relationships in Ping'an and engendered feelings of discontent and envy between households, relations between Longji and Ping'an villages were much more clear-cut and well-defined, with everyone in unanimous agreement that Longji was very far from Ping'an: developmentally, materially, and economically. Attempts to promote tourism to Longji village emerged in fits and starts; in the summer of 2008, construction began on a direct road to Longji from the main scenic area road, and there was talk of an outside investor turning the entire village into an "ecomuseum" (*shengtai bowuguan*), loosely following the model of village-based ecomuseums in Guizhou funded by the Norwegian government.[10]

By 2011, Longji was deemed an official "scenic spot" within the Longji Scenic Area and renamed as the Longji Old Village Cultural Terraced Fields Scenic Spot (Longji Gu Zhuang Titian Wenhua Guanjingqu) (see Chio 2013).[11] Its touristic transformation was complete with a parking lot and entry ticket gate, financed largely through the efforts of a local Longsheng county government official. Other changes to Longji village included the construction of two viewpoints above the village proper, as well as directional signs throughout the village pointing toward the parking lot, an ecological museum (housed in the former school), a water wheel and mill, and "the oldest home in Longji," which was labeled a "Cultural Model Home of Longji Ecomuseum." In the home, farm tools and other material objects were labeled and displayed for tourists to examine, and tour groups were hosted by a local woman, who would prepare oil tea in advance of their arrival. Actual tourist visits were still relatively low, however, compared to Ping'an, according to a few shopkeepers in Longji who sold water and other snacks at one of the viewpoints, but they were hopeful that over time the village would become a popular attraction in its own right. The heavy emphasis on Zhuang culture and traditional lifeways in Longji village was intended to mark this village's difference from its more well-known and more modern neighbor Ping'an.

Another visual reminder of the opportunities in Ping'an were the ethnic Yao women who came every morning from the neighboring villages of Zhongliu and Huangluo, which were also within the Longji Scenic Area. They wore black pleated skirts, red or pink shirts, and their long hair wrapped in a topknot covered with an embroidered black cloth square. These women sold souvenirs, posed for photographs, performed folk songs on request, and would offer to take tourists on hikes through the mountains to other villages, including Dazhai (which was located in the Jinkeng Red Yao Terraced Fields Scenic Spot, another main scenic spot within the Longji Scenic Area). Other residents from Longji, Zhongliu, Dazhai, and neighboring villages would come to Ping'an on occasion to sell goods such as tea, bamboo shoots, pork, and beef to guesthouses, restaurants, and tourists. Ping'an was the region's biggest market, given the number of hotels, tourists, and higher amounts of disposable income among its residents. Relations between the Yao communities in the scenic region and the Zhuang in Ping'an were generally sympathetic but not entirely welcoming; the naming of the scenic spots as Zhuang terraced fields in Ping'an and Yao terraced fields around the village of Dazhai is only one reminder of how important clear ethnic distinctions are to tourism. Separate ethnic designations of what are essentially similar systems of terraced fields suggests that in the competitive tourism economy, any and every difference is potentially valuable.

As stated earlier, it was not only area locals who moved to Ping'an for economic opportunities; a number of entrepreneurs from other parts of Guangxi (such as Longsheng, Guilin, Yangshuo) and from farther places like Beijing, Shenzhen, and even Seattle were a noticeable presence in the village. The increasing arrival of people, from tourists to migrant workers and investors (who are migratory in their own way), exacerbated competition and senses of a growing sociopolitical gulf between all of these stakeholders in the tourism enterprise. One notable case was a Chinese-American travel agency owner and professional photographer based in Seattle who opened a luxury hotel in 2007. Until this point, the most expensive rooms in the village cost, at most, ¥300 a night during the high season (the Golden Weeks) and less during the rest of the year, but the new hotel reported its prices at around ¥2,000 or more per room (inclusive of meals). Many village residents were curious to see exactly how a hotel room could cost so much, but unfortunately for the people of Ping'an, the hotel came complete with a locked front gate, accessible only by buzzer, security cameras, and a raised construction that allowed guests inside a sweeping view of the terraced fields but those outside only a glimpse at the stone railing around the elevated balcony (figure 5.3).[12]

The construction of the hotel reflected, perhaps, a desire to achieve visual, photographic domination over the landscape. Much like how the "starchitecture" of pre-Olympics Beijing was constructed to be seen from above, through a mediating lens, in Ping'an many hotels and balconies, including the photography booths, literally placed tourists above the landscape, which could then be viewed as static and subordinate. In

FIGURE 5.3. Hotels in Ping'an are clustered along the path to the viewpoint for looking at the Seven Stars with Moon landscape, which is the more well-known view; the last large building on the upper left is the most expensive hotel in the village (2007). Photo by the author.

effect, "such photographic practices [of landscape] thus demonstrate how the environment is to be viewed, as dominated by humans and subject to their mastery" (Urry 2000, 87). These spaces only reinforced an ongoing problem, however: village residents felt excluded from the celebration of their landscape, which they considered the product of their ingenuity and labor. The photographic "domination" of the landscape in Ping'an by the gated balcony of a hotel owned by an outsider to the village suggested yet another external exertion of power over the community. Within a few months of this hotel's opening, villagers remarked to me that no one except the staff (at first only one of whom was a local woman, hired as a cleaner) and guests could enter. The villagers who were hired as porters to carry luggage up from the parking lot were allowed only as far as the front door. This total exclusion from the hotel space was new to the village residents. Family-run guesthouses were more typically a semiporous border zone between the public and the private, the home and the hotel; the tourist's dining room often also served as a family living room. Friends and relatives would relax, chat, watch TV, and otherwise use their hotel and restaurant spaces whenever tourists were not around, although it was tacitly agreed that when tourists were present, village residents would move out of the center of a room, either to one side or go outside. The physical distance created by the new luxury hotel's construction reinforced for the villagers the socioeconomic differences between them, the tourists, and the nonlocal business entrepreneurs who came to Ping'an.

By offering such an exclusive secluded space for tourists who wanted to "get away from it all" within a village as densely populated yet geographically small as Ping'an, the inference was that perhaps Ping'an, the terraced fields, and rural Zhuang minority life were best experienced from a distance, from an elevated, walled-off balcony. As a symbol of power, the balcony and the hotel reinforced the social inequalities of tourism. The visuality of the balcony can be traced back to mid-nineteenth-century Britain, and perhaps not entirely coincidentally with the rise of the European Grand Tour and modern tourism, when "the upper class . . . [stood] visibly on their balconies and [overlooked] the 'other.' The balcony took on special significance in nineteenth-century life and literature as the place from which one could gaze but not be touched, could participate in the crowd yet be separate from it. . . . According to [Walter] Benjamin the balcony demonstrates superiority over the crowd, as the observer 'scrutinizes the throng' [1969, 173]" (Urry 2000, 94–95). In Ping'an, the balcony had a recent history and was a relatively new feature of tourism in the village. This luxury hotel's balcony was unique in its exclusivity and position in the village, but many other hotels in Ping'an also had balconies by 2008 (figure 5.4). Indeed, by this time, having a balcony for guest use was considered a necessary element of a successful hotel-restaurant business.

While most houses in Ping'an traditionally included a flat outdoor space (usually made of bamboo poles strapped together and propped against the roof or side of the house) for drying foods and doing other chores, the first balcony for tourists was built in the late 1990s by Ying, the owner-manager of the original Li Qing guesthouse, who was one of Lao's sons-in-law. Ying explained that he decided to try to build a balcony outside the guesthouse after seeing how popular they were with foreign tourists in Yangshuo; however, as the Li Qing guesthouse was perched over a steep slope, he

FIGURE 5.4. Balconies in Ping'an compete for views, space, and tourists. The smallest, lower-middle balcony was the first to be built in the village, attached to the old Li Qing guesthouse (2008). Photo by the author.

had trouble at first with designing a balcony out of wood that would be structurally sound but still maintain the look of the village. Eventually, Ying devised a way to use steel rebar and concrete to construct supports for the balcony and then wrapped the concrete pillars with wooden planks to cover up the original material. When the balcony was complete, he said, income at the Li Qing guesthouse nearly doubled in one year.

By 2008, almost every new hotel-restaurant construction project included a balcony, if not for general shared use then for private guest use directly attached to guestrooms. Families who were building new guesthouses would often first build a large, flat space over the hillside's steep slopes if they didn't have a wide enough plot of land to use as the foundation (see figure 5.4; the large unfinished concrete surface in the middle right of the image is one such newly constructed flat space). The idea would be to first use the flat, open balcony as an outdoor restaurant and then, when they had enough money, to build a hotel on top. The balcony was a fitting architectural manifestation of how Ping'an should be experienced, touristically, since the village's main attraction was *looking at* (and more precisely *looking down upon*) the terraced fields. This type of sightseeing tied a particular behavior to notions of how the land should be experienced and consumed: visually.[13] Therefore, construction projects in Ping'an centered on how to make the experience of looking more enjoyable for tourists and profitable for business owners. The outdoor balcony restaurant and private balconies attached to guestrooms were obvious solutions, where tourists could enjoy the view while also spending money. Just as guesthouses were often also living spaces for village residents, when there were no tourists present, most balconies were also public-private spaces for playing cards, eating meals, and even hula-hooping. But with the increase in more professionally run hotels and guesthouses, usually started by experienced entrepreneurs from other places, some balconies were gradually regulated to be for tourist use only. The luxury hotel balcony, gated off from the village paths and raised above eye level, marked the limits of the "contact zone" in Ping'an, where the "thick co-presence" (Urry 2002a, 259) of tourists and locals, residents and outsiders, even neighbor and neighbor, was wearing quite thin.

UPPER JIDAO: FINDING SPECIAL CHARACTERISTICS

The situation in Upper Jidao was equally tense and rife with unmet expectations and frustrations, though around different issues. Unlike in Ping'an, instead of a process of in-migration from neighboring regions and villages, the residents of neighboring Lower Jidao simply seemed to be left out of Upper Jidao's developments. Indeed, provincial-level government plans and funding specifically targeted Upper Jidao as the tourism destination. From conception these projects, including the World Bank's eventual Guizhou Cultural and Natural Heritage Protection and Development Program, aimed at separating selected villages according to certain features and characteristics. But they effectively left out, or left behind, the other villages and communities in the area. In the *Rural Tourism Plan, 2006–2020*, published by the Guizhou Tourism Bureau (2006, 41), a "control plan" for tourism in Upper Jidao outlined specific aspects of intended development, including the protection of natural resources, construction of infrastructure, and marketing of tourism products.

Mention of Lower Jidao was made in passing within the document, which gives only brief acknowledgment to the existence of Lower Jidao when reporting village population: "The village is divided into two parts: Jidao Upper Village and Jidao Lower Village. The total population of the village [here referring to Upper and Lower Jidao] is up to 1,037, including 220 families, all of which are Miao minority" (ibid., 41). The description of the control plan continues by outlining the various components of the changes to be made in Upper Jidao. In every provincial-level government publication on tourism in the Bala River region I obtained, only Upper Jidao village is mentioned in the development plans, and often Lower Jidao is simply left off the map. Some documents referred to Upper Jidao as "Jidao village," altogether ignoring the existence of Lower Jidao, or simply by the destination name "Jidao Miao Village," which lumped them together but did not acknowledge how funding or plans were allocated.

The problems of selecting one village out of many for tourism development was not unnoticed by government officials; Xiao Qianhui (2005, 213), Party Secretary and director of the newspaper office for *China Tourism News*, said in a paper given at the 2004 International Forum on Guizhou Rural Tourism (later published in the forum proceedings) that while "there may be over 10,000 natural villages in Qiandongnan Prefecture; yet there may be only 50 out of them that would have the conditions to develop rural tourism, which is a very small number among them. . . . When rural tourism grows vigorously in Nanhua Village, how about the other over 9000 villages?" His proposed solution was to implement a "division of labor"—to allow for and facilitate the migration of villagers from one village to another "to be their assistants, actors, logistic service base for providing farm productions and the like for the front-line villages" (ibid., 214). This is precisely what happened, somewhat organically, in Ping'an over time. After all, Xiao continued, many young people from the popular tourism village of Upper Langde migrated to urban centers like Beijing, Guiyang, and Shenzhen for work (and "such a migration is a normal phenomenon," he noted), leaving behind a tourism destination without a "backbone performing team" (i.e., only the elderly and infirm are left). Xiao suggested simply inviting other villagers from Nanmeng or other nearby communities to perform and share in the profits (ibid., 214).

For tourism villages with a "permanent presence" of tourists like Ping'an, the in-migration of potential employees was possible because as established destinations, these villages could reasonably expect tourist arrivals. For Upper Jidao, however, because it was just beginning to participate in tourism and had yet to really earn any profits from it, the notion of sharing labor and earnings with any other village was counterintuitive, to say the least. The net result was a doubling of the social tensions in Upper Jidao: first, to mitigate, to some extent, the unhappiness of their neighbors (in many cases, their relations) in Lower Jidao lest this anger and resentment cause more damage to their own tourism; and second, to continually strive to be different from the other villages earmarked as tourism destinations along the Bala River. Since Upper Jidao is extremely close to the most popular and well-known tourism villages in the region, if not in the entire province (Upper Langde, Xijiang, and Nanhua), this physical nearness had to be combated with the creation of greater differences from the tourist attractions offered in these well-known villages.[14] Moreover, after 2008, their greatest competition came from Xijiang, which is not in the Bala River area. Xijiang, technically a township, had been redeveloped with provincial and county funds into a scenic area, and was now managed and run by a tourism development company in conjunction with government offices; it has since obtained a national "AAAA" rating as a tourism region.[15] With Xijiang on the map, so to speak, tourists simply went there and no longer passed through the Bala River area, villagers said.

As I learned through my household survey in Upper Jidao in 2006, villagers overwhelmingly agreed that they were interested in doing tourism as a source of income and wages. When it came to what kind of tourism activities they considered best or most suitable to them, people expressed a sincere desire to be different from Upper Langde and Nanhua, both of which relied upon prearranged dance performances and charged flat fees of ¥300 to ¥800 to tour groups who booked shows in advance. Upper Jidao should not become a song-and-dance village like Upper Langde or Nanhua, I was told repeatedly, because there was no need for another such attraction in the Bala River area. The 2006 village subcommittee head of Upper Jidao, Chun, summarized the situation in more proactive terms: what they needed to do, he said, was "get out the special characteristics" of Upper Jidao (*ba tese gao chulai*). "When other villages are a step ahead [of us]," he added, "we're behind them; [therefore] we can't follow the old road, and instead we need to find our own special characteristics." This feeling of the need to be different was pervasive throughout tourism development programs but especially in the marketing of rural ethnic places for tourism.

This ability to be different, or characteristically special, was emphasized early on in the original plans for the Bala River Demonstration Project for Rural Tourism. According to a paper prepared for the 2004 International Forum on Guizhou Rural Tourism by the (then) vice governor for Qiandongnan, Li Zaiyong, the Bala River project delineated very specific, differing tourism "characteristics" for each of the seven villages involved (Li Zaiyong 2005). Table 5.1 is adapted from the published version of his paper (note that Jidao and Langde in the table refer to the upper villages of each, respectively). According to Li Zaiyong (ibid., 185), the principles behind this table included "seeking differences from the same group of tourism attractions; demonstrating special features through comparison; and pinpointing the key points through selection." The purpose of creating a table like this one was therefore to explicitly make these seven villages be *more different* from each other.

Table 5.1 is a visual reminder of how villages were to draw lines between and keep their distance from each other. An interview with Wang Qiao, Party Secretary of the Kaili Municipal Tourism Bureau in 2006, revealed a similar approach to tourism development; Wang repeatedly emphasized to me that the Bala River villages must not be the same. Even national-level tourism officials pointed out the "problems" of sameness. In his paper given at the 2004 International Forum on Guizhou Rural Tourism and published in the forum proceedings, Xiao Qianhui (2005, 212), from *China Tourism News*, described the situation as follows: "When we came in Guizhou, we found there were too many common points existing between different ethnic villages and different ethnic groups here. Only the professionals could see where the differences [were] between them; yet it was difficult for the ordinary tourists to find the differences between them. . . . The greatest threat in our rural tourism would be the sameness in a thousand villages. If all the villages should have the same face, it is unnecessary for tourists to visit them one by one."

Being recognizably the same as your neighbors becomes a burden within the tourism worldview, where the perpetual search for difference, between tourist and toured, or this tourist village and that one down the road, necessitates a distancing of self from the others. But finding and developing the necessary differences between these villages was easier said

TABLE 5.1. Characteristics and work divisions planned for the Bala River Demonstration Project Area, 2005

Village Name	Characteristics	Work Division and Positioning
Huai'enbao	Ancient postal road built in late Ming and early Qing dynasties and located at the entrance to the Demonstration Project Area	Providing comprehensive tourism services
Nanhua	Miao songs and dances	Displays of the Miao songs and dances
[Upper] Jidao	Ancient building structures, history and culture	Showing tourists the hundred-year granary and the hundred-year path; performance of ancient (hundred-year) songs
[Upper] Langde	Miao songs and dances; ancient building complex; liquor-drinking customs	Showing tourists the ancient traditional Miao buildings; performances of the Miao songs and dances
Jiaomeng	The Miao Copper Drum Dance; specialty agriculture; water-buffalo fights; cockfights, bird fights	Specialty agriculture for sightseeing; services at the spots along the hiking route of Maomaohe–Jiaomeng–Nanmeng–Langde
Nanmeng	Homeland of *lusheng* art	Performances of *lusheng*; services at the spots along the hiking route of Jiaomeng–Nanmeng–Langde
Maomaohe	A village famous nationwide for its good sanitation; the entrance to the Demonstration Area	Exhibition of Miao embroideries; leisure tours and holiday making; comprehensive supporting services

Source: Adapted from Li Zaiyong 2005, 185.

than done; an official from Maomaohe village reported in 2006 that tourism to his village had decreased since 2002. When asked why, he said it was because promoting seven tourism villages was too much—"We are all the same," the official exclaimed, "so why would any tourist go to seven of the same places? Historically, socially, culturally, we are all the same Miao!"

The vision of tourism development proposed by government tourism bureaus and consultants required that the villages along the Bala River, considered by scholars and residents of the region to be cut of the same Miao ethnic minority cloth, now had to create differences not only between themselves and mainstream Han society but also between each other as well. This problem of "sameness" was not unique to China, of course, and potential solutions have been created in other rural tourism programs, such as the One Village One Product movement that originated in Japan.[16] This approach focused on creating one specialty product per village to encourage tourists to visit multiple villages, thus expanding the tourism map by creating consumable differences between villages. The economic success of this project in certain regions of Japan is well-documented on the program's website. Particularly in Asian tourism contexts, the "one village, one product" model fits within already existing ideas about the desirability of local specialties and gift-giving (Graburn 1983).

Chinese tourism promotions and marketing were awash in the language of special characteristics (*tese*) and special products (*techan*). In 2006, the Guiyang-based Highland Research Institute (Gaodi Yanjiu Suo) funded seven villages in Qiandongnan, including Upper Jidao, to create their own special products as part of a program to develop local economies and promote local goods in regional marketplaces. Some villages used the ¥10,000 grant to improve upon and advertise a product they were already known for, such as paper-making in Shiban village. Others, like Upper Jidao, used the funds to purchase new items, in this case multiple large *lusheng* for use in their tourism performances. Chinese domestic tourists visiting both Upper Jidao and Ping'an frequently asked for special products, especially foods, so villagers also developed standard replies to these inquiries. In Upper Jidao, the local specialty was sour-soup fish (*suantang yu,* a tomato-based fish hotpot); the sour-soup flavor was widely associated with the Miao ethnic group, to the point where even the international fast-food chain KFC once offered a Miao Mountain Sour Soup Double Chicken Burger (figure 5.5).[17] In Ping'an, the foods named by residents as

FIGURE 5.5. A KFC advertisement for the Miao Mountain Sour Soup Double Chicken Burger inside the Xizhimen subway station in Beijing features a background image from Upper Langde, Guizhou (2007). Photo by the author.

local specialties included bamboo rice and smoked pork. In both villages, the local alcoholic brew was also evoked as a specialty. In Upper Jidao, it was distilled from rice or corn; in Ping'an, it was usually made from sweet potatoes, and many families also made their own sweet rice wine.

In general, Upper Jidao needed to offer something different from the other tourist villages nearby, but it also needed to adopt certain features to meet and fulfill expected tourist demands. As a result, villagers struggled with the double-edged sword of sameness: while wanting to differentiate their own attractions from the similar Miao cultural performances and festival attire in nearby villages, the village also needed to *look* more like a "real" tourist village to attract more tourists. Tourists arriving in Upper Jidao sometimes complained that they couldn't *see* what was so unique about the place—a complaint that led to the occasional refusal of tourists to pay entrance fees or to stay for a meal. The village needed more obvious, familiar elements to explicitly signal to tourists that this was a place that could be visited. Even as some plans detailed how Upper Jidao would be different, village residents were nevertheless encouraged to practice and prepare folk song-and-dance performances, despite the fact that such shows were already commonly offered in Upper Langde and Nanhua.

These performances, in effect, made Upper Jidao into a *real* tourism village. Residents of Upper Jidao often emphasized that their shows were different, however, because they included "ancient songs" (*gu ge*) performed by elderly village residents. This was partly the result of out-migration and a lack of younger adults in the village, but this circumstance was reshaped as an advantage in the current tourism market. Ultimately, Upper Jidao sought to be similar enough to existing tourism models to participate in the industry but unique enough to offer a slightly different experience.

The selected Bala River villages also had to be immediately recognizable visually as destinations. To start, the provincial and municipal governments erected matching road signs on the highway through the region and placed wooden placards at the entrance to each village to visually brand the Bala River region as a tourism destination. Because the original road into Jidao was tucked in a bend, however, residents worried that the village would be missed. Thus they increased the number of signs on the highway (see figure 1.4). When the highway was rebuilt in 2008 and 2009, new decorated parking lots were built as a part of the entrances to the tourism villages in the Bala River area that fell within Kaili municipality; these visually similar areas signaled even more strongly to passing traffic that these particular villages were worth visiting (figure 5.6).

There were other visual elements, or recognizable architectural styles and structures that indicated the presence of a village for tourism in Guizhou.[18] These included wind-and-rain bridges (*fengyu qiao*, which Nanhua and Upper Langde both had), an arched entryway into the village (*zhaimen*; at first, one was constructed only at the entrance to Upper Jidao by the riverside and was not visible from the highway), a large dancing ground for *lusheng* performances (the original space was renovated in 2004; in 2006 and 2007, additional fields were appropriated for the construction of a larger one that was completed in 2008), a parking lot, and a village museum. Much of the money from the New Socialist Countryside program and development funds from Ningbo were spent on building these features in Upper Jidao. The new, larger performance space came first, and the village museum/cultural center shortly thereafter. But by the summer of 2008, tensions between Upper Jidao and Lower Jidao had worsened, spurred on by the increased number of tour groups visiting Upper Jidao. One woman from Upper Jidao told me that she had heard rumors about leaders from Lower Jidao renting a digger to start construc-

FIGURE 5.6. A new decorative parking lot for Jidao was completed as a part of the 2008 highway project along the Bala River. This lot was located at the roadside entrance to both Upper Jidao and Lower Jidao, and the wooden gates displayed the name of the village ("Jidao" on the smaller, right side, and "Jidao Miao Village" on the larger, left gate). The carved stone wall features a mural of Xijiang, Jidao, and other villages promoted as tourism destinations in the Bala River area. In the carving, wooden houses are tucked in among tall trees and steep hillsides (2010). Photo by the author.

tion on their own performance ground in their village to compete with Upper Jidao.

Nonetheless, the plans and ideas imagined for Upper Jidao went even further than a museum and performance space. As early as 2006, my host in Upper Jidao, Teacher Pan, envisioned "rafting on the river, covered huts on the riverbank, and also more things for sale in the village along a commercial street, or small bars and shops, so when tourists arrive and are thirsty or tired, they can have a cup of tea." He declared that a tourist village needed "something to look at, something to buy, and something to be entertained by" for the tourist, with the ideal end result that "villagers can have some income." Tourism to Upper Jidao was not entirely focused on landscape appreciation, as in Ping'an, because its landscape was by and large no different than that surrounding every other village along the Bala River. Therefore, Upper Jidao would have to develop its own products to address tourist expectations, who hoped to see and enjoy a rural ethnic Miao cultural environment—but in ways *different from* how Miao cultural life could be seen and enjoyed in nearby villages like Nanhua or Upper Langde.

Upper Jidao was still going to be a Miao village for tourists, just with different activities and "special characteristics" to demonstrate its Miao identity. The work chart (see table 5.1) of characteristics and divisions planned for the area was intended create these specific differences, while suggesting that these seven villages were all worth a visit. After the redevelopment and opening of the Xijiang Thousand Households Miao Village in 2008, however, tourist numbers to the Bala River region villages dropped significantly, to the point that by 2012, one Upper Jidao resident who taught in the elementary school in Nanhua said that Nanhua had stopped doing tourism almost entirely. Tourist numbers to Upper Jidao had also declined by 2012, although because of the influx of funds from the World Bank project and from private donors, there were still a number of construction projects ongoing in the village, including the building of additional guestrooms in local homes and a new parking lot, and the creation of an exhibition of embroidery inside the cultural center. A very large, multistory building was also under construction in Lower Jidao along the riverside in 2012, which some Upper Jidao residents surmised would be turned into a hotel.

Being a recognizable part of a recognized ethnic minority group remains important for political representation in a centralized state system that maintains an exact count and decisive role in naming the nation's constituent ethnic communities. On the ground, however, tourism development and maintenance requires a negotiation of difference. The residents of Upper Jidao and Ping'an are officially acknowledged by the state as ethnic minorities, and the cultural traditions of each village are promoted as part of the tourism experience in each place. Ethnic and rural identity thus becomes an integral component of how differences are produced in tourism, ostensibly for the economic benefit of the destination communities. For Ping'an and Upper Jidao, tourism has brought not only new enterprises and economies but also new ways of thinking about community, belonging, and the future. In Ping'an, tourism and its relative success has introduced psychological distances between families, neighbors, and other stakeholders crowded into the village's tourism industry; in Upper Jidao, however, the tensions with Lower Jidao and the emphasis on creating differences between villages has demonstrated that a certain kind of distance is necessary for tourism development. Nevertheless, because of tourism, both of these communities are evermore interlinked and interdependent with their neighboring villages by virtue of being destinations. As villagers expressed a sense of distance from their neighbors or their ethnic communities, these perceived distances continued to impart very real implications for village socialities and subjectivities.

KEEPING YOUR DISTANCE

Rural ethnic tourism in China revolves around three primary axes of difference: rural-urban, ethnic minority–mainstream majority, and poor-rich. These binaries were experienced and expressed in various ways as they came to bear on local, regional, and national relationships between individual, community, and ethnic identities within and beyond Ping'an and Upper Jidao. Of course, these binaries of socioeconomic difference are not unique to China, but they have been increasingly adopted for promoting tourism *and* rural development, and more often than not, at the same time. In the discursive construction of what constituted development and progress in China, extending Louisa Schein's concept of "internal orientalism," rural, poor, and ethnic minority existed at one end of the apparent one-way street toward urban, rich, and mainstream. Indeed, as the examples of Upper Jidao and Ping'an show, the process of tourism *as* development functioned to mainstream the ethnic minority, not to erase or eliminate ethnic distinctiveness but rather to render it into popular, nationally shared forms and variations (such as sour soup–flavored dishes and standard expectations of rural vernacular architecture).

This distancing of populations (rural-urban, minority-mainstream, poor-rich) within the scope of the nation also affects tourist behaviors and the perception of tourists by destination community residents. In Joan Laxson's (1991) study of tourist opinions at Native American sites in the U.S. Southwest, she found that rather than being a contact zone across differences, museum and other public cultural performances became ways for tourists to reinforce their original ideas and beliefs about Native Americans. Some tourists were well aware of the differences between themselves and Native cultures and admitted to feeling more comfortable at a distance: a young woman at the Pueblo Cultural Center in Albuquerque, New Mexico, told her: "The only way I feel comfortable learning about it (Pueblo culture) or knowing about it is through something like (novels by Tony Hillerman). Something that lets you keep your distance" (Laxson 1991, 367). Distance becomes a desired aspect of consumption for this tourist, much as the popularity of balconies in Ping'an allows tourists to "control" the land through possession of a privileged viewing position. Other tourists might feel more comfortable "looking at, buying, and being entertained by" rural ethnic minority life through a front-row seat at the edge of a performance ground (to evoke Teacher Pan's formula). In response, given the concerns of village residents in Upper Jidao over being able to provide an appropriate and satisfactory experience for tourists, they were worried about not being different *enough* to fulfill tourist desires.

Whether it was people in Ping'an talking about who was responsible for the maintenance of the terraced fields or government officials and residents in the Bala River region wondering how to increase tourist flows to all seven villages, their comments reflect a shift in senses of identity, community, and connectedness among rural ethnic minority populations in China. This shift is part of a more fundamental transformation of how differences are being experienced and categorized in meaningful ways. The logic of this shift reveals the underlying assumptions of projects such as the work chart for the Bala River villages (see table 5.1) and the insistence of Ping'an residents on their need to become more ethnic in light of competition from their neighbors (see chapter 1). But this means of rationalizing difference into a handful of tourist activities or naming strategies in order to create *distinctions* illuminates how differences become instrumentalized within certain forms and assertions of power. By systematically organizing differences and labeling them as such, in a method not unlike that of natural history (Pratt 2008 [1992], 24–36), differences themselves became naturalized as universal types and forms, rather than as cultural or historically contingent.[19] In this way, Upper Jidao *becomes* the village of Miao ancient songs; Ping'an *becomes* the village of Zhuang terraced fields.

Ethnic identity is malleable to the politics and, increasingly, to the economics of an era. During China's Ethnic Classification project of the 1950s and 1960s, the purpose of distinguishing between ethnic minority groups was to reduce difference into a finite number of governable groups with the goal of integrating all into a seamless map of national progress and social development. Nowadays, however, differences (visual differences in particular) are invoked to keep ethnic communities apart for purposes of economic growth via tourism. For tourism purposes, once the basic fact of difference is established along ethnic lines and usually through naming, the "repertoire" or "options" (Bunten 2008, Waters 1990, and Wood 1998) available in these cultural and ethnic identities gradually became "filled up" with meaning through very material means, such as architecture, performance, clothing, and landscape. Ultimately, the desired end result is that the "Other" in tourism—village residents—is supposed to be somewhat close to the tourist (by leading a modern life through the successful execution of national development programs and able to provide acceptable eating and sleeping conditions to tourists) but distant enough to render culture and customs into acceptable varieties of song-and-dance performances, a few "local" flavors at dinner, and traditional handicrafts.

Domestic tourism in China continues to seek out and codify the internal "Other" to expand tourism industries and opportunities. For tourism village residents, the process of doing tourism was also a process of being able to be different in ways appropriate to national discourses about tourism, belonging, and identity. More than just development, this is a project in understanding how and why tourists come to a rural ethnic minority village and in negotiating what happens when tourism comes to one or two villages but perhaps not to others. The sensation of the distances between communities increases as a result of concrete social, economic, and political changes while these very communities are simultaneously becoming more and more interdependent on one another for economic growth and social progress. In both Ping'an and Upper Jidao, socioeconomic development meant increased opportunities to not stay in one's natal village, or at least to imagine a life elsewhere in China. With this, the ability to be mobile took on increasingly significant resonances in terms of productive labor (as a migrant worker) and consumption (as a tourist).

In Upper Jidao and Ping'an, "the cultural economy of distance" (Appadurai 1996, 71) traded socialist narratives of unidirectional social progress and development for an ethnic identity that could be enjoyed, shared cultural traits for consumable local specialties, and income-earning opportunities for the imagination of a life that would allow for leisure travel. The transformations taking place in Ping'an and Upper Jidao were not only internal. Incidents of sabotage raised questions of competition, unmet expectations, jealousy, and disappointment that involved stakeholders from the village to the nation. The significance of tracing these relationships beyond the limits of the village is apparent. For tourism to succeed in Ping'an and Upper Jidao, these villages depend upon provincial and national funds, support, and infrastructure. If these tourism industries are to fail, it would also be through the combined failure of the many parties involved.

By understanding the interaction between physical distances, socioeconomic disparities, and cultural distinctiveness, the desire for difference in tourism—or as one travel magazine editor in Beijing put it, "tourism that can be different" (*chayi xing de lüyou*)—translates into the ability to be different on the part of tourism village residents. Whereas tourism in Ping'an drew increased numbers of "outsiders" into the village's socioeconomic sphere, thereby forcing all parties to take stock of how to distinguish themselves, Upper Jidao struggled to establish its purpose within the forces of rural ethnic tourism plans and discourses that demanded difference. Both sets of circumstances strained social and personal relations, and the resultant changes were noticeably manifest in visual practices in each village. Hotel and restaurant owners in Ping'an competed to lure tourists with the best views via balconies, while officials and leaders in Upper Jidao, Kaili, and Guizhou planned and constructed new facilities to make the village look more like a tourist destination while trying to imagine a different way to attract tourists. The distances and differences at play in these villages provide the guiding outlines of the landscape of travel in China today, which above all is about the connectivity of these communities to national goals of progress and modernization.

CONCLUSION

Upper Jidao, Meet Ping'an

In June 2007, I invited the members of the Upper Jidao Tourism Association to visit Ping'an; it would be a second trip to the Longji Scenic Area for Teacher Pan and Fa, and the first for the other association members. Through this trip, I came to fully realize how complicated tourism is as a lived practice. As I spent time with the Upper Jidao residents in Ping'an, listening to their observations and taking note of their questions, I saw how doing tourism was reconfiguring the social, cultural, and political values of being ethnic and being rural for them. Participation in tourism had become not only a new means of earning an income, but another way of taking part in the construction and creation of one's own modern identity. Of course, this process has not been without problems.

National campaigns to Open Up the West and to build a New Socialist Countryside articulate current discourses of rural socioeconomic development and national unity among (and between) the country's officially recognized ethnic groups. Beyond national cohesion, however, these programs also have sought to transform individual subjectivities, most noticeably in the push for a "quality population" (*suzhi renkou*) and "civilized tourism" (*wenming lüyou*). They tapped into, and drew upon for justification, shared, dominant discourses on mobility, where domestic migrants are disparaged and domestic tourists are desirable.[1] These policies have had the effect of encouraging rural ethnic Chinese people to learn how to be rural and how to be ethnic in very specific ways. My analysis in this book has focused on how various discourses and experiences of learning to be rural and ethnic have been negotiated through the accumulation and communication of *visual* knowledge, resulting in a particular politics of appearance at work in tourism villages. Thus tourism has become the actual context in which learned identities are displayed, performed, and commodified for economic gain and personal growth.

By exploring the effects of mobility and visuality across scales—from the personal to the public and from the village to the nation—being mobile and being seen are clearly shown to be integral to local understandings of the perils and possibilities latent in tourism. But as a lived experience, tourism is a messy business in which individual aspirations may collide with communal plans. Undulating tensions between collective ambitions for rural tourism and individual goals for a life worth living punctuated the often fraught relationships between the myriad stakeholders involved. Tourism development programs such as those undertaken in Upper Jidao depended upon the assumption that a village could, and would, work together as a cohesive social, political, and economic unit. Perhaps out of practicality, these plans frequently overlooked the range of individual opinions, perspectives, desires, and interests that exist in any one village. Admittedly, as the history of tourism in Ping'an demonstrates, once tourism becomes a steady and predictable source of income, most families and households will choose to participate in the industry, but not without exacerbating some, and sometimes new, inequalities. The landscape of travel in which these village communities seek out their place in contemporary China has been continually outlined by the negotiation of opportunities and ambitions by individuals and within social collectivities.

The study tour I organized in 2007 illustrated in real time the complexities of tourism in rural ethnic China. I offered to pay for the members of the Upper Jidao Tourism Association to visit Ping'an. Here, my role as a foreign ethnographer shifted from being an active participant-observer to a proactive initiator. After months of seeing "the other" village in my video footage (Chio 2011a), I hoped that some residents of Upper Jidao and Ping'an would finally get to meet each other in person and discuss tourism in face-to-face conversation. I imagined the trip would include a significant amount of interaction between villagers, without the agenda of an international development program, consultants, or government officials.

Much of what I anticipated never came to light. In the end, the short two-day trip showed me how mobility, visuality, and the learning curve of tourism are deeply complicated in Ping'an and Upper Jidao. Residents of both villages are juggling the expectations for better tourism posed by government and industry stakeholders alongside their own aspirations for better lives. After the trip, I began to better comprehend how mobility and immobility are two sides of the same coin, how ethnicity can be simultaneously creative and formulaic, and how tourism is always both sacred and profane. Indeed, the trip forced me to remember that from the perspective of the villagers, it was the potential of tourism to improve upon their everyday, normal, and ordinary lives that mattered the most.

YOUR MOBILITY DEFEATS YOUR TOURISM

My idea to invite people from Upper Jidao on a trip to Ping'an was hardly new, given that Teacher Pan and Fa had both gone on a government-sponsored study trip in 2004, which had included a stop in Ping'an.[2] Sharing my video footage from Ping'an with residents of Upper Jidao only increased our mutual enthusiasm for another study trip. In spring 2007, I told Fu, that year's village subcommittee leader and the head of the tourism association, that I would provide ¥4,000 for transport, lodging, food, and incidental costs for the trip. A manager in the Longji Scenic Area management company generously agreed to waive the entry ticket fees for the group. Fu arranged for a driver and a van. Everyone in the tourism association was enthusiastic and excited about the trip, Fu assured me.

The first problem was with scheduling. It had been a very busy year for Upper Jidao, as the village was at the center of a number of government projects, including the ongoing provincial rural tourism plans and the concurrent New Socialist Countryside development program. Upper Jidao was also involved with a rural development NGO that held occasional retreats and conferences for village representatives. Individual opportunities and obligations placed additional demands on residents. Qin, the most active female member of the tourism association and the village clinician, had been offered an office job with a company that sold the flavor base for "Miao" sour-soup fish hotpot. This would give her the chance to live in Kaili, where she had lived as a child and teenager and where her mother still resided. Qin left Upper Jidao with her daughter in March 2007, thinking it would be a good way for her daughter to attend preschool and for her to save a bit of money. We talked on the phone occasionally, and I asked her about the job and living in the city again. The work was fine, if a bit boring, Qin opined; she mostly just answered the phone. Her daughter was doing well in preschool, but Qin claimed she wasn't saving much money at all since there were too many things to buy in Kaili.

In addition, Qin said, people in the village kept calling her back. Like many young adults in rural communities, she desired more than what a village livelihood could provide. But her education and communication skills, developed largely because she'd grown up and gone to school in Kaili, were now her greatest assets to the village. Everyone in Upper Jidao village relied on her when tour groups or government officials requested a local tour guide. Over the May 1 Golden Week holiday that year, she recalled, she was told to return to the village; one tour guide specifically requested Qin to show a group around, adding that if Qin wasn't there, the group would not come. Since Kaili was only about forty minutes away from Upper Jidao by public bus, Qin felt obliged to return as often as possible, even though the travel back and forth disrupted her office job. Another time, she said, someone called Teacher Pan to say that a group of tourists was going to visit the village and wanted a local guide, but Teacher Pan was in Guiyang attending another meeting. So Teacher Pan called Qin; she was in Kaili but Teacher Pan nonetheless told her to return to the village to "take care of it," she said.

Qin and Teacher Pan were always in the middle of arrangements for tourists coming to Upper Jidao. Their absence from the village simply did not figure into the tourism plans from the perspective of tour agencies and local government officials. By late May 2007, Qin told me that she was thinking about quitting her job in Kaili and moving back to the village, but her boss wanted her to stay and offered her a raise of somewhere between ¥300 and ¥500, on top of her ¥800 monthly salary, meals, and housing. The village women begged her to return, she added, saying they needed her to be a tour guide and to resume her services as the village clinician. Some women in the village had said, "Don't leave, we need you for shots, and for tourism; we'll tie you up and not let you go," Qin recalled, laughing.

After this conversation with Qin, I realized that for the residents of

Upper Jidao, their mobility was defeating their tourism. The increased ability, and desire, among residents to leave was a problem in sustaining village tourism. To be fair, both Qin and Teacher Pan had gained their abilities to do the work of tourism through their extensive experiences outside of the village. They both had "seen the world." But now, if they weren't "there" in the village, the ability of the entire village to do tourism suffered because the current arrangements depended heavily upon just a few individuals. If Teacher Pan was in Guiyang at a conference, Qin in Kaili at her job, Fu (the village subcommittee leader in 2007) in the township at a government meeting, who was left to do tourism? When tour guides wanted to bring groups to the village or government officials were showing off the village as a successful demonstration project to visiting delegates and consultants, they would contact Teacher Pan a day or two in advance to arrange their visit. This advance notice was more convenient for both the village residents and the visitors; Teacher Pan would organize a few people to be prepared on the given day (such as Qin to guide the tourists, a few women to wear Miao festival dress, and perhaps a meal to be served in someone's home), and the visitors could then be certain of having a more satisfying experience in the village through an encounter with local hosts. As was implied by the tour guide who threatened to not bring a group if Qin could not guide them, only certain individuals within the village were considered suitable for certain tasks. Neither Qin nor Teacher Pan wanted to disappoint the tourists, the guides, or the other village residents, who in turn accepted these separate roles as the status quo. In the way that these arrangements were made, the expectation was that rural villagers were simply always "there." All of the programs and plans for tourism development rested on a fundamental assumption of rural immobility; Teacher Pan, Fu, and Qin were never expected to actually *go* anywhere.

If it was difficult to find the right people in Upper Jidao, it was nearly impossible to find a few days during which the entire tourism association was available for a trip to Ping'an. I hadn't expected such scheduling conflicts, and I humbly realized that I also attributed immobility to the village residents by assuming that it would be fairly straightforward for them to find time for the trip. Fu and I traded dates constantly. Fu was often at local government meetings or in other villages installing satellite dishes and telephone lines for his day job with China Telecom. Teacher

Pan frequently was called to meetings with the tourism bureau in Kaili or Guiyang. Qin had not yet decided if she would stay in Kaili or return to the village and kept to her scheduled work hours in the office. By mid-June, we still had not settled on a date. In a state of minor desperation, I called everyone I knew from Upper Jidao on June 19 and suggested meeting in Ping'an in two days. I left messages for Fu and Teacher Pan; in the evening, Fu returned my call and said he would check the dates with the others. Teacher Pan said that he and Qin needed to be in Guiyang by June 24 for a meeting with the NGO but otherwise were free. If the others could come, it would be a short two-day trip to Ping'an.

On the morning of June 20, Fu called and confirmed that everyone would be able to make it. There were a few more people than expected, he said—about eleven instead of six or seven. Was that okay? I agreed, knowing that the question was more of a statement anyway. Fu sent a text message to me around 8:30 A.M. on the morning of June 21; they were on their way, having left Upper Jidao by hired van at 6 A.M. I exchanged multiple text messages with Fu and with the supervisor at the scenic area management company to arrange for the group's entry to the region. I began making arrangements for rooms in the guesthouse where I stayed, for dinner that evening with the guesthouse family, and for another dinner the following evening with a few members of the Ping'an village committee. The people I spoke with about joining the Upper Jidao Tourism Association for a meal were all individuals who knew about my research; I envisioned a few interesting conversations between the groups. What I had perhaps not wanted to admit to myself was that the people from either village might not be that interested in talking to each other.

The group from Upper Jidao arrived around 8:30 P.M. on June 21, exhausted from their fourteen-hour drive across two provincial borders (having taken a wrong turn into Hunan), with little luggage but two *lusheng*. As we walked up the dark path from the parking lot to the guesthouse, Jian, the father of the family who owned the place and whom I knew quite well, declined to join us for dinner, saying he had been invited elsewhere. Jian's sons showed the group their rooms, and we proceeded to dinner in the small restaurant run by the family a few steps away. Disappointed at Jian's absence and my failure to make more of an effort to include him, I concentrated on the meal, which did not impress the visitors from Upper Jidao. The chicken hotpot and bamboo chicken weren't very flavorful, Qin confessed, and the "wild vegetables" (*yecai*), promoted as a local specialty in Ping'an, was what they fed to pigs (*zhucao*) in Upper Jidao, she whispered.[3] The men found the local liquor, distilled from sweet potatoes, to be far too weak for their taste and asked to buy a few bottles of commercial Erguotou (a common brand of liquor) instead.

Su, the girlfriend of Jian's eldest son, had prepared the meal and stayed to chat. When I asked her where the rest of the family was, she said perhaps they felt too embarrassed, or simply out of place, to join. Jian's two sons did appear as the meal ended, and I tried to direct Teacher Pan's and Fu's questions about Ping'an to them. Qin asked me how much a meal like this cost, and I replied around ¥200. Shocked, Qin said she couldn't imagine a meal like this costing that much. In Upper Jidao, she mused, for ¥200 you would be served chicken, homemade sausage, smoked pork, fish if available, scrambled eggs, plus cabbage and spinach. Rice and liquor were also included, she added, not charged separately like in Ping'an. Later, Qin and Teacher Pan asked Su about the souvenirs she sold at the side of the restaurant. The various training programs and meetings held in Guizhou about rural tourism always emphasized the importance of selling handmade, locally crafted items. Teacher Pan asked Su if the things she sold were handmade. She replied, evasively, that some were, but some were not. It was nice to have handmade products to display, Su continued, but they were harder to sell because handmade goods were too expensive for most tourists—a problem that Upper Jidao had also encountered.[4]

Before turning in for the night, I chatted with Qin about her first impressions of Ping'an. She was a bit disappointed, she admitted. Here, Qin said, they "really know how to make money" (*hen hui zhuan qian*). Besides the overpriced food, she explained, the bathrooms in this particular guesthouse lacked sinks or buckets for collecting water, the water from the tap was a bit musty, although the price of the room (about ¥20 per person) seemed fair to her. I tried to explain that this was a more basic family-owned guesthouse; tomorrow we would walk past some of the higher-end, more modern hotels. I asked Fu for his opinion of Ping'an thus far, and he said what I had surmised. The food was passable (*mama huhu*) but not great, and the portions were quite small. The weakness of the alcohol, however, he realized was a good thing—it meant that more people might be willing to try it, especially the sweet rice wine, because it wasn't so potent. Since the businesses here charged for alcohol separately, he reasoned, the more people who drank, and the more they drank, the more money a restaurant could make from selling it.

THE ECONOMICS OF BEING ETHNIC

The next day started promptly. By 7 A.M., everyone was awake and ready for breakfast. Su had also gotten up early to prepare breakfast for the group: stir-fried rice noodles and oil tea, a concoction of green tea leaves stir-fried in oil, then steeped in water and poured over puffed rice. Fu offered to cook the rice noodles, partly I suspected because of his dissatisfaction with the food from the previous night but also because of his own personal interest in cooking. No one from Upper Jidao had ever tasted oil tea before, a dish commonly advertised in the village as a local specialty, and the verdict was not positive. Reluctant to offend Su, their hosts, and me, the men spoke in Miao to each other. When I asked directly what they thought of it, Teacher Pan hesitantly answered: "They say the tea is too bitter."

After breakfast, we headed off toward viewpoint 2 to see the landscape known as Seven Stars and Moon. The morning was already clear and sunny, indicating a very hot afternoon to come. As we walked through the village, we passed the guesthouse where I'd arranged for dinner that evening. It was the home of an extended family whom I'd gotten to know quite well, and who were related to the women's representative of the Ping'an village committee. I confirmed with them that a few members of the village committee, including perhaps the village leader, would join us for dinner. I added that the group from Upper Jidao had brought along two *lusheng* and might even be willing to perform, in hopes of increasing the village committee's motivation to stop by. Other villagers in Ping'an had seen the *lusheng* the previous night, and throughout the day many people stopped to ask if the group from Upper Jidao would give a performance. I replied it was up to them; a performance was not scheduled into the visit, but they must have decided to bring the instruments along for a reason.

While we walked, Teacher Pan and Fu paid close attention to the houses and architecture in Ping'an, finding the general "look" of the village acceptable. Qin pointed out that there was less visible concrete in Ping'an than in some of the other tourist villages near Upper Jidao, and we examined the ways in which the concrete hotels were covered in wooden planks. She added that as they'd driven into the area yesterday afternoon, she had not thought much of the villages they passed on the road because they looked shabby and not particularly attractive, so she was impressed by how big and modern the hotels in Ping'an were. Then she mentioned that she was no longer going to Guiyang for the NGO meeting right after this trip; instead, Teacher Pan and Fu had enrolled Qin in a two-week-long training program for tour guides in Kaili organized by the prefectural government, which was taking place at the same time.

When we reached the photo booth, where the minority models I knew worked, we paused for a bit to admire the terraced fields and take pictures. The models were getting dressed and made up for the day, and when Qin realized what they were there for, she asked them if they didn't feel embarrassed (*buhao yisi*) when charging tourists to pose with them for photographs. The models replied by asking, rhetorically, how anyone could possibly feel embarrassed by *work*. Qin marveled to me at how openly commercialized tourism work in Ping'an really was. She said to the models that she should learn how to make money when photographed, since tour guides frequently asked her to pose. Once, she recalled, a tour guide had come to Upper Jidao with a group and asked her to put on Miao festival attire so the tourists could take pictures. The guide offered to pay, but Qin was quite busy that day and didn't really want to do it—however, she felt obligated and agreed anyway. Afterward, Qin said, the guide handed her ¥10, which she felt was so little for the amount of effort and time she'd expended that she didn't want the money after all.

Realizing that Qin and the others from Upper Jidao were ethnically Miao, Yuan, the model who wore a stylized Miao costume, asked Qin questions about Miao customs. Yuan wanted more information so that she could give better descriptions of Miao culture to tourists who asked her questions. Qin animatedly began describing traditional festivals, such as Miao New Year, and styles of dress as I had heard her do before for tourists in Upper Jidao. If Qin felt any sense of surprise by the fact that she was describing her own cultural traditions to a non-Miao woman whose job it was to pose in a stylized Miao costume, she did not express it. In fact, I realized while listening to Qin describe being Miao to these models that truly there was nothing special at all about looking, posing, or appearing to be ethnic in this configuration of tourism, ethnicity, and economy. Qin was learning from the models how to better commercialize her work in tourism, as the models learned from her how to be more ethnic.

The rest of the group milled around the photo booth area, and the owners of the booth were quick to suggest that we take a group photograph with the models. Teacher Pan and Fu hesitated, and I offered to buy photographs for each member of the group as a souvenir (figure C.1). Afterward, some of the men decided to pose individually with a few of the models as well. I watched as the residents of Upper Jidao became tourists—sightseeing, enjoying the view, taking pictures, and joking with each other about their pictures. Fu had borrowed a digital camera from his brother for the trip, and Teacher Pan had brought along a point-and-shoot film camera I'd given him early on in my fieldwork as a thank-you present.

Once our photos were taken, we continued on to the top of viewpoint 2, where Fu and Teacher Pan glanced at the range of souvenirs for sale (postcards, photo books, key rings, snacks, and other trinkets), before leading the group along the path connecting viewpoints 1 and 2. The path wound between and above the terraced fields, and Qin commented this kind of walking through fields must be what tourism consultants meant by "real" ecological tourism (*shengtai lüyou*). In Upper Jidao, the local government tourism bureau, with funding from the province, had erected a few wooden signs that read, in English and Chinese, "Ecological Path" (*shengtai budao*) along the farmer paths above the village to encourage tourists to explore the hillsides. There had also been talk of creating walking trails between all seven villages in the Bala River tourism zone, and by 2012 one path between Nanhua and Lower Jidao was nearly complete. For Qin, this walk in the fields around Ping'an village was her first real experience of what constituted an "ecological" tourist activity.

Before long, a group of Yao women from the nearby village of Zhongliu passed us; they were on their way to Ping'an for the day. When I explained that these women had walked about an hour and half to get to Ping'an, Qin asked, "Why do they come here?" I could only reply, "To make money." Teacher Pan, Fu, and the others reached viewpoint 1 first and waited there for Qin and me to catch up. As it was close to 11 A.M., when the majority of tourists on day tours from Guilin typically arrive in Ping'an, a number of other Yao women were also at viewpoint 1 waiting for tourists. They recognized me and suggested that I pay for a performance for my friends; they would unravel their long hair and sing a few traditional folk songs, they

龙脊梯田留影

桂林留念

2007.06.22

七星伴月

FIGURE C.1. During their visit to Ping'an, members of the Upper Jidao Tourism Association pose for a souvenir photo with the models and the author (2007). The Chinese text on the right reads, "Longji Terraced Fields Souvenir Photo," and in the box, "Guilin Souvenir." At the bottom it reads, "Seven Stars with Moon." Courtesy of the author.

said. I agreed after negotiating on the price. The women lined up in a row and began explaining how the Yao valued long hair on women, cutting it only once as a woman approaches marriage (around eighteen, these women said) and often keeping it covered until marriage. I wondered how interesting this was to the group from Upper Jidao, where women also typically kept long hair and would also wind it up into a topknot for special occasions (though, of course, the types and styles of head coverings, as well as the techniques for securing the hair, were different). But a show was a show, and the Yao women's performance was punctuated by the Upper Jidao group, as individual men posed for pictures behind the Yao women (figure C.2).

When the Yao women began to sing traditional folk songs (*shan ge*, literally "mountain songs"), some of the men from Upper Jidao lined up opposite them and responded to the Yao songs with their own Miao ones. Call-and-response singing (*dui ge*) is frequently attributed to traditional

FIGURE C.2. Members of the Upper Jidao Tourism Association pose for a photograph with Yao women who come to Ping'an daily from the neighboring village of Zhongliu (2007). Photo by the author.

ethnic minority courtship practices in southwestern China, and it is commonly performed in ethnic shows and films. Part of the preparations for tourism in Upper Jidao included organizing groups of men and women to practice and perform call-and-response singing for tourists in the forms of courtship songs (*qing ge*) and "ancient songs" (*gu ge*). It was a moment of parallel ethnic forms meeting face to face. Both the Yao women and the Miao men knew that such songs were evoked in the mainstream media as representative parts of their own traditional practices; they knew how the performance of these songs was valued in tourist experiences; and they knew that they were each singing in languages and styles unfamiliar to the other (figure C.3). Nevertheless, "being ethnic" in this touristic context became a total sensory experience for everyone involved—"ethnicity" here was entertaining and deeply personal, as each group drew upon its own practices and skills to participate in the encounter.

As we chatted with each other at viewpoint 1, the men from Upper

FIGURE C.3. Men from Upper Jidao sing in response to the Yao women's song (2007). Photo by the author.

Jidao jokingly referenced familiar storylines of love and sex in their conversations with the Yao women—from winking at the notion of women not being allowed to "show their hair" to asking if Yao young men were allowed to "visit" young women at home, in an allusion to another well-known ethnic stereotype of "free" love among some minorities in China, such as the Mosuo, or Na, of Yunnan (Walsh 2001 and 2005). The joviality from both sides was reminiscent of the "sweet talk" of the models. But unlike the models whose interactions with tourists are decidedly, and deliberately, unbalanced and unequal, in this instance I wondered if the performances of the Yao women and of the Miao men somehow could cancel out the staged nature of their encounter. These men seemed quite pleased to be able to contribute something to the performance, just as they had perhaps thought that they could do by bringing a few *lusheng* with them to Ping'an. They were not simply performing ethnicity but in fact anticipating and planning ahead for how they could, and would, be ethnic in Ping'an. Singing with the Yao women and carrying two *lusheng* in case they might perform were ways for the group from Upper Jidao to be a part of the economy of being ethnic in tourism, whether it was in their home village or another tourism destination.

It was past noon when we returned to the village, and I went with Fu to find a place that could prepare lunch for us. I wanted to eat somewhere run by another local, Ping'an family, but because I hadn't arranged anything in advance, the guesthouse we ended up at was overwhelmed by our order to feed eleven people. It was a long and tedious wait lasting well over an hour. We sat down to eat shortly after 2 P.M., with Fu and the others frustrated from hunger but also cognizant of the amount of work required to feed a group of hungry tourists. Qin and I discussed why prices for food surprised her—costs were high here due to overhead (such as having a space large enough for a restaurant and purchasing furniture, dishes, and disposable chopsticks). Combined with relatively low volume per household (most family guesthouses, I explained, served at most one or two groups of tourists a day), the simple reality was that for the residents of Ping'an, tourism was difficult to manage and sustain at a household level. It wasn't worth it to keep a lot of fresh food on hand, if you weren't certain you would have tourists on any given day. As a result, if a group of tourists did arrive (as we did on this day), it was difficult to prepare everything in a reasonable amount of time. During lunch and dinner time, guesthouse owners often ran to their neighbors to borrow (or buy) food to serve to guests—an extra pot of rice, a chicken, tofu, or even just some vegetables. Some families had begun making and selling bamboo rice for other restaurants in the village. The constant uncertainty, as well as the ebb and flow of tourists, reinforced for Qin what she knew already: it would be nearly impossible to hold a salaried job and run a tourism-related business or, in her case, to always be available as a tour guide. In Ping'an, the prices are higher than in Upper Jidao, I continued, because here they calculated the cost of the materials and their time into the amounts. In Upper Jidao, the cost of the food and beverages consumed by tourists thus far was seen as relatively minor and insignificant because in Upper Jidao they generally only served what foods they had available in the village. Guesthouses and restaurants in Ping'an, however, regularly purchased meat and vegetables, and by 2012 a number of small shops in the village sold foods brought in from wholesale markets in Longsheng and Guilin, to provide a greater variety of dishes to tourists.

The food at lunch was disappointing again, and I wondered if the Upper Jidao group would leave thinking that the food in Ping'an was simply inedible. I suggested, half-heartedly, that perhaps we should wander around the village a bit more, but the heat and the early start left us all feeling sluggish and unmotivated. We returned to our guesthouse to rest, and around 5:30 P.M., three of the models came over to drop off the printed, laminated group photographs we'd taken earlier that morning. They asked to see Miao clothes, some of which Qin had brought with her. The models' keen interest in learning more about Miao culture was contagious. For them, knowing more about the people represented by the ethnic costumes they wore would be good for their business, which, after all, relied on sweet talk and being able to be what tourists saw. For the group from Upper Jidao, the models' interest in Miao cultural traditions reinforced their confidence in being interesting and desirable for tourism.

Qin described the Miao New Year festival, explaining how the women sew silver adornments onto the fabric of the jackets worn as a part of the festival attire, men play *lusheng*, and the whole village gathers to dance during the three days of celebration. Without missing a beat, the men who had brought *lusheng* to Ping'an and who were known as talented *lusheng* musicians pushed aside the table they were using to play cards and proceeded to demonstrate *lusheng* dancing. Their transformation was astonishing: they went from quietly smoking and playing cards to being light-on-their-feet *lusheng* musicians and dancers. The second floor of the guesthouse became a stage as the men played and the models tried to emulate their footwork (figure C.4).

The piercing sound of the *lusheng* drew Jian's sons upstairs. One of Jian's sons began explaining construction techniques to Fu, who asked how the guesthouses were built to accommodate so many guestrooms upstairs. The son said that the actual frame of the house was altered to allow for additional walls and rooms to be built on the upper floor. Fu wanted to learn more about architecture and construction because two of the biggest projects happening in Upper Jidao at the time included a cultural center that would also provide some office space, as well as renewed plans to build a hotel in the village (which ultimately was not completed), supported by funds obtained from the China National Tourism Administration (CNTA) by the former director of the Guizhou Tourism Bureau. They discussed the high cost of such materials as wood, furniture, and

FIGURE C.4. *Lusheng* musicians from Upper
Jidao perform in a guesthouse in Ping'an
(2007). Photo by the author.

bedding for guestrooms. When it was time for dinner, I reminded the
group that we were eating with some of the local leadership from Ping'an.
Before dinner, Qin decided to change into her Miao clothes and put her
hair up in a topknot with a flower. Then we trooped off to the other guesthouse where I had arranged for the meal.

"WHERE ARE YOU?"

Earlier that afternoon, I had gone to replace my order of "wild vegetables"
at dinner with cabbage and other greens, having seen the reaction of the
Upper Jidao group to the dish the previous night. When we arrived for
dinner, three tables were set and the food nearly ready; this particular
family frequently took in large tour groups and ran a very well-organized
operation.[5] But the only people present were the guesthouse family members. Seeing the women's representative from the village committee, I
asked her where the other committee members were—perhaps they were

on their way? She replied, half-apologetically but in a matter-of-fact tone, that they were not coming; she would represent the entire committee. Disappointed, I pressed her for a reason, thinking that I could still go out and personally ask individual committee members to come over, even just for a short while. She responded in vague terms that the committee was dining with the management company. I offered to wait, if they were finishing up a meeting, and finally she stated in no uncertain terms that no one else was coming. They weren't going to have dinner here, nor were they going to stop by later to meet the group from Upper Jidao; they had other plans, she said. It wasn't necessarily to be interpreted as a deliberate slight to me or the Upper Jidao group, but more so the simple fact that when it came to priorities for the Ping'an village leadership, the tourism association from Upper Jidao and I were less important than the scenic area's management company. Embarrassed, I told Teacher Pan and Fu that the committee members would not be joining us. Since there was plenty of food, I invited the family running the guesthouse as well as the restaurant entrepreneur from Henan, who leased the lower floor of the house and ran a large restaurant there, to join us.

Despite my own frustrations, the conversation between the Upper Jidao group and the guesthouse owners was lively and spirited. Everyone toasted each other's success in tourism and talked about how to make tourism work in a village. Fu was particularly enthusiastic, first because the food was finally to his liking but also because the atmosphere was talkative and engaged. Toward the end of the meal, Teacher Pan's cell phone rang, and he answered—it was someone from the Kaili Tourism Bureau calling to make sure that the tourism association would be back in Upper Jidao tomorrow. After he hung up, Teacher Pan said that an official from the bureau had called in the afternoon as well and had been shocked to learn that no one, or more specifically no one from the tourism association, was in Upper Jidao. Everyone was here in Ping'an.

The tourism bureau planned to bring a group of Japanese tourism consultants to a number of demonstration villages tomorrow and had called Teacher Pan in the afternoon as a courtesy to tell him to be prepared for their arrival the following day. Fu interrupted Teacher Pan, chuckling, and said that the conversation Teacher Pan had had was farcical. "Where are you?" the official had asked Teacher Pan. Teacher Pan had replied, "I'm in Guangxi." "What about Fu?" they had asked. "He's also in

Guangxi." "What about Qin?" the official had countered. "She's here with us too," Teacher Pan had responded. Fu doubled over with laughter as he exclaimed: "Every single village leader [from Upper Jidao] is out of the village right now!" The tourism bureau of Kaili did not find this at all amusing and demanded that they, the villagers, figure out a solution. Teacher Pan had no choice but to promise to be in Upper Jidao by the evening of the next day to meet the consultants. It meant that they would have a very early start to their long journey back tomorrow.

Most of the group from Upper Jidao returned to our guesthouse after they finished eating; only Teacher Pan, Fu, Qin, and I stayed behind. When the others had left, Fu turned to me and said that some of the others from the tourism association "didn't know how to ask questions" as he put it, but the experience of being here in Ping'an was still good for them, even if they were quiet and kept to themselves. Fu knew I was disappointed at the lack of interaction between the group from Upper Jidao and residents in Ping'an, and he was trying to reassure me of the trip's overall value to them. We eventually headed back to our rooms, where we talked briefly with Jian's family. Qin wanted to purchase some souvenirs and asked Su to show her what was available. Fu and I settled up payments and receipts; because I'd paid for the meals and rooms in Ping'an, I gave him what he owed the driver, as well as money for meals on the road. When I went to bed, exhausted, the men were playing cards and smoking.

Everyone woke up early the next morning, and by 6 A.M. the group was at the parking lot, getting settled into the van for the long drive back to Upper Jidao. Qin called me a few days later to say that the tour guide training program in Kaili was going well and that many of the instructors had also visited Ping'an before, so they had a lot to talk about. She had so many questions to ask now that she had experienced what tourism was like in Ping'an, she said. The trainees would take a certification exam in two weeks, and afterward she wanted to teach some of the other women in Upper Jidao how to be guides.

THE TOURISM LEARNING CURVE

The abrupt end to Upper Jidao's study tour in Ping'an was, in retrospect, quite fitting to the circumstances faced by the tourism association in 2007. They were *busy*—busy attending meetings about tourism, busy working out plans and budgets for tourism, busy being trained and taught about tourism, and busy demonstrating to government officials and policy makers how the village residents were doing tourism. Qin's enthusiasm for the tour guide training program in Kaili partially reassured me that the trip hadn't been a total waste of time and effort for the eleven people who had ridden in a van for nearly twenty-five hours to visit Ping'an for just thirty-six hours. Nevertheless, I wondered what they had learned, and I worried that the people in Ping'an would consider the whole thing no more, and no less, than any other group of tourists stopping by to take a photograph of the terraces and eat a meal or two.

After all, could doing tourism really be learned? What would one study if one wanted to study how to do tourism? Qin had honed in on the pricing mechanisms at work in Ping'an—on how every single item or service was calculated in terms of costs and benefits. Fu wanted to learn how to build guesthouses that still resembled "wooden houses" but could accommodate more rooms. But, somehow, their hurried departure from Ping'an left me feeling unconvinced that learning all of these things could make tourism work in Upper Jidao. Surely, I thought, what Upper Jidao needed was more basic infrastructure, such as a sewage system, hot water heaters, and a bridge structurally sound enough to hold the weight of a tour bus. My skepticism nagged at me. Learning how to price souvenir handicrafts they didn't have, build rooms for tourists who didn't stay the night, or prepare for meetings with consultants who didn't know what life was like in the village could hardly be useful at this point.

However, from the conversations I had with Qin, Teacher Pan, and Fu after the study tour, I understood that what stayed with them about their trip to Ping'an was the experience of seeing people do tourism in ways that were somewhat different from what they had been told about and practiced in Upper Jidao. Many aspects of tourism that had been planned for Upper Jidao existed in Ping'an, such as posing for photographs, performances, and preparing meals. That said, everything in Ping'an differed slightly from what Upper Jidao was expecting. People in Ping'an didn't work together as a village; rather, it was each family, and each business owner, for themselves. Qin's attention to the differences between what she experienced in a tourism village like Ping'an and what she expected from tourism in Upper Jidao made me aware of the fact that tourism was no longer just something that happened when tourists arrived; instead, it was something to be *actively* created and constructed. Thus, my study of Upper Jidao and Ping'an has focused the various ways in which tourism is done and understood—from individual stories of migration and return, to the efforts expended on making a village "look good," to the unintended conflicts that arise throughout the process. All these are happening during a moment in contemporary, postreform China in which ethnic differences are continually made over as reassuringly familiar forms, leisure and travel are considered a part of raising the quality of the Chinese people, and rural development is envisaged as a critical component of the nation's future.

As the study tour made clear, tourism is a messy business—for Upper Jidao and Ping'an, their tourisms fundamentally rested upon a commonly assumed structure of urban mobility and rural immobility. When the entire tourism association for Upper Jidao was away, they were told to hurry back to be there for the visitors, who wanted to have a full experience of "being there" in the village with villagers. Rural ethnic tourism thusly conceived could not function if rural people continued to be mobile; that was why, from the national and provincial governments' perspectives, tourism was intended to increase wage-earning opportunities in rural villages so that rural people would stop leaving their home villages. In this kind of tourism, mobility depended upon immobility; having tourists travel to a village meant village residents could not, or should not, travel away. But in this formula lay an inherent contradiction, because as these villages modernized and developed along the lines espoused by the state, the residents found and desired more chances to travel. Mobility was ordered by these opportunities and logics, and it was through these imagined possibilities of who could and could not travel, and for what reasons, that certain structures of belonging and opportunity took shape and were made meaningful.

When examining the constituent parts of tourism, it is crucial to understand that for the residents of these villages, their experiences in the mainstream economies of tourism reach beyond the momentary encounter with tourists to encompass learning how to be distinctly modern as rural and ethnic subjects in contemporary China. This was a part of their own experiences in travel, their mobility in other words, but also their engagement with the visual practices of tourism. Visuality becomes not only learning how to recognize what "looks good" but also a process of determining the limits and range of the value of ethnicity and identity. When ethnic identities are literally worn on one's sleeve, it is vital to take seriously the process by which visual knowledge is communicated and translated into ideas, stereotypes, and expectations. New configurations of belonging emerge when ethnicity is mainstreamed into familiar types that are easily reproducible in tourism marketing and promotions. New senses of cultural ownership and pride may come to shape new ways of being, and looking, ethnic. More critical ethnography needs to be done on the efficacy of the visual and the politics of appearance in preempting, prompting, and promoting social change. An analytical focus on mobility and visuality thus unravels the tangled knot of economic imperatives, social aspirations, and cultural celebrations of ethnic tourism that is implicated in the lives and livelihoods of rural ethnic minority Chinese villagers.

Indeed, village residents made tourism meaningful to themselves because of its potential to transform their everyday, ordinary lives and livelihoods. In 2012, tourism in Ping'an was as strong as ever, to the point where more and more local families were leasing out their guesthouses and restaurants to outside entrepreneurs or building bigger, more modern hotels. The building boom was partly the result of a county-level directive to build a series of concrete houses throughout the village as a means of fire prevention, in response to a fire that had broken out in the center of the village in September 2010.[6] Fortunately, that fire caused no injuries to people, but it was enough to convince villagers and the county government that something had to be done. The density of buildings in Ping'an, coupled with increasing use of and demand for hot water, electricity, and propane (for cooking and on-demand hot water), meant that the risk of another fire was extremely high. The county sketched a plan to take down a number of older wooden houses in the center of the village, to be replaced with concrete ones, and provided some financial support to families to complete these constructions. The family I always lived with in the village was one such household who received some financial assistance. With the support, they finished five new en suite guestrooms on the bottom level of a large concrete structure, and I was the first guest to stay overnight. Amusingly, the rest of the building was unfinished; the rooms were on the first level, above which was a tile and concrete area used as a restaurant. Although a third story had been built (providing a ceiling for the restaurant), the top level was entirely exposed, without walls or a roof. But the family had invested so much money in their new building that they had to continue serving meals and offering rooms to tourists in the unfinished building in hopes of saving enough to complete the top floor. Car ownership, which was practically nonexistent during the early 2000s, was now common in 2012, and for the first time, instead of waiting for the public bus, I negotiated a ride with a local family when I needed to leave the village.

In Upper Jidao, the village was again under construction in 2012, but this time with funds from the World Bank project. Tensions between Upper Jidao and Lower Jidao had been somewhat overshadowed by other uneasy situations within Upper Jidao: through a private donor, money and furnishings had been provided to two households in the village to build guestrooms. Qin's new house was thus designed to suit her dual roles in the village, as clinician and tour guide. The ground floor was given over to her clinic, with a separate room for storing medicines, a computer and printer for keeping track of village residents' cooperative health insurance dues and benefits, and a third room intended as an examination room. The middle level was her living space, with the kitchen, living room, a modern bathroom with indoor plumbing and hot water, and bedrooms. The top floor featured six double rooms, plus a large bathroom with a flushing toilet and shower stall. In 2011 she began hosting overnight tourists, many of whom were American students introduced to Upper Jidao through Zhang Xiaosong, who had coordinated many of the early efforts to develop tourism throughout rural Guizhou and was now based at Guizhou Normal University. Qin's home was even more frequently visited by an ever expanding network of friends and relatives—often friends of friends or colleagues of friends of friends from Kaili—who had heard that she was now running a *nong jia le* and who would, Qin complained, simply show up on short notice and expect to be treated to a meal. When I asked if they paid, as tourists at a *nong jia le* are expected to do, she simply sighed and said she wouldn't feel right asking friends to pay.

The other family who received money to build guestrooms in their house worked much more slowly and had yet to complete their rooms in mid-2012. It took time, they said, and they had to do all of the construction work themselves. There were a number of personal and communal concerns and disputes circulating in the background—from envy at the relative success of Qin's guestrooms (and the money that she was presumed to be making from hosting foreign tourists) to exasperation over the overall lack of tourists coming to the village (and thus the reluctance of some villagers to *do more tourism*) to the pressing, quotidian need for sources of income. Although community participation was lauded as a key component of the development programs since 2002, many village residents were averse to investing their time and labor into something that did not necessarily address their immediate economic and family situations. Tourism had noticeably waned in recent years, with the redevelopment of Xijiang nearby, and many of the village leadership I knew in 2007 had left Upper Jidao or stopped doing tourism by 2012. Fu now lived in Kaili, selling construction materials, Fa, who had been involved with tourism in the mid-2000s after he returned to the village, was busy growing and selling vegetables for local markets, and Teacher Pan had stepped out of tourism work entirely. Nevertheless, the World Bank project was pushed forward, funding continued to arrive, and village paths were dug up to lay pipes for a more integrated sewage system, a new parking lot was under construction by the riverside, and computer-generated images circulated of the new fanciful wooden decorative coverings that each house would receive to make the village look even better for tourists.[7]

In sum, this ethnography of Ping'an and Upper Jidao villages is a study of the learning curve of tourism, in which the end goal of tourism is to construct not only a better place to tour but also, and more important, a better place to *live*. This objective aligns with the discourses of economic development and poverty alleviation espoused in tourism plans promoted by local, provincial, and national governments, international agencies, and academics alike. But in practice, from the perspective of village residents, tourism has been about much more than just economic development. Their understandings of tourism reached deeply into their senses of belonging and opportunity, and in turn, it was through tourism that these communities found ways of asserting, and contesting, their place in contemporary China. I have argued for the necessity of situating tourism within the complex of relationships imaginable and possible in China today—what I call a landscape of travel. Entangled in tourism are intricate interdependencies between ethnicity, imagery, economy, and travel that shape contemporary rural social lives and livelihoods. It is precisely this complicated mess of obligations, relations, and expectations that rendered the study trip to Ping'an somewhat disappointing, yet ultimately revealing, to me. I had hoped that the group from Upper Jidao could simply learn by experiencing tourism in Ping'an, but I realized that this was to be a long process of learning by doing.

The work of tourism in villages such as Ping'an and Upper Jidao is clearly not yet done. Future research must contend with the social effects and consequences of tourism policies, especially in terms of village resident grievances. Only by breaking apart the host-guest divide in tourism theory and acknowledging that the relationship between the tourist and the toured may be only one of many relationships affecting destination communities, does an ethnography of touristed villages like Ping'an and Upper Jidao contribute to a more contextually rich and theoretically sophisticated understanding of these places where travel is both labor and leisure.

GLOSSARY OF CHINESE CHARACTERS

a'mei 阿妹
a'ge 阿哥

bainian guwu 百年古屋
bainian liangcang 百年粮仓

chengshi hua 城市化
cunweiyuan hui 村委员会

dagong 打工
duanwu jie 端午节
dui ge 对歌

fei nongye 非农业
fen jia 分家
fengjing 风景
fengyu qiao 风雨桥

gaige kaifang 改革开放
gao lüyou 搞旅游
geti hu 个体户

gu ge 古歌
Guizhou sheng (Guizhou province)
    贵州省
Guangxi Zhuangzu Zizhi Qu (Guangxi
    Zhuang Autonomous Region)
    广西壮族自治区
guanjing qu 观景区
guanjing tai 观景台
Guilin Longji Titian Jingqu
    桂林龙脊梯田景区
Guilinhua 桂林话

hexie shehui 和谐社会
Huangluo Yao zhai 黄洛瑶寨
hukou 户口

jianshe shehui zhuyi xin nongcun
    建设社会主义新农村
jian shi mian 见世面
Jidao Miao zhai 季刀苗寨
Jidao Shangzhai 季刀上寨

jie dai shi 接待室

Jinkeng Hong Yao Titian Guanjingqu
   金坑红瑶梯田观景区

jingqu 景区

jingdian 景点

jingji tounao 经济头脑

Jiu Long Wu Hu 九龙五虎

jiujiu 鬏鬏

Kailihua 凯利话

kexue fazhan 科学发展

la ke 拉客

laoban 老板

Longji Gu Zhuang Titian
   Wenhua Guanjingqu
   龙脊古壮梯田文化观景区

lusheng 芦笙

lüyou xiehui 旅游协会

Miao jia le 苗家乐

Miao yifu 苗衣服

minsu 民俗

minzu fengge 民族风格

minzu shibie 民族识别

minzu zhuyi 民族主义

nong jia le 农家乐

nongcun 农村

nongmin 农民

nongmin gong 农民工

nongye 农业

Ping'an zhai 平安寨

Ping'an Zhuangzu Titian Guanjingqu
   平安壮族梯田观景区

putonghua 普通话

Qi Xing Ban Yue 七星伴月

Qiandongnan Miaozu Dongzu Zizhi
   Zhou (Qiandongnan Miao and
   Dong Autonomous Prefecture)
   黔东南苗族侗族自治州

qing ge 情歌

qingming jie 清明节

renkou suzhi 人口素质

san nong wenti 三农问题

shan ge 山歌

shaoshu minzu 少数民族

shengtai bowuguan 生态博物馆

shengtai budao 生态步道

shengtai lüyou 生态旅游

sheng zhuang 盛装

suantang yu 酸汤鱼

suzhi 素质

techan 特产

tese 特色

tian zui 甜嘴

tiao ge chang 跳歌场

tiao lusheng 跳芦笙

tuji 土鸡

tusheng tuzhang 土生土长

waidi ren 外地人

waimao 外貌

wenming 文明

wenming lüyou 文明旅游

xiansheng 先生

xiaozu 小组

xibu da kaifa 西部大开发

xifang 西方

Xijiang Qianhu Miaozhai
西江千户苗寨

xingzheng cun 行政村

yecai 野菜

yiwu gongzuo fuwu dui
义务工作服务队

yuan shengtai 原生态

zhaimen 寨门

zhishi qingnian 知识青年

Zhongguo xiangcun you 中国乡村游

zhongqiu jie 中秋节

zhucao 猪草

zhutong fan 竹筒饭

ziran cun 自然村

NOTES

1   Because this discussion was at the time a preliminary exploration for the Chinese publishers, I was asked not to use the company's real name.

2   Of these 1.4 billion trips, 576 million were taken by urban Chinese and 818 million by rural Chinese. Statistics for 2007 reported 1.6 billion domestic travelers, or 1.2 trips per person, of which 612 million were by urban Chinese and 998 million by rural Chinese. For more statistics on tourism in China, see tables 2.5 and 2.6 in chapter 2 of this volume.

3   I am following the English translations of names provided on a map of the scenic area, available on the website of the region's tourism management company (www.txljw.com). The full name of the region is Guilin Longji Titian Jingqu (Guilin Longji Terraced Fields Scenic Area), which I shorten to Longji Scenic Area in this book. Generally, *jingqu* can be translated as "scenic area" or, in some cases, "scenic spot." *Jingdian* is also a common term for "scenic spot" (see Nyíri 2006, 7). However, within the Longji Scenic Area there were three additional *guanjingqu* (corresponding with Ping'an, Dazhai, and Longji villages, which are translated as "spots" on the company map available at www.txljw.com/dt/dtlj/). Thus I distinguish these second-level *guanjingqu* as "scenic spots" because they are contained within the larger scenic area. Each of these three scenic spots has multiple *jingdian* (also translatable as "scenic spots" but which the official company map calls "viewpoints") within the villages. For clarity, throughout this book I refer to the larger Longji Terraced Fields as a scenic area, each village as a scenic spot, and the specific *jingdian* in each village as viewpoints.

4   Officially, the World Bank loan agreement is called the Guizhou Cultural and Natural Heritage Protection and Development Project. It was approved in 2009.

5   Much has been written on visual research methods and collaboration using pho-

tography, video, and other media (including drawing) in anthropological and social science research; the literature is too extensive to list here. For a fuller discussion of my own methods, see Chio 2011a. A few works that guided my own efforts and thinking have included Blumenfield Kedar 2010; Collier and Collier 1986; Deger 2006; Harper 2002; Jackson 2004; Lozada 2006; and Turner 1992. On the history of travel films, see Ruoff 2002 and 2006.

6 Oakes and Schein (2006, 22) go on to argue that there is a need to "push beyond the formulation of media providing the material for imagining elsewhere(s)." They point out two contemporary phenomena that demonstrate different arenas where imagining and ideas about the self are formed: in renegotiations of one's subjectivity based upon imagined geographical "scales" (provincial, regional, national identities) and the influence of translocal businesses and industries, like tourism, on self-perceptions of connectedness and networks of belonging and action.

7 Wasserstrom (2010, 122) cites Chang 2009 in making this claim; following national statistics in China, in 2003 the number of internal migrants, defined as persons not living in the place of their household registration, was 140 million (Huang and Zhan 2005). By 2008 the number of migrant workers (*nongmin gong*) was calculated at 225 million (NBS 2009).

INTRODUCTION

1 For descriptions of this government program and its policies, see the special report "Rural Development: Building a New Socialist Countryside," available online at http://english.gov.cn/special/rd_index.htm.

2 Oakes 1998 provides a comprehensive account of tourism development in Guizhou up through the mid-1990s; Donaldson 2007 compares tourism development policies recently enacted in Guizhou with those in neighboring Yunnan.

3 The scholarly literature on Chinese migration, both internal and international, is large; see, for example, Fan 2005; Huang and Zhan 2005; Xin Liu 1997; Nyíri 2005a, 2005b, and 2010; Ong 1999; Ong and Nonini 1997; Solinger 1999; Sun 2002; and L. Zhang 2001. Xin Liu 1997 and, more recently, Nyíri 2010 offer readings of migration in the context of social mobility and national desires that have greatly informed my understanding.

4 Chinese statistics on domestic tourism are based on the number of tickets sold at official tourism destinations; thus this number of 1.4 billion trips taken references the number of tickets sold (Nyíri 2010, 62). Given that the official population of China in 2004 was 1.34 billion people, this number indicates that at least some Chinese were taking repeat trips that year.

5 These statistics from 2010 were taken from the China Statistical Yearbook 2011 and reported on the website www.china.org.cn, which describes itself as "the authorized government portal site to China, China.org.cn is published under the auspices of the State Council Information Office and the China International Publishing Group (CIPG) in Beijing" (from www.china.org.cn/2009-09/28/content_18620394.htm).

6 The full text of the Universal Declaration of Human Rights by the United Nations is available online at www.un.org/en/documents/udhr/index.shtml.

7 "Landscape" plays a key analytical and conceptual role in a number of disciplines,

and my usage of the term is limited here to the ways in which it has been directly useful for understanding tourism in rural ethnic China. To that end, I have drawn on theorizations of landscape from a number of disciplines, from art history to geography. A few key works that have influenced this book include Bender 1993; Cosgrove 1984 and 2006; Hendry 1999; Hirsch and O'Hanlon 1995; Ingold 1993; Meinig 1979; Mitchell 2002; and Tilley 1994.

8   These are ethnoscapes, mediascapes, technoscapes, financescapes, and ideoscapes (see Appadurai 1996, 33).

9   On landscaping as an act of power, see Urry 2000, 80–93; see also Mitchell 2002 and Pratt 2008 [1992] on imperialism and visuality.

10 Tim Ingold's (1993) influential concept of "taskscape," which derives form and meaning through human activity, is very relevant to my analysis of doing tourism as a landscape of travel because of the focus on action and embedded relations through human movements and skills; however, in doing tourism, as is shown in later chapters, the representational power of landscape is a serious matter that is contested by tourism village residents and other stakeholders not only as activity but also as image. Therefore, the term "landscape" is still more appropriate for drawing out the specific strands of power and agency at work in this ethnographic study.

11 Martin Jay has called these ways of seeing "scopic regimes of modernity," using the example of Western European painting. His analysis of three "scopic regimes" (a term coined by Christian Metz) aims to "understand the multiple implications of sight in ways that are now only beginning to be appreciated" (Jay 1988, 4). The three models of scopic regimes that he addresses are Cartesian perspectivalism, "the art of describing" (following Alpers 1983), and the baroque. Of these three models, Jay (1988, 5) argues that it is the first, Cartesian perspectivalism, which has been regarded as "the reigning visual model of modernity . . . because it best expressed the 'natural' experience of sight valorized by the scientific world view." This combination of science, nature, and the production of visual images has proven to be ripe for theoretical inquiry. Indeed, Mitchell 1994 calls this the "pictorial turn," or the critique of the image, in academic scholarship, with its disciplinary genealogy rooted in the critical writings of Benjamin 1969, Debord 1983, and Baudrillard 1988, as just a few examples of key works that have paid attention to how images and vision are thoroughly socialized and thus socially significant (see also Crary 1990, 2001; Jay 1993; and Levin 1993 for analytical studies of vision in modern thought and the modern era).

12 In the fields of art history and visual studies, critical approaches to landscape imagery have unpacked the power relations embedded in representations of landscape; see, for example, DeLue and Elkins 2008, and Mitchell 2002.

13 Following this argument, Julia Harrison (2003) has shown through detailed, longitudinal interviews with Canadians before and after tours that tourism is not a separate sphere of experience but rather fully integrated into the passage of everyday time through anticipation and planning (before tour) and, later, storytelling and memory (after tour).

14 The latter point has been persuasively argued in Graburn with Barthel-Bouchier 2001, MacCannell 1999 [1976]) and 2001, and Urry 2002b [1990].

15 From Deborah Poole's (1997, 10) work on the meanings and movements of Andean images, I take "visual economy" to encompass the cultural systems of technolo-

gies, manufacture, and circulation "through which graphic images are appraised, interpreted, and assigned historical, scientific, and aesthetic worth." Touristic images and representations include postcards and advertisements; see Crouch and Lübbren 2003; Desmond 2001; Kahn 2011; and Selwyn 1996.

16 On a similar process in urban China, see Broudehoux 2004 and 2007 for an incisive critique of the spectacularization of architecture in Beijing before the 2008 Olympics and the relationships of this visual spectacle to regimes of power, international attention, and authoritarian control.

17 See, for example, see the *Guidelines for Landscape and Visual Impact Assessment* published by the Landscape Institute (2002).

18 "Visual effect" is defined as "change in the appearance of the landscape as a result of development. This can be positive (improvement) or negative (detraction)." Visual amenity is defined as "the value of a particular area or view in terms of what is seen" (Landscape Institute 2002, 121).

19 Roads are both symbols of and necessary components of modernization, in China and elsewhere of course. As Julie Chu (2010, 51–52) has noted of a highway built in rural Fujian, despite the fact that the construction of the road required "the loss of productive agricultural land and the major alteration of one of their [sacred] mountains," when she took a photograph of the road, a villager next to her commented on how "pretty" the road was and added that with the new, more convenient access to the city, "it won't seem so far from here to there."

1. SIMILAR, WITH MINOR DIFFERENCES

1 The Chinese phrase for "ethnic minority" is *shaoshu minzu*. The Chinese concept of *minzu* is notoriously difficult to translate, as it bears reference to both the notion of cultural nationalism in terms of a unified entity and the groups that make up a nation (and the social and cultural differences between these groups) (Harrell 2001, 38). Some scholars and official government writings on *shaoshu minzu* translate this phrase as "minority nationality," following early Chinese Communist usage taken from Soviet ideas of nationality. I acknowledge the difficulties raised by this translation, noting in particular Thomas Mullaney's discussion of the semantic work on *minzu* (2004a, 232fn1), Chris Berry (1992) (who translates *minzu* as "race"), Prasenjit Duara (1995), Stevan Harrell, ed. (1995 and 2001), and Yingjin Zhang (1997). Nowadays, the English-language website of the Central People's Government of China also refers to the different *shaoshu minzu* in China as ethnic minorities.

2 The following history of Ping'an is drawn largely from Lao's written account, as well as from other scholarly sources.

3 For a comparative study of folklore and cultural change in Ping'an and two surrounding villages, see Xu Ganli 2006.

4 On the creation of the Zhuang as a political and ethnic category in China, see Kaup 2000.

5 Administratively changing place names to reflect "local" characteristics has been a popular strategy in tourism development, particularly in Yunnan. The city of Simao was renamed "Pu'er" to promote the eponymous tea; the city of Zhongdian

was renamed "Shangri-la" as a means of increasing its visibility in tourism promotions (Hillman 2003 and Kolås 2008).

6   Some scholars translate *minzu shibie* as "nationalities classification," following the early Chinese Communist usages of Soviet ideas of "nationality" for *minzu* as drawn from writings by Joseph Stalin (Gladney 1996; Harrell 2001, 39; and Leibold 2007, 150–55). However, I believe that given current constructions of *minzu* in China today, the term "ethnic" better represents how these identities are being discussed and imagined; I am following arguments and perspectives discussed in depth in Harrell ed. 1995 and 2001, Mullaney 2004b and 2011, Mackerras 2004, Tapp 2012, and others in this move (translating *minzu* as "ethnic/ethnicity" rather than "nationality").

7   This "civilizing project" did not assume that all barbarians were equally capable of being civilized into the Chinese political and cultural center, and therefore some groups, notably in the empire's southwestern regions, "were readily divided into raw (*sheng*) and cooked (*shu*), according to whether they were cultured enough to accept moral edification and eventual civilization" (Harrell 1995, 19). Ming and Qing dynasty records even describe how the Miao as a group were divided into the "Raw Miao" and "Cooked Miao," where the latter had taken on some Chinese cultural customs and the former resisted pacification, assimilation, and state control (Diamond 1995, 100).

8   See Hostetler 2001 and Deal and Hostetler 2003.

9   For example, take the emergence of the Chinese as the "yellow race"—a term first used by Europeans but brought back to China by missionaries (Dikötter 1992, 55).

10   As James Leibold (2007, 29) has written: "The increased threat of Western imperialism following the Opium War and the ineffectiveness of the Manchu court in stemming the decline of the empire following the Taiping Rebellion created a crisis of political authority in Qing China.... This political crisis was accompanied by an epistemological shift in how difference was conceptualized in China."

11   Attention to racial differences and the representation of barbarian populations within China continued during the Republican era; William Schaefer (2003) has demonstrated how images and verbal descriptions of "the savage" and racialized otherness in short stories and illustrated magazines of the Republican era brought into question the very nature of representational forms in the conjunction of technological advances, new Chinese nationalism, and continued colonial presence. Race and ethnic otherness in China during this period developed into an amalgamation of comparative interests in defining differences between China and the West, as well as an inward turn to applying these categories to the "barbarians" within China itself.

12   During the early years of the Communist government, the policy of autonomous local government was open to any groups who self-identified and submitted their group status to the central government; the policy was called "names follows the bearer's will" (*ming cong zhu ren*, Gros 2004), which was a "stance of avowed nonintervention by the state into questions of ethnic appellations" (Mullaney 2004a, 210).

13   Mullaney 2011 provides a detailed history of the classification project in Yunnan and the extensive conceptual links between the project as it was completed and earlier classifications of ethnicity and identity from both Republican-era sources and foreign missionaries. The case of the Tai/Dai-Lue in southern Yunnan is nota-

ble in China's southwest, in that prior to the Chinese Communist classification project, there was a political structure and solidarity among the Tai/Dai-Lue that included territory now divided between China, Myanmar, Laos, and Thailand. This political structure had to contend with the process of classifying the "Dai" an ethnic minority *within* China. See Hsieh 1995 and S. Davis 2005.

14　Morgan devised his schema of the evolutionary development of human social organizations and values in his earlier research on the Iroquois (see Morgan 1962 [1851]), and it greatly influenced concepts of human social evolution theorized by Herbert Spencer (1897), as well as arguments on social class and economic modes of production put forth by Karl Marx and Friedrich Engels—namely Engels's *The Origin of the Family, Private Property, and the State* (1972 [1884]).

15　Karsten Krüger (2003) has written a comprehensive history and analysis of these films and their production, based on field research and interviews he conducted with Yang Guanghai, one of the principal producers and filmmakers in this project. The three main film studios in China at the time were the August First Film Studio, the Beijing Scientific and Educational Film Studio, and the Central Documentary and News Reel Film Studio. Of the ethnographic films produced between 1957 and 1966, the August First and Beijing Scientific and Educational Film studios played the most central role, perhaps as a result of many discussions held at the time regarding the intended purposes of creating specifically ethnographic films and the debate over the importance of authenticity in these films.

16　Through the efforts of Karsten Krüger and others, eleven of the films were remastered, translated into English, and distributed internationally first by the Institute for Media and Knowledge and later by the German National Library of Science and Technology (in Hannover) under the title "The Chinese Historical Ethnographic Film Series 1957–1966." These included *The Kawa* (1958), *The Li* (1958), *The Ewenki on the Banks of the Argun River* (1959), *The Kucong People* (1960), *The Dulong People* (1960–61), *The Serf System of the Town of Shahliq* (1960, 1962), *The Jingpo* (1960, 1962), *The Oroqen* (1963), *The Hunting and Fishing Life of the Hezhe* (1965), *The "Azhu" Marriage System of the Naxi (Moso) from Yongning* (1965), and *Naxi Art and Culture in Lijiang* (1966). See also Alexander 2005 and Chio dir. 2003.

17　Moreover, the limited distribution of these ethnic classification films begs the question of what types of films were considered appropriate for public distribution and which qualities of scientific documentary filmmaking made its products unsuitable or undesirable for a mass audience.

18　Many of these films about the struggles and livelihoods of ethnic minorities in Communist China from the 1950s and 1960s remain hugely popular in contemporary China and have become romantic, nostalgic anchors for the ethnic tourism industry in certain destinations, such as in Dali, Yunnan (Notar 2006, 47–79), and in Yangshuo, Guangxi, with the creation of a nighttime performance extravaganza (directed by Zhang Yimou) based loosely on the film *Third Sister Liu*.

19　Berry 1992 provides a critical reading of the conflation of race, or Han majority identity, and nation in the term *minzu* and its deployment in art, literature, and film criticism in China as a distinguishing feature of Chinese productions.

20　According to Michael Oppitz, the ethnographic films of the 1950s and 1960s from China hold little to no value as documents of minority ethnicities as compared to contemporary feature film representations of ethnic minorities in China. Oppitz (1989, 25) has written: "The films documented the tribal societies, of which they should be about, less than the ideological attitudes of the Han Chinese in the era after 1949. When seen against such products from the 'Exotification-Factory,' contemporary fiction films from China conversely appear to be real ethnographic documents."

21 Other examples of minority song and dance performances being remade to convey socialist messages include a 1965 picture book featuring folk songs such as "How I Want to See Chairman Mao" (Uyghur) and "We Have Electric Lights Now" (Owenki) (Schein 2000, 87).

22 See Diamond 1995, Oakes 1998, Rack 2005, and Schein 2000.

23 Social science researchers such as Fei Xiaotong (1981) played an important role in the administration and fieldwork investigations of the classification project and laid the groundwork for the establishment of "nationalities institutes" during this period. On the establishment of anthropology in China, see Guldin 1994 and Guldin ed. 1986. Publications by non-Chinese scholars on the subject of ethnic identity formation in contemporary China include, for example, Blum 2001; Gladney 1996 and 2004; Harrell ed. 1995; Harrell 2001; Heberer 2007; Kaup 2000; Lipman 1997; Litzinger 1995, 1998, and 2000; McCarthy 2009; Rack 2005; Rudelson 1997; Schein 2000; and Wellens 2010.

24 There is also a growing body of scholarship emerging on the conceptual similarities and differences between Han identity and notions of "whiteness" (Mullaney et al. 2012). Blum (2001, 57–58) offers some interesting convergences and divergences between Han identity and "whiteness," pointing out the importance of understanding the discursive formations of these categories in their historical contexts (i.e., differing concepts of "blood" and "color" in China and, say, the United States).

25 The term *lusheng* is also used to refer to specific dances that accompany the playing of the instrument; in general, people would say *tiao lusheng* to indicate both the playing of *lusheng* and dancing. Traditionally men play *lusheng* and women dance in a circular formation around the men during festivals and other village events. *Tiao lusheng* is a common feature of most Miao tourism performances.

26 For analysis and case studies of ethnic tourism see, among others, Bruner 2005, Hitchcock 1995, MacCannell 1999 [1976], Swain 1989 [1977], Tilley 1997, Walsh 2005, and Yang and Wall 2008.

27 Edward Bruner (2005, 1–7) has written about his role as a middleman in tours to Indonesia, and his eventual "failure" to maintain the proper boundaries as conceived by the travel agency director who had hired him as a tour guide. Bruner relies upon the early work of Dean MacCannell on the notions of front and backstage authenticity in his story to defend and justify his "failure" at boundary maintenance; MacCannell later published, in 2008, a pointed rejoinder on his role in Bruner's story.

28 See Bruner 2005, Cohen 2001, Hitchcock 1999, and Picard 1996.

29 See Hitchcock 1995, Tilley 1997, Kirshenblatt-Gimblett 1998 and 2006, and Thomas 1999.

30 On tourist motivations, see Cohen 1979, Graburn with Barthel-Bouchier 2001, MacCannell 1999 [1976], and N. Wang 1999; on anxiety, modernity, and the marketing of "the ethnic" in the genre of world music, see Feld 2000.

31 See Schaefer 2010 on nostalgia, photography, and the rural in China; see also P. Young 2008 on loss and longing in early twentieth-century tourism to Brittany, France.

32 Critical tourism studies have considered nostalgia in a number of ways—as the impetus for touring (MacCannell 1999 [1976]), as the sought-after object of tourist practices (Graburn 1995 and N. Wang 1999), and as the gloss applied to destinations to promote tourist activities (see Bruner 2005, 33–70 and 145–68). Graham Dann (1996, 219) has even outlined the "register" of nostalgia tourism as a particular form of language play that emphasizes nostalgic yearning and desires. Ning Wang (1999, 360) elaborates on the relationship between authenticity and nostalgia, writing: "The ideal of authenticity can be characterized by either nostalgia or romanticism. It is nostalgic because it idealizes the ways of life in which people are supposed to be freer, more innocent, more spontaneous, purer, and truer to themselves than usual (such ways of life are usually supposed to exist in the past or in childhood). People are nostalgic about these ways of life because they want to relive them in the form of tourism at least temporally, empathetically, and symbolically."

33 Svetlana Boym (2002) has distinguished between what she calls *reflective* and *restorative* nostalgia, where the former dwells upon longing, loss, and ruins, while the latter emphasizes rebuilding and refilling gaps in memory. See also K. Stewart 1988.

34 As Susan Stewart (1993 [1984], 135) has explained, "we need and desire souvenirs of events that are reportable, events whose materiality has escaped us, events that thereby exist on through the invention of narrative." Of course, classic works on photography and memory, such as Roland Barthes's *Camera Lucida* (1982 [1980]) and Susan Sontag's *On Photography* (2001 [1977]) also discuss emotions of nostalgia and longing, manifest in the materiality of the photograph.

35 David Lowenthal (1996, 86–87) has described two such situations in the United States: "'We have to learn how to be Indian again,' said a Pueblo craftswoman. 'First the whites came and stripped us. Then, they come again and "find" us. Now, we are paid to behave the way we did when they tried to get rid of us.' Since whites expect Indians to be steeped in tradition simply because they are Indian, Indians must trade on this image. . . . [Second] for example, many whites construe the new Native American casino enterprises as a sad lapse from traditional tribal values. Financial mogul Donald Trump pooh-poohed the wealthy Pequots, whose Connecticut casino had trumped his own, as not looking to him like 'real' Indians. They had looked Indian enough, they retorted, when they were poor."

36 The phrase "ethnic options" was coined by Mary Waters (1990) in her study of white ethnic identities in the United States and later applied to tourism studied by Robert E. Wood (1997). Alexis Celeste Bunten (2008) developed a similar idea of the ethnic "repertoire" in tourism encounters, where tourism workers draw upon a predetermined set of behaviors and practices in order to be successfully ethnic in tourism.

37 Taman Mini theme park in Indonesia is commonly cited as a prime example of a state agenda for tourism; see Adams 2005 and 2006; Bruner 2005, 211–30; Errington 1998; Hitchcock 1995 and 1998; and Wood 1997.

38 For analyses of these parks, see Anagnost 1993 and 1997; Bruner 2005, 211–30; Gladney 2004, 28–50; Oakes 2006b; Stanley 1998; and Stanley and Chung 1995.

39 See Tamar Gordon's 2005 film *Global Villages: The Globalization of Ethnic Display* for a vivid documentary portrayal of some of the parks and their employees.

40 In the Zhuang village in the Beijing park, for example, a sign stated that some of the photographs included inside the house had been taken by researchers from

the Central Institute of Nationality Studies during trips to the Longsheng region, including visits to Ping'an village, between May and September 1998.

41 See also Cable 2008, Jing Li 2003, Sun and Bao 2007a; L. Yang, Wall, and Smith 2008; and Tan, Cheung, and Yang 2001 for studies of Manchunman village.

42 Luo Yongchang (2006a) compared four ethnic tourism villages, noting the types of attractions available (from "daily life activities" to "village scenery"), the ways in which tourism was started (through government and/or private investment, or by the villagers themselves), and some of the problems encountered (low profits, declining visitor numbers, etc.) in each village. Specifically, these were Basha Miao Village and Upper Langde Miao Village in Guizhou, Ping'an village in Guangxi, and the Dai villages in Yunnan.

43 On tourism and poverty alleviation in China, see Huang H. 2006, Luk 2005, Wei Min 2005, and Wei Xiao'an 2003; a more conceptual approach to poverty tourism is developed in Scheyvens 2001.

44 Margaret Swain (2001) has argued for an approach to ethnic tourism framed by the concept of cosmopolitanism, to better understand the multiple identities inhabited by ethnic tourism stakeholders who commoditize ethnicity precisely for the purposes of engaging with, and in, the global networks of capital embodied in tourism.

45 On China's national tourism rating system, see Nyíri 2006.

46 See Chio 2013 for a discussion of how the naming of these villages, in the context of tourism, exemplifies and exacerbates local efforts to "claim heritage" in the context of tourism and economic competition.

47 Wen Tong (2002) reported 710 persons in 156 households; Huang Haizhu (2006) reported 792 persons in 180 households.

48 For example, Chinese scholars working in Ping'an have published on the development of family-run inns (Liang 2005, Meng 2007, and Wen 2002), community participation in tourism (Sha, Wu, and Wang 2007; and Wu and Ye 2005), folk customs and cultural change (Wu and Lu 2005, Mao C. 2006, Xu Ganli 2005 and 2006, and Xue 2008), and problems encountered in tourism, including ecological studies and government policy (Cheng et al. 2002, Huang H. 2006, Su and Chen 2005, Wei and Wu 2006, and Yang G. 2002).

49 Judith Shapiro (2001, 106–14) provides an account of hillside terracing and forced agricultural production in the model village of Dazhai, Shanxi during this era.

50 Lao could not remember where exactly these foreign tourists were from; most residents I asked assumed they were from Hong Kong, although a few people told me they were "really foreign," as in North American or European.

51 Guilin was one of the first cities in China to be developed and designated for tourism in the early 1980s, so it is not entirely surprising that local officials in Longsheng also began discussing tourism so soon after China's reform and opening in the late 1970s.

52 "Mountain People Also Use Foreign Money" is a direct translation of the title as reported by Lao (in Chinese, he wrote *Shanli ren ye hui yong yangqian*).

53 Urry's tourist gaze has since been challenged in MacCannell 2001, 29, which describes a second tourist gaze that knows and acknowledges the existence of the unseen and unsaid in tourism. Graburn with Barthel-Bouchier 2001, 153, following Parrinello 1993, notes that tourism in general, not limited to sightseeing or photography, is part of a hermeneutic "sociocultural circle" of experience, reintegration and feedback.

54 I have seen images of the terraced fields around Ping'an (both photographs and drawings) reproduced on packets of tissues, bamboo coasters, in anthropology textbooks, and in in-house advertisements for China Central Television, in addition to postcards, photo books, and the like.

55 This is the individual walk-up price. Tour group tickets are discounted by 50 percent.

56 Ticket sales from 1998 to 2000 were handled by the Longji Tourism Development Company, which was run by the county government. From 2001 on, ticket sales were handled by the Guilin Longsheng Hot Springs Tourism Company, Ltd.

57 This average is based off numbers from my own household survey in Ping'an.

58 Sources of water in Ping'an included natural springs and streams, cisterns, and an artificial reservoir. The regulation of water use was a huge point of contention between the villagers and the company—of course, both parties agreed that there needed to be enough water to flood the terraces every spring (which was always the busiest season) and run businesses. But, quite simply, there wasn't enough water to go around; the natural sources depended upon rainwater, and water usage was not taxed or otherwise managed. Each year, villagers told me, they would have to wait later and later into the spring or early summer to have enough water to flood the terraces; many photography tours that came to Ping'an in April and May left disappointed. Plans to regulate water collection and usage included a project to cement over all of the original gutters and water troughs between the terraces (which would prevent water loss through absorption but also altered the system of water flow) and to build two new large cisterns high up in the hillside.

59 Thanks to Jessica Anderson Turner for telling me about this development. By September 2010, this director had already left Ping'an and set up his business in Yangshuo, the much more popular and much larger tourism destination just south of Guilin. The space built for his performances was left in Ping'an, and at the time residents were not certain how they might use the space in the future.

60 Tourism in Upper Langde has been widely studied; see Donaldson 2007; Oakes 1998, 193–204, and 2006a; Wang Xiaomei 2007; and Zhou X. 1999.

61 In China, the distinction between "natural" and "administrative" villages can be important when understanding local-level community relations. Following Xing et al. 2006: "A natural village occurs when households cluster together, forming a small community. An administrative village is a region consisting of several villages designated by the state as a unit for administrative purposes" (ibid., viii). Thus, in the case of Jidao, Jidao is the administrative village name of two natural villages, known simply as Upper Jidao and Lower Jidao.

62 The overwhelming majority of people living in Upper Jidao are ethnically Miao; marriage is strictly patrilocal, so most married women living in Upper Jidao are from other villages. I did, however, meet two young wives who were non-Miao and who had met their husbands while working in Kaili or elsewhere. On occasion these women would wear Miao festival clothes and perform.

63 In other domestic government publications—namely, Guizhou Tourism Bureau 2006 and Kaili Shi Fupin Kaifa Bangongshi 2006—the population of Jidao village as a whole is provided, referring to both Upper and Lower Jidao.

64 Articles addressing the New Socialist Countryside program and rural tourism development include Wang and Wang 2006 and Zhou J. 2007; Yu D. 2008, Luo 2006b, and Zhou X. 1999 on tourism and community participation in Upper

Langde; Li N. 2007, Luo 2006a, and Qian 2005 on cultural change and poverty alleviation strategies in ethnic tourism; Liu Xiaohui 2007 and Li, Yu, and Dai 2006 on small business ventures in tourism, such as family-run inns; and Mo 2006 on historical tourism resources in Guizhou.

65   It should be reiterated that in many of these national and provincial-level reports and documents about the Bala River Demonstration Project for Rural Tourism, the distinction of "Upper" or "Lower" Jidao is not typically used; rather just "Jidao" is named. This oversight on the part of provincial, national, and international funders, I believe, has had serious consequences for the residents of Jidao village. Of course, there are more than seven villages along the Bala River, but only these seven were chosen for inclusion in the project.

66   It was from this curiosity on the villagers' behalf to know more about places like Ping'an that I developed my collaborative video viewing methodology (see Chio 2011a).

67   The Libo National Nature Reserve was included in a national bid for inscription on the UNESCO World Natural Heritage list, which was successfully granted in 2007 as part of the "South China Karst" World Natural Heritage region.

68   The corporatization of rural village tourism through such arrangements between government offices, private companies, and village units is a typical model for development in China; it was also used to infuse the Longji Scenic Area with money for development in 2001, as described earlier in this chapter.

69   By comparison, in 2007 the average cost of a bed in a family-run guesthouse in Ping'an was ¥25 a night, with shared facilities; in Upper Langde, just a mile from Upper Jidao, a bed in the village hostel was ¥10 to ¥15 a night. In some of the higher-end hotels in Kaili, the closest major city, rooms were around ¥150 to ¥200 a night in 2006.

70   Jidao village had also been included in other recent rural poverty studies and projects, including a program sponsored by the international organization Oxfam in the late 1990s (Oxfam International 2009), the Ford Foundation, and as a case study in a report on ethnic minorities, migration, and poverty by China Development Brief (Perrement 2006).

71   I repeatedly asked government officials and residents of Upper Jidao why Upper Jidao was chosen for tourism development rather than Lower Jidao or both. Most residents of Upper Jidao said that the international experts invited in 2002 and 2004 had decided that Upper Jidao was better, whereas Zhang Xiaosong hinted that Lower Jidao was less organized, in terms of leadership, and as a result it had been more difficult to work with the villagers there. The few people from Lower Jidao whom I asked about this typically responded, brusquely, that they had no idea why Upper Jidao had been chosen as the tourism focus.

72   See Chio 2012 for a discussion of locally recorded videos of Miao cultural life in Guizhou.

73   In the village most people spoke Miao to each other, and when engaging with non-Miao speakers, they spoke a local dialect, Kailihua.

74   Much later, in 2012, I was told that the developer had spent about the first half of his allotted amount, built the hotel frame, received the remainder of the amount, and used those funds for another project in another village. When asked why the developer wasn't forced to complete the hotel, Teacher Pan, Qin, and others in Upper Jidao shrugged and said there wasn't anything they could do about it.

75 See Oakes 1999 for a case study of a more business-oriented handicrafts production.
76 Unfortunately I have not met the donor in person; this description is based on what Qin and other village women have told me over the years.
77 Qin actually presented the piece to Zoellick on the occasion of his visit to Guizhou; I also received one in 2009 from the former director of the Guizhou Tourism Bureau, Yang Shengming.

2. PEASANT FAMILY HAPPINESS

1 See Park 2008 for a study of *nong jia le* tourism outside Beijing.
2 This phrase has also been translated as "Joyous Village Life" (Donaldson 2007), "Delights in Farm Guesthouses" (Park 2008), "Happy Farmer's Home" (Gao, Huang, and Huang 2009), "happy country home" (Oakes 2011), and as "rural resorts" in the state-run *China Daily* newspaper (Nilsson 2010), although I prefer "peasant family happiness," also used in Blanchard 2007. The logic for my translation is explained in this chapter, although to maintain consistency and draw attention to the particular historical and cultural context of the phrase, I use the Chinese *nong jia le* throughout.
3 These definitions have been taken from Guizhou Statistical Bureau 2007.
4 For general statistical review of national conditions in 2006, see People's Daily Online 2007.
5 These "civilized behavior" promotions included campaigns to practice waiting in line at bus stops and basic English-language lessons for residents and taxi drivers in Beijing. Problems in the tourism industry have garnered the attention of state politicians. A national law regulating travel agencies was approved in April 2013 and took effect beginning on October 1, 2013, at the start of the National Day holiday, while in September 2013 updated guidelines for tourist behavior were issued by the CNTA ("China's First Tourism Law Comes into Effect, Tourists Issued Manner Guides," online at www.cnn.com/2013/10/03/travel/new-china-tourism-law/, accessed October 29, 2013).
6 Of course, the idea that tourism could be harnessed for national development circulated in China as early as the late 1970s; Honggen Xiao (2005) has analyzed discourses of tourism and development in five speeches by Deng Xiaoping given between October 1978 and July 1979.
7 See Sofield and Li 1998a and 1998b. For example, the practice of landscape painting coupled with poetic inscriptions continues to inform contemporary travel patterns and valuations of the idea of "being there" in Chinese tourism practices (on landscape and travel in China, see Petersen 1995, Strassberg 1994, as well as Nyíri 2006 and 2010; for an assessment of Chinese outbound tourism, see Arlt 2006).
8 Many studies of tourism have viewed the phenomenon as an outgrowth of a distinctly Western, Euro-American historical condition rooted in nineteenth-century perspectives on leisure, modernity, individual subjectivity, and the meaning of travel. Classic examples include Veblen 2009 [1899], Boorstin 2012 [1962], and MacCannell 1999 [1976], which remain important for understanding tourism and leisure practices in society. However, as useful as they may be for sorting through the diversity of reasons for travel, formulaic classifications of tourist experiences (i.e., Cohen 1979 and N. Wang 1999) are often insufficient for examining "other"

tourisms that are neither based in nor emergent from the West. For critiques of the Western bias in tourism studies, see Alneng 2002; Y. Chan 2006; Ghimire 2001; Graburn 1983 and 1995; Lew and Yu, eds. 1995; Nyíri 2006; and Winter 2007 and 2009.

9   See Chan and Zhang 1999 and F. Wang 2005 for detailed studies of the *hukou* system.

10 See such films as Dai Sijie's *Balzac and the Little Chinese Seamstress* and Zhang Nuanxing's *Sacrificed Youth*. Chris Berry (1992) and Yingjin Zhang (1997), along with Ester Yau (1989), have all discussed *Sacrificed Youth*, the story of a young Han woman sent to a Dai village during the Cultural Revolution. Berry, Zhang, and Yau differ in their conclusions, but nonetheless all agree that the portrait of Dai culture and society presented in this film is generally one of a positive, desirable light and that the narrator of the film experiences a positive outcome to her time "sent-down." Davies 2005 provides a more nuanced analysis of reactions to the publication of a book of photographs from the *zhiqing* era, which ranged from nostalgia to regret; see also Davies 2007.

11 See Ghimire and Zhou 2001; Lew et al., eds. 2002; Li and Jia 2004; Qiao 1995; Oakes 1998; Xiao Q. 2005; and Zhang W. 1997.

12 Class A enterprises could do business directly with overseas tour operators; Class B could receive international tourists organized by Class A agencies. Class C enterprises were limited to organizing domestic tours, though Class A and Class B agencies also engaged in domestic tour businesses as well (Gang Xu 1999, 77fn15). The deposit amounts required were ¥600,000 for Class A businesses, ¥200,000 for Class B, and ¥100,000 for Class C agencies (Ghimire and Zhou 2001, 97).

13 The exact sources and methodologies used to gather this data is unclear; the statistical yearbooks do not specify precisely how these numbers were calculated. However, according to Gang Xu (1999), when statistics on domestic tourism were first collected in the early 1990s, these numbers were based on the number of tickets sold at major sightseeing destinations. Pál Nyíri (2010) has also reported the same counting method for calculating tourist trips taken—namely based on the sale of tickets at tourism destinations (*jingqu*) officially recognized by the government. The original charts also provide an explanation regarding urban/rural tourist ratios—namely that "rate is the ratio that the total amount of the urban citizens or the rural habitants compares to the urban population or the rural population" (CNTA 2008a). For clarity, I have not included these numbers.

14 See Gao, Huang, and Huang 2009 for a general review of rural tourism in China since 1978; for specific examples of poverty alleviation and tourism development in Guizhou and Yunnan, see Donaldson 2007, Luk 2005, Oakes 1998, and Sun and Bao 2007a, 2007b, and 2007c.

15 A number of the Communist-era documentary films discussed in chapter 1 explicitly discuss religious practices among ethnic minorities in China as superstitions in need of eradication; the films on the Uyghur ethnic group and the Naxi are particularly good examples of this.

16 While I use "peasant" as a translation for *nongmin* (as do Chu 2010, Hathaway 2010, Murphy 2004, Oakes 2011, Zhang and Donaldson 2010, and others when examining Chinese discourses on rural development and social transformation), when I am discussing people in Ping'an and Upper Jidao, I use "village resident"

or "villager" in recognition of the diversity of occupations, livelihoods, individual histories, and kin relations in each community.

17 See Su 2009, 81–117, for a general overview of the construction of the Chinese peasant historically and in light of more recent development goals.

18 Julie Chu (2010, 64–65) provides a case from Fujian, where residents of Longyan, a rural area by classification, had "mainly relied on nonagricultural and translocal kinds of labor before the Second World War," so they found that "the reclassification of most people as peasants was experienced as an extremely artificial imposition from above and their confinement to compulsory agricultural work in the countryside as a dramatic narrowing of their social world and life chances under Mao."

19 According to Gao, Huang, and Huang (2009, 440), this formulation was first posited by social scientists in the late 1980s as an analytical framework for addressing and solving problems in China's rural development.

20 Chu 2010 calls this the "moral career of the peasant," in which it has been impossible for the category and the term to be dissociated from perceptions of social and economic backwardness. For a comparative study of development plans, including the role of tourism, in Yunnan and Guizhou throughout the 2000s, see Donaldson 2011.

21 The "West" in this campaign encompassed everything from parts of northeastern Jilin to the Tibet Autonomous Region (Goodman 2004, 5–10).

22 See He 2005, Li and Jia 2004, Shi 2005, Yang and Hui 2005, and Zhang P. 2005.

23 These are the Guangxi Zhuang Autonomous Region, Ningxia Mongolian Autonomous Region, Tibet Autonomous Region, Inner Mongolia Autonomous Region, and Xinjiang Uyghur Autonomous Region.

24 The convergence of ethnic minority development and tourism development, particularly in the late 1990s to early 2000s, has been well studied; see S. Davis 2005, Hillman 2003, Kolås 2008, Oakes 1998, Mueggler 2002, Notar 2006, Schein 2000, and Swain 2001.

25 See, for example, Anagnost 2004, Hoffman 2003, Kipnis 2006, Murphy 2004, and Nyíri 2010 as well as a special section of the journal *positions* 17, no. 3 (2009): 523–642.

26 On women migrant workers, *suzhi*, and subjectivity, see, for example, Gaetano and Jacka 2004 and Yan 2008.

27 Official Chinese government documents and statements on the 11th Five Year Plan can be read in English online at "Key Points of the 11th Five-Year Guidelines," www.china.org.cn/english/2006lh/160403.htm, and "China Mapping Out 11th Five Year Guidelines," www.china.org.cn/english/features/guideline/156529.htm. In Chinese, the five areas focused on in the New Socialist Countryside program were *shengchan fazhan, shenghuo fuyu, xiangfen wenming, cunrong zhengjie,* and *guanli minzhu.* Official reports and statements on the campaign can be found online at, "Building a New Socialist Countryside," www.china.org.cn/english/zhuanti/country/159776.htm. See also China (Official Government Website) 2006.

28 This report is available online at "Socialist Countryside Should Not Be Mere Exercise in Vanity," online at www.china.org.cn/english/2007lh/201767.htm.

29 The complete law, "Law of the PRC on Urban and Rural Planning," can be accessed online at www.china.org.cn/china/LegislationsForm2001-2010/2011-02/11/content_21899292.htm.

30 On some of the problems of the New Socialist Countryside policy, see also Perry 2011.

31 These projects were all noted in a preliminary plan, completed in 2006; none of these specific items were ever built (as of 2012). A new performance space and cultural center were constructed in 2008, although by 2010, the performance space had been repurposed by the original land-use owners to build a new house.

32 Gorsuch (2003) adopts this idea of a "ritual of reassurance" from Linda Ellerbee (2000).

33 The Central Spiritual Civilization Steering Committee (www.wenming.cn) is an office of the Communist Party of China charged with maintaining and improving the level of civilized behavior and thought in China.

34 See Chio 2010 and Nyíri 2010, 88–96, for details on the 2006 guidelines. Updated guidelines were issued in September 2013 for outbound Chinese tourists and can be found online (CNTA 2013).

35 See Sha and Wang 2006, Shao 2007, and Wang and Bai 2006.

36 This was published originally in *Qiushi* (*Seeking Truth* no. 1 [2007]), the ideological journal of the Chinese Communist Party (cited in Blanchard 2007), and in magazines such as *Zhongguo Nongcun Keji* (*China Rural Science and Technology* no. 9 [2007]: 48–50). It was also published online on the official website of the Chinese government (www.gov.cn), which is the version referenced here (Shao 2007).

37 In addition to *miao jia le* in Guizhou, this convention has also been observed in ethnic Dai regions in Yunnan, where *nong jia le* tourism businesses are called *dai jia le* (J. Li 2005 and Sun and Bao 2007a).

38 "Farmer" often seems to be the easier term to use as a translation for *nongmin*; however, as Myron Cohen (1993, 160) has pointed out, the term "farmer" doesn't suggest the "Other" as much as "peasant" still does; moreover, "farmer" is functionally inappropriate given the occupational diversity of rural residents (see also Zhang and Donaldson 2010).

39 Nostalgia for the rural village extends beyond just tourism, of course; see Schaefer 2010 for a close reading of documentary photographs of Chinese villages and "the cultural politics of blankness" in contemporary Chinese art.

3. LEAVE THE FIELDS WITHOUT LEAVING THE COUNTRYSIDE

1 This sentiment was even more present in Ping'an. There I realized I was one of many—hundreds it seemed—scholars, students, and journalists who had come to this village to gather data about rural life from the residents.

2 Julie Chu (2006, 401, emphasis in the original) also notes that for the subjects of her research in Longyan, Fujian, "as state-classified peasants for four decades, the rural Fuzhounese were precisely *not* the kind of subjects authorized to chart moral careers as mobile cosmopolitans."

3 The scholarly literature on internal migration and the experience of migrants in China is vast; see, for example, see Chan and Zhang 1999, Fan 2005, Huang and Zhan 2003, Jacka 2006, Murphy 2002, Pun 2005, Solinger 1999, W. Sun 2006, Yan 2008, and L. Zhang 2001.

4 For example, see studies on the effects of migration on sending communities in rural Jiangxi (Murphy 2002); patterns of migration and identity discourse among

communities within Anhui, an area of China commonly associated with supplying female nannies and caretakers for urban households in Beijing, Shanghai, and other cities (W. Sun 2006, 2008, and 2009); and changing notions of personal development and desire among female domestic workers (Yan 2008).

5   Yan Hairong (2008, 44) argues that "if Modernity and Progress reside in the city, and if the city monopolizes modern culture, the countryside is the city's emaciated other. It is in this discursive context that the countryside cannot function as the locus of a modern identity," thus necessitating the city as a part of the rural imagination.

6   For studies of migrants in tourism destinations, see Bookman 2006; Castellanos 2007, 2008, and 2010; Castellanos and Boehm 2008; and Lindquist 2009.

7   After all, for the "global underclass that struggles to make sense of the world it inhabits in different ways . . . [t]hese processes of sense making should be situated not only in relation to capitalist expansion and state power, but also in the context of the desires and emotions that drive migration and tourism" (Lindquist 2009, 150).

8   R. V. Bianchi (2000) has dubbed these persons "migrant-tourist workers," based on research conducted in the Mediterranean, and similar studies have also been done in New Zealand and Sweden on seasonal employees at ski resorts and hotels (Boon 2006 and Lundmark 2006).

9   The social significances of ethnic clothing, including posing for pictures with people in costume or renting a costume to wear oneself, is explored in chapter 4.

10   Ze's description of tourism in Upper Jidao was quite precise, and exactly what many travel media photographers sought to reproduce in their images. Women in Upper Jidao were often asked to put on Miao clothes (*Miao yifu*), tie up their hair into topknots (*jiujiu*) decorated with a flower in front, and then go into the rice paddies and pose in action shots of planting rice seedlings or other farming activities.

11   The distinction between rice and wheat, while certainly simplistic and reductive, is a common one used throughout China to distinguish between northern and southern regions and peoples.

12   As tourism increased in Upper Jidao, and in particular because more and more U.S. college students had become involved in Upper Jidao's development through study abroad exchange programs organized by Zhang Xiaosong at Guizhou Normal University, the foods deemed more palatable to foreign tastes—namely, scrambled eggs and fried potatoes—were also offered to me whenever I visited.

13   The region around Ping'an was a major producer of lumber for the domestic markets until 1998, when forestry was heavily restricted by national law. Many Ping'an villagers recalled hauling cut tree trunks through the mountains as one of the few sources of cash income in the region in the 1980s and early 1990s. Thus, Mei explained, she felt she "knew" the lumber business and could take that knowledge elsewhere to create her own opportunities.

14   By this, I mean that some of those who migrated from Ping'an and Upper Jidao had been recruited directly in the villages, traveled on privately organized buses with a group of other recruits, and were taken directly to whatever work site (often a factory) and employed as a group; these migrants did not have to strike out on their own to find work, although many I knew from Upper Jidao did end up leaving their initial jobs and finding work elsewhere.

15   Ironically, this particular man's youngest son was also a recently returned migrant, who had worked for many years in Jiangsu in construction and soon would begin building a new hotel for his family. Everyone agreed that it was a good thing this man's son knew more about concrete and rebar construction; he was more knowledgeable about modern building techniques. In his own case, then, the migrant experiences of this man's son were considered beneficial to the family business.

16   During the 17th Party Congress in 2007, then President Hu Jintao made a statement to the effect that the household registration system may be dismantled, or changed significantly, in the near future. In essays and discussions from *East Asia Forum*, scholars have surmised that although the language of household registration may be erased, the lasting effects and social prejudices associated with *hukou* may persist quite a bit longer (K. Chan 2010, Kong 2010, Tao 2010, and J. Young 2010), because this system administratively bound residents to a geographical place (a township or city) in China and granted residents their rights and access to education, medical care, social security, employment, and so on. Migrant workers do not fit into the *hukou* system and are commonly referred to as the so-called "floating population."

17   Elsewhere, Urry (2002a, 271) has written of the importance of critically examining mobility as "the analysis of why people travel, and whether they should travel in the way they currently do, [which] is to interrogate a complex set of social practices, social practices that involve old *and* emerging technologies that reconstruct notions of proximity and distance, closeness and farness, stasis and movements, the body and the other."

18   Diane Austin-Broos (1997 and 2005) has conceptualized what she calls the "politics of moral orders," which are the modalities of power at work in the "order of values and meanings through which subjects are defined within a cultural milieu" (Austin-Broos 1997, 8). In these politics, "subjects sustain themselves through modes of representation and practice that can mediate, criticize, or reinforce larger orders of governance" (ibid., 12). I am extending her framework toward my consideration of the orders of mobility at work in rural China.

4. "TAKE A PICTURE WITH US"

1   On tourism in Upper Langde, see Donaldson 2007 and 2011; Oakes 1998, 2006a, and 2011; Yu D. 2008; and Zhou X. 1999.

2   See Adler 1989, MacCannell 1999 [1976] and 2011, Urry 2002b [1990], and van den Abeele 1980 on sightseeing and tourism.

3   By "media" here, I mean television, film, print media, and of course, the Web; see Kerwin 2010 for an analysis of images of the Miao on tourism websites.

4   Tourism and social change in Lijiang have been extensively researched ever since the inscription of the "old town" district on the UNESCO World Heritage Site list in 1997. See Chao 2012, Peters 2001, Su and Teo 2011, and Y. Wang 2007.

5   For a captivating documentary portrait of this phenomenon in Beijing, see the 2009 film *New Beijing: Reinventing a City*, directed by Georgia Wallace-Crabbe.

6   There are a series of "hundred year" features of Upper Jidao that have been particularly targeted as valuable and worth promoting as a part of the village's tourism.

These are the "hundred year houses," "hundred year granaries," "hundred year trees" (*bainian gushu*), and "hundred year ancient songs" (*bainian gu ge*). Many of these features are actually older than one hundred years, as Teacher Pan was quick to point out, but naming them as such provides for continuity.

7   It is possible that if this particular household had not had a home right on the river that was so immediately *visible* to tourists arriving from the highway, they might not have been the subject of so much criticism. This possibility was openly speculated, but of course no one could say for sure what might have been.

8   The desire for visual continuity is not new or unique to rural China, of course; many UNESCO World Heritage–listed regions around the world have strict guidelines on how buildings (residential and commercial) can or cannot be altered, inside and out, for the purpose of historical preservation.

9   Families with two or more sons typically would eventually split once the sons married. If the family did not have enough land or money to build an entirely new house for one of the sons, they would create new spaces within the existing house by adding walls so that the two sons and their families could engage in their everyday household activities relatively independently of one another. A family split of this kind also indicates that the finances are no longer managed together.

10   This particular series was called *Ethnic Odyssey* and featured, in total, sixteen episodes on fifteen different ethnic minority groups in China. It is now available as a DVD box set, distributed by China International TV Corporation.

11   Such images are ubiquitous, and women from Upper Jidao wearing festival clothes have been photographed for numerous publications, including the Japan Airlines in-flight magazine, the Chinese edition of *Marie Claire*, and *Hidden China*, a glossy coffee-table book of photographs (Meniconzi 2008).

12   None of this is unique to Upper Jidao, or China, for matter. The desiring gaze of documentary filmmakers and tourists affects people and architecture around the globe; see Stasch 2011 on the case of "tree houses" and photography in New Guinea. Of course, to be truly successful in tourism, rural destinations have to change and adapt to urban living standards in order to accommodate tourists; leading Chinese tourism scholar and policy maker Wei Xiao'an has called this "urban life in the countryside" (Wei 2005, 165).

13   More precisely, this style of architecture is known as *diaojiaolou*, commonly translated as "wooden stilted houses," in reference to how the living areas of the house are built above ground level, where animals are kept. *Diaojiaolou* are found throughout Buyi, Dong, Miao, Shui, Tujia, and Zhuang ethnic minority communities in Guangxi, Guizhou, and neighboring areas in southwestern China.

14   I refer to the clothing worn by the minority models as "costumes" rather than "clothes" or "clothing," to differentiate between the intended purposes of these different types of ethnic minority attire.

15   See figure 4.6 for an example of the local Zhuang clothes (a shirt, long pants, and terry-cloth headdress) worn by women in the village when they guided tourists, when they were working as porters and hosting guests in their hotels or restaurants, and sometimes, among the older women especially, as day-to-day clothing. These Zhuang clothes were usually machine-made of synthetic materials but this did not, to my knowledge, take away their "Zhuang-ness" for the women who wore them or the tourists who viewed the women in the clothing.

16 Village residents told me that in previous years, some enterprising photo booth owners had also brought peacocks and monkeys to Ping'an to be photographed with tourists, but these businesses had left by the time I arrived.

17 See, for example, Kahn 2000 and 2011 on touristic images of Tahiti and recent debates over nuclear testing; see also Ness 2005 on tourism and locational violence through the analysis of the visual landscape of the Pearl Farm Beach Resort in the southern Philippines.

18 Questions of power and photography are pervasive in the history of anthropology and in anthropological analysis; see, for example, Cohen, Nir, and Almagor 1992; Crowe 2003; Edwards 2001; MacDougall 2006; Pinney and Petersen 2003; and Poole 1997.

19 Hyde's (2007, 128–49) concept of the "transactional exchange" informs her nuanced reading of the performance of "being ethnic" put on by non-ethnic minority women in sex work, and also of the regimes of power informing current discourses of HIV/AIDs, Chinese modernity, and ethnic identities. As far as I know, the models in Ping'an were not engaged in any type of sex work; I have been asked whether this might have occurred in Ping'an between models and tourists, and over the course of my fieldwork, I never encountered nor heard of it in the village (neither from other villagers nor from the models themselves). Although theoretically there are interesting conceptual links between the study of sex work, the economic exchange of emotions, and sweet talk in minority model photography, I am reluctant to assume, ipso facto, that the models I studied were necessarily doing anything more than posing (although Hyde 2007 and Walsh 2005 do document various cases of sex workers using national stereotypes about ethnic minorities as sexually "free" in popular ethnic tourism destinations by donning ethnic costumes).

20 Hyde (2007, 118) elaborates: "The Han women represent and perform Tai-ness for a Han audience in order to achieve secondary gains in their own economic status, personal freedoms, desires, and amusements."

21 Hyde develops this analytic by drawing from Louisa Schein's (1996 and 1997) work on the fusing of desire into the sexual and the political through the engendering of ethnic groups, as well as from Judith Butler's (1990) critical approach to the performativity of gender.

22 The particular group of models I followed tended to wear, by their own description, Dong, Miao, Tibetan, Yao, and Zhuang costumes most regularly. To be honest, I couldn't really tell the difference between most of the costumes (except for differences in color).

23 By comparison, a hotel worker in the village earned about ¥500 a month; recently returned migrant workers I met said that factory labor in South China's industrial zones at the time paid around ¥800 to ¥1,000 a month for basic nontechnical labor.

24 See the work of Åshild Kolås (2008, 82) on the appeal of "playing" with ethnic and social identities in Chinese tourism, which she points out is enjoyed by tourists, locals, and migrant workers in the Shangri-la area of Yunnan; Beth Notar (2006, 61–64) has called this a practice of "romantic reembodiment" for Han Chinese tourists visiting Dali, Yunnan. David MacDougall (2006, 164–69) has also written about the appeal of dressing up for photographs among middle-class domestic tourists in India.

25 Xin Liu (2002) has analyzed the terminology of "boss" and "miss" (*xiaojie*) in

relation to businessmen and female escorts in China's business culture; addressing a man as "boss" carries with it an immediate acknowledgment of respect and inequality in social status between the parties involved.

26 Wedding photography is a huge business in China and Taiwan (see Adrian 2003 and Li Xin dir. 2005). Engaged to be married or recently married couples will go to professional studios for these pictures, and this is often considered part of "being married." Thus, by joking that they will "be engaged" once their picture is taken together, male tourists are deliberately referencing what is considered a traditional marriage practice as well as the supposed sexual availability of ethnic minority women. It is also possible to "get married" to an ethnic woman at ethnic theme parks and during various song-and-dance performances at tourism destinations; having pictures taken together is often a central part of this process.

27 Pigs are culturally considered constitutive of Chinese households; as is frequently pointed out, the Chinese character for "family" (家) is composed of the character for "hog" or "swine" (豕) under the radical for "roof" (宀).

28 Erik Cohen, Yeshayahu Nir and Uri Almagor (1992) have compared social relationships at instances of the photographic encounter, or what they term "stranger-local interactions" in photography. They argue that ambiguity is a key feature of photographer-photographee interaction. The ambiguity of the relationship can be either unilateral (for example, a photographer who believes she or he is taking a "candid" photograph of a subject who does not know the photographer is there) or mutual (the most extreme version of this would be a posed portrait, in which both the photographer and photographee are highly cognizant of the exchange and agree to participate in the act) (ibid., 214–15). But, they explain, "the ambiguity in the [photographer-photographee interaction] is most pronounced in situations where the photographer defines his relationship to the photographee as a unilateral one and engages in taking a 'candid' picture of the subject who appears to be unaware of, or unconcerned with, the photographer's endeavor. The subject, however, perceives it as a mutual relationship and reacts to such an attempt, for example, by fear, anger, a smile, or by a consciously struck pose" (ibid., 215).

29 See Hammond et al. 2009 for an analysis of anthropology textbook covers.

30 By appearing in pictures of the terraces, local women countered the "disemplacement" brought about by the development of Ping'an as a tourism destination, a process that, as Sally Ann Ness (2005, 120) has argued, occurs "in persons as they experience the material transformation and scenic rendering of a location."

31 As mentioned earlier, one minority model I knew was from Ping'an, although she left the job after a couple of months to study hairdressing in Guilin. Yuan, the model considered by the others the best at sweet talk, was actually from a Zhuang village near Ping'an, so she was considered more local than the other models (who were not Zhuang and from farther away). Although Yuan had relatives in Ping'an, and her mother and sister were often around working in the guesthouses, Yuan chose to live and eat with the other models in the house provided by the photo booth owners.

32 Notar (2006, 60) has reported a similar sentiment among young Bai performers outside Dali who found "the tourism-related work both easier and more glamorous than the fishing and farming work of their parents."

33 See the work of Olivier Evrard and Prasit Leepreecha (2009, 250) for a similar case in contemporary Thai domestic tourism.

5. THE ABILITY TO BE DIFFERENT

1   After the holiday week was over, I asked Teacher Pan how many tourists had visited; he estimated about twenty to thirty people per day, or no more than two hundred people throughout the week. The village had tried to collect an entrance fee of ¥10 per person, but many tourists, Teacher Pan said, had been turned off by the fee and left, or, as the village clinician Qin later told me, they would try to sneak around the main entrance using other paths. I observed at least one group of cars driving into the village, only to drive back out within ten minutes; Qin said these visitors had refused to pay the entrance fee.

2   It is important to state that there was no proof that residents from Lower Jidao had blocked the road or slashed the sign, but the manner in which Upper Jidao residents on the whole believed this to be the case was revealing of their perspective on village relations after the tourism plans began.

3   This kind of "cleaning up" of the look of a village also happened in Upper Jidao in summer 2008. There, the local government sent in a few people to demolish a row of brick pigsties that butted up against the village's new performance ground. When I visited in July 2008, I was told that the families had refused to take down the sties themselves because, in their opinion, the government compensation offered was too low (about ¥2,500 to be split between four or five households). The new village subcommittee leader was incapable of brokering an agreement and eventually acquiesced to the government's demands. Doing so meant that hired laborers from elsewhere knocked down the sties, leaving the rubble behind. As far as I could ascertain, the families received no compensation.

4   It is worth noting that the issue of public toilets in Ping'an was often discussed; village residents found it frustrating and mildly annoying when tourists, who were not their customers, asked to use the facilities in a village home, hotel, or restaurant. There are public toilets in only three places in Ping'an—at the parking lot and at each of the two viewpoints.

5   See, for example, Sun and Bao 2007a, 2007b, and 2007c; Nyíri 2006; Wen 2002; and Xu Ganli 2005.

6   My use of the concept of distances here draws on Ning Wang's (2001) invocation of Simmel's (1950) "appeal of distance" as applied to tourism studies, as well as John Urry's (2007) mobilities paradigm.

7   For example, Erik Cohen (1979) schematically analyzed different modes of tourist experiences.

8   I am, of course, drawing on the idea of "time-space compression," as articulated by David Harvey (1990), in thinking through how social relations within Ping'an and Upper Jidao have been affected by both physical transport changes regionally and the ongoing pressures of tourism to emphasize cultural difference as a valuable commodity.

9   The idea of "the stranger" is so obviously relevant to the concept of the tourist that perhaps for this reason it has received fairly little investigation in tourism studies (Dann 1996, 13), and the figure of "the stranger" is frequently evoked in tourism studies as an apt conceptual definition of the "modern-man-in-general"-as-tourist; see the work of Eeva Jokinen and Soile Veijola (1997, 29–30), following, of course, that of Dean MacCannell 1999 [1976], 1. Graham Dann (1996) has pointed out that in the early theorizations of the tourist by Erik Cohen (1979), Cohen only makes

explicit the relationship between being a tourist and being a stranger in a paper about expatriates. Similarly, Dennison Nash (1996, 47–48) has also made passing reference to the concept of strangerhood in his chapter on theories of tourism as a personal transition.

10 Information about the Norwegian-Chinese joint ecomuseums can be found on the website of the Norwegian Embassy in China (www.norway.cn). See a paper by Yang Shengming (2005, 14), where she mentions that "the Chinese and the Norwegian Governments have established with joint efforts four ecological village museums in Guizhou." See also the work of Li Jiqia (2005), who has examined this project in Guizhou, and that of Peter Davis (2011, 236–47) on ecomuseums across China.

11 The change from using "ancient" to "old" in the English translation of the name for Longji village was something I noticed on official maps in 2012.

12 I offer a more extended discussion of hotels and the politics of heritage in Ping'an in Chio 2013. To be fair, when I raised the issue of the exclusivity and price of the high-end hotel with one village woman, she rightly pointed out to me that the hotel had opened up Ping'an to tourists who otherwise probably wouldn't come to the village, let alone stay overnight, so she did not perceive of the hotel as competition (Chio 2013, 155).

13 The platforms where the minority models work were another example of this; but these structures, haphazardly constructed, were deemed unsightly by the management and county government officials in 2008 and forcibly taken down that spring. Some platforms had reappeared again in 2012, however.

14 Upper Langde is administratively connected with Lower Langde; however, from anecdotal evidence, it appears that the economic differences between Upper and Lower Langde are more balanced because of Lower Langde's position on the main road through the area and its role as the administrative center for a cluster of villages in the area. Furthermore, as has been demonstrated in studies of the profit-sharing system used in Upper Langde tourism (see Wang X. 2007 and Yu D. 2008), the profits made by each household in Upper Langde from tourism are, relatively, not that great. Nanhua village, just four kilometers from Upper Jidao, had been developed with funds from the Kaili municipal government and "opened" to tourism in 1997.

15 For reports on Xijiang's redevelopment and subsequent economic boom, see articles from *China Daily* (Nilsson 2010), the U.S. National Public Radio program *Marketplace* (Schmitz 2012), and Yu Lintao (2012), as well as the scenic area development company website (see www.xjqhmz.com). In addition to being included in the World Bank project loan in Guizhou for cultural and natural heritage, Xijiang is also a part of a UNESCO China Culture and Development Partnership Framework project (see www.unescobej.org/culture/culture-and-development/china-culture-and-development-partnership-framework, accessed on December 13, 2012).

16 Information on Japan's One Village One Product movement can be found online at www.ovop.jp.

17 The village in the background of the advertisement is actually Upper Langde village; it is recognizable from the location of the buildings and paths around the performance space.

18 Thanks to Nelson Graburn, who first pointed out to me the formulaic structure of building tourism villages in terms of certain key components.

19 To understand how difference is transformed and used within certain forms and assertions of power, I am drawing on Mary Louise Pratt's reading of Michel Foucault's study of knowledge, nature, being human, and categories in *The Order of Things* (1994 [1970]), in light of Pratt's own analysis of the work and productions of seventeenth-, eighteenth-, and nineteenth-century botanists and naturalists, many of whom traveled to colonies in the New World as part of their labors (Pratt 2008 [1992], 24–36). Pratt argues that the way in which natural history turned difference into a "system of variables" allowed European male colonialists to "subsume history and culture into natural." Moreover, "the (lettered, male, European) eye that held the system could familiarize ('naturalize') new sites/sights immediately upon contact, by incorporating them into the language of the system. The differences of distance factored themselves out of the picture: with respect to mimosas, Greece could be the same as Venezuela, West Africa or Japan; the label 'granitic peaks' can apply identically to Eastern Europe, the Andes or the American West" (ibid., 31).

CONCLUSION

1 As noted in previous chapters, following arguments by Xin Liu (1997) and Pál Nyíri (2006 and 2009), overseas Chinese migrants are typically considered at the top of the "social-spatial hierarchy."

2 Village clinician and de facto tour guide Qin had been invited then as well but was too far along in her pregnancy for the long bus rides on winding mountain roads.

3 The "wild vegetables" served at this time were sweet potato leaves, so to be exact, they were not "wild" but simply different from the more familiar types of cabbage usually offered.

4 Some businesses in Ping'an did sell handmade goods; these were mostly from the neighboring Yao villages or, increasingly, brought into Ping'an by traders and collectors who specialized in ethnic handicrafts from Guizhou or other parts of rural Guangxi.

5 They had the advantage of being a larger extended household, including grandparents, their two sons, two daughters-in-law, as well as aunts and other relatives hired to help out at their family guesthouse. Over the next few years, however, this family gradually leased out more of their business and space to the restaurant manager from Henan, who served the day tours from Guilin. The sons, their wives, and children, then moved to the county seat, Longsheng, where the children attended school. These families would come back to the village only on weekends and during school holidays.

6 The concrete houses were strategically situated throughout the village to control the spread of a fire, if one were to break out.

7 According to a status report published in December 2012, progress on the World Bank's Guizhou Cultural and Natural Heritage Protection and Development project was rated as "unsatisfactory" overall. The reasons given included "insufficient commitment to the project's participatory approach and inadequate assistance provided to local communities" leading to a situation where many "physical works" (i.e., construction and renovations) were "being carried out by outside contractors rather than the villagers themselves" (World Bank 2012b, 1). This was certainly the case in July 2012 when I visited Upper Jidao, where village residents

were participating as manual laborers on some of the projects, which were in turn managed by outside contractors mostly from Kaili. That said, most village residents were not experienced at executing large construction projects, nor did they have the means to rent the necessary equipment (such as diggers, etc.), so there was not much of an expectation, locally, that they *could* in fact carry out these projects on their own. In the June 2013 status report, progress was still unsatisfactory and a risk rating of "substantial" had been added; however, in the overview the report noted that in the January 2013 midterm review, it had been agreed to scale back both the project development objectives and the key performance indicators to help the project's progress improve (World Bank 2013, 1–2).

REFERENCES

Authors' names are represented here as they appear on the title page of their publications, with a comma indicating when a name has been inverted for alphabetization by surname. Names that were represented on the title page with surname first do not require a comma.

Adams, Kathleen M. 2005. "The Genesis of Touristic Imagery: Politics and Poetics in the Creation of a Remote Indonesian Island Destination." *Tourist Studies* 4 (2): 115–35.
———. 2006. *Art as Politics: Re-crafting Identities, Tourism, and Power in Tana Toraja, Indonesia.* Honolulu: University of Hawai'i Press.
Adler, Judith. 1989. "The Origins of Sightseeing." *Annals of Tourism Research* 16: 7–29.
Adrian, Bonnie. 2003. *Framing the Bride: Globalizing Beauty and Romance in Taiwan's Bridal Industry.* Berkeley: University of California Press.
Alexander, John R. 2005. "Visualizing Ethnicity, Solidifying History: Documentary Ethnographic Filmmaking in China, 1957–1966." MA thesis, University of California–Berkeley.
All China Data Center. 2012. *China Yearly Macro-Economics Statistics (National).* Accessed July 19, 2013. http://chinadataonline.org/member/macroy/macroytshow.asp?code=A0501.
Alneng, Victor. 2002. "The Modern Does Not Cater for Natives: Travel Ethnography and the Conventions of Form." *Tourist Studies* 2 (2): 119–42.
Alpers, Svetlana. 1983. *The Art of Describing: Dutch Art in the Seventeenth Century.* Chicago: University of Chicago Press.
AlSayyad, Nezar, ed. 2001. *Consuming Tradition, Manufacturing Heritage: Global Norms and Urban Forms in the Age of Tourism.* London: Routledge.
Amit, Vered. 2007. "Structures and Dispositions of Travel and Movement." In *Going First Class? New Approaches to Privileged Travel and Movement,* edited by Vered Amit, 1–14. New York: Berghahn Books.

Anagnost, Ann. 1993. "The Nationscape: Movement in the Field of Vision." *Positions* 1 (3): 585–606.

———. 1997. *National Past-Times: Narrative, Representation, and Power in Modern China.* Durham: Duke University Press.

———. 2004. "The Corporeal Politics of Quality (*Suzhi*)." *Public Culture* 16 (2): 189–208.

Appadurai, Arjun. 1996. *Modernity at Large: Cultural Dimensions of Globalization.* Minneapolis: University of Minnesota Press.

Arlt, Wolfgang. 2006. *China's Outbound Tourism.* London: Routledge.

Austin-Broos, Diane. 1997. *Jamaica Genesis: Religion and the Politics of Moral Orders.* Chicago: University of Chicago Press.

———. 2005. "The Politics of Moral Order: A Brief Anatomy of Racing." *Social Analysis* 49 (2): 182–90.

Barth, Frederik, ed. 1969. *Ethnic Groups and Boundaries: The Social Organization of Cultural Differences.* London: George Allen and Unwin.

Barthes, Roland. 1982 [1980]. *Camera Lucida: Reflections on Photography,* translated by Richard Howard. New York: Hill and Wang.

Baudrillard, Jean. 1988. "Simulacra and Simulations." In *Selected Writings,* edited by Mark Poster, 166–84. Palo Alto: Stanford University Press.

Bender, Barbara, ed. 1993. *Landscape: Politics and Perspectives.* Oxford: Berg Publishers.

Benjamin, Walter. 1969. "The Work of Art in the Age of Mechanical Reproduction." In *Illuminations,* 217–51. New York: Shocken.

Berry, Chris. 1992. "'Race': Chinese Film and the Politics of Nationalism." *Cinema Journal* (Winter): 45–58.

Bianchi, R. V. 2000. "Migrant Tourist-Workers: Exploring the 'Contact Zones' of Post-Industrial Tourism." *Current Issues in Tourism* 3 (2): 107–37.

Blanchard, Ben. 2007. "No Early Harvest in China's Rural Tourism Push." Reuters, February 28. Accessed July 29, 2013. www.reuters.com/article/2007/03/01/us-china-parliament-tourism-idUSPEK30992320070301.

Blum, Susan D. 2001. *Portraits of "Primitives": Ordering Human Kinds in the Chinese Nation.* New York: Rowman & Littlefield.

Blumenfield Kedar, Tami. 2010. "Scenes from Yongning: Media Creation in China's Na Villages." PhD diss., University of Washington.

Bookman, Milica Z. 2006. *Tourists, Migrants, and Refugees: Population Movements in Third World Development.* Boulder: Lynne Rienner Publishers.

Boon, Bronwyn. 2006. "When Leisure and Work Are Allies: The Case of Skiers and Tourist Resort Hotels." *Career Development International* 11 (7): 594–608.

Boorstin, Daniel. 2012 [1962]. *The Image: A Guide to Pseudo-Events in America.* New York: Vintage.

Bourdieu, Pierre. 1977. *Outline of a Theory of Practice,* translated by Richard Nice. Cambridge: Cambridge University Press.

Boym, Svetlana. 2002. *The Future of Nostalgia.* New York: Basic Books.

Bray, David. 2012. "Urban Planning Goes Rural: Conceptualizing the 'New Village.'" Paper presented at the Australian National University, China in the World Workshop on Rural Urbanization, Zhongdian, July 15–17, 2012.

Broudehoux, Anne-Marie. 2004. *The Making and Selling of Post-Mao Beijing.* London: Routledge.

———. 2007. "Spectacular Beijing: The Conspicuous Construction of an Urban Metropolis." *Journal of Urban Affairs* 29 (4): 383–99.

Bruner, Edward M. 2005. *Culture on Tour: Ethnographies of Travel.* Chicago: University of Chicago Press.

Bunten, Alexis Celeste. 2008. "Sharing Culture or Selling Out? Developing the Commodified Persona in the Heritage Industry." *American Ethnologist* 35 (3): 380–95.

———. 2010. "More Like Ourselves: Indigenous Capitalism through Tourism." *American Indian Quarterly* 43 (3): 285–311.

Butler, Judith. 1990. *Gender Trouble: Feminism and the Subversion of Identity.* New York: Routledge.

Cable, Monica. 2008. "Will the Real Dai Please Stand Up: Conflicting Displays of Identity in Ethnic Tourism." *Journal of Heritage Tourism* 3 (4): 267–76.

Cai Fuyou. 1987. "Analysis and Appraisal of Stalin's Definition of a 'Nation.'" *Social Sciences in China* 8 (1): 209–21.

Cartier, Carolyn. 2005. "Introduction: Touristed Landscapes/Seductions of Place." In *Seductions of Place: Geographical Perspectives on Globalization and Touristed Landscapes,* edited by Carolyn Cartier and Alan A. Lew, 1–20. London: Routledge.

Cartier, Carolyn, and Alan A. Lew, eds. 2005. *Seductions of Place: Geographical Perspectives on Globalization and Touristed Landscapes.* London: Routledge.

Castellanos, M. Bianet. 2007. "Adolescent Migration to Cancún: Reconfiguring Maya Households and Gender Relations in Mexico's Yucatán Peninsula." *Frontiers* 28 (3): 1–27.

———. 2008. "Constructing the Family: Mexican Migration and the State." *Latin American Perspectives* 35 (1): 64–77.

———. 2010. *A Return to Servitude: Maya Migration and the Tourist Trade in Cancún.* Minneapolis: University of Minnesota Press.

Castellanos, M. Bianet, and Deborah A. Boehm. 2008. "Engendering Mexican Migration: Articulating Gender, Regions, Circuits." *Latin American Perspectives* 35 (1): 5–15.

Chan, Kam Wing. 2010. "Making Real Hukou Reform in China." *East Asia Forum.* Accessed December 16, 2012. www.eastasiaforum.org/2010/03/03/making-real-hukou-reform-in-china/.

Chan, Kam Wing, and Li Zhang. 1999. "The Hukou System and Rural-Urban Migration in China: Processes and Changes." *China Quarterly* 16: 818–55.

Chan, Yuk Wah. 2006. "Coming of Age of the Chinese Tourists: The Emergence of Non-Western Tourism and Host-Guest Interactions in Vietnam's Border Tourism." *Tourist Studies* 6 (3): 187–206.

Chang, Leslie T. 2009. *Factory Girls: From Village to City in a Changing China.* New York: Spiegel and Grau.

Chao, Emily. 2012. *Lijiang Stories: Shamans, Taxi Drivers, and Runaway Brides in Reform-Era China.* Seattle: University of Washington Press.

Cheng Guanwen, Wang Dunqiu, Qin Ligong, Kong Yunduo, Yan Qikun, and Qin Guohui. 2002. "Ecoenvironmental Protection of Ecotourist Development in Longji Terraced Landscape, Guangxi." *Journal of Guilin Institute of Technology* 22 (1): 94–98.

Cheung, Siu-Woo. 1995. "Millenarianism, Christian Movements, and Ethnic Change among the Miao in Southwest China." In *Cultural Encounters on China's Ethnic Frontiers,* edited by Stevan Harrell, 217–47. Seattle: University of Washington Press.

———. 1996. "Representation and Negotiation of Ge Identities in Southeast Guizhou." In *Negotiating Ethnicities in China and Taiwan,* edited by Melissa Brown, 240–73. Berkeley: Institute of East Asian Studies, University of California Press.

China (Official Government Website). 2006. *Facts and Figures: China's Drive to Build New Socialist Countryside.* Accessed February 2, 2009. www.gov.cn/english/2006-03/05/content_218920.htm.

Chio, Jenny. 2009. "The Internal Expansion of China: Tourism and the Production of Distance." In *Asia on Tour: Exploring the Rise of Asian Tourism*, edited by Tim Winter, Peggy Teo, and T. C. Chang, 207–20. London: Routledge.

———. 2010. "China's Campaign for Civilized Tourism: What to Do When Tourists Behave Badly." *Anthropology News* (November): 14–15. Arlington, VA: American Anthropological Association.

———. 2011a. "Know Yourself: Making the Visual Work in Tourism Research." In *Fieldwork in Tourism: Methods, Issues, and Reflections*, edited by C. Michael Hall, 209–19. London: Routledge.

———. 2011b. "Leave the Fields without Leaving the Countryside: Mobility and Modernity in Rural, Ethnic China." *Identities: Global Studies in Culture and Power* 18 (6): 551–75.

———. 2012. "'Village Videos' and the Visual Mainstream in Rural, Ethnic Guizhou." In *Mapping Media in China: Region, Province, Locality*, edited by Wanning Sun and Jenny Chio, 79–93. London: Routledge.

———. 2013. "Good Fences Make Good Neighbors: Claiming Heritage in the Longji Terraced Fields Scenic Area." In *Cultural Heritage Politics in China*, edited by Tami Blumenfield and Helaine Silverman, 143–60. New York: Springer.

Chio, Jenny, dir. 2003. *Film the People: National Minorities in Ethnographic Films in the People's Republic of China, 1957–1966* (digital video, 22 minutes). MA thesis, Goldsmiths College, University of London.

———. 2013. *Nong Jia Le Peasant Family Happiness* (digital video, 70 minutes). Distributed by Berkeley Media, LLC.

Chou Chou, dir. 2006. *Anayi* (film, 96 minutes). Beijing: China State Administration for Radio, Film, and Television.

Chu, Julie Y. 2006. "To Be 'Emplaced': Fuzhounese Migration and the Politics of Destination." *Identities: Global Studies in Culture and Power* 13 (3): 395–425.

———. 2010. *Cosmologies of Credit: Transnational Mobility and the Politics of Destination in China.* Durham: Duke University Press.

Clark, Paul. 1987. "Ethnic Minorities and Chinese Film: Cinema and the Exotic." *East-West Film Journal* 1 (2): 15–31.

Clarke, Samuel R. 1911. *Among the Tribes in South-West China.* London: Morgan & Scott, Ltd.

Clifford, James. 1997. *Routes: Travel and Translation in the Late Twentieth Century.* Cambridge: Harvard University Press.

CNN (Cable News Network). 2013. "China's First Tourism Law Comes into Effect, Tourists Issued Manner Guides." Accessed October 29, 2013. www.cnn.com/2013/10/03/travel/new-china-tourism-law/.

CNTA (China National Tourism Administration). 2005. *The Yearbook of China Tourism.* Beijing: China Tourism Press.

———. 2007. *The Yearbook of China Tourism.* Beijing: China Tourism Press.

———. 2008a. "Major Statistics of Domestic Tourism 2005." Accessed July 29, 2013. http://en.cnta.gov.cn/html/2008-11/2008-11-9-21-40-54934.html.

———. 2008b. "Major Statistics of Domestic Tourism 2007." Accessed August 3, 2008. www.cnta.gov.cn/html/2008-6/2008-6-2-21-29-3-319.html.

———. 2008c. "2008 nian 'Shi Yi' Huangjing zhou lüyou tongji baogao" (2008 October

1 Golden Week tourism statistics report). Accessed July 27, 2010. www.cnta.gov.cn/html/2008-10/2008-10-6-17-23-95229.html.

———. 2013. "Tisheng Zhongguo gongmin chujinglü wenming suzhi ziliao xiazai" (Raise the quality of Chinese outbound tourists download). Accessed October 20, 2013. www.cnta.gov.cn/html/2013-7/2013-7-15-9-58-46078.html.

CNTA and Zhongguo Wenming Xie. 2006. "Tisheng Zhongguo gongmin lüyou wenming suzhi xingdong jihua" (Plan to raise the civilized tourism quality of Chinese citizens). Accessed August 17, 2006. www.cnta.gov.cn/Upfiles/200681784098.doc.

Cohen, Erik. 1979. "A Phenomenology of Tourist Experiences." *Sociology* 13 (2): 179–201.

———. 2001. "Ethnic Tourism in Southeast Asia." In *Tourism, Anthropology, and China*, edited by Tan Chee-Beng, Sidney C. H. Cheung, and Yang Hui, 27–54. Bangkok: White Lotus Press.

Cohen, Erik, Yeshayahu Nir, and Uri Almagor. 1992. "Stranger-Local Interaction in Photography." *Annals of Tourism Research* 19: 213–33.

Cohen, Myron. 1993. "Cultural and Political Inventions in Modern China: The Case of the Chinese 'Peasants.'" *Daedalus* 122 (2): 151–70.

Collier Jr., John, and Malcolm Collier. 1986. *Visual Anthropology: Photography as a Research Method*. Albuquerque: University of New Mexico Press.

Comaroff, John L., and Jean Comaroff. 2009. *Ethnicity, Inc.* Chicago: University of Chicago Press.

Cosgrove, Denis E. 1984. *Social Formation and Symbolic Landscape*. Madison: University of Wisconsin Press.

———. 2006. "Modernity, Community, and the Landscape Idea." *Journal of Material Culture* 11 (1/2): 49–66.

Crary, Jonathan. 1990. *Techniques of the Observer*. Cambridge: MIT Press.

———. 2001. *Suspensions of Perception*. Cambridge: MIT Press.

Cresswell, Tim. 2006. *On the Move: Mobility in the Modern Western World*. New York: Routledge.

Crouch, David, and Nina Lübbren, eds. 2003. *Visual Culture and Tourism*. Oxford: Berg.

Crowe, Darryn. 2003. "Objectivity, Photography, and Ethnography." *Critical Studies <=> Critical Methodologies* 3 (4): 470–85.

Dai Sijie, dir. 2002. *Balzac and the Little Chinese Seamstress* (film, 111 minutes). Empire Pictures.

Dann, Graham. 1996. *The Language of Tourism: A Sociolinguistic Perspective*. Wallingford, UK: CAB International.

Daugstad, Karoline. 2008. "Negotiating Landscape in Rural Tourism." *Annals of Tourism Research* 35 (2): 402–36.

Davies, David J. 2005. "Old *Zhiqing* Photos: Nostalgia and the Spirit of the Cultural Revolution." *China Review* 5 (2): 97–123.

———. 2007. "Visible *Zhiqing*: The Visual Culture of Nostalgia among China's *Zhiqing* Generation." In *Re-envisioning the Chinese Revolution*, edited by Guobin Yang and Ching Kwan Lee, 166–92. Stanford: Stanford University Press.

Davis, Peter. 2011. *Ecomuseums: A Sense of Place*, second edition. London: Continuum International Publishing Group.

Davis, Sara L. M. 2005. *Song and Silence: Ethnic Revitalization on China's Southwest Border*. New York: Columbia University Press.

Deal, David M., and Laura Hostetler. 2003. *The Art of Ethnography: A Chinese "Miao" Album*. Seattle: University of Washington Press.

Debord, Guy. 1983. *Society of the Spectacle*. New York: Zone Books.

Deger, Jennifer. 2006. *Shimmering Screens: Making Media in an Aboriginal Community*. Minneapolis: University of Minnesota Press.

DeLue, Rachael Ziady, and James Elkins, eds. 2008. *Landscape Theory*. London: Routledge.

Desmond, Jane. 2001. *Staging Tourism: Bodies on Display from Waikiki to Sea World*. Chicago: University of Chicago Press.

Diamond, Norma. 1995. "Defining the Miao: Ming, Qing, and Contemporary Views." In *Cultural Encounters on China's Ethnic Frontiers*, edited by Stevan Harrell, 92–116. Seattle: University of Washington Press.

Dikötter, Frank. 1992. *The Discourse of Race in Modern China*. Stanford: Stanford University Press.

Donaldson, John. 2007. "Tourism, Development, and Poverty Reduction in Guizhou and Yunnan." *China Quarterly* 190: 333–51.

———. 2011. *Small Works: Poverty and Economic Development in Southwestern China*. Ithaca, NY: Cornell University Press.

Duara, Prasenjit. 1995. *Rescuing History from the Nation: Questioning Narratives of Modern China*. Chicago: University of Chicago Press.

Durkheim, Emile. 1912. *Elementary Forms of Religious Life*. London: Allen and Unwin.

Edwards, Elizabeth. 2001. *Raw Histories: Photography, Anthropology, and Museums*. Oxford: Berg.

Ellerbee, Linda. 2000. "No Shit! There I Was . . ." In *A Woman's Path: Women's Best Spiritual Travel Writing*, edited by Lucy McCauley, Amy G. Carlson, and Jennifer Leo, 60–68. San Francisco: Traveler's Tales.

Engels, Friedrich. 1972 [1884]. *The Origin of the Family, Private Property, and the State*. New York: International Publishers.

Errington, Shelly. 1998. *The Death of Authentic Primitive Art and Other Tales of Progress*. Berkeley: University of California Press.

Evrard, Olivier, and Prasit Leepreecha. 2009. "Staging the Nation, Exploring the Margins: Domestic Tourism and Its Political Implications in Northern Thailand." In *Asia on Tour: Exploring the Rise of Asian Tourism*, edited by Tim Winter, Peggy Teo, and T. C. Chang, 239–53. London: Routledge.

Fan, C. Cindy. 2005. "Interprovincial Migration, Population Redistribution, and Regional Development in China: 1990 and 2000 Census Comparisons." *Professional Geographer* 57 (2): 295–311.

Fei Xiaotong. 1981. *Toward a People's Anthropology*. Beijing: New World Press.

Feld, Steven. 2000. "A Sweet Lullaby for World Music." *Public Culture* 12 (1): 145–71.

Fodor's. 2007. *Fodor's China*, fifth edition. New York: Random House.

Foster, Hal, ed. 1988. *Vision and Visuality*. Seattle: Bay Press.

Foucault, Michel. 1994 [1970]. *The Order of Things: An Archaeology of the Human Sciences*. New York: Random House.

Friedman, Sara L. 2006. "Watching *Twin Bracelets* in China: The Role of Spectatorship and Identification in an Ethnographic Analysis of Film Reception." *Cultural Anthropology* 21 (4): 603–32.

Gaetano, Arianne M., and Tamara Jacka, eds. 2004. *On the Move: Women and Rural-to-Urban Migration in China*. New York: Columbia University Press.

Gao, Shunli, Songshan Huang, and Yucheng Huang. 2009. "Rural Tourism Development in China." *International Journal of Tourism Research* 11 (5): 439–50.

Ghimire, Krishna B., ed. 2001. *The Native Tourist: Mass Tourism within Developing Countries*. London: Earthscan Publications.

Ghimire, Krishna B., and Li Zhou. 2001. "The Economic Role of National Tourism in China." In *The Native Tourist: Mass Tourism within Developing Countries*, edited by Krishna B. Ghimire, 86–108. London: Earthscan Publications.

Gladney, Dru. 1994. "Representing Nationality in China: Refiguring Majority/Minority Identities." *Journal of Asian Studies* 53 (1): 93–123.

———. 1996. *Muslim Chinese: Ethnic Nationalism in the People's Republic*. Cambridge: Harvard University Press.

———. 2004. *Dislocating China: Muslims, Minorities, and Other Subaltern Subjects*. Chicago: University of Chicago Press.

Goffman, Erving. 1990 [1959]. *The Presentation of Self in Everyday Life*. New York: Anchor Books.

Goldsmith, Belinda. 2008. "Ethnic Children Faked at Games Opening." Reuters, August 15. Accessed July 29, 2013. www.reuters.com/article/2008/08/15/idINIndia -35019820080815.

Goodman, David S. G. 2004. "The Campaign to 'Open Up the West': National, Provincial-level and Local Perspectives." *China Quarterly Special Issues New Series, No. 5*, edited by David S. G. Goodman, 3–20. Cambridge: Cambridge University Press.

Gordon, Tamar, dir. 2005. *Global Villages: The Globalization of Ethnic Display* (digital video, 59 minutes). National Film Network.

Gorsuch, Anne. 2003. "'There's No Place Like Home:' Soviet Tourism in Late Stalinism." *Slavic Review* 62 (4): 760–85.

Graburn, Nelson. 1983. *To Pray, Pay, and Play: The Cultural Structure of Japanese Domestic Tourism*. Aix-en-Provence: Centre des Hautes Etudes Touristiques (Les Cahiers du Tourisme).

———. 1989 [1977]. "Tourism: The Sacred Journey." In *Hosts and Guests: The Anthropology of Tourism*, second edition, edited by Valene L. Smith, 21–36. Philadelphia: University of Pennsylvania Press.

———. 1995. "Tourism, Modernity and Nostalgia." In *The Future of Anthropology: Its Relevance to the Contemporary World*, edited by Akbar Ahmed and Cris Shore, 158–75. London: Athlone.

Graburn, Nelson, ed. 1976. *Ethnic and Tourist Arts: Cultural Expressions from the Fourth World*. Berkeley: University of California Press.

Graburn, Nelson, with Diane Barthel-Bouchier. 2001. "Relocating the Tourist." *International Sociology* 16 (2): 147–58.

Greenblatt, Stephen, with Ines Županov, Reinhard Meyer-Kalkus, Heike Paul, Pál Nyíri, and Frederike Pannewick. 2009. *Cultural Mobility: A Manifesto*. Cambridge: Cambridge University Press.

Gros, Stéphane. 2004. "The Politics of Names: The Identification of the Dulong (Drung) of Northwest Yunnan." *China Information* 18: 275–302.

Guangxi Statistical Bureau. 2007. *Guangxi Statistical Yearbook*. Beijing: China Statistics Press.

Guilin Shi Qikexing Lüyou Guihua Zixun Youxian Gongsi. 2008. *Longsheng Gezu Zizhi Xian Ping'an Titian Jingqu guanjingtai—Xiujianxing xiangxi guihua ji Huangluo Yao zhai lüyou guihua xiubian* (Longsheng Multi-Ethnic Autonomous County Ping'an Terraced Fields Scenic Area viewpoints—Construction details plan and Huangluo Yao village renovation plan). Internal document.

Guilin Statistical Committee. 2007. *Guilin jingji tongji nianjian* (Guilin economy statistical yearbook). Beijing: China Statistics Press.

Guizhou Statistical Bureau. 2007. *Guizhou Statistical Yearbook*. Beijing: China Statistics Press.

Guizhou Tourism Bureau. 2006. *Rural Tourism Plan, 2006–2020*. Guiyang: Guizhou Provincial Tourism Administration.

Guldin, Gregory Eliyu. 1994. *The Saga of Anthropology in China: From Malinowski to Moscow to Mao*. Armonk, NY: M. E. Sharpe.

———, ed. 1986. *Anthropology in China: Defining the Discipline*. Armonk, NY: M. E. Sharpe.

Guo Henqi, dir. 2010. *Xinbao* (New Castle) (digital video, 112 minutes).

Guo, Jianbin. 2012. "'Family' vs. 'State' in Media Ritual: Fieldwork in an Ethnic Minority Village in Yunnan Province," translated by Jingjing Chen. In *Mapping Media in China: Region, Province, Locality*, edited by Wanning Sun and Jenny Chio, 94–106. London: Routledge.

Hammond, Joyce D., Jeff Brummel, Cristina Buckingham, Dani Dolan, Lauren Irish, Elissa Menzel, and Charles Noard. 2009. "Interrogating Cultural Anthropology Text Covers: Intended Messages, Received Meanings." *Visual Anthropology Review* 25 (2): 150–71.

Harper, Douglas. 2002. "Talking about Pictures: A Case for Photo-Elicitation." *Visual Studies* 17 (1): 13–26.

Harrell, Stevan. 1995. "Introduction: Civilizing Projects and the Reaction to Them." In *Cultural Encounters on China's Ethnic Frontiers*, edited by Stevan Harrell, 3–36. Seattle: University of Washington Press.

———. 2001. *Ways of Being Ethnic in Southwest China*. Seattle: University of Washington Press.

Harrell, Stevan, ed. 1995. *Cultural Encounters on China's Ethnic Frontiers*. Seattle: University of Washington Press.

———. 2001. *Perspectives on the Yi of Southwest China*. Berkeley: University of California Press.

Harrison, Julia. 2003. *Being a Tourist: Finding Meaning in Pleasure Travel*. Vancouver: University of British Columbia Press.

Harvey, David. 1990. *The Condition of Postmodernity: An Enquiry into the Origins of Cultural Change*. Malden, MA: Blackwell.

Hathaway, Michael. 2010. "The Emergence of Indigeneity: Public Intellectuals and an Indigenous Space in Southwest China." *Cultural Anthropology* 25 (2): 301–33.

Hayford, Charles W. 1998. "The Storm over the Peasant: Orientalism and Rhetoric in Construing China." In *Contesting the Master Narrative: Essays in Social History*, edited by Jeffrey Cox and Shelton Stromquist, 150–72. Iowa City: University of Iowa Press.

He Jingming. 2005. "Zhong wai xiangcun lüyou yanjiu: Duibi, fansi yu zhanwang" (China and foreign rural tourism research: Comparisons, similarities, and prospects). *Nongcun jingji* (Village economy) 1: 126–27.

Heberer, Thomas. 1989. *China and Its National Minorities—Autonomy or Assimilation?* Armonk, NY: M. E. Sharpe.

———. 2007. *Doing Business in Rural China: Liangshan's New Ethnic Entrepreneurs*. Seattle: University of Washington Press.

Hendry, Joy. 1999. "Pine, Ponds, and Pebble: Gardens and Visual Culture." In *Rethinking*

Visual Anthropology, edited by Marcus Banks and Howard Morphy, 240–55. New Haven: Yale University Press.

Hillman, Ben. 2003. "Paradise under Construction: Minorities, Myths, and Modernity in Northwest Yunnan." *Asian Ethnicity* 4 (2): 175–88.

Hirsch, Eric. 1995. "Introduction—Landscape: Between Space and Place." In *The Anthropology of Landscape: Perspectives on Place and Space,* edited by Eric Hirsch and Michael O'Hanlon, 1–30. Oxford: Clarendon Press.

Hirsch, Eric, and Michael O'Hanlon, eds. 1995. *The Anthropology of Landscape: Perspectives on Place and Space.* Oxford: Clarendon Press.

Hitchcock, Michael. 1995. "The Indonesian Cultural Village Museum and Its Forebears." *Journal of Museum Ethnography* 7: 17–24.

———. 1998. "Tourism, Taman Mini, and National Identity." *Indonesia and the Malay World* 26 (75): 124–35.

———. 1999. "Tourism and Ethnicity: Situational Perspectives." *International Journal of Tourism Research* 1: 17–32.

Hitchcock, Michael, Nick Stanley, and Siu Kung Chung. 1997. "The South-east Asian 'Living Museum' and Its Antecedents." In *Tourists and Tourism: Identifying with People and Places,* edited by Simone Abram, Jacqueline Waldren, and Donald V. L. Macleod, 197–221. Oxford: Berg.

Hoffman, Lisa. 2003. "Enterprising Cities and Citizens: The Re-figuring of Urban Spaces and the Making of Post-Mao Professionals." *Provincial China* 8 (1): 5–26.

Hom Cary, Stephanie. 2004. "The Tourist Moment." *Annals of Tourism Research* 31 (1): 61–77.

Hostetler, Laura. 2001. *Qing Colonial Enterprise: Ethnography and Cartography in Early Modern China.* Chicago: University of Chicago Press.

Hsieh, Shih-chung. 1995. "On the Dynamics of Tai/Dai-Lue Ethnicity: An Ethnohistorical Analysis." In *Cultural Encounters on China's Ethnic Frontiers,* edited by Stevan Harrell, 301–28. Seattle: University of Washington Press.

Huang Haizhu. 2006. "Minzu lüyou duoyuan liyi zhuti fei hexie yinsu tantao—Yi Guangxi Longsheng Ping'an cun weilie" (Inquiry into multiple stakeholders and unharmonious elements in ethnic tourism—The example of Ping'an, Guangxi). *Guangxi Social Sciences* 10: 68–71.

Huang Ping and Zhan Shaohun. 2005. *Internal Migration in China: Linking It to Development.* Accessed April 6, 2009. http://hdr.undp.org/docs/network/hdr_net/China_internal_%20migration_development_poverty_alleviation.pdf.

Hyde, Sandra Teresa. 2007. *Eating Spring Rice: The Cultural Politics of AIDS in Southwest China.* Berkeley: University of California Press.

Ingold, Tim. 1993. "The Temporality of Landscape." *World Archaeology* 25 (2): 152–74.

Jacka, Tamara. 2006. *Rural Women in Urban China: Gender, Migration, and Social Change.* Armonk, NY: M.E. Sharpe.

Jackson Jr., John L. 2004. "An Ethnographic *Film*flam: Giving Gifts, Doing Research, and Videotaping the Native Subject/Object." *American Anthropologist* 106 (1): 32–42.

Jay, Martin. 1988. "Scopic Regimes of Modernity." In *Vision and Visuality,* edited by Hal Foster, 3–29. Seattle: Bay Press.

———. 1993. *Downcast Eyes: The Denigration of Vision in Twentieth Century French Thought.* Berkeley: University of California Press.

Jokinen, Eeva, and Soile Veijola. 1997. "The Disoriented Tourist: The Figuration of the Tourist in Contemporary Cultural Critique." In *Touring Cultures: Transforma-*

tions of Travel and Theory, edited by Chris Rojek and John Urry, 23–51. London: Routledge.

Kahn, Miriam. 2000. "Tahiti Intertwined: Ancestral Land, Tourist Postcard, and Nuclear Test Site." *American Anthropologist* 102 (1): 7–26.

———.2011. *Tahiti beyond the Postcard: Power, Place, and Everyday Life*. Seattle: University of Washington Press.

Kaili Shi Fupin Kaifa Bangongshi. 2006. *Guizhou sheng Kaili shi Sankeshu zhen Jidao cun shehui zhuyi xin nongcun jianshe guihua* (Guizhou province Kaili municipality Sankeshu township Jidao village New Socialist Countryside construction plans). Internal document.

Kaup, Katherine Palmer. 2000. *Creating the Zhuang: Ethnic Politics in China*. Boulder: Lynne Rienner Publishers.

Kerwin, Kaitlin. 2010. "Exoticism and Authenticity in Pictures: Representation of the Miao Ethnicity through Pictures on Tourism Web Sites." MA thesis, University of Washington.

Kipnis, Andrew. 1995. "Within and against Peasantness: Backwardness and Filiality in Rural China." *Comparative Studies in Society and History* 37 (1): 110–35.

———. 2006. "*Suzhi*: A Keyword Approach." *The China Quarterly* 186: 295–313.

Kirshenblatt-Gimblett, Barbara. 1998. *Destination Culture: Tourism, Museums, and Heritage*. Berkeley: University of California Press.

———. 2006. "World Heritage and Cultural Economics." In *Museum Frictions: Public Cultures/Global Transformations*, edited by Ivan Karp, Corinne A. Kratz, Lynn Szwaja, and Tomás Ybarra-Frausto, 161–202. Durham: Duke University Press.

Kolås, Åshild. 2008. *Tourism and Tibetan Culture in Transition: A Place Called Shangrila*. London: Routledge.

Kong, Sherry Tao. 2010. "China's Migrant Problem: The Need for Hukou Reform." *East Asia Forum*. Accessed December 16, 2012. www.eastasiaforum.org/2010/01/29/chinas-migrant-problem-the-need-for-hukou-reform/.

Kottak, Conrad Phillip. 2006. *Anthropology: The Exploration of Human Diversity*, twelfth edition. New York: McGraw Hill Higher Education.

Krüger, Karsten. 2003. *Exotische Landschaften und ethnische Grenzzonen—Die Nationalen Minderheiten* (shaoshu minzu) *Chinas im Film* (Exotic landscapes and ethnic borders—China's national minorities in film). Göttingen: IKO Verlag für Interkulturelle Kommunikation.

Kuan, Teresa. 2008. "Adjusting the Bonds of Love: Parenting, Expertise, and Social Change in a Chinese City." PhD diss., University of Southern California.

The Landscape Institute with the Institute of Environmental Management and Assessment. 2002. *Guidelines for Landscape and Visual Impact Assessment*. London: Spon Press.

Laxson, Joan D. 1991. "How 'We' See 'Them': Tourism and Native Americans." *Annals of Tourism Research* 18: 365–91.

Leach, Edmund. 1961. *Rethinking Anthropology*. London: Athlone Press.

Leibold, James. 2007. *Reconfiguring Chinese Nationalism: How the Qing Frontier and Its Indigenes Became Chinese*. New York: Palgrave Macmillan.

Levin, David Michael. 1993. *Modernity and the Hegemony of Vision*. Berkeley: University of California Press.

Lew, Alan, and Lawrence Yu, eds. 1995. *Tourism in China: Geographic, Political, and Economic Perspectives*. Boulder: Westview Press.

Lew, Alan, Lawrence Yu, Zhang Guangrui, and John Ap, eds. 2002. *Tourism in China*. London: Routledge.

Lewis, Peirce E. 1979. "Axioms for Reading the Landscape." In *The Interpretation of Ordinary Landscapes*, edited by D. W. Meinig, 11–32. Oxford: Oxford University Press.

Li, Jing. 2003. "Playing upon Fantasy: Women, Ethnic Tourism, and the Politics of Identity Construction in Contemporary Xishuang Banna, China." *Tourism Recreation Research* 28 (2): 51–65.

Li Jiqia. 2005. "Guizhou Ecological Museum: A Successful Example of International Cultural Cooperation between the Government of China and Norway." In *Xiangcun lüyou—Fan pinkun zhanlü de shixian* (Rural tourism: A strategy for poverty alleviation), edited by Yang Shengming, 252–59. Guiyang: Guizhou Renmin Chubanshe.

Li Junmei, Yu Weixiang, and Dai Cheng. 2006. "Research on Rural Households Hotels' Development in the West of China—A Case Study in Guizhou Province." *Journal of Mountain Agriculture and Biology* 25 (6): 536–39.

Li Nan. 2007. "Characteristic Tourism of Minority Culture in Guizhou." *Guizhou Ethnic Studies* 27 (1): 83–85.

Li Xin, dir. 2005. *Face Value* (digital video, 30 minutes). Göttingen: Institute for Knowledge and Media.

Li Zaiyong. 2005. "Introduction to the Work of the Rural Tourism Demonstration Project Area of the Bala River Valley in Guizhou." In *Xiangcun lüyou—Fan pinkun zhanlü de shixian* (Rural tourism: A strategy for poverty alleviation), edited by Yang Shengming, 184–88. Guiyang: Guizhou Renmin Chubanshe.

Li Zhou and Jia Jianhua. 2004. *Lüyouye dui Zhongguo nongcun he nongmin de yingxiang yanjiu* (Research on the influence of tourism industries on China's villages and peasants). Beijing: Zhongguo Nongye Chubanshe.

Li Zhuangming. 1997. "'Shi Qi Nian' shaoshu minzu ticai dianying zhong de wenhua shidian yu zhuti" ("Seventeen Years" ethnic minority films in cultural perspectives and themes). In *Lun Zhongguo shaoshu minzu dianying di wu ji Zhongguo Jinji Baihua Dianying Jie xueshu yantaohui wenji* (Proceedings of discussions about China's ethnic minority films at the Fifth Golden Rooster and Hundred Flowers Film Festival Symposium), edited by Zhongguo Dianying Jie Xiehui (Association of Chinese Film Festivals), 172–85. Beijing: Zhongguo Dianying Chubanshe.

Liang Zhongrong. 2005. "A Study of Developing Family Inn Industry in Dragon Ridge Terrace Scenic Spot." *Journal of Lingling University* 26 (3): 49–51.

Lin Hesheng. 2007. "Nong jia le shidai de zhexue sikao" (Philosophical thoughts on the era of *nong jia le*). *Zhonggong Sichuan sheng ji jiguan dangxiao xuebao* (Chinese Communist Party School of Sichuan Journal) 1: 87–90.

Lindquist, Johan A. 2009. *The Anxieties of Mobility: Migration and Tourism in the Indonesian Borderlands*. Honolulu: University of Hawai'i Press.

Lipman, Jonathan N. 1997. *Familiar Strangers: A History of Muslims in Northwest China*. Seattle: University of Washington Press.

Litzinger, Ralph. 1995. "Making Histories: Contending Conceptions of the Yao Past." In *Cultural Encounters on China's Ethnic Frontiers*, edited by Stevan Harrell, 117–39. Seattle: University of Washington Press.

———. 1998. "Memory Work: Reconstituting the Ethnic in Post-Mao China." *Cultural Anthropology* 13 (2): 224–55.

———. 2000. *Other Chinas: The Yao and the Politics of National Belonging*. Durham: Duke University Press.

Liu Xiaohui. 2007. "Dui Guizhou lüyou mudidi fazhan xiaoxing lüyou jingying zuzhi de sikao" (Thoughts on developing small tour operators in Guizhou's tourism destinations). *Social Sciences in Guizhou* 206 (2): 152–54, 163.

Liu, Xin. 1997. "Space, Mobility, and Flexibility: Chinese Villages and Scholars Negotiate Power at Home and Abroad." In *Ungrounded Empires: The Cultural Politics of Modern Chinese Transnationalism*, edited by Aihwa Ong and Donald Nonini, 91–114. London: Routledge.

———. 2002. *The Otherness of Self: A Genealogy of the Self in Contemporary China*. Ann Arbor: University of Michigan Press.

Lora-Wainwright, Anna. 2012. "Rural China in Ruins: The Rush to Urbanize China's Countryside Is Opening a Moral Battleground." *Anthropology Today* 28 (4): 8–13.

Lowenthal, David. 1996. *Possessed by the Past: The Heritage Crusade and the Spoils of History*. New York: Free Press.

Lozada, Ernesto. 2006. "Framing Globalization: Wedding Pictures, Funeral Photography, and Family Snapshots in Rural China." *Visual Anthropology* 19: 87–103.

Luk, Tak-Chuen. 2005. "The Poverty of Tourism under Mobilizational Developmentalism in China." *Visual Anthropology* 18: 257–89.

Lundmark, Linda. 2006. "Mobility, Migration, and Seasonal Tourism Employment: Evidence from Swedish Mountain Municipalities." *Scandinavian Journal of Hospitality and Tourism* 6 (3): 197–213.

Luo Yongchang. 2006a. "The Choose [sic] of Policy on the Tourism Development of Ethnic Village." *Guizhou Ethnic Studies* 26 (4): 32–37.

———. 2006b. "Guanyu Guizhou minzu cunzhai lüyou kaifa de jige wenti" (On a few problems about Guizhou ethnic village tourism development). *Social Sciences in Guizhou* 201 (3): 47–49.

Macartney, Jane. 2006. "Chinese Told to Mind Their Manners." *Ottawa Citizen*, August 18, D15.

MacCannell, Dean. 1999 [1976]. *The Tourist: A New Theory of the Leisure Class*. Berkeley: University of California Press.

———. 2001. "Tourist Agency." *Tourist Studies* 1 (1): 23–37.

———. 2008. "Why It Was Never Really about Authenticity." *Soc* 45 (4): 334–37.

———. 2011. *The Ethics of Sightseeing*. Berkeley: University of California Press.

MacDougall, David. 2006. *The Corporeal Image: Film, Ethnography, and the Senses*. Princeton, NJ: Princeton University Press.

Mackerras, Colin. 2004. "Conclusion: Some Major Issues in Ethnic Classification." *China Information* 18: 303–13.

Malkki, Liisa. 1992. "National Geographic: The Rooting of Peoples and the Territorialization of National Identity among Scholars and Refugees." *Cultural Anthropology* 7 (1): 24–44.

Mao Changrong. 2006. "Study on the Impact of the Tourism Development on the Culture of Traditional Villages." *Journal of Nanjing Xiaozhuang University* 4: 91–95.

Mao Zedong. 1975. "Report on an Investigation of the Peasant Movement in Hunan, March 1927." In *Selected Works of Mao Tse-tung*, volume 1, 23–29. Beijing: Foreign Languages Press.

Massey, Doreen. 1993. "Power-Geometry and a Progressive Sense of Place." In *Mapping the Futures: Local Cultures, Global Change*, edited by Jon Bird, Berry Curtis, Tim Putnam, George Robertson, and Lisa Tickner, 59–69. London: Routledge.

McCarthy, Susan. 2009. *Communist Multiculturalism: Ethnic Revival in Southwest China*. Seattle: University of Washington Press.

Meinig, Donald W., ed. 1979. *The Interpretation of Ordinary Landscapes: Geographical Essays*. Oxford: Oxford University Press.

Meng Fang. 2007. "Guilin jiating lüguan jingying guanli duibi yanjiu—Yi Yangshuo he Longsheng Ping'an weilei" (Guilin family guesthouse operations and management comparative research—The examples of Yangshuo and Longsheng Ping'an). *Journal of Guangxi University* 29: 244–45.

Meniconzi, Alessandra. 2008. *Hidden China*. Potsdam: H. F. Ullmann.

Minca, Claudio, and Tim Oakes, eds. 2006. *Travels in Paradox: Remapping Tourism*. Lanham, MD: Rowman and Littlefield.

Mirzoeff, Nicholas. 2011. *The Right to Look: A Counterhistory of Visuality*. Durham: Duke University Press.

Mitchell, W.J.T. 1994. *Picture Theory: Essays on Verbal and Visual Representation*. Chicago: University of Chicago Press.

———, ed. 2002. *Landscape and Power*. Chicago: University of Chicago Press.

———. 2005. *What Do Pictures Want? The Lives and Loves of Images*. Chicago: University of Chicago Press.

Mo Zigang. 2006. "Historical and Cultural Resources and the Development of Guizhou Tourism." *Journal of Guizhou University for Ethnic Minorities* 1: 109–12.

Morgan, Lewis Henry. 1962 [1851]. *League of the Iroquois*. New York: Corinth Books.

———. 1963 [1877]. *Ancient Society; or, Researches in the Lines of Human Progress from Savagery through Barbarism to Civilization*. Cleveland: World Publications.

Moseley, George, trans. 1966. *The Party and the National Question in China*. Cambridge: MIT Press.

Mueggler, Eric. 2002. "Dancing Fools: Politics of Culture and Place in a 'Traditional Nationality Festival.'" *Modern China* 28 (1): 3–38.

Mullaney, Thomas S. 2004a. "Ethnic Classification Writ Large: The 1954 Yunnan Province Ethnic Classification Project and Its Foundations in Republican Era Taxonomic Thought." *China Information* 18: 207–41.

———. 2004b. "Introduction: 55 + 1 = 1 or the Strange Calculus of Chinese Nationhood." *China Information* 18: 197–205.

———. 2011. *Coming to Terms with the Nation: Ethnic Classification in Modern China*. Berkeley: University of California Press.

Mullaney, Thomas S., James Leibold, Stéphane Gros, and Eric Vanden Bussche, eds. 2012. *Critical Han Studies: The History, Representation, and Identity of China's Majority*. Berkeley: University of California Press.

Murphy, Rachel. 2002. *How Migrant Labor Is Changing Rural China*. Cambridge: Cambridge University Press.

———. 2004. "Turning Peasants into Modern Chinese Citizens: 'Population Quality' Discourse, Demographic Transition, and Primary Education." *China Quarterly* 177: 1–20.

Nash, Dennison. 1996. *The Anthropology of Tourism*. New York: Pergamon.

National Bureau of Statistics of China (NBS). 2009. "2008 nianmo quanguo nongmingong zongliang wei 22542 wan ren" (225.42 million migrant workers at the end of 2008). Accessed December 14, 2012. www.stats.gov.cn/tjfx/fxbg/t20090325_402547406.htm.

———. 2011. *China Statistical Yearbook*. China Statistics Press. Accessed October 11, 2012. http://chinadataonline.org/member/yearbooknew/yearbook/Aayearbook.aspx?ybcode=F88F0EDoC6279E70148150AA6B635573&key=en.

Ness, Sally Ann. 2003. *Where Asia Smiles: An Ethnography of Philippine Tourism*. Philadelphia: University of Pennsylvania Press.

———. 2005. "Tourism-Terrorism: The Landscaping of Consumption and the Darker Side of Place." *American Ethnologist* 32 (1): 118–40.

Nilsson, Erik. 2010. "Custom-made Culture." *China Daily*. Accessed December 13, 2012. www.chinadaily.com.cn/cndy/2010-08/05/content_11098892.htm.

Nora, Pierre. 1989. "Between Memory and History: Les Lieux de Memoire." *Representations* 26: 7–24.

Norway (Official Site in China). 2004. "Eco-museums in Guizhou: Preserving a Unique Lifestyle in China." Accessed August 2, 2013. www.norway.cn/ARKIV/News-and-events/Environment-and-Development/Development_Cooperation/ecomuseum/.

Notar, Beth E. 2006. *Displacing Desire: Travel and Popular Culture in China*. Honolulu: University of Hawai'i Press.

Nyíri, Pál. 2001. "Expatriating Is Patriotic? The Discourse on 'New Migrants' in the People's Republic of China and Identity Construction among Recent Migrants from the PRC." *Journal of Ethnic and Migration Studies* 27 (4): 635–53.

———. 2003. "Chinese Migration to Eastern Europe." *International Migration* 41 (3): 239–65.

———. 2005a. "The 'New Migrant': State and Market Constructions of Modernity and Patriotism." In *China Inside Out*, edited by Pál Nyíri and Joana Breidenbach, 141–76. Budapest: Central European University Press.

———. 2005b. "Scenic Spot Europe: Chinese Travelers on the Western Periphery." Accessed March 25, 2005. www.espacestemps.net/document1224.html.

———. 2006. *Scenic Spots: Chinese Tourism, the State, and Cultural Authority*. Seattle: University of Washington Press.

———. 2009. "Between Encouragement and Control: Tourism, Modernity, and Discipline in China." In *Asia on Tour: Exploring the Rise of Asian Tourism*, edited by Tim Winter, Peggy Teo, and T. C. Chang, 153–69. London: Routledge.

———. 2010. *Mobility and Cultural Authority in Contemporary China*. Seattle: University of Washington Press.

Nyíri, Pál, and Joana Breidenbach. 2008. "The Altai Road: Visions of Development across the Russian-Chinese Border." *Development and Change* 39 (1): 123–45.

Oakes, Tim. 1998. *Tourism and Modernity in China*. London: Routledge.

———. 1999. "Bathing in the Far Village: Globalization, Transnational Capital, and the Cultural Politics of Modernity in China." *Positions* 7 (2): 307–42.

———. 2006a. "Get Real! On Being Yourself and Being a Tourist." In *Travels in Paradox: Remapping Tourism*, edited by Claudio Minca and Tim Oakes, 229–50. Lanham, MD: Rowman and Littlefield.

———. 2006b. "The Village as Theme Park: Mimesis and Authenticity in Chinese Tourism." In *Translocal China: Linkages, Identities, and the Reimagining of Space*, edited by Tim Oakes and Louisa Schein, 166–92. London: Routledge.

———. 2011. "Laser Tag and Other Rural Diversions: The Village as China's Urban Playground." *Harvard Asia Quarterly* 13 (3): 25–30.

Oakes, Tim, and Louisa Schein. 2006. "Translocal China: An Introduction." In *Translo-

cal China: Linkages, Identities, and the Reimagining of Space, edited by Tim Oakes and Louisa Schein, 1–35. London: Routledge.

One Village, One Product. Accessed August 2, 2013. www.ovop.jp.

Ong, Aihwa. 1999. *Flexible Citizenship: The Cultural Logics of Transnationality.* Durham: Duke University Press.

Ong, Aihwa, and Donald M. Nonini, eds. 1997. *Ungrounded Empires: The Cultural Politics of Modern Chinese Transnationalism.* New York: Routledge.

Oppitz, Michael. 1989. *Kunst der Genauigkeit* (Art of Accuracy). Munich: Trickster.

Oxfam International. 2009. "Turning a New Leaf: Fighting Poverty in China." Accessed April 19, 2009. www.oxfam.org/en/development/china-turning-a-new-leaf.

Park, Choong-Hwan. 2008. "Delights in Farm Guesthouses: Nongjiale Tourism, Rural Development, and the Regime of Leisure-Pleasure in Post-Mao China." PhD diss., University of California–Santa Barbara.

Parrinello, Giuli Liebman. 1993. "Motivation and Anticipation in Post-Industrial Tourism." *Annals of Tourism Research* 20: 233–49.

People's Daily Online. 2007. *Statistical Review of 2006.* Accessed August 2, 2013. http://english.peopledaily.com.cn/200703/02/eng20070302_353783.html.

Perrement, Matt. 2006. "On the Margins: Migration among Miao, Yi, and Tibetan People in China (A Special Report by China Development Brief)." Accessed August 2, 2013. www.chinadevelopmentbrief.com/node/673.

Perry, Elizabeth J. 2011. "From Mass Campaigns to Managed Campaigns: Constructing a New Socialist Countryside." In *Mao's Invisible Hand: The Political Foundations of Adaptive Governance in China,* edited by Sebastian Heilmann and Elizabeth J. Perry, 30–61. Cambridge: Harvard University Press.

Peters, Heather. 2001. "Making Tourism Work for Heritage Preservation: Lijiang—A Case Study." In *Tourism, Anthropology, and China,* edited by Tan Chee-Beng, Sidney C. H. Cheung, and Yang Hui, 313–32. Bangkok: White Lotus Press.

Petersen, Ying Yang. 1995. "The Chinese Landscape as a Tourist Attraction: Image and Reality." In *Tourism in China: Geographic, Political, and Economic Perspectives,* edited by Alan A. Lew and Lawrence Yu, 141–54. Boulder: Westview Press.

Picard, Michel. 1996. *Bali: Cultural Tourism and Touristic Culture,* translated by Diana Darling. Singapore: Archipelago Press.

Pinney, Christopher, and Nicholas Petersen, eds. 2003. *Photography's Other Histories.* Durham: Duke University Press.

Podolefsky, Aaron, Peter Brown, and Scott Lacy. 2008. *Applying Cultural Anthropology: An Introductory Reader,* eighth edition. New York: McGraw Hill.

Poole, Deborah. 1997. *Vision, Race, and Modernity: A Visual Economy of the Andean Image World.* Princeton, NJ: Princeton University Press.

Pratt, Mary Louise. 2008 [1992]. *Imperial Eyes: Travel Writing and Transculturation,* second edition. London: Routledge.

Pun Ngai. 2005. *Made in China: Women Factory Workers in a Global Workplace.* Durham: Duke University Press.

Qian Jin. 2005. "Development of Countryside Tourism and Anti-poverty Strategy in Guizhou." *Guizhou caijing xueyuan xuebao* (Guizhou College of Finance Journal) 2: 61–65.

Qiao Yuxia. 1995. "Domestic Tourism in China: Policies and Development." In *Tourism in China: Geographic, Political, and Economic Perspectives,* edited by Alan A. Lew and Lawrence Yu, 121–30. Boulder: Westview Press.

Rack, Mary. 2005. *Ethnic Distinctions, Local Meanings: Negotiating Cultural Identities in China*. London: Pluto Press.

Rhoda, Richard. 1983. "Rural Development and Urban Migration: Can We Keep Them Down on the Farm?" *International Migration Review* 17 (1): 34–64.

Rudelson, Justin Jon. 1997. *Oasis Identities: Uyghur Nationalism along China's Silk Road*. New York: Columbia University Press.

Ruoff, Jeffery. 2002. "Around the World in Eighty Minutes: The Travel Lecture Film." *Visual Anthropology* 15: 91–114.

———, ed. 2006. *Virtual Voyages: Cinema and Travel*. Durham: Duke University Press.

Sautman, Barry. 1999. "Ethnic Law and Minority Rights in China: Progress and Constraints." *Law and Policy* 23 (3): 283–314.

Schaefer, William. 2003. "Shanghai Savage." *Positions* 11 (1): 91–133.

———. 2010. "Poor and Blank: History's Mark and the Photographies of Displacement." *Representations* 10: 1–34.

Schein, Louisa. 1996. "The Other Goes to the Market: The State, the Nation, and Unruliness in Contemporary China." *Identities: Global Studies in Culture and Power* 2 (3): 197–222.

———. 1997. "Gender and Internal Orientalism in China." *Modern China* 23 (1): 69–78.

———. 1999. "Performing Modernity." *Cultural Anthropology* 14 (3): 361–95.

———. 2000. *Minority Rules: The Miao and the Feminine in China's Cultural Politics*. Durham: Duke University Press

———. 2006. "Negotiating Scale: Miao Women at a Distance." In *Translocal China: Linkages, Identities, and the Reimagining of Space*, edited by Tim Oakes and Louisa Schein, 213–37. London: Routledge.

Scheyvens, Regina. 2001. "Poverty Tourism." *Development Bulletin* 55: 18–21.

Schmitz, Rob. 2012. "The End of the Great Migration: China's Workers Return Home." *National Public Radio*. Accessed December 13, 2012. www.marketplace.org/topics/world/end-great-migration-chinas-workers-return-home.

Selwyn, Tom, ed. 1996. *The Tourist Image: Myths and Myth Making in Tourism*. Chichester, UK: John Wiley and Sons.

Sesser, Stan, and Mei Fong. 2006. "Hu Wants You." *Wall Street Journal*, April 22, 2006.

Sha Hang and Wang Qing. 2006. "Fazhan xiangcun lüyou tuidong xin nongcun jianshe" (Develop rural tourism, promote building a new countryside). *Hongqi Wengao* 23: 20–22.

Sha Yao, Wu Zongjun, and Wang Xulian. 2007. "Longji Titian Jingqu Ping'an cunzhai jumin lüyou ganzhi diaocha fenxi" (Resident perceptions of tourism in Longji Terraced Fields Scenic Area Ping'an village). *Coastal Enterprises and Science & Technology* 2: n.p.

Shao Qiwei. 2007. "Fazhan xiangcun lüyou cujin xin nongcun jianshe" (Develop rural tourism, promote building a new countryside). Accessed August 1, 2013. www.gov. cn/jrzg/2007-01/01/content_485625.htm.

Shapiro, Judith. 2001. *Mao's War against Nature: Politics and the Environment in Revolutionary China*. Cambridge: Cambridge University Press.

Shi Peihua. 2005. "Fazhan xiangcun lüyou de jidian sikao" (A few thoughts on developing rural tourism). *Dangdai Guizhou* (Contemporary Guizhou) 6: 10–11.

Simmel, Georg. 1950. "The Stranger." In *The Sociology of Georg Simmel*, translated by Kurt H. Wolff, 402–8. Glencoe, IL: Free Press.

Smith, Valene L. 1989 [1977]. "Introduction." In *Hosts and Guests: The Anthropology of*

Tourism, second edition, edited by Valene L. Smith, 1–17. Philadelphia: University of Pennsylvania Press.

———, ed. 1989 [1977]. *Hosts and Guests: The Anthropology of Tourism*, second edition. Philadelphia: University of Pennsylvania Press.

Sofield, Trevor H. B., and Fung Mei Sarah Li. 1998a. "Historical Methodology and Sustainability: An 800-Year-Old Festival from China." *Journal of Sustainable Tourism* 6 (4): 267–92.

———. 1998b. "Tourism Development and Cultural Policies in China." *Annals of Tourism Research* 25 (2): 362–92.

Solinger, Dorothy. 1999. *Contesting Citizenship in Urban China: Peasant Migrants, the State, and the Logic of the Market*. Berkeley: University of California Press.

Sontag, Susan. 2001 [1977]. *On Photography*. New York: Picador.

Spencer, Herbert. 1897. *The Principles of Sociology*. New York: Appleton.

Stanley, Nick. 1998. *Being Ourselves for You: The Global Display of Cultures*. London: Middlesex University Press.

Stanley, Nick, and Siu King Chung. 1995. "Representing the Past as the Future: The Shenzhen Chinese Folk Culture Villages and the Marketing of Chinese Identity." *Journal of Museum Ethnography* 7: 25–40.

Stasch, Rupert. 2011. "The Camera and the House: The Semiotics of New Guinea 'Tree-Houses' in Global Visual Culture." *Comparative Studies in Society and History* 53 (1): 75–112.

Stewart, Kathleen. 1988. "Nostalgia—A Polemic." *Cultural Anthropology* 3 (3): 227–41.

Stewart, Susan. 1993 [1984]. *On Longing: Narratives of the Miniature, the Gigantic, the Souvenir, the Collection*. Durham: Duke University Press.

Strassberg, Richard, trans. 1994. *Inscribed Landscapes: Travel Writing from Imperial China*. Berkeley: University of California Press.

Su, Minzi. 2009. *China's Rural Development Policy: Exploring the "New Socialist Countryside."* Boulder: Lynne Rienner.

Su, Xiaobo, and Peggy Teo. 2011. *The Politics of Heritage Tourism in China: A View from Lijiang*. London: Routledge.

Su Li, dir. 1960. *Liu San Jie* (Third Sister Liu) (film, 130 minutes). Changchun: Changchun Film Studio.

Su Weibin and Chen Shangling. 2005. "Problems Existing in Longsheng's Rural Tourism and Measures to Deal With." *Journal of Guilin Institute of Tourism* 16 (3): 36–38.

Sun Jiuxia, ed. 2007. *Anthropological Tourism Studies in China: Case Studies of Community Participation*. Armonk, NY: M.E. Sharpe.

Sun Jiuxia and Bao Jigang. 2007a. "Anthropological Tourism Analysis on Community Participation: The Case Study of Arcadia in Yangshuo." In *Anthropological Tourism Studies in China: Case Studies of Community Participation, Chinese Sociology, and Anthropology* 39 (3): 69–89.

———. 2007b. "Anthropological Tourism Analysis on Community Participation: The Case Study of Dai Village in Xishuangbanna." In *Anthropological Tourism Studies in China: Case Studies of Community Participation, Chinese Sociology, and Anthropology* 39 (3): 28–49.

———. 2007c. "Anthropological Tourism Analysis on Community Participation: The Case Study of Yulong River in Yangshuo." In *Anthropological Tourism Studies in China: Case Studies of Community Participation, Chinese Sociology, and Anthropology* 39 (3): 50–68.

Sun, Wanning. 2002. *Leaving China: Media, Migration, and Transnational Imagination*. Lanham, MD: Rowman and Littlefield.

———. 2006. "The Leaving of Anhui: The Southward Journey of the Knowledge Class." In *Translocal China: Linkages, Identities, and the Reimagining of Space*, edited by Tim Oakes and Louisa Schein, 238–61. London: Routledge.

———. 2008. "'Just Looking': Domestic Workers' Consumption Habits and a Latent Geography of Beijing." *Gender, Place, and Culture* 15 (5): 475–88.

———. 2009. *Maid in China: Media, Mobility, and a New Semiotic of Power*. London: Routledge.

Swain, Margaret B. 1989 [1977]. "Gender Roles in Indigenous Tourism: Kuna *Mola*, Kuna Yala, and Cultural Survival." In *Hosts and Guests: The Anthropology of Tourism*, second edition, edited by Valene L. Smith, 83–104. Philadelphia: University of Pennsylvania Press.

———. 1995. "Père Vial and the Gnip'a: Orientalist Scholarship and the Christian Project." In *Cultural Encounters on China's Ethnic Frontiers*, edited by Stevan Harrell, 140–85. Seattle: University of Washington Press.

———. 2001. "Cosmopolitan Tourism and Minority Politics in the Stone Forest." In *Tourism, Anthropology, and China*, edited by Tan Chee-Beng, Sidney C. H. Cheung, and Yang Hui, 125–46. Bangkok: White Lotus Press.

———. 2011. "Commoditized Ethnicity for Tourism Development in Yunnan." In *Moving Mountains: Ethnicity and Livelihoods in Highland China, Vietnam, and Laos*, edited by Jean Michaud and Tim Forsyth, 173–92. Vancouver: University of British Columbia Press.

Tan Chee-Beng, Sidney C. H. Cheung, and Yang Hui, eds. 2001. *Tourism, Anthropology, and China*. Bangkok: White Lotus Press.

Tang, R. 1990. "Guonei lüyou" (Domestic tourism). In *Zhongguo lüyou jingji yanjiu* (China tourism economics research), edited by S. Sun, 143–81. Beijing: Renmin Chubanshe.

Tao, Ran. 2010. "Achieving Real Progress in China's Hukou Reform." *East Asia Forum*. Accessed December 16, 2012. www.eastasiaforum.org/2010/02/08/achieving-real-progress-in-chinas-hukou-reform/.

Tapp, Nicholas. 2012. "The Han Joker in the Pack: Some Issues of Culture and Identity from the *Minzu* Literature." In *Critical Han Studies*, edited by Thomas S. Mullaney et al., 147–70. Berkeley: University of California Press.

Thomas, Nicholas. 1999. *Possessions: Indigenous Art/Colonial Culture*. London: Thames and Hudson.

Tilley, Christopher. 1994. *A Phenomenology of Landscape: Places, Paths, and Monuments*. Oxford: Berg Publishers.

———. 1997. "Performing Culture in the Global Village." *Critique of Anthropology* 17(1): 67–89.

Tucker, Hazel. 2003. *Living with Tourism: Negotiating Identities in a Turkish Village*. London: Routledge.

———. 2010. "Peasant-Entrepreneurs: A Longitudinal Ethnography." *Annals of Tourism Research* 37 (4): 927–46.

Turner, Jessica Anderson. 2010. "Cultural Performances in the Guangxi Tourism Commons: A Study of Music, Place, and Ethnicity in Southern China." PhD diss., Indiana University.

Turner, Terence. 1992. "Defiant Images: The Kayapo Appropriation of Video." *Anthropology Today* 8 (6): 5–16.

UNWTO (World Tourism Organization). 2003. *Reducing Poverty through Tourism Development: Bala River Valley, Guizhou China.* Accessed February 23, 2009. www .world-tourism.org/regional/east_asia_&_pacific/image_country/guizhou.htm.

———. 2006. *Poverty Alleviation through Tourism—A Compilation of Good Practices.* Madrid: UNWTO.

Urry, John. 2000. *Sociology beyond Societies: Mobilities for the Twenty-First Century.* London: Routledge.

———. 2002a. "Mobility and Proximity." *Sociology* 36 (2): 255–74.

———. 2002b [1990]. *The Tourist Gaze.* London: Sage Publications.

———. 2003. *Global Complexity.* Cambridge: Polity Press.

———. 2007. *Mobilities.* Cambridge: Polity Press.

van den Abeele, Georges. 1980. "Sightseers: The Tourist as Theorist." *Diacritics* 10 (4): 2–14.

van den Berghe, Pierre L., and Charles F. Keyes. 1984. "Introduction: Tourism and Re-created Ethnicity." *Annals of Tourism Research* 11: 343–52.

Veblen, Thorstein. 2009 [1899]. *The Theory of the Leisure Class.* Oxford: Oxford University Press.

Wallace-Crabbe, Georgia, dir. 2009. *New Beijing: Reinventing a City* (digital video, 52 minutes). Film Projects.

Walsh, Eileen Rose. 2001. "Living with the Myth of Matriarchy: The Mosuo and Tourism." In *Tourism, Anthropology, and China,* edited by Tan Chee-Beng, Sidney C. H. Cheung, and Yang Hui, 93–124. Bangkok: White Lotus Press.

———. 2005. "From Nü Guo to Nü'er Guo: Negotiating Desire in the Land of the Mosuo." *Modern China* 31 (4): 448–86.

Wang, Fei-ling. 2005. *Organizing through Division and Exclusion: China's Hukou System.* Stanford: Stanford University Press.

Wang Jiayi, dir. 1959. *Wu Duo Jin Hua* (Five Golden Flowers) (film, 96 minutes). Changchun: Changchun Film Studio.

Wang Lei. 1983. "The Definition of 'Nation' and the Formation of the Han Nationality." *Social Sciences in China* 4 (2): 167–87.

Wang, Ning. 1999. "Rethinking Authenticity in Tourist Experiences." *Annals of Tourism Research* 26 (2): 349–70.

———. 2001. *Tourism and Modernity: A Sociological Analysis.* London: Elsevier.

Wang Shijin and Bai Yongping. 2006. "Guanyu shehui zhuyi xin nongcun jianshe de xiangcun lüyou fazhan silu" (Approaches to rural tourism development in the building of a New Socialist Countryside). *Guangxi Social Sciences* 11: 5–7.

Wang Tiansheng and Wang Yao. 2006. "Some Problems about Constructing New Village in Guizhou." *Guizhou Agricultural Sciences* 34 (4): 5–9.

Wang Xiaomei. 2007. "Mirroring Modernization: Between the Miao and Outsiders in the Villages of Jidao and Langde, Guizhou Province, Southwestern China." MA thesis, Clark University.

Wang Yongchang. 2006. "Tourism Trends to Countryside: Funds Funnel to Farmers." *China Pictorial.* Accessed August 2, 2013. www.rmhb.com.cn/chpic/htdocs/ english/200610/7-1.htm.

Wang, Yu. 2007. "Customized Authenticity Begins at Home." *Annals of Tourism Research* 34 (3): 789–804.

Wasserstrom, Jeffrey. 2010. *China in the Twenty-First Century: What Everyone Needs to Know*. Oxford: Oxford University Press.

Waters, Mary. 1990. *Ethnic Options: Choosing Identities in America*. Berkeley: University of California Press.

Wei Jiayu and Wu Zhongjun. 2006. "Longsheng minzu yinshi wenhua lüyou kaifa yanjiu" (Longsheng minority food culture tourism development research). *Journal of Guilin College of Aerospace Technology* 2: 38–40.

Wei Min. 2005. "A Research on the Development Strategy of Tourism Economic Growth." *China Business Review* 4 (9): 76–78.

Wei Xiao'an. 2003. "Xiaokang shenghuo yu xiaokang lüyou" (Well-off life and well-off tourism). *Tourism Tribune* 18 (2): 5–6.

———. 2005. "Development of Tri-Agricultural Tourism in China." In *Xiangcun lüyou: Fan pinkun zhanlü de shixian* (Rural tourism: A strategy for poverty alleviation), edited by Yang Shengming, 160–76. Guiyang: Guizhou Renmin Chubanshe.

Wellens, Koen. 2010. *Religious Revival in the Tibetan Borderlands: The Premi of Southwest China*. Seattle: University of Washington Press.

Wen Tong. 2002. "On Developing Family Inn Industry: A Case Study of Dragon Ridge Terrace Scenic Spot." *Tourism Tribune* 17: 26–30.

Williams, Raymond. 1975. *The Country and the City*. Oxford: Oxford University Press.

Winter, Tim. 2007. "Rethinking Tourism in Asia." *Annals of Tourism Research* 34 (1): 27–44.

———. 2009. "Conclusion: Recasting Tourism Theory towards an Asian Future." In *Asia on Tour: Exploring the Rise of Asian Tourism*, edited by Tim Winter, Peggy Teo, and T. C. Chang, 315–25. London: Routledge.

Wood, Robert E. 1997. "Tourism and the State: Ethnic Options and Constructions of Otherness." In *Tourism, Ethnicity, and the State in Asian and Pacific Societies*, edited by Michel Picard and Robert E. Wood, 1–34. Honolulu: University of Hawai'i Press.

———. 1998. "Touristic Ethnicity: A Brief Itinerary." *Ethnic and Racial Studies* 21 (2): 218–41.

World Bank. 2007. "Strategic Environmental Assessment Study: Tourism Development in the Province of Guizhou, China." Accessed August 2, 2013. http://siteresources.worldbank.org/INTEAPREGTOPENVIRONMENT/Resources/Guizhou_SEA_FINAL.pdf.

———. 2008. "China—Guizhou Cultural and Natural Heritage Protection and Development Project: Indigenous Peoples Plan." Accessed July 29, 2013. http://documents.worldbank.org/curated/en/2008/04/9559433/china-guizhou-cultural-natural-heritage-protection-development-project-indigenous-peoples-plan.

———. 2009. *Project Agreement for Loan 7693-CN Conformed*. Accessed July 29, 2013. http://documents.worldbank.org/curated/en/2009/06/10840623/project-agreement-loan-7693-cn-conformed.

———. 2011. *Implementation Status and Results: China, CN-Guizhou Cultural and Natural Heritage Protection and Development, Sequence 02*. Accessed October 19, 2013. http://documents.worldbank.org/curated/en/2011/03/13869131/china-cn-guizhou-cultural-natural-heritage-protection-development-p091950-implementation-status-results-report-sequence-02.

———. 2012a. *Implementation Status and Results: China, CN-Guizhou Cultural and Natural Heritage Protection and Development, Sequence 03*. Accessed May 15, 2012. http://documents.worldbank.org/curated/en/2012/02/15852289/china-cn-guizhou

-cultural-natural-heritage-protection-development-p091950-implementation
-status-results-report-sequence-03.

———. 2012b. *Implementation Status and Results: China, CN-Guizhou Cultural and Natural Heritage Protection and Development, Sequence 04.* Accessed December 17, 2012. http://documents.worldbank.org/curated/en/2012/12/17052151/china-cn -guizhou-cultural-natural-heritage-protection-development-p091950-implemen tation-status-results-report-sequence-04.

———. 2013. *China-CN-Guizhou Cultural and Natural Heritage Protection and Development: P091950-Implementation Status Results Report: Sequence 05.* Accessed July 29, 2013. http://documents.worldbank.org/curated/en/2013/06/17920155/china-cn -guizhou-cultural-natural-heritage-protection-development-p091950-implemen tation-status-results-report-sequence-05.

Wu Nanlan. 2007. "Socialist Countryside Should Not Be Mere Exercise in Vanity." Accessed November 30, 2012. www.china.org.cn/english/2007lh/201767.htm.

Wu Zhongjun and Lu Jun. 2005. "Planning Festivals for Nationality Tourism." *Journal of Guizhou Normal College* 19 (3): 117–21.

Wu Zhongjun and Ye Ye. 2005. "The Discuss about Ethical Community Tourism Benefit Distribution and Validity of Resident's Participation—Take Guilin Longsheng Longji Terrace Scenic Spot Ping'an As Example." *Journal of Guangxi Economic Management Cadre College* 17 (3): 51–55.

Xiao, Honggen. 2005. "The Discourse of Power: Deng Xiaoping and Tourism Development in China." *Tourism Management* 27: 803–14.

Xiao Qianhui. 2005. "Evaluation, Unique Features, Divisions of Labor and Management and Operational Models for the Development of Rural Tourism in Guizhou Province." In *Xiangcun lüyou—Fan pinkun zhanlü de shixian* (Rural tourism: A strategy for poverty alleviation), edited by Yang Shengming, 210–15. Guiyang: Guizhou Renmin Chubanshe.

Xin Jing Bao. 2006. "Guonei lü wenming le, chujing lü cai wenming" (Only when domestic tourism is civilized, can overseas tourism be civilized). Accessed October 22, 2006. www.godpp.gov.cn/wmpl_/2006-09/18/content_8058810.htm.

Xing, Li, Shenggen Fan, Xiaopeng Lou, and Xiaobo Zhang. 2006. *Village Inequality in Western China: Implications for Development Strategy in Lagging Regions.* DSGD Discussion Paper No. 31. Washington, D.C.: International Food Policy Research Institute.

Xinhua News. 2005. "Zhongguo lüyouju: 2006 nian lüyou zhuti wei 'Zhongguo xiangcun you'" (CNTA: 2006 tourism theme is "China Rural Tourism"). Accessed August 1, 2013. http://news.xinhuanet.com/fortune/2005-12/28/content_3980908.htm.

———. 2006a. "Chinese Tourists Urged to Behave." Accessed October 10, 2006. www .chinadaily.com.cn/china/2006-10/09/content_704315.htm.

———. 2006b. "Gov't: Travelers Must Improve Their Manners." Accessed October 3, 2006. http://news.xinhuanet.com/english/2006-10/02/content_5165301.htm.

Xu, Gang. 1999. *Tourism and Local Economic Development in China: Case Studies of Guilin, Suzhou, and Beidaihe.* Richmond: Curzon Press.

Xu Ganli. 2005. "The Exploration and Evaluation of the Folklore Tourism in Longji, Guangxi province." *Guangxi minzu yanjiu* (Guangxi ethnic minority research) 2: 195–201.

———. 2006. *Minzu lüyou yu minzu wenhua bianqian: Guibei Zhuang, Yao san cun kao-*

cha (Ethnic tourism and ethnic cultural change: Research in three northern Guilin Zhuang and Yao villages). Beijing: Minzu Chubanshe.

Xue Jing. 2008. "Guangxi Longsheng Titian Jingqu lüyou gongyipin de baohu ji kaifa xianzhuang yanjiu" (Research on Guangxi Longsheng Terraced Fields Scenic Area tourism handicrafts preservation and development conditions). *Journal of Chongqing University of Science and Technology* 2: 91–92.

Yan Hairong. 2008. *New Masters, New Servants: Migration, Development, and Women Workers in China*. Durham: Duke University Press.

Yang Chaoji and Hui Li. 2005. "Xiangcun lüyou: Huanjie xibu 'san nong' wenti de yi zhong changshi" (Rural tourism: An attempt to solve the "three rural" problems of the west). *Ascent* 24 (2): 50–52.

Yang Guoliang. 2002. "Seeing the Government's Leading Role from Tourism Development of Longsheng County after China's Entry of WTO." *Gui Hai Tribune* 18 (5): 55–57.

Yang Hui, Liu Chun, Liu Yongqing, and Duan Ying. 2001. "Man-chun-man Village at the Crossroads: Conservation and Vicissitudes of Ethnic Cultures during the Development of Tourism." In *Tourism, Anthropology, and China*, edited by Tan Chee-Beng, Sidney C. H. Cheung, and Yang Hui, 167–78. Bangkok: White Lotus Press.

Yang, Li, and Geoffrey Wall. 2009. "Ethnic Tourism: A Framework and an Application." *Tourism Management* 30: 559–70.

Yang, Li, Geoffrey Wall, and Stephen L. J. Smith. 2008. "Ethnic Tourism Development: Chinese Government Perspectives." *Annals of Tourism Research* 35 (3): 751–71.

Yang Shengming. 2005. "Rural Tourism—A Strategy for Poverty Elimination." In *Xiangcun lüyou—Fan pinkun zhanlü de shixianm* (Rural tourism: A strategy for poverty alleviation), edited by Yang Shengming, 144–49. Guiyang: Guizhou Renmin Chubanshe.

———, ed. 2005. *Xiangcun lüyou—Fan pinkun zhanlü de shixian* (Rural tourism: A strategy for poverty alleviation). Guiyang: Guizhou Renmin Chubanshe.

Yang Yongjin. 2007. *Nong jia le: Lüyou jingying zhinan* (*Nong jia le*: Tourism operation guidebook). Beijing: Nongye Chubanshe.

Yau, Esther. 1989. "Is China the End of Hermeneutics? Or, Political and Cultural Usages of Non-Han Women in Mainland Chinese Films." *Discourse* 2: 115–36.

You Zhong. 1985. *Zhongguo xinan minzu shi* (History of China's southwestern minorities). Kunming: Yunnan Renmin Chubanshe.

Young, Jason. 2010. "China's Hukou System Impinges on Development and Civic Rights." *East Asia Forum*. Accessed December 16, 2012. www.eastasiaforum.org/2010/08/14/chinas-hukou-system-impinges-on-development-and-civic-rights/.

Young, Patrick. 2008. "Of Pardons, Loss, and Longing: The Tourist's Pursuit of Originality in Brittany, 1890–1935." *French Historical Studies* 30 (2): 269–304.

Yu Dazhong. 2008. "The Pattern of Upper Lang-de Village: The Practice and Thinking of Ethnic Community Involvement in Tourism Development." *Journal of Kaili University* 5: 1–5.

Yu Lintao. 2012. "A Taste of the Southwest: Miao culture in Guizhou Toasts to Tourism." *Beijing Review*. Accessed December 13, 2012. www.bjreview.com.cn/culture/txt/2012-08/06/content_473463.htm.

Zhang, Li. 2001. *Strangers in the City: Reconfigurations of Space, Power, and Social Networks within China's Floating Population*. Stanford: Stanford University Press.

Zhang Nuanxing, dir. 1985. *Sacrificed Youth* (film, 96 minutes). Beijing College Youth Film Studio.

Zhang Peng. 2005. "Lun xiangcun lüyou de kechixu fazhan" (Discussion on the sustainable development of rural tourism). *Journal of Southeast Guizhou National Teacher's College* 23 (1): 29–30.

Zhang, Q. Forrest, and John A. Donaldson. 2010. "From Peasants to Farmers: Peasant Differentiation, Labor Regimes, and Land-Rights Institutions in China's Agrarian Tradition." *Politics and Society* 38 (4): 458–89.

Zhang Rui. 2006. "Chinese Tourists' Bad Behavior to Be Curbed." Accessed October 8, 2006. www.china.org.cn/english/2006/Oct/183079.htm.

Zhang Tan. 2008. "A New Economic Community for Modern Rural Development." In *International Forum on Rural Tourism Final Report: Guiyang, Guizhou China, 4–6 September 2006*, 177–83. Madrid: World Tourism Organization.

Zhang Wen. 1997. "China's Domestic Tourism: Impetus, Development, and Trends." *Tourism Management* 15 (8): 565–71.

Zhang Xiaosong. 2005. "Bala He: Xiangcun lüyou de xuexi yu tansuo" (Bala River: Rural tourism studies and explorations). *Dangdai Guizhou* (Contemporary Guizhou) 6: 17–18.

Zhang, Yingjin. 1997. "From 'Minority Film' to 'Minority Discourse': Questions of Nationhood and Ethnicity in Chinese Cinema." In *Transnational Chinese Cinemas: Identity, Nationhood, Gender*, edited by Sheldon Hsiao-peng Lu, 81–104. Honolulu: University of Hawai'i Press.

Zhongguo Wang. 2011. "Zhongguo nongmingong zongshu yida 2.42 yi shouru wunian zengzhang yibei" (China's migrant worker number reach 242 million, revenue doubles in five years). Accessed October 22, 2012. www.china.com.cn/policy/txt/2011-02/14/content_21915392.htm.

Zhongguo Wenming Wang. 2006a. "Beijing Qingnian Bao: Waiguo ren zenme kan Zhongguo youke" (Beijing Youth Daily: How do foreigners view Chinese tourists?). Accessed October 22, 2006. www.godpp.gov.cn/cjzc_/2006-09/18/content_8061060.htm.

———. 2006b. "Chujing lüyou wenming xingwei zhinan; guonei lüyou wenming xingwei zhinan" (Overseas tourism civilized behavior guidelines; domestic tourism civilized behavior guidelines). Accessed October 3, 2006. www.godpp.gov.cn/2006-10/02/content_8182277.htm.

———. 2006c. "Tisheng gongmin lüyou wenming suzhi dajia tan" (Let's discuss raising citizens' civilized tourism quality). Accessed September 2, 2006. www.godpp.gov.cn/2006-09/01/content_7925965.htm.

Zhou Jun. 2007. "Reflection on Country Tourism and Construction of Socialism New Countryside—Having Yunshe Village as Example, Which Located at Jiangkou County in Guizhou Province." *Journal of South-Central University for Nationalities* 27 (2): 25–28.

Zhou Xing. 1999. "'Cunzhai bowuguan': Minsu wenhua zhanshi de tupuo yu wenti" ("Village museums": Breakthroughs and problems in folk culture exhibitions). In *Liang'an minsu wenhua xueshu yanlunhui wenji* (Straits Folk Culture Symposium Proceedings), n.p. Taipei: Taiwan Zhengfu Wenhua Chubanshe.

INDEX

Lightning Source UK Ltd.
Milton Keynes UK
UKHW04f1002021018
329681UK00002B/129/P